# Conservation and Productivity
## of Natural Waters

SYMPOSIA OF THE ZOOLOGICAL SOCIETY OF LONDON

NUMBER 29

# Conservation and Productivity
# of Natural Waters

*(The Proceedings of a Symposium organized jointly by the
British Ecological Society and the Zoological Society of London,
held at The Zoological Society of London on 22 and 23 October, 1970)*

*Edited by*

R. W. EDWARDS

*Department of Applied Biology, The University of Wales Institute of Science and
Technology, Cardiff, Wales*

D. J. GARROD

*Fisheries Laboratory, Lowestoft,
Suffolk, England*

*Published for*

THE ZOOLOGICAL SOCIETY OF LONDON

BY

ACADEMIC PRESS

1972

ACADEMIC PRESS INC. (LONDON) LTD.

24/28 Oval Road

London NW1


U.S. *Edition published by*

ACADEMIC PRESS INC.

111 Fifth Avenue,

New York, New York 10003

Second Printing 1977

Library of Congress Catalog Card Number: 79-172369

ISBN: 0-12-613329-8


PRINTED IN GREAT BRITAIN BY
J. W. ARROWSMITH LTD., BRISTOL

71361

# CONTRIBUTORS

ALABASTER, J. S., *Water Pollution Research Laboratory of the Department of the Environment, Stevenage, Hertfordshire, England* (p. 87)

BERRIE, A. D., *Department of Zoology, University of Reading, Reading, England* (p. 69)

BEVERTON, R. J. H., *Natural Environment Research Council, London, England* (p. 297)

BIRKETT, L., *Fisheries Laboratory, Lowestoft, Suffolk, England* (p. 259)

CLAYDEN, A. D., *Faculty of Medicine, University of Sheffield, Sheffield, England\** (p. 161)

COLE, H. A., *Fisheries Laboratory, Lowestoft, Suffolk, England* (p. 157)

COLEBROOK, J. M., *Oceanographic Laboratory, Edinburgh, Scotland* (p. 203)

CORNER, E. D. S., *Marine Biological Association Laboratory, Plymouth, Devon, England* (p. 185)

CURRIE, R. I., *Dunstaffnage Marine Research Laboratory, Oban, Scotland* (p. 285)

CUSHING, D. H., *Fisheries Laboratory, Lowestoft, Suffolk, England* (p. 213)

GARLAND, J. H. N., *Water Pollution Research Laboratory of the Department of the Environment, Stevenage, Hertfordshire, England* (p. 21)

GARROD, D. J., *Fisheries Laboratory, Lowestoft, Suffolk, England* (p. 161)

HART, I. C., *Water Pollution Research Laboratory of the Department of the Environment, Stevenage, Hertfordshire, England* (p. 21)

JEFFERIES, D. F., *Fisheries Radiobiological Laboratory, Lowestoft, Suffolk, England* (p. 271)

LE CREN, E. D., *Freshwater Biological Association, The River Laboratory, East Stoke, Wareham, Dorset, England* (p. 115)

MORGAN, N. C., *Nature Conservancy, Edinburgh, Scotland* (p. 135)

OWENS, M., *Water Pollution Research Laboratory of the Department of the Environment, Stevenage, Hertfordshire, England* (p. 21)

PENTREATH, R. J., *Fisheries Radiobiological Laboratory, Lowestoft, Suffolk, England* (p. 271)

PRESTON, A., *Fisheries Radiobiological Laboratory, Lowestoft, Suffolk, England* (p. 271)

SOLBÉ, J. F. DE L. G., *Water Pollution Research Laboratory of the Department of the Environment, Stevenage, Hertfordshire, England* (p. 87)

* Present address: Glamorgan County Council, Cardiff, Wales.

v

STEEL, J. A., *Metropolitan Water Board, Queen Elizabeth II Reservoir, West Molesey, Surrey, England* (p. 41)

WHITTON, B. A., *Department of Botany, University of Durham, Durham, England* (p. 3)

WOOD, G., *Water Pollution Research Laboratory of the Department of the Environment, Stevenage, Hertfordshire, England* (p. 21)

ZIJLSTRA, J. J., *Rijksinstituut voor Visserijonderzoek, IJmuiden, Netherlands* (p. 233)

# ORGANIZERS AND CHAIRMEN

## ORGANIZERS

R. W. EDWARDS and D. J. GARROD *on behalf of the Zoological Society of London*

## CHAIRMEN OF SESSIONS

I. R. H. ALLAN, *Ministry of Agriculture, Fisheries and Food, London, England*

R. J. H. BEVERTON, *Natural Environmental Research Council, London, England*

H. A. COLE, *Fisheries Laboratory, Lowestoft, Suffolk, England*

R. W. EDWARDS, *Department of Applied Biology, The University of Wales Institute of Science and Technology, Cardiff, Wales*

# CONTENTS

CONTRIBUTORS . . . . . . . . . .  v

ORGANIZERS AND CHAIRMEN OF SESSIONS . . . . .  vii

## FRESHWATER

### Environmental Limits of Plants in Flowing Waters

#### B. A. WHITTON

Synopsis . . . . . . . . . . .  3
Introduction . . . . . . . . . . .  3
Limits in extreme environments . . . . . . .  4
   Temperature . . . . . . . . . .  4
   Acidic environments . . . . . . . . .  7
   Toxic substances . . . . . . . . .  9
   Light climate . . . . . . . . . .  10
   Dissolved oxygen . . . . . . . . .  11
Comparison of methods for describing extreme environments . .  13
Discussion and conclusions . . . . . . . .  15
Acknowledgements . . . . . . . . .  16
References . . . . . . . . . . .  16

### Nutrient Budgets in Rivers

#### M. OWENS, J. H. N. GARLAND, I. C. HART and G. WOOD

Synopsis . . . . . . . . . . .  21
Introduction . . . . . . . . . . .  21
Nitrogen and chloride budget studies in the Rivers Great Ouse and
   Trent . . . . . . . . . . .  23
Yields of inorganic nitrogen and chloride from other catchment areas .  25
Yields of nitrogen and chloride from hypothetical catchments . .  28
Calculation of seasonal variations of inorganic nitrogen and chloride
   in any river . . . . . . . . . .  31
Conclusions . . . . . . . . . . .  38
Acknowledgements . . . . . . . . .  39
References . . . . . . . . . . .  39

# The Application of Fundamental Limnological Research in Water Supply System Design and Management

## J. A. STEEL

Synopsis . . . . . . . . . . . 41
Introduction. . . . . . . . . . . 41
Dissolved oxygen and energy requirements for de-stratified reservoirs . 44
    Dissolved oxygen demands . . . . . . . . 44
    Energetics of mixing . . . . . . . . . 46
    A mixing experiment . . . . . . . . . 50
Effects of mixing on the biocoenosis . . . . . . 51
    Phytoplankton production . . . . . . . . 51
    Herbivorous zooplankton . . . . . . . . 57
    Inter-relation between phytoplankton, zooplankton and "input" energy in a "jetted" reservoir . . . . . . . 58
    Some qualitative observations on buoyant algae, mixing and grazing . 60
Conclusion . . . . . . . . . . . 61
List of symbols used . . . . . . . . . 65
References . . . . . . . . . . . 66

# Productivity of the River Thames at Reading

## A. D. BERRIE

Synopsis . . . . . . . . . . . 69
Introduction. . . . . . . . . . . 69
Physical and chemical conditions . . . . . . . 72
Plants . . . . . . . . . . . 72
    Phytoplankton . . . . . . . . . . 72
    Benthic algae . . . . . . . . . . 74
    Aquatic macrophytes . . . . . . . . . 75
    Trees . . . . . . . . . . . 75
    Leaf decomposition . . . . . . . . . 75
Invertebrates . . . . . . . . . . 77
    Macrobenthos . . . . . . . . . . 77
    Chironomidae . . . . . . . . . . 78
    Zooplankton . . . . . . . . . . 78
Fish . . . . . . . . . . . 79
    Population estimates . . . . . . . . . 79
    Fecundity . . . . . . . . . . 79
    Production . . . . . . . . . . 80
    Energy requirements . . . . . . . . . 81
Discussion . . . . . . . . . . . 82
    Influence of the River Kennet . . . . . . . 82
    Fauna of *Nuphar* beds . . . . . . . . 84
    Fish problems . . . . . . . . . . 84
Acknowledgements . . . . . . . . . 85
References . . . . . . . . . . . 85

# An Approach to the Problem of Pollution and Fisheries

J. S. ALABASTER, J. H. N. GARLAND, I. C. HART
and J. F. DE L. G. SOLBÉ

Synopsis . . . . . . . . . . . 87
Introduction. . . . . . . . . . . 87
Extent of the problem in the United Kingdom . . . . 88
Factors to consider in attempting correlation of toxicity with the status
  of fisheries . . . . . . . . . . 89
  Effect of mixtures of poisons . . . . . . . 89
  Comparison of susceptibility of trout and coarse fish . . . 91
  Relation between long- and short-term effects of poisons . . 94
  Fluctuations in toxicity . . . . . . . . . 94
Investigations relating the presence and absence of fisheries to water
  toxicity . . . . . . . . . . . 96
  Direct measurements of toxicity (River Cam) . . . . 96
  Predicted toxicity . . . . . . . . . 97
Discussion . . . . . . . . . . . 110
Summary . . . . . . . . . . . 112
Acknowledgements . . . . . . . . . 112
References . . . . . . . . . . . 113

# Fish Production in Freshwaters

E. D. LE CREN

Synopsis . . . . . . . . . . . 115
Introduction. . . . . . . . . . . 115
The relationships of production to other parameters . . . 116
Methods of estimating fish production . . . . . . 119
Estimates of production. . . . . . . . . 121
Factors affecting fish production . . . . . . . 125
  General productivity . . . . . . . . . 125
  Species composition . . . . . . . . . 126
  Intra-specific factors . . . . . . . . . 126
Conclusions for conservation and management . . . . . 128
Discussion and conclusions . . . . . . . . 130
Acknowledgements . . . . . . . . . 131
References . . . . . . . . . . . 131

# Problems of the Conservation of Freshwater Ecosystems

N. C. MORGAN

Synopsis . . . . . . . . . . . 135
Introduction. . . . . . . . . . . 135

CONTENTS

Selection of Nature Reserves . . . . . . . 136
  The United Kingdom . . . . . . . . 136
  Project Mar . . . . . . . . . . 137
  Project Aqua . . . . . . . . . . 137
Conservation of rare species . . . . . . . . 137
Water abstraction and regulation . . . . . . . 138
  Reservoirs . . . . . . . . . . 138
  Irrigation . . . . . . . . . . . 142
  Abstraction from chalk aquifers . . . . . . 142
Multiple use of open waters . . . . . . . . 143
  Disturbance . . . . . . . . . . 144
  Pollution . . . . . . . . . . . 144
  Mechanical destruction of habitat . . . . . . 144
  Wildfowl introductions . . . . . . . . 145
Pollution . . . . . . . . . . . 145
Effects of agriculture and forestry . . . . . . . 146
  Insecticides . . . . . . . . . . 146
  Herbicides . . . . . . . . . . 146
  Nutrients from farmland . . . . . . . . 146
Changes in the amounts of aquatic vegetation . . . . 148
  Increases . . . . . . . . . . . 148
  Decreases . . . . . . . . . . . 148
Herbicides . . . . . . . . . . . 150
Conclusions . . . . . . . . . . . 151
Acknowledgements . . . . . . . . . 152
References . . . . . . . . . . . 152

# MARINE

## Introduction

### H. A. COLE . . . . 157

## Current Biological Problems in the Conservation of Deep-Sea Fishery Resources

### D. J. GARROD and A. D. CLAYDEN

Synopsis . . . . . . . . . . 161
Introduction. . . . . . . . . . . 161
The cod fisheries of the north Atlantic 1946–1968 . . . . 162
  Distribution . . . . . . . . . . 162
  The development of the distant-water cod fisheries . . . 165
The management problem . . . . . . . . 168
A time-varied multi-stock model of the north Atlantic cod fishery 170
Application of the model to investigate management strategies . 173
The risk of biological overfishing in the north Atlantic cod stocks . 178
Concluding remarks . . . . . . . . . 180
Summary . . . . . . . . . . . 182
References . . . . . . . . . . . 183

# Laboratory Studies Related to Zooplankton Production in the Sea

## E. D. S. CORNER

Synopsis . . . . . . . . . . . 185
Introduction. . . . . . . . . . . 185
Food and feeding . . . . . . . . . 185
Metabolic rate . . . . . . . . . . 188
Assimilation of food . . . . . . . . . 193
Growth efficiency . . . . . . . . . 193
Daily ration . . . . . . . . . . 194
Conclusions . . . . . . . . . . . 197
References . . . . . . . . . . . 198

# Changes in the Distribution and Abundance of Zooplankton in the North Sea, 1948–1969

## J. M. COLEBROOK

Synopsis . . . . . . . . . . . 203
Introduction and material . . . . . . . . 203
Results . . . . . . . . . . . . 205
Discussion . . . . . . . . . . . 209
References . . . . . . . . . . . 212

# The Production Cycle and the Numbers of Marine Fish

## D. H. CUSHING

Synopsis . . . . . . . . . . . 213
Introduction. . . . . . . . . . . 213
The single process governing the numbers of marine fish . . . 213
The plaice of the southern North Sea . . . . . . 219
Larval drift . . . . . . . . . . 219
Timing of the primary production cycle . . . . . 222
The timing of spawning and the production cycle in relation to subsequent recruitment . . . . . . . . . 227
Summary . . . . . . . . . . . 229
References . . . . . . . . . . . 230

# On the Importance of the Waddensea as a Nursery Area in Relation to the Conservation of the Southern North Sea Fishery Resources

## J. J. ZIJLSTRA

Synopsis . . . . . . . . . . . 233
The problem. . . . . . . . . . . 233

Size and conditions of the Waddensea in relation to other coastal areas     237
    Physical characteristics   .     .     .     .     .     .     .     .     237
    The benthic fauna   .     .     .     .     .     .     .     .     240
The research programme   .     .     .     .     .     .     .     .     241
Results   .     .     .     .     .     .     .     .     .     .     245
Discussion   .     .     .     .     .     .     .     .     .     .     248
Summary   .     .     .     .     .     .     .     .     .     .     255
Acknowledgements   .     .     .     .     .     .     .     .     256
References   .     .     .     .     .     .     .     .     .     .     256

# Some Relationships Between the Food Intake and Growth of Young Fish

## L. BIRKETT

Synopsis   .     .     .     .     .     .     .     .     .     .     259
Introduction.   .     .     .     .     .     .     .     .     .     259
Utilization of food—the efficiency concept   .     .     .     .     .     260
Variance of the net efficiency, $E$, in experiments   .     .     .     .     261
Relationship between rate of gain and feeding rate   .     .     .     .     264
Discussion   .     .     .     .     .     .     .     .     .     .     266
Summary   .     .     .     .     .     .     .     .     .     .     267
References   .     .     .     .     .     .     .     .     .     .     268

# The Possible Contributions of Radioecology to Marine Productivity Studies

## A. PRESTON, D. F. JEFFERIES and R. J. PENTREATH

Synopsis   .     .     .     .     .     .     .     .     .     .     271
Introduction.   .     .     .     .     .     .     .     .     .     271
Movement of water   .     .     .     .     .     .     .     .     271
Sediment transport   .     .     .     .     .     .     .     .     274
Biological reconcentration   .     .     .     .     .     .     .     275
    Estimates of food consumption   .     .     .     .     .     .     276
    Trace element pathways to fish   .     .     .     .     .     .     279
    Biological availability.   .     .     .     .     .     .     .     281
Summary   .     .     .     .     .     .     .     .     .     .     282
References   .     .     .     .     .     .     .     .     .     .     283

# The Potential Productivity of Waters on the West Coast of Scotland

## R. I. CURRIE

Synopsis   .     .     .     .     .     .     .     .     .     .     285
Coastal waters of the west coast of Scotland   .     .     .     .     285
The west coast fisheries .   .     .     .     .     .     .     .     287

Improvement of productivity . . . . . . . 289
    Objectives. . . . . . . . . 289
    Present status of cultivation . . . . . . 290
    Research in cultivation techniques . . . . . 290
Natural organic cycle of the west coast lochs . . . . . 291
Foreseeable developments . . . . . . . . 292
    Replenishment or supplementation of natural stocks . . . 292
    Low density "free range" cultivation . . . . . . 292
    High density cultivation . . . . . . . . 293
    "Intensive" cultivation . . . . . . . . 293
Legal aspects . . . . . . . . . . 294
Pollution . . . . . . . . . . . 294
Summary . . . . . . . . . . . 295
References . . . . . . . . . . . 295

## Chairman's Concluding Remarks

### R. J. H. BEVERTON

Some non-biological interests in the conservation and productivity of
    the coastal marine environment . . . . . . 297


AUTHOR INDEX . . . . . . . . . 301


SYSTEMATIC INDEX . . . . . . . . . 307


SUBJECT INDEX . . . . . . . . . 311

# Freshwater

*Symp. zool. Soc. Lond.* (1972) No. 29, 3–19.

# ENVIRONMENTAL LIMITS OF PLANTS IN FLOWING WATERS

## B. A. WHITTON

*Department of Botany, University of Durham, Durham, England*

### SYNOPSIS

A review is presented summarizing the literature and some unpublished data on attached photosynthetic plants in certain extreme flowing water environments.

With upper temperature limits, it is possible to compare situations occurring naturally and those arising as a result of pollution. Such comparisons show up obvious anomalies. The limits of plants under low pH conditions and high levels of heavy metals are also reviewed, although with these extremes the data are insufficient for comparison of natural and polluted conditions. Sections of a more speculative nature are added on light climate and dissolved oxygen as factors which at high and low levels may limit the growth of plants.

The attached river and stream plants tolerant of the extreme environments are mostly simple algae, but the particular taxa involved are not the same for each extreme. *Ulothrix* is probably the genus quoted from the widest range of habitats, some forms being reported from relatively high temperatures, low pH values, high concentrations of several different heavy metals and very low levels of dissolved oxygen. Although there is no record of a vascular plant more tolerant of an extreme environment than an alga or moss, there are a few records of these organisms at sites where algal and moss species diversity is very low.

The quantitative methods which have been used for comparing the effects of extreme environments on plants fall into four main categories: use of toxicity tests; use of diversity indices; measurement of primary production; measurement of standing crops. These methods do not necessarily give similar results. An improvement in methods of quantifying the extent to which an environment is extreme is important if the significance of environmental limits of plants in natural and polluted waters is to be evaluated. Such an approach will prove useful both in interpreting the complex ecosystems of more typical rivers, and in helping to predict the effects of new pollutants. It is hoped that it may also aid planning for the deliberate introduction of species into polluted rivers and streams.

## INTRODUCTION

One of the main requirements in drawing up plans for the management of rivers and streams is a sound understanding of the factors influencing the distribution and behaviour of the organisms present. The difficulties involved in determining the relative contribution of these various factors in particular situations are all too well known. Yet biologists are not infrequently asked to predict the effects of an environmental change like a new pollutant entering a river, and they would probably be asked such questions much more often if it were widely believed that they could supply the answers.

The purpose of this review on attached photosynthetic plants in flowing waters is to summarize the data available on their occurrence in certain extreme environments. Information from such situations can be a useful aid in analysing the complex ecosystems of more typical rivers and streams. A comparison of extremes occurring naturally and as a result of man's activities may also prove of considerable value in predicting both short and long-term effects of pollution.

The extreme limits of many physical and chemical factors tolerated by organisms anywhere on earth are now known quite well (Brock 1969), although this is less true if one particular habitat is considered, like flowing water. Brock defined an extreme taxonomically: it is an environment with a very low species diversity. As discussed later, it is possible to describe extreme environments quantitatively, but this review is largely dependent simply on data from sites with an obvious reduction in the number of species present as compared with more typical sites.

The organisms occupying the extremes discussed by Brock (1969) are mostly morphologically very simple. The limits tolerated by the various groups of more complex plants like the angiosperms are only poorly known, but those tolerated by some animals, especially fish, are known much better (see Wilber, 1969). Among the extremes occurring naturally, the most pronounced instances of some, like high temperatures and low pH values, are characteristically in flowing waters, whereas those of others, such as some ionic extremes, are found in ponds and lakes. Usually pollution may be expected to raise the level of any potentially inhibitory factor more in lakes than rivers. For instance, an intermittent addition of copper sulphate to a lake can lead to the accumulation of high levels of copper in the mud (Macken-thun & Cooley, 1952), but accumulation to such an extent would not be expected in a river.

LIMITS IN EXTREME ENVIRONMENTS

*Temperature*

High temperature is the only extreme where it is possible to compare a range of both natural and polluted waters. In recent years data have been accumulated on the upper thermal limits tolerated by organisms in the effluents from naturally occurring hot springs. The uppermost limit for the blue-green alga *Synechococcus lividus* is about 74°C (Peary & Castenholz, 1964), while that for some other photosynthetic groups is: purple sulphur bacteria, 60°C; diatoms, 50°C; green algae, 48°C

(Castenholz, 1969b). Maximal growth rates at temperatures above 45°C occur mainly with procaryotic organisms. Only a few eucaryotic organisms tolerate temperatures above this. Laboratory studies of blue-green algae from thermal springs have shown clearly that various strains of a single species may have different temperature optima (Peary & Castenholz, 1964). Similar studies have apparently not been made on other groups, but the extensive list of diatoms occurring above 35°C given by Stockner (1967) includes many species which are also quite common at much lower temperatures, so it seems possible that high temperature strains may occur in a range of morphological types also within this phylum. Among the green algae, Stockner reported *Mougeotia* sp. at 47°C, and there are several other records of Conjugales at temperatures over 40°. There are a few observations in the older literature on mosses and angiosperms in the cooler parts of thermal springs, but none of the modern accounts discuss these groups.

Under acidic conditions blue–green algae are absent, and the upper temperature limit is much lower. In a study of over 150 acid thermal areas, *Cyanidium caldarium*, an eucaryotic alga of uncertain relationships, was found to have an upper thermal limit of 55–57°C by Doemel & Brock (1970). These authors found in a laboratory study of photosynthesis that $^{14}CO_2$ incorporation shows a sharp temperature optimum at 45°C, irrespective of whether the natural population came from 30°, 39°, 49° or 56°C. There is no incorporation of $^{14}CO_2$ at 60°C. Ascione, Southwick & Fresco (1966) did however show that *Cyanidium* survives for many hours at temperatures higher than the maximum permitting growth, in contrast to the behaviour of *Synechococcus lividus* observed by Peary & Castenholz (1964). A variety of flagellate algae occupy the temperature niche in acidic streams below that of *Cyanidium* (Brock, 1969).

Observations on solar-heated aquatic environments over 35° are few (Castenholz, 1969b), and almost non-existent for flowing waters. More data on such environments would be of great help in predicting the changes likely to result from thermal pollution in temperate rivers. For instance, drainage channels in hot desert regions might provide examples of water chemistry (although not of light climate) more comparable to lowland nutrient-rich rivers in temperate regions than do most of the hot springs of telluric origin.

Examples of obvious floristic changes in rivers whose temperature regime has been altered by thermal pollution have been known for a long while. Weiss & Murray (1909) summarized earlier records in the Reddish Canal, Manchester, of several plants native to warmer climates, notably *Naias graminea*, *Chara braunii* and *Compsopogon*. Sládečková

(1969) gave a list of algae occurring on cooling towers, where the
initial water temperature was about 40°C. The list consists of Oscillatoriaceae, Ulotrichales and Cladophoraceae. Trembley (1965) studied
the effects of thermal discharges on algae on slides placed in the
Delaware River. He found that in the heated areas there were fewer
species, and that they were represented by more individuals. During the
periods when the temperature exceeded 34·5°C for long periods, there
occurred an increase in the number of blue–green algal species. The
present author has observed that where part of the River Wear,
England, used to be diverted for cooling purposes, the dominant algae
(in summer) at 35°C were species of Oscillatoriaceae, in contrast to
a diverse flora of green algae and diatoms in the main river and also
at lower temperatures in the diverted water.

Two further studies on the effects of thermal pollution on attached
algae in rivers were reported in detail by Patrick (1969). The results of
one of these are difficult to interpret since a source of organic pollution
entered the river near the source of thermal pollution. The other survey,
carried out on the Green River, near Philadelphia, showed a great
reduction in the number of species present, even though the temperature
of the thermally polluted water at the time ranged only between 26°
and 28°C. The four very common algae included *Compsopogon coeruleus*,
a member of the Rhodophyta not mentioned in the literature on thermal
spring algae. The extreme summer temperature at this site was 36°C.

Anderson (1969) summarized results of a detailed study on the
effects of a heated effluent on the vascular plants in the Patuxent
River, Maryland. Among the submerged species, a large population of
*Ruppia maritima* was replaced by *Potamogeton perfoliatus* in the region
of the effluent, where temperatures reached 35°C. While the lethal
temperature for *Ruppia maritima* may not have been reached, the
critical temperature for vegetative growth may have been exceeded.

Some data on adaptation of *Synechococcus lividus* to an upward
temperature change are included in Peary & Castenholz (1964). As
pointed out by Anderson (1969) research on the temperature tolerance
of aquatic angiosperms goes back to Sachs (1864), who studied
*Vallisneria spiralis* and *Ceratophyllum demersum*. The former had a
temperature tolerance of 45°C for 10 min and the latter of 50°C.
Sachs concluded that aquatic plants were more easily damaged than
terrestrial ones. With vascular plants from other habitats, several
studies (Lyutova, Zavadskaya, Luknitskaya & Feldman, 1967;
Denko, 1967) have shown that high cultivation temperatures raise the
temperature of cell death. Anderson (1969) studied the oxygen consumption of *Potamogeton perfoliatus* taken from the Patuxent River,

Maryland, using material from sites both above and below a source of thermal pollution. Measurements were made between 25° and 45°C. Oxygen consumption was found to increase with rise in temperature in leaves collected both from heated and non-heated water. Oxygen consumption and the $Q_{10}$ value were greater between 30° and 40°C in plants taken from non-heated water than in plants taken from heated water. However it was concluded that plants growing in heated water were probably not temperature tolerant ecotypes. Immature leaves had the same oxygen consumption, and adaptation occurred during the development of each leaf. The lethal temperature for plants from both heated and non-heated sites was 45°C.

Waters with a low temperature do not represent an extreme environment for algae and bryophytes, as a wide range of species exist under such conditions. Some taxa are however favoured especially by low temperatures. Strøm (1924) reported that some algae frequent ice-cold mountain waters e.g. *Hydrurus foetidus, Prasiola fluviatilis*. Whitford (1969) mentioned that in North Carolina there are a number of winter species, belonging to the Chrysophyta, which grow and reproduce below 10°C. The present author has observed that palmelloid growths Chrysophyta are sometimes abundant in upland streams in north-east England when temperatures are only just above freezing. Physiological aspects of algal growth at low temperature were reviewed by Fogg (1969).

*Acidic environments*

Most authors treating acidic environments describe them in terms of pH only, and the only work on stream plants using both pH and total acidity is that of Bennett (1969).

Extreme acidic environments not resulting from man's activities are mostly associated with thermal springs, and, as mentioned above, at the higher temperatures only a single species is found, *Cyanidium caldarium*. The optimum pH for growth of this organism is 2·0, no growth occurs above pH 5·0, but growth still occurs well at pH 1·0 (Ascione et al., 1966). Brock (1969) reported that cultures adjusted to pH 7·0 rapidly reduce the pH towards 2·0.

It is uncertain to what extent acidic flowing waters occur naturally other than those associated with thermal springs. Williams (1968) reported a value of pH 4·0 for a major tributary of the Amazon, so it seems possible that values lower than this may occur in some Amazonian brown-water streams. White, Hem & Waring (1963) reported the chemical composition of two acid (c. pH 2·4) non-thermal springs not closely associated with a mine. Bennett (1969) suggested that drainage from coal seams and the subsequent contamination of water has probably been occurring since the exposure of coal to the air by natural erosion. Unfortunately the floristic accounts of non-thermal acid streams deal only with man-induced ones, which have probably been flowing for at the most not much more than a century. Lackey (1938) gave a detailed list of organisms occurring in acid mine drainages in Indiana and West Virginia, although, as pointed out by Brock (1969), no studies were carried out to show that the species were optimally adapted to these pH values, or that they were even growing there. The following is a summary of the filamentous algae found by Lackey in an examination of 62 sites where pH values were less than 4·0 (the number of sites at which each species was found and the minimum pH are given): *Ulothrix zonata*, 17, pH 2·4; *Mougeotia* sp., 4, pH 2·6; *Desmidium* sp., 2, pH 1·8; *Phaeothamnion* sp., 7, pH 2·6. In addition to the Chlorophyta and Chrysophyta, three other algal phyla were found: Cryptophyta, Euglenophyta, Bacillariophyta. The last two phyla were represented by many occurrences. One species, *Euglena mutabilis*, occurred at the great majority of sites (53 out of 62).

More recent studies on acid mine drainages which give some data on the algae are those of Joseph (1953) and Bennett (1969). Bennett's survey was especially detailed. He sampled 17 sites for one year at bimonthly intervals. Eight of these sites were acid creeks, and these had a total algal flora of 107 species, of which 25 were restricted to this habitat. In addition to the phyla found by Lackey (1938), a few Cyanophyta were found also. Among the Chlorophyta, representatives especially of the orders Volvocales, Ulotrichales and Microsporales had a tolerance for high levels of mine pollution. Bennett could find no evidence that any of the chemical factors other than those associated with total acidity (pH, iron) were limiting or controlling factors. While pH was considered a good indicator, total acidity seemed to have the controlling influence on the algal flora. At a particular pH a greater reduction in the total number of species was observed at the higher levels of total acidity. It was suggested that total acidity could become high enough in water coming from a mine to eliminate all algae. However, some algae, like *Euglena mutabilis*, may grow at very high levels of total acidity.

Lackey (1938) included details of other organisms. No liverworts were found in the acid waters, and only a very few mosses. The only pteridophyte actually growing in the water was *Isoetes*, but *Equisetum arvense* was found in mud only a few inches from a stream whose pH was 3·2. *Typha latifolia* was observed in several streams, but no other angiosperm was actually growing in the water.

In a small acid stream associated with the coal-field near Durham, England, the author has found the dominant organism to be a moss, *Drepanocladus fluitans*. Except under high flow conditions the pH of this stream remains more or less constant for 100 m at about pH 2·6. For the first 10 m below the source the moss exists as protonema only, mixed with four species of algae (*Stichococcus* sp., *Euglena mutabilis*, *Eunotia exigua*, unidentified chrysophyte), whereas for the remaining stretch before the stream enters a wood, the moss exists as the typical adult leafy form in an almost pure stand. The reason for this transition is not obvious.

### Toxic substances

High concentrations of many substances are probably at times responsible for reducing floristic diversity in polluted waters. Often several different toxic substances are present in a river at the same time, and it is then extremely difficult to estimate the contribution of one particular agent like a detergent or a heavy metal. Fjerdingstad's (1964, 1965) reviews provide a good starting point for searching the older literature on algae and pollutants. The present account deals only with heavy metals.

The period for which plant populations in streams may have come into contact with high levels of heavy metals varies greatly. There are situations where local metal bearing rocks have probably influenced the water chemistry over periods on the geological time-scale. Some of the chemically most exceptional waters are associated with thermal springs (White *et al.*, 1963), but there has been no systematic attempt to relate the distribution of plants in these springs to the metal chemistry of the water. On the shorter historical scale there are waters where the activities of man have increased the levels of heavy metals over periods of a century or more, as in the streams draining old mine tips. In some cases of industrial pollution contamination is intermittent, or perhaps may occur only once.

In spite of the extensive literature on toxicity of heavy metals to freshwater algae (reviewed by Whitton in press), no account has yet been given which adequately describes the limits of particular metals tolerated by particular plants in particular habitats. The main reason for this is that it is seldom clear in what forms the metal is present at a particular site. Steemann-Nielsen & Wium-Anderson (1970) showed that in the absence of chelating agent, a level of copper as low as 12·5 $\mu$g/l causes a marked lag in the growth of cultures of *Nitzschia palea*, a species which some field studies (Schroeder, 1939) have indicated is relatively resistant to copper. Besides the level of chelating agent, others factors which have been shown to influence metal toxicity are hardness of the medium and temperature (Patrick, 1962) and presence or absence of light (Whitton, 1968). Many analyses in the literature of levels of heavy metal in streams must include metal in suspension as well as in true solution. Whitton (in press) concluded from observations on streams in North Wales that high levels of zinc in stream sediments were not toxic to *Cladophora*, whereas zinc in solution is usually highly toxic to this alga (Whitton, 1970b).

Although the absolute levels of metals limiting plant growth combined with details of the forms in which the metals are occurring are not available, it is nevertheless often easy to see that metals are having a marked effect on the flora. Weimann (1952) found that in the Nordrhein–Westfalen region small Tetrasporales and Protococci, *Stigeoclonium tenue* and a few Cyanophyceae were very resistant to metallic poisons. Butcher (1955) found that in the River Churnet wastes from a copper factory greatly reduced the flora. A microflora returned in great quantity five miles downstream of the source of pollution, with *Chlorococcum*, *Achnanthes affinis* and *Stigeoclonium tenue* as the dominant species, instead of the normal succession of *Nitzschia palea–Cocconeis*. E. R. Morgan and the author (unpublished data) have found that streams in North Wales draining old mine tips and carrying levels of zinc greater than about 1·5 mg/l have a very reduced flora. At one silted site there were only three species: *Ulothrix* sp. 6 μm (width), *Mougeotia* sp. 6 μm, *Lyngbya* sp. 1·8 μm.

The limits of zinc, copper and lead tolerated in a standard test medium by 25 species of Chlorophyta from flowing waters were studied by Whitton (1970a). *Microspora* and *Ulothrix* spp. tended to be relatively resistant to all three metals, whilst *Oedogonium* spp. tended to be relatively sensitive. Conjugales were on the whole intermediate in their resistance to copper and lead, but showed a wide range of behaviour with regard to zinc, from relatively sensitive to very resistant.

### Light climate

It is uncertain to what extent high intensities of light (photosynthetically active and ultra-violet) are an extreme environment in the sense used here. According to Landsberg, Lippman, Paffen & Troll (1965) the region of the earth receiving the highest total annual radiation is the Southern Sudan, but there appear to be no floristic accounts of streams in this region, nor for that matter of any in other regions receiving very high total annual radiation. However some studies on thermal springs do provide examples of habitats subject to high light intensities during part of the year. Castenholz (1969b) concluded that inhibition of *Synechococcus* may sometimes be reached at the level of the individual cell, though many cells making up the algal layer may not even become light saturated during the very high mid-day intensities because of self-shading. On the other hand other observations by the same author suggest that growth of the blue-green algal layer as a whole may sometimes be limited by very high light intensities. R. W. Castenholz (personal communication) has studied two sites where the blue-green algal layer lies under a layer of flexibacteria. In one example, a *Synechococcus* layer lies under an orange flexibacterium over the temperature range from 40° to 53°C in areas exposed to full sunlight during the time of year when solar radiation is highest.

Man has greatly increased the levels of light reaching many streams and rivers by cutting down vegetation along the banks. It is well known that the occurrence of some algae is favoured by shaded conditions, and the occurrence of others by high light intensities (Blum, 1956). At present it does not appear possible to make any generalization about the effect of greatly increased light intensities on species diversity in streams. A greatly decreased light intensity due to pollution by suspended matter may be expected to reduce species diversity, but again there appears to have been no thorough quantitative investigation of such an effect.

Intermittent reduction of light to below compensation point for long periods due to high flows of turbid water probably also constitutes an environmental extreme. A laboratory study by the author on algae taken from the River Wear, and incubated in the dark in shaken flasks for two months at 20°, showed that in about one quarter of the species tested, at least a few cells remained alive. Those that survived were mostly unicellular forms (green algae, diatoms), but included one filamentous species, *Ulothrix* sp. (8 $\mu$m).

It seems probable that some river angiosperms may depend for a few weeks each spring on foods stored in the subterranean organs, before their upright shoots reach levels where photosynthesis exceeds respiration. In rivers where this situation occurs the plant can presumably spread only by vegetative means and not by seed, so if a new habitat is created, introduction of suitable species may be expected to occur only if planted deliberately.

### Dissolved oxygen

Dissolved oxygen has largely been neglected as an environmental factor of possible significance for photosynthetic plants in streams. Nevertheless, due to man's activities, very high and very low levels are now probably much more widespread than they were in prehistoric times. The following speculative section is presented simply in the hopes that it will stimulate investigation as to whether or not high and low oxygen levels have any marked selective effects on these plants.

In some rivers receiving artificial enrichment with mineral nutrients, levels of dissolved oxygen frequently approach and occasionally exceed 200% for short periods. The only data available on effects of high dissolved oxygen levels on the growth of aerobic photosynthetic organisms is for blue–green algae. Gusev (1962) found with cultures of *Anabaena variabilis*, grown in medium containing nitrate, that concentrations of dissolved oxygen greater than 180% were always harmful. Development during day one to four after inoculation was possible only when the concentration of dissolved oxygen did not exceed 120%. Reducing the partial pressure of oxygen sharply increased the yield of alga. More recently it has been shown (Stewart, Haystead & Pearson, 1969) that reducing the partial pressure of oxygen increases both $^{14}CO_2$ and nitrogen fixation in *Anabaena flos-aquae*. The possibility should be considered therefore that high dissolved oxygen values, perhaps in conjunction with the high light intensities and/or high redox conditions, lead to the relatively poor development of blue–green algae in eutrophic fast-flowing waters, as compared with their abundance in eutrophic lakes.

There are few data on dissolved oxygen levels in those natural habitats where they might be expected to be low, as, for instance, in acidic springs where sulphate has been produced by oxidation of hydrogen sulphide. The oxygen levels in effluents from such springs would be expected to be raised rapidly by contact with the air, and therefore of only very local influence on plant growth. In contrast, the oxygen levels in rivers receiving high organic pollution are sometimes low for many kilometres. The possibility that these low levels may be an important factor influencing the growth of attached plants has not been investigated experimentally. Examples are however quite well known of algae which can tolerate periods of anaerobiosis. Gibbs (1962), and Laing (1940) concluded that the rhizomes of *Nuphar advenum* and some other aquatic angiosperms can respire anaerobically for long periods. The limits for photosynthetic organisms on estuarine muds of pH and Eh were described in detail by Baas Becking & Wood (1955). Attached algae which have been found by the author in the River Tees at Stockton on various substrata submerged for part of the tidal cycle include blue–green algae, green algae, diatoms, *Porphyridium cruentum* and *Vaucheria* sp. Dissolved oxygen levels at this site range between 0 and 10%.

COMPARISON OF METHODS FOR DESCRIBING EXTREME ENVIRONMENTS

There are numerous other observations in the literature on particular environmental limits of particular taxa. The significance of such data is not always obvious due to the lack of suitable quantitative methods for comparing different situations. How extreme is one habitat as compared with another? The definition of an extreme environment as one with a low species diversity is a useful starting point for comparing habitats like thermal springs and acid mine drainages. However, if such studies are to be used both as a step in the study of factors influencing organisms in more typical waters, and also in the prediction of likely effects of new sources of pollution then it would seem important to develop quantitative approaches. Storrs et al. (1968) have suggested that "the lack of quantitative methods for measuring the relationship between water quality and aquatic ecology is probably the single most important pollution problem today".

The methods which have been used for comparing the effects of extreme environments on plants fall into four main categories: use of toxicity tests; use of diversity indices; measurement of primary production; measurement of standing crops. The use of toxicity tests has already been mentioned. Those which have been developed for river algae have been concerned both with comparing the toxicities of a range of waters to standard test organisms (Anon., 1964) and also with comparing the limits of particular toxic substances tolerated in one standard test medium by a range of algae (Whitton, 1970a).

The most common approach to comparing various environments where one factor has an overwhelming influence is to make use of a species diversity index. A successful application of diversity indices to thermal spring data has been made by Kullberg (1968). He used both the dominance–diversity approach of Whittaker (1965) and the species diversity index of Margalef (1951; 1958) to describe the changes in algal communities along the temperature gradients. Scattered representation along the gradients was more prevalent among the minor species than the dominants. Diversity indices showed a marked increase on passing down the gradient.

With the use of a species diversity index, an extreme environment in the sense of Brock (1969) could be quantified by stating that it is one with an index lower than a particular value. Such an application of the diversity index poses various problems. In most rivers many more species of diatoms are recognized than any other phylum, and any factor influencing these will therefore have an especially marked effect. If a pollutant does not enter at the source of a stream, it will be particularly difficult to evaluate the data because of washdown from upstream.

The widely used index of Margalef is probably not adequate if flowing waters of very different types are to be compared. Dickman (1969) tested the effect of an agent (germanium dioxide) with selective toxicity to lake periphyton by measuring diversity based on volume rather than numbers. In the study of Kullberg (1968) the size of population sampled was approximately constant, and if species diversity indices are to be used more widely, the influence of size of population on the index will need detailed study for each type of habitat. Wilhm (1968) discussed the use of diversity index minimizing the effect of sample size, where the contribution to total diversity by rare species is small. He suggested that "biomass numbers" be used, or, preferably, energy flow units. Dickman (1968) has approached such an ideal for lake plankton. He included "productivity" in a diversity index, with productivity measured by multiplying, for each species, mean sample density and biomass times the annual turnover for that species.

As with all stream situations, standardization of sampling from site to site poses many problems. The use of glass slides for monitoring the microflora of streams has often been advocated, and the particular application of periphyton to pollution studies has been discussed by von Tümpling (1968).

Quantitative estimates of primary production and standing crops of attached plants in flowing waters of an extreme nature are few, but some data has been obtained along hot spring temperature gradients. Brock (1967a) made quantitative measurements of photosynthesis (using $^{14}CO_2$) and chlorophyll at a series of stations with blue–green algae dominant along a gradient from 30° to 70°C. There was no simple correlation between standing crop and photosynthesis; a low standing crop found at the lower temperatures might have been due to grazing by animals. At temperatures close to the upper limit for algal growth, the standing crop was low, although the photosynthetic efficiency was high, and the algae were optimally adapted to the temperature at which they were living. Stockner (1968a) made estimates of primary production and respiration in the run-off streams of a hot spring (37°C) throughout one year, using the diurnal oxygen curve technique. Rates of primary production were less than found by Brock (1967a), but slightly higher than published values from other aquatic ecosystems.

Whilst there are no primary production data from other extreme flowing water habitats, it seems probable that rates of primary production are usually reduced rather than increased as they are in at least those thermal sites mentioned above. The effects of acid mine wastes on phytoplankton were studied by Johnson et al. (1968) on three Northern Ontario lakes. They found that two polluted lakes had, as compared with the unpolluted lake, reduced numbers of species and reduced primary productivity. They suggested that the level of inorganic carbon under the low pH conditions was an important contributory factor to this situation.

### DISCUSSION AND CONCLUSIONS

The attached river and stream plants tolerant of the most extreme environments are mostly simple algae, but the particular taxa involved are not the same for each extreme. *Ulothrix* is probably the genus quoted from the widest range of extreme environments, some forms being reported from relatively high temperatures, low pH values, high concentrations of several different heavy metals and very low levels of dissolved oxygen. Mosses may form a significant component of some extreme environments, especially those due to some heavy metals. Although there is no record of a vascular plant more tolerant of an extreme than an alga or a moss, there are a few records of these organisms at sites where algal and moss species diversity is very low.

It was suggested earlier that studies of the environmental limits of different groups of plants in extreme environments will prove especially useful in two ways: as a step towards understanding the complex ecosystems of more typical rivers and streams, and in prediction of the likely effects of pollution on such waters. However care needs to be taken in interpreting the results of some studies on extreme environments. Frequently more than one factor occurs at an extreme level, although it is usually only the most obvious one which is considered. For instance, waters with a very high acidity frequently also carry high levels of heavy metals. Comparison of a large number of sites is needed, like that carried out by Doemel & Brock (1970) for *Cyanidium caldarium*, before it can be assumed reliably which factors are of overwhelming importance in determining the presence of an organism at a particular site with low species diversity.

Sometimes the literature indicates an obvious difference in the floras from extreme environments resulting from pollution and from those occurring naturally. The results of Patrick (1969) mentioned earlier provide an example. She reported a great reduction in algal species diversity in a thermally polluted river, but the temperatures quoted were well below those occurring naturally in flowing waters elsewhere. More data on naturally occurring extreme environments, combined with an improvement in the quantitative methods used for describing both these and those due to pollution would no doubt show up further differences. Such an approach would also permit comparison with other environments not treated as extremes here, like those receiving very high enrichment by nitrates and phosphates.

Prediction of the long-term effects of pollution depends on a knowledge of the ability of the species to adapt to changed environmental parameters, and also on the likelihood of adapted species being introduced to the site. Brock (1967b) concluded that, in general, the temperature optima of organisms are not easily changed by mutation. Studies on physiological and genetic adaptation of stream plants to extreme environments are too few for any more detailed attempt at generalization. Studies on the long-distance dispersal of microorganisms are also too few for prediction of the time interval before a full microbial flora adapted to a new environment is introduced and becomes established. Stockner (1968b) described a 500-year old core deposited by a thermal stream which showed a gradual increase with time in number of species of diatoms present, the present diatom assemblage being reached only 75–85 years ago. However he stressed the possibility that disturbance might have confused interpretation of this core, so these results should be treated simply as an example of the type of data which should be sought. Observations on thermally polluted sites where alien macrophytes have become introduced have sometimes shown good evidence that the new species have been introduced accidently by man, as in the case of the Reddish Canal surveyed by Weiss & Murray (1909). In view of this it would seem wise to make a deliberate introduction into any markedly changed environment of a range of "desirable" plants whose environmental limits and other biological features like ability to accumulate toxic materials are clearly understood, rather than just waiting to see what happens.

## ACKNOWLEDGEMENTS

I am most grateful to the Natural Environment Research Council for a grant during the period when the previously unpublished observations were made. Among the many people who have been most helpful in discussion are E. R. Morgan, M. K. Hughes and M. Richardson.

## REFERENCES

Anderson, R. R. (1969). Temperature and rooted aquatic plants. *Chesapeake Sci.* **10**: 157–164.
Anon. (1964). *Industrial Water.* Book of ASTM Standards, D-2037-64T. Philadelphia, Amer. Soc. Test. Mat., 1964, part 23, 765 pp.

Ascione, R., Southwick, W. & Fresco, J. R. (1966). Laboratory culturing of a thermophilic alga at high temperature. *Science, N.Y.* **153**: 752–754.
Baas Becking, L. G. M. & Wood, E. J. F. (1955). Biological processes in the estuarine environment I, II. Ecology of the sulphur cycle. *Proc. K. ned. Akad. Wet.* **58**: 160–172, 173–181.
Bennett, H. D. (1969). Algae in relation to mine water. *Castanea* **34**: 306–328.
Blum, J. L. (1956). The ecology of river algae. *Bact. Rev.* **22**: 291–341.
Brock, T. D. (1967a). Relationship between standing crop and primary productivity along a hot spring thermal gradient. *Ecology* **48**: 566–571.
Brock, T. D. (1967b). Life at high temperatures. *Science, N.Y.* **158**: 1012–1019.
Brock, T. D. (1969). Microbial growth under extreme environments. *Symp. Soc. gen. Microbiol.* **19**: 15–41.
Butcher, R. W. (1955). Relation between the biology and the polluted condition of the Trent. *Verh. int. Verein theor. angew. Limnol.* **12**: 823–827.
Castenholz, R. W. (1968). The behavior of *Oscillatoria terebriformis* in hot springs. *J. Phycol.* **4**: 132–139.
Castenholz, R. W. (1969a). The thermophilic cyanophytes of Iceland and the upper temperature limit. *J. Phycol.* **5**: 360–368.
Castenholz, R. W. (1969b). Thermophilic blue–green algae and the thermal environment. *Bact. Rev.* **33**: 476–505.
Denko, E. I. (1967). The influence of cultivation temperature on cellular resistance of *Cabomba aquatica* Aubl. to various agents. In *The cell and environmental temperature*. Troshin, A. S. (ed.) London: Pergamon Press.
Dickman, M. (1968). Some indices of diversity. *Ecology* **49**: 1191–1193.
Dickman, M. (1969). A quantitative method for assessing the toxic effects of some water soluble substances, based on changes in periphyton community structure. *Water Research* **3**: 963–972.
Doemel, W. N. & Brock, T. D. (1970). The upper temperature limit of *Cyanidium caldarium*. *Arch. Mikrobiol.* **72**: 326–332.
Fjerdingstad, E. (1964). Pollution of streams estimated by benthal phytomicroorganisms. I. A saprobic system based on communities and ecological factors. *Int. Revue ges. Hydrobiol.* **49**: 63–131.
Fjerdingstad, E. (1965). Taxonomy and saprobic valency of benthic phytomicroorganisms. *Int. Revue ges. Hydrobiol.* **50**: 475–604.
Fogg, G. E. (1969). Survival of algae under adverse conditions. *Symp. Soc. exp. Biol.* **23**: 123–142.
Gibbs, M. (1962). Fermentation. In *Physiology and biochemistry of algae:* 91–98. Lewin, R. A. (ed). New York and London: Academic Press.
Gusev, M. V. (1962). The influence of dissolved oxygen on the development of blue–green algae. (In Russian). *Dokl. Akad. Nauk SSSR* **147**: 947–950. Translated in (1963) *Dokl. Akad. Nauk SSSR Biol. Sci. Sect. (Transl.)* **147**: 1358–1360.
Johnson, M. G., Michalski, M. F. P. & Christie, A. E. (1968). Effects of acid mine waters on phytoplankton in Northern Ontario lakes. *Publs Ont. Wat. Resources Commn Div. Res.* No. 30: 1–59.
Joseph, J. M. (1953). Microbiological study of acid mine waters. Preliminary report. *Ohio J. Sci.* **53**: 123–127.
Kullberg, R. G. (1968). Algal diversity in several thermal spring effluents. *Ecology* **49**: 751–755.
Lackey, J. B. (1938). The flora and fauna of surface water polluted by acid mine drainage. *U.S. Public Health Rep.* **53**: 1499–1507.

B

18    B. A. WHITTON

Laing, H. E. (1940). Respiration of the rhizomes of *Nuphar advenum* and other water plants. *Am. J. Bot.* **27**: 574–581.
Landsberg, H. E., Lippman, H., Paffen, Kh. & Troll, C. (1965). *World maps of climatology*, Second Edition. Springer–Verlag. New York Inc.
Lyutova, M. I., Zavadskaya, I. G., Luknitskaya, A. F. & Feldman, N. L. (1967). Temperature adaptation of cells of marine and freshwater algae. In *The cell and environmental temperature*. Troshin, A. S. (ed). London: Pergamon Press.
Mackenthun, K. M. & Cooley, H. L. (1952). The biological effect of copper sulphate treatment on lake ecology. *Trans. Wisc. Acad. Sci. Arts Lett.* **41**: 177–187.
Margalef, R. (1951). Diversidad de especies en las communidades naturales. *Publnes Inst. Biol. apl. Barcelona* **9**: 5–27.
Margalef, R. (1958). La teorie de la informacion en ecologia. *Mems R. Acad. Cienc. Artes Barcelona* **32**: 373–499.
Patrick, R. (1962). Algae as indicators of pollution. In *Biological problems in water pollution*, 3rd Seminar, U.S. Department of Health, Education and Welfare, Cincinnati.
Patrick, R. (1969). Some effects of temperature on freshwater algae. In *Biological aspects of thermal pollution*: 161–185. (Krenkel, P. A. and Parker, F. L., eds). Vanderbilt University Press, U.S.A.
Peary, J. & Castenholz, R. W. (1964). Temperature strains of a thermophilic blue–green alga. *Nature, Lond.* **202**: 720–721.
Sachs, J. (1864). *Flora N.R.* **22**: 139–215.
Schroeder, H. (1939). Die Algenflora der Mulde: ein Beitrag zur Biologie saprober Flusse. *Pflanzenforschung* **21**: 1–88.
Sládečková, A. (1969). Control of slimes and algae in cooling towers. *Verh. int. Verein. theor. angew. Limnol.* **17**: 532–538.
Steemann-Nielsen, E. & Wium-Anderson, S. (1970). Copper ions as poison in the sea and freshwater. *Mar. Biol.* **6**: 93–97.
Stewart, W. D. P., Haystead, A. & Pearson, H. W. (1969). Nitrogenase activity in heterocysts of blue–green algae. *Nature, Lond.* **224**: 266–228.
Stockner, J. G. (1967). Observations of thermophilic algal communities in Mount Rainier and Yellowstone National Parks. *Limnol. Oceanog.* **12**: 13–17.
Stockner, J. G. (1968a). Algal growth and primary productivity in a thermal stream. *J. Fish. Res. Bd. Can.* **25**: 2037–2058.
Stockner, J. G. (1968b). The ecology of a diatom community in a thermal stream. *Br. Phycol. Bull.* **3**: 501–514.
Storrs, P. N., Pearson, E. A., Ludwig, H. F., Walsh, R. & Stann, E. J. (1968). Estuarine water quality and biologic population indices. *Int. Conf. Wat. Poll. Res.* **4**: 128–129.
Strom, K. M. (1924). Studies in the ecology and geographical distribution of freshwater algae and plankton. *Revue algol.* **1**: 127–155.
Trembley, F. J. (1965). Effects of cooling water from steam–electric power plants on stream biota. In *Biological problems in water pollution*: 334–335. U.S. Dept. Health, Education and Welfare, 999 WP–25. Washington, D.C., U.S. Government Printing Office.
von Tümpling, W. (1968). Suggested classification of water quality based on biological characteristics. *Int. Conf. Wat. Poll. Res.* **4**: 279–290.
Weimann, R. (1952). Abwassertypen in Nordrhein–Westfalen. *Schweiz. Z. Hydrol.* **14**: 272–433.

Weiss, F. E. & Murray, H. (1909). On the occurrence of some alien aquatic plants in the Reddish Canal. *Mems Proc. Manchester Lit. Phil. Soc.* **53** (No. 14): 1–8.

White, D. E., Hem, J. D. & Waring, G. A. (1963). Chemical composition of sub-surface waters. *Prof. Pap. U.S. geol. Surv.* No. 440–F.

Whitford, L. A. (1969). Discussion (on "Some effects of temperature on fresh-water algae"). In *Biological aspects of thermal pollution*: 186–190. Krenkel, P. A. and Parker, F. L. (eds). Vanderbilt University Press, U.S.A.

Whitford, L. A. & Schumacher, G. J. (1961). Effect of current on mineral uptake and respiration by a fresh-water alga. *Limnol. Oceanogr.* **6**: 423–425.

Whittaker, R. H. (1965). Dominance and diversity in land plant communities. *Science, N.Y.* **147**: 250–260.

Whitton, B. A. (1968). Effect of light on toxicity of various substances to *Anacystis nidulans. Pl. Cell Physiol., Tokyo* **9**: 23–26.

Whitton, B. A. (1970a). Toxicity of zinc, copper and lead to Chlorophyta from flowing waters. *Arch. Mikrobiol.* **72**: 353–360.

Whitton, B. A. (1970b). Biology of *Cladophora* in fresh-waters. *Wat. Res.* **4**: 457–476.

Whitton, B. A. (in press). Toxicity of heavy metals to freshwater algae. *Phykos.*

Wilber, C. G. (1969). *The biological aspects of water pollution.* Illinois, U.S.A.: C. C. Thomas.

Wilhm, J. L. (1968). Use of biomass units in Shannon's formula. *Ecology* **49**: 153–156.

Williams, P. M. (1968). Organic and inorganic constituents of the Amazon River. *Nature, Lond.* **213**: 937–938.

*Symp. zool. Soc. Lond.* (1972) No. 29, 21–40.

# NUTRIENT BUDGETS IN RIVERS

M. OWENS, J. H. N. GARLAND, I. C. HART and G. WOOD

*Water Pollution Research Laboratory of the Department of the Environment,
Stevenage, Hertfordshire, England*

## SYNOPSIS

In order to meet the future demands for water by the population and by industry there will be an increasing need to obtain water from surface sources. Many of these will provide water of indifferent or doubtful quality and therefore various remedial measures will have to be undertaken before it can be used. These measures will depend on the probable use, and on the existing and probable future quality of the water. For the authorities responsible for controlling and planning the most efficient use of water resources a knowledge of the sources of materials which affect water quality is essential before decisions concerning establishment of treatment works for the removal of the offending material from effluents and waste waters can be made.

The quantities of materials derived from various sources can be estimated either by making direct determination of the loads from various sources in a particular catchment, in the manner illustrated by studies carried out in the River Great Ouse which drains a primarily rural area, and the River Trent which drains a more industrialized and urbanized area, or by making use of published information and experience of yields derived from the differing sources in other catchments to predict the likely concentration of polluting materials in river systems. Sewage effluents and land drainage are shown to be important sources. The relations between the quantities of inorganic nitrogen and chloride derived from land and the quantities of nitrogenous and potassium fertilizers (applied as potassium chloride) are examined. The average concentrations of inorganic nitrogen and chloride in the drainage water are shown to be inversely related to the residual run-off of water from the catchment.

A simple method of prediction of the average water quality and its variations at a particular site in a river, based on population density and land use within the catchment is described and illustrated with reference to total inorganic nitrogen and chloride.

## INTRODUCTION

In order to meet future demands for water by the population and by industry there will be an increasing need to obtain water from surface sources. Many of these will provide water of indifferent or doubtful quality, having been polluted from a wide variety of sources, and therefore various remedial measures will have to be undertaken before such water can be used. These measures will depend on the probable use and on the existing and probable future quality of the water.

When attempting to evaluate the impact of waste discharges on the quality of the receiving water, it is necessary to consider the effects of different kinds of pollutants. These can be categorized as:

(a) Those which neither serve as plant nutrients nor are assimilated like oxygen-demanding wastes but remain unchanged and may therefore be described as persistent or conservative substances which become detrimental to water quality as their concentrations rise. Many of the minerals, such as sodium, calcium, magnesium, boron, bicarbonate, chloride, and sulphate, which adversely affect the suitability of a given water for irrigation purposes, fall into this category. Some of these minerals are however required in trace amounts for algal and plant growth.

(b) Those such as nitrogen and phosphorus which can serve as plant nutrients.

(c) Those which are oxygen-demanding.

A knowledge of both the concentration of the pollutant present and the load (the quantity or mass transported) is essential for quality considerations. Concentrations are important when the river water is used for direct potable supply, irrigation, fisheries, and some industrial needs; loads can be the more important of the two factors when water is pumped from a river to a storage reservoir or when the river discharges directly into a lake.

A knowledge of the sources of pollutants which affect water quality adversely is essential before decisions can be made by the responsible authorities concerning the establishment of treatment works for the removal of the offending material either from the water or from the effluents discharged to the water. Pollutants are derived from many sources within a catchment area. These can be categorized as: (a) *diffuse sources* such as rainfall, run-off, drainage from agricultural land and urban areas, droppings from animals and birds and leaf-fall, and (b) *point sources* such as sewage effluents and industrial wastes.

The proportions of pollutants derived from these various sources can be estimated either by making direct determinations of the loads from these sources in a particular catchment or by making use of published information and experience of yields derived in other catchments to calculate the likely loads carried.

The work described in this paper is concerned with the elucidation of the magnitude and effects on water quality of the principal sources in a river catchment of (a) chloride, as an example of a conservative material and (b) inorganic nitrogen, as an example of a nutrient of biological significance. Budgets have been prepared for chloride and nitrogen flows in two rivers—the Great Ouse, which is primarily a rural river, and the Trent, which drains a more industrialized and urbanized area. For simplicity all the nitrogen and chloride derived from sources other than industry and sewage effluents are classified as coming from land-drainage. A simple method of estimating water quality at a particular site in a river based on population density and

land use within the catchment, is described and illustrated with reference
to chloride and inorganic nitrogen.

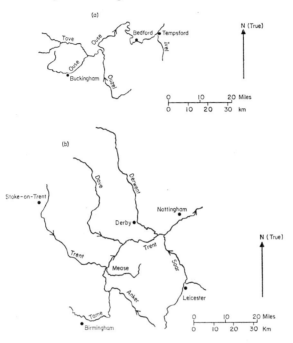

FIG. 1.a. Map of Great Ouse System. b. Map of River Trent System.

### NITROGEN AND CHLORIDE BUDGET STUDIES IN
### THE RIVERS GREAT OUSE AND TRENT

The Great Ouse drains the rich agricultural land of Oxfordshire,
Buckinghamshire, Bedfordshire, and Huntingdonshire and passes
through the Fens before discharging into the Wash. The present
study was confined to an 80-km stretch from the headwaters to
Tempsford about 16 km below Bedford (Fig. 1a). Its average flow at
Tempsford is about $0.8 \times 10^6$ m³/day; it receives many sewage
effluents and is used extensively for water supply. Water is also pumped
from it and stored in Grafham Water, a large multipurpose reservoir.

The River Trent is one of England's major river systems flowing
in a broad arc west to east across the Midlands (Fig. 1b) and discharging
into the Humber. Its average flow at Nottingham is $7 \times 10^6$ m³/day
and it embraces a complete spectrum of water quality from the clean
Derbyshire trout streams to the grossly polluted water-courses draining
the industrial areas of Birmingham and Stoke.

The concentrations of inorganic nitrogen and chloride present in samples of the water collected weekly from the Great Ouse at Tempsford and the River Trent at Nottingham were determined, river flows recorded, and the mass or load transported (the product of the concentration and the river flow) calculated. Many of the sewage effluents discharged into these two rivers within the study areas were sampled on a number of occasions and their contents of inorganic nitrogen and chloride determined. When estimating the contribution from sewage effluents to the total mass flow of nutrients in the river, the concentration of each in the remainder of the discharges was taken as an average value of those sampled. In the Great Ouse system about 21% of the inorganic nitrogen and 17% of the chloride were derived from effluents whereas in the Trent about 65% of the nitrogen and 17% of the chloride came from this source (Table I). The proportion of chloride derived from sewage effluent in the River Trent is low because of a very large industrial input of chloride, about 169 tonnes/day, to the Upper Trent from the River Sow and Amerton Brook. If allowance is made for this industrial contribution then the proportion derived from effluents becomes 40%.

TABLE I

*Some characteristics of the catchments of the Rivers Great Ouse and Trent, together with mass flows of inorganic nitrogen and chloride*

|  | Great Ouse | Trent |
|---|---|---|
| Mean flow (m³/day) | $9 \cdot 7 \times 10^5$ | $77 \cdot 4 \times 10^5$ |
| Catchment area (ha) | $16 \cdot 6 \times 10^4$ | $74 \cdot 8 \times 10^4$ |
| Population | $0 \cdot 3 \times 10^6$ | $5 \cdot 2 \times 10^6$ |
| Population density (persons/ha) | $1 \cdot 8$ | $6 \cdot 8$ |
| Sewage effluent (m³/day) | $6 \cdot 5 \times 10^4$ | $127 \times 10^4$ |
| Inorganic nitrogen |  |  |
| load from effluent (kg/day) | $1 \cdot 8 \times 10^3$ | $35 \cdot 8 \times 10^3$ |
| load in river (kg/day) | $7 \cdot 1 \times 10^3$ | $55 \times 10^3$ |
| percentage from effluent | 25 | 65 |
| Chloride |  |  |
| load from effluent (kg/day) | $6 \cdot 8 \times 10^3$ | $122 \cdot 7 \times 10^3$ |
| load in river (kg/day) | $39 \cdot 7 \times 10^3$ | $740 \times 10^3$ |
| percentage from effluent | 17 | 17 |

The results shown in Table I indicate that in a river draining primarily an agricultural area, land drainage is the major source of nitrogen and chloride but that in industrialized and urbanized catchments the major proportions of these ions are derived from effluents. This accords with recent results in Canada (Neil, Johnson & Owen, 1967), the USA (Task Group Report 2610P, 1967), and in the UK (Owens, 1970), all of which indicated that land drainage is an important source of nitrogen. Owens (1970) calculated that a population density of about three persons/ha was required before the contributions of nitrogen derived from sewage effluents and land drainage were of equal proportions and that when the population reached six persons/ha sewage effluent would contribute 67% of the nitrogen.

### YIELDS OF INORGANIC NITROGEN AND CHLORIDE
### FROM OTHER CATCHMENT AREAS

Annual loads of nitrogen and chloride have also been calculated from data available for a number of other rivers in England and Wales. The contribution from sewage effluents was calculated by assuming that they contained 28 mg/l inorganic nitrogen and 100 mg/l chloride, the mean concentrations found in a number of sewage effluents that have been examined. If the residual masses of nitrogen and chloride, those not accounted for by contributions from sewage effluents, can be assumed to be derived from land drainage then the annual loads derived per unit of catchment area can be calculated. These ranged from 1 to 23 with a mean of 11·3 kg nitrogen/ha year and from 50 to 400 with a mean of 106 kg chloride/ha year.

Similar yields have been reported in other studies. Sawyer (1947) found that agricultural drainage in the Madison area, Wisconsin, contributed 7·5 kg nitrogen/ha year. The yields of nitrogen from several rural streams near Toronto varied from 3·2 to 7·7 kg/ha year. Feth (1966) analysed the nitrate nitrogen load of 109 rivers in the USA and found yields which varied from 0·04 to 3·6 kg/ha year. Minshall, Nichols & Witzel (1969) observed that the annual nitrogen losses in the base flow of streams in south western Wisconsin ranged from 0·6 to 5·0 with a mean of 1·2 kg/ha year.

The estimated average rates of chloride loss in run-off in 11 rivers draining a $142 \times 10^6$ km$^2$ area in the western United States ranged from $9 \times 10^6$ to $601 \times 10^6$ kg/year, corresponding to losses per unit of catchment area of 0·5 to 150 with a mean of 17 kg/ha year (Van Denburgh & Feth, 1965).

It would be expected that these yields would be affected by soil type, land use, varying rates of fertilizer application, water content of the soil, rainfall, rates of run-off per unit of catchment area, and proximity to the sea. In the UK catchment area studies described above, the yield of nitrogen was relatively independent of the quantity of nitrogenous fertilizer applied in the catchment, yields tending to increase only slightly, and not significantly, with increasing quantity

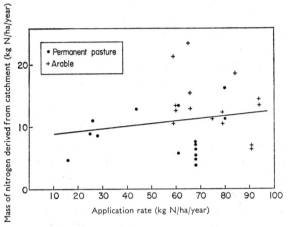

FIG. 2. Relation between annual yields of inorganic nitrogen and quantity of nitrogenous fertilizer applied to different river catchments.

of fertilizer applied (Fig. 2). Furthermore the loads of nitrogen carried at any flow by some rivers in the UK have not increased despite considerable increases in the quantities of nitrogenous fertilizer applied in their catchments (Owens, 1970). Yields of chloride were also only slightly dependent on the quantity of potassium fertilizers applied which in the UK are mostly potassium chloride. It must be emphasized however that the rates of application of fertilizer were derived from county figures and do not necessarily reflect those which would be directly applicable to the catchment.

Yields are affected by different land uses; for example average yields of 1·4 to 3·5 kg nitrogen/ha year have been reported for sparsely populated afforested catchment areas (Sylvester, 1961); whereas yields of 2·8 to 26 kg nitrogen/ha year (85% nitrate) have been reported for surface irrigation return flows (Sylvester & Seabloom, 1963). Drainage from urban areas can contribute 9·5 kg/ha year (Sylvester & Anderson, 1964). Owens (1970) has shown that the yield of nitrogen was slightly dependent on land use; the mean quantities of nitrogen derived in drainage from arable, grassland, and rough grazing being 13, 8, and 4 kg/ha respectively. The information relating to land use was based on counties rather than on river catchment basins but the results tended to support the view that nitrogen loads in run-off from

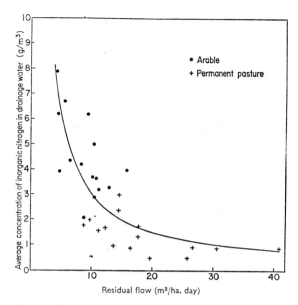

FIG. 3. Relation between the average inorganic nitrogen content of "drainage water" and the residual run-off from different river catchments.

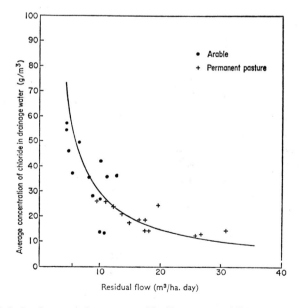

FIG. 4. Relation between the average chloride content of "drainage water" and the residual run-off from different river catchments.

permanent grassland may be less than those from arable land, presumably because of the more efficient use of nitrogen by the grass.

In order to determine the effect of run-off on the annual yields of nitrogen and chloride from the catchment area, the average concentrations of these elements in the drainage water were calculated by dividing the estimated annual loads by the estimated annual run-off from the catchment (taken as the total river flow minus the volume of sewage effluent discharged). The average concentrations appear to be inversely related to the quantity of water draining from the catchments (Figs 3 and 4).

The ranges of average concentrations in the drainage water from the different catchments are 0·5 to 8 mg/l for nitrogen and 14 to 60 mg/l for chloride. The calculated regression lines are shown in Figs 3 and 4 and correspond to mean annual loads from all the catchments of 11·2 and 106 kg/ha of nitrogen and chloride respectively. The relation shown in Fig. 3 suggests that in rivers like the River Stour in Essex, in which the nitrate content has aroused a great deal of interest and which has a small residual run-off of water from the catchment, about 2·0 m³/ha day on average, then the drainage water would be expected to have an average inorganic nitrogen content of about 15 mg/l. Although Feth (1966) has also shown that the average nitrate concentrations in 109 American rivers varied inversely with areal discharge (i.e. drainage), the differences in concentrations were small, varying from a high of 0·8 mg/l for areas with low areal discharge (0·35 m³/ha day) to a low of 0·5 mg/l for areas with high discharge (14·2 m³/ha day) and these indicated that the annual loads derived from the catchments tended to increase with increase in discharge. No explanation can be offered for this seeming difference in behaviour between British and American catchments.

It must be emphasized that, although it is likely that the figures presented here give a general indication of the yields of nitrogen and chloride from land, more detailed investigations in well-defined catchments are required to establish the precise influence of land-use, fertilizer application, and run-off on the concentrations of nitrogen and chloride in the drainage water.

## YIELDS OF NITROGEN AND CHLORIDE FROM
## HYPOTHETICAL CATCHMENTS

It was stated earlier that it is possible to make use of information derived from other catchments to calculate the approximate proportions of nitrogen and chloride that would be derived from the various sources in any catchment. For this it is necessary to know the contributions per person of these elements in sewage effluents, the quantities derived from land, the population of the catchment area or the volume of the sewage effluent discharged, and the area of the catchment. It is then possible by means of a simple population density–land drainage relationship to estimate the quantities of nitrogen and chloride derived from the two sources and also the total mass transported in any river.

Thus

| Mass entering or transported by a river per unit time | = | Mass from effluents in catchment per unit time | + | Mass from land drainage in catchment per unit time |
|---|---|---|---|---|

or

$$M_R = M_E + M_L \qquad (1)$$

It might be necessary in certain catchments to expand this to include a contribution $M_I$ from industrial sources.

The mass from sewage effluents in the catchment can be written

$$M_E = n \times \bar{P} = Q_E \times \bar{C}_E \qquad (2)$$

where $n$ is the population of the catchment area, $\bar{P}$ is the average contribution of nitrogen or chloride per person in the effluent per unit time, $Q_E$ is the volume of sewage effluent discharged per unit time, and $\bar{C}_E$ is the average concentration of nitrogen or chloride in the effluent in consistent units.

The mass entering from the land ($M_L$) can be calculated by multiplying the average yield of nitrogen or chloride per unit of catchment area per unit time ($\bar{Y}$) by the area of the catchment ($A$) in consistent units.

Thus

$$M_L = [A \times \bar{Y}]. \qquad (3)$$

The mass transported by the river is therefore

or
$$M_R = [n \times \bar{P}] + [A \times \bar{Y}] \qquad (4)$$
$$M_R = [Q_E \times \bar{C}_E] + [A \times \bar{Y}]. \qquad (5)$$

The mass entering from the land can also be calculated as the product of the residual flow from the land ($Q_L$) and the concentration ($C_L$) of nitrogen or chloride in the drainage water.

Thus

$$M_L = Q_L \times C_L \tag{6}$$

and the mass transported by the river is

$$M_R = [Q_E \times \bar{C}_E] + [Q_L \times C_L], \tag{7}$$

where $Q_L = Q_R - Q_E$ ($Q_R$ is the river flow and $Q_E$ the effluent discharge).

Equations 4 or 7 can therefore be used to calculate the proportions of the total load of inorganic nitrogen or chloride transported by the river that are derived from the two sources.

If $[n \times \bar{P}]$ and $[A \times \bar{Y}]$ are estimated in annual quantities or $Q_E$ and $Q_L$ are the total annual flows of effluent and drainage, then by dividing both sides of Equations 4 or 7 by $Q_R$, the total annual flow of the river, the average or mean concentration of nitrogen or chloride $(\bar{C}_R)$ in the river is obtained. If the masses from sewage effluent and land drainage are calculated on a daily basis then division of both sides of Equations 4 or 7 by the mean daily flow $\bar{Q}_R$ will again yield the mean concentration $\bar{C}_R$ in the river water.

The mean concentration of inorganic nitrogen in a number of sewage effluents was about 28 mg/l and that of chloride about 100 mg/l corresponding to contributions of 7 g inorganic nitrogen and 23 g chloride per person per day. The average loads of nitrogen and chloride from the catchment areas were 11·3 and 106 kg/ha year or about 30 and 290 g/ha day. Equations 4 and 7 can be written for nitrogen on a daily basis as

$$M_R = 7n + 30A \qquad \text{g/day} \tag{8}$$

or

$$M_R = 28Q_E + Q_L C_L \quad \text{g/day} \tag{9}$$

and chloride as

$$M_R = 23n + 290A \qquad \text{g/day} \tag{10}$$

or

$$M_R = 100Q_E + Q_L C_L \text{ g/day.} \tag{11}$$

Thus for example from a catchment of 100 ha and a population of 1000 the total mass of nitrogen entering the river each day will be

$$M_R = [7 \times 1000] + [100 \times 30] = 10\cdot0 \text{ kg/day,}$$

about 70% of which is obviously derived from sewage effluents. If the mean daily flow of the river to which this mass is discharged is 1000 m³ then the mean concentration of nitrogen in the river will be 10·0 mg/l.

CALCULATION OF SEASONAL VARIATIONS OF
INORGANIC NITROGEN AND CHLORIDE IN ANY RIVER

While it is of value to know the magnitude of the average concentration of any ion in a river water, this concentration does vary and it would be of greater use to be able to calculate this expected variation.

The volume of sewage effluent discharged daily and its content of nitrogen and chloride are relatively constant. Observations made at two-monthly intervals at 20 sewage works in the Great Ouse catchment area over a period of one year show a variation in discharge from 2620 to 2980 with a mean of 2710 $m^3/h$ and variation in concentration from 22 to 34 mg nitrogen/l with a mean of 28 mg/l, and from 90 to 120 mg chloride/l with a mean of 100 mg/l. These data suggest that the flow of sewage effluents and their contributions of nitrogen and chloride might in the first instance be accepted as constants. Therefore any change in the concentration of these substances in river water must be brought about by a varying flow and mass derived from the land. This varying mass can be calculated by multiplying the varying residual flow by the estimated mean concentration in the water draining from the land. This concentration is obtained from the relation shown in Figs 3 and 4 between mean concentration and mean residual run-off for a number of different catchments. It is assumed in the first instance that the concentrations of inorganic nitrogen and chloride in the drainage water remain constant. Some evidence to support this is given by Cooke & Williams (1970) who showed that the monthly average concentrations of oxidized nitrogen in drainage water at Woburn were fairly constant. It should be pointed out however that in the same paper considerable variations in the monthly average concentrations of nitrogen in the drainage at Saxmundham are reported. This variation could be simulated by estimating the concentration present in the drainage water corresponding to any particular residual flow from the land from Figs 3 and 4 and multiplying this by that flow.

It is postulated that since the mass derived from effluents is relatively constant then the variation in mass flow as a function of flow in any river can be simulated by allowing the mass derived in drainage from the land to vary directly with the flow of drainage water. This hypothesis is not at variance with the data for different catchments shown in Figs 3 and 4, for although these suggest that the annual mass (expressed on a daily basis) derived from the land is independent of the flow, it would still be possible to observe seasonal variations in the quantities derived from land in any single catchment according to variations in run-off and still attain the same annual mass as other catchments

If

$$\bar{C}_L = \frac{A\bar{Y}}{\bar{Q}_L} = \frac{A\bar{Y}}{\bar{Q}_R - \bar{Q}_E}$$

where $\bar{Q}_L$ is the mean residual run-off

$\bar{Q}_R$ is the mean river flow

$\bar{Q}_E$ is the mean effluent flow

and $\bar{Q}_R - \bar{Q}_E$ is constant for any one year.

Then $M_L$, the mass derived from run-off in auy catchment, is given by

$$\bar{C}_L \cdot Q_L = \frac{A\bar{Y} \cdot Q_L}{\bar{Q}_R - \bar{Q}_E} = \frac{A\bar{Y}(Q_R - Q_E)}{\bar{Q}_R - \bar{Q}_E}. \tag{12}$$

Thus the mass transported by the river is

$$M_R = C_R \cdot Q_R = n\bar{P} + A\bar{Y}\left(\frac{Q_R - Q_E}{\bar{Q}_R - \bar{Q}_E}\right) \tag{13}$$

or

$$M_R = C_R \cdot Q_R = n\bar{P} + \bar{C}_L \cdot Q_L = n\bar{P} + \bar{C}_L(Q_R - Q_E) \tag{14}$$

and

$$C_R = \frac{n\bar{P} + \bar{C}_L(Q_R - Q_E)}{Q_R} \tag{15}$$

where $C_R$ is the concentration corresponding to the river flow $Q_R$. When

$$Q_R = \bar{Q}_R$$

$C_R \cdot Q_R$ is the mean mass flow.

Equation 13 can be written as

$$M_R = M_E + M_L\frac{Q_R - Q_E}{\bar{Q}_R - \bar{Q}_E}$$

$$= M_E + \frac{M_L \cdot Q_R}{\bar{Q}_R - \bar{Q}_E} - \frac{M_L \cdot Q_E}{\bar{Q}_R - \bar{Q}_E}$$

$$= \left[M_E - \frac{M_L \cdot Q_E}{\bar{Q}_R - \bar{Q}_E}\right] + \frac{M_L \cdot Q_R}{\bar{Q}_R - \bar{Q}_E}$$

which suggests that a linear relationship should exist between mass flow and river flow with an intercept on the mass axis of $M_E - (M_L Q_E)/(\bar{Q}_R - \bar{Q}_E)$ and a slope of $M_L/(\bar{Q}_R - \bar{Q}_E)$. The slope is thus the average concentration of nitrogen or chloride in the drainage water.

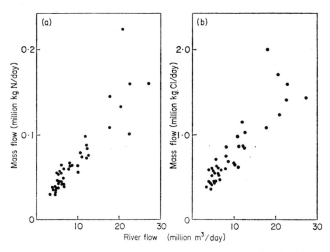

FIG. 5. Mass flows of (a) inorganic nitrogen and (b) chloride in the River Trent.

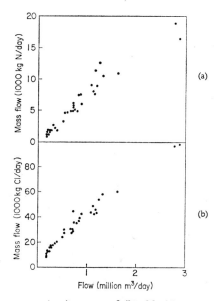

FIG. 6. Mass flows of (a) inorganic nitrogen and (b) chloride in the River Great Ouse.

For this model to apply to the mass flows of inorganic nitrogen and chloride in the Great Ouse and Trent systems, the mass flows of these substances, when plotted against the corresponding river flow, should yield a straight line. That this is the case is shown in Figs 5 and 6.

This simple empirical model has been used to predict the monthly mean concentrations of chloride in both the rivers Great Ouse and Trent. Since it was known that there was a considerable industrial input of chloride in the Upper Trent, Equation 15 was expanded to

$$C_R = \frac{M_E + M_I + (Q_R - Q_E - Q_I)\bar{C}_L}{Q_R} \qquad (16)$$

where $M_I$ is the mass of chloride derived from industry (kg/day) and $Q_I$ is the volume of the industrial discharges (m³/day).

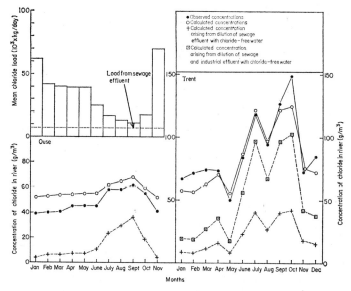

FIG. 7. Comparison of calculated and observed average monthly concentrations of chloride in the Rivers Great Ouse and Trent. The monthly mass flows in the Great Ouse together with that derived from sewage effluent are also shown.

Figure 7 compares the calculated concentration of chloride with that observed in the rivers Great Ouse and Trent. While reasonable agreement was obtained between the calculated and observed monthly means in the River Trent, in the Great Ouse the calculated values exceeded those observed. If however allowance is made for the considerable variation in the concentration of chloride present in drainage water shown in Fig. 4, then the measure of agreement is not unreasonable. Seasonal trends in concentration were reproduced. Precise information on drainage for a particular catchment would obviously improve the accuracy of the calculated concentrations for the river draining that catchment.

When however this model was used to calculate the monthly mean concentrations of inorganic nitrogen an interesting feature emerged. While there was reasonable agreement with observed values during winter, spring, and late autumn months when the flows were high, the calculated concentrations during the summer, a time of low flows, were considerably greater than those actually observed (Fig. 8). In fact the concentration of inorganic nitrogen observed at these times was less than would have been expected from dilution of sewage effluent with nitrogen-free water. The maximum quantity unaccounted for or lost corresponds to about 1200 kg/day ($0.75$ g/m$^2$ day) in the Great Ouse and 25 000 kg/day ($1.4$ g/m$^2$ day) in the River Trent.

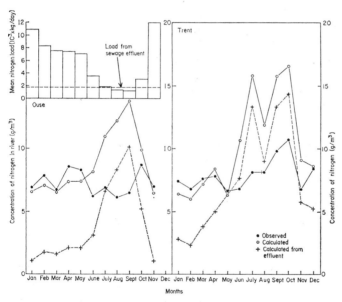

Fig. 8. Comparison of calculated and observed average monthly concentrations of inorganic nitrogen in the Rivers Great Ouse and Trent. The total mass flows in the Great Ouse together with that derived from sewage effluent are also shown.

The apparent losses of inorganic nitrogen in these rivers might be accounted for, in part at least, by seasonal variations in the volume and the concentrations of inorganic nitrogen present in the sewage effluents discharged, though either the volume of effluent discharged or its content of inorganic nitrogen would have to be approximately halved to account for the losses observed. It is suggested that the losses are real, however, for even if the contribution from land drainage has been overestimated, greater concentrations of inorganic nitrogen than those actually found would have been expected merely from dilution of the effluent by nitrogen-free water. Quite obviously however the estimated quantities lost in each river should be considered only as estimates and they do not have any precise meaning.

Similar losses of inorganic nitrogen during the summer months appear to have occurred in other rivers. In the Sangamon River, Illinois (Illinois State Water Survey, 1968) the monthly mass transported ranges from 152 to 17 400 kg/day. The maximum load is carried at time of maximum stream discharge in the Spring, and the minimum at time of low flows in September and October. The quantity of nitrate nitrogen derived from sewage effluent was said to be between 150 and 170 kg/day which accounts for the total mass transported by the river during the latter month. The volume of sewage effluent discharged was about 2000 $m^3$/day while the river flow was 73 000 $m^3$/day. It seems unlikely that the 71 000 $m^3$ of dilution water available would contain no inorganic nitrogen and therefore the true loss of inorganic nitrogen is even greater than seems apparent from these figures.

In the River Stour about 200 kg N/day are transported by the low flows during the summer months (Figs 1 and 2, Tomlinson, 1970). The volume of sewage effluent discharged is about 8400 $m^3$/day and thus the quantity derived from the effluents would be about 235 kg N/day, assuming that the effluent contained 28 mg/l inorganic nitrogen. The flow in the river at this time is 34 500 $m^3$/day and again it seems unlikely that the considerable quantity of dilution water available, whether it be from run-off or from ground water, which is more probable in this area, would be completely devoid of inorganic nitrogen.

In the Rivers Chelmer and Blackwater the quantities of inorganic nitrogen transported at times of low summer flows in 1968 were about 168 and 286 kg/day for flows of 54 000 and 45 600 $m^3$/day respectively. The quantities of inorganic nitrogen derived from sewage effluent in each river amounted to 400 and 350 kg/day for flows of 14 000 and 12 700 $m^3$/day. Again it seems unlikely that the considerable volumes of dilution water available in each river would be devoid of inorganic nitrogen and thus in the Rivers Stour, Chelmer, and Blackwater considerable losses of inorganic nitrogen occur.

Hoather (1966) reported an apparent loss of chloride from the River Great Ouse during a period of extreme low flow in September 1959. The average chloride concentration was 65 mg/l and the mass transported by the river was about 2300 kg/day. About 10 000 kg/day with a concentration of about 70–100 mg/l would have been expected from sewage effluents. While it might be expected that water taken for irrigation would reduce the mass of chloride transported, it should not affect the concentration present. A similar observation was made by Carter (1963) for the River Lee. No explanation of this phenomenon was given but it was suggested that there was soakage from the river into the surrounding soil because of its low water content, together with a like amount of replenishment of the river from springs rising from the river bed.

The losses of inorganic nitrogen in the Great Ouse could be due, in part, to uptake by aquatic plants. If the plant biomass present was equivalent to 200 g dry plant material per $m^2$, an average for rivers in Southern England, then with an estimated area of the river of about 160 ha and a growing season of 160 days, about 200 kg N/day would be utilized. Algal growth in June and July could account for a similar loss. It is difficult to quantify losses to aquatic plants and algae in the River Trent but even though the mass per unit area may be considerably less than that present in the Great Ouse, the total mass present in the estimated 1800 ha area of the river is almost certainly no less than that present in the Great Ouse and therefore the quantity of inorganic nitrogen utilized would be about 200 kg/day.

Losses of nitrogen particularly in the form of nitrate have been observed in rivers in the UK, when the water above the mud deposits contained appreciable concentrations of dissolved oxygen, and it seems likely that denitrification was occurring in the mud. In laboratory experiments losses of nitrate-nitrogen ranging from 40 to 720 mg/$m^2$ day at 10–15°C have been observed with deposits derived from activated sludge and muds from rivers and the Thames Estuary (Department of Scientific and Industrial Research, 1963, 1964). The rate was temperature dependent, the rate of loss increasing with increasing temperature. Vollenweider (1968) also reports losses of nitrogen ranging from 5 to 56 mg/$m^2$ day to the muds of various lakes in Switzerland. Assuming mud surfaces of 160 and 1800 ha in the experimental areas of the Great Ouse and River Trent, denitrification could account for losses between 60 and 1150 kg nitrogen/day in the Great Ouse and in the River Trent between 600 and 23 000 kg/day.

Significant quantities of the nitrogen present in a stream or lake as ammoniacal nitrogen may be lost to the atmosphere as gaseous ammonia, owing to natural degasification processes under favourable conditions of temperature and pH value (Stratton, 1968, 1969) and also depending on the degree of turbulence of the water and overlying air and on the concentration of ammoniacal nitrogen. At a pH of

7·5 to 8·3, the summer range in the Great Ouse and Trent, a temperature of 20°C, and an ammoniacal nitrogen content of 1 mg/l, the rate of loss would be about 6–10 mg nitrogen/m² day. This could give rise to losses of about 10 and 100 kg/day in the Ouse and Trent respectively. If the concentration of ammoniacal nitrogen was about 2 to 3 mg/l, as might be the case in the River Trent, then about 300 kg/day could be lost by this means. The rate of loss increases with increase in temperature by about 6% per degree Celsius.

It would seem therefore that the simple method of calculating loads, based on population density and land use, is of considerable value and it can be expanded to allow calculation not only of mean concentrations but also the seasonal variations in concentrations of certain substances in river waters. It seems particularly applicable to conservative substances such as chlorides, but in order to allow for the likely concentrations of biologically utilizable substances, such as nitrogen, the simple model is not adequate and must be expanded to include a "sink". Thus Equation 15 may be written

$$C_R = \frac{n\bar{P} + \bar{C}_L(Q_R - Q_E) - M_N}{Q_R}$$

where $M_N$ is the mass of nitrogen utilized by plants, or lost by denitrification or degasification processes. Further detailed work in many more river catchments is required to ascertain the magnitude of these sinks and to determine how environmental factors affect them. It seems unlikely however that such observational studies will be able to determine the importance of the many possible mechanisms involved without supporting experimental work.

### CONCLUSIONS

1. In rivers such as the Great Ouse which drain primarily agricultural land the major source of inorganic nitrogen and chloride is land drainage whereas in urbanized and industrialized catchments effluents are the major source.

2. Mean loads derived from land for a number of catchments in England and Wales have been estimated at 11·3 kg inorganic nitrogen/ ha year and 106 kg chloride/ha year.

3. Mean loads derived from land are relatively independent of the quantity of fertilizer applied to the catchments; inorganic nitrogen increased on average from 9·0 to only 12·6 kg/ha year as the quantity of nitrogenous fertilizer applied increased from 16 to nearly 100 kg/ha year.

4. Average concentrations of inorganic nitrogen and chloride in the drainage waters from these catchments appeared to be inversely related to the residual run-off per unit of catchment.

5. A simple relation between population density and land use has been used to calculate (a) the proportions of inorganic nitrogen and chloride derived from various sources within a catchment and (b) the average and varying concentrations of these substances in the river water.

6. Reasonable agreement throughout the year between calculated and observed chloride concentrations was obtained for both the River Great Ouse and the River Trent.

7. In both rivers calculated concentrations of inorganic nitrogen generally exceeded those observed during the summer months, while reasonable agreement was obtained at other times of the year.

8. Possible explanations of this discrepancy between calculated and observed concentrations of inorganic nitrogen are discussed, including utilization by aquatic plants and algae, denitrification, and loss of gaseous ammonia. Further work is required to elucidate the magnitudes of processes contributing to this nitrogen loss or "sink".

It is hoped that this paper has demonstrated the values of nutrient or chemical budget studies, which are an essential part of successful river management.

## ACKNOWLEDGEMENTS

The authors wish to thank the Pollution Prevention Officers of the River Authorities, Dr H. Clay (Great Ouse River Authority) and Mr W. F. Lester (Trent River Authority), who submitted data for the chemical survey of rivers. Misses Dear, Furness, and Harrison and Messrs Maris and Tozer (WPRL) assisted in processing the data.

## REFERENCES

Carter, G. (1963). The Rivers Thames and Lee—chloride content and hardness. *Proc. Soc. Wat. Treat. Exam.* **12**: 226–229.

Cooke, G. W. & Williams, R. J. B. (1970). Losses of nitrogen and phosphorus from agricultural land. *Wat. Treat. Exam.* **19**: 253–276.

Department of Scientific and Industrial Research (1963). *Water Pollution Research 1962*: 88. London: H.M. Stationery Office.

Department of Scientific and Industrial Research (1964). *Water Pollution Research 1963*: 108. London: H.M. Stationery Office.

Feth, J. H. (1966). Nitrogen compounds in natural waters—a review. *Wat. Resour. Res.* **2**: 41–58.

Hoather, R. C. (1966). Chemical characteristics of river waters. *Proc. Soc. Wat. Treat. Exam.* **15**: 34–49.

Illinois State Water Survey (1968). *Interim report on the presence of nitrate in Illinois surface waters.*

Minshall, N., Nichols, M. S. & Witzel, S. A. (1969). Plant nutrients in base flow of streams in southwestern Wisconsin. *Wat. Resour. Res.* **5**: 706–713.

Neil, J. H., Johnson, N. G. & Owen, G. E. (1967). Yields and sources of nitrogen from several Lake Ontario watersheds. *Proc. Conf. Gr. Lakes Res.* No. 10, 375–389.

Owens, M. (1970). Nutrient balances in rivers. *Wat. Treat. Exam.* **19**: 239–252.

Sawyer, C. N. (1947). Fertilization of lakes by agricultural and urban drainage. *J. New Engl. Wat. Wks. Ass.* **61**: 109–127.

Stratton, F. E. (1968). Ammonia losses from streams. *J. sanit. Engng Div. Am. Soc. civ. Engrs* **94**: 1085–1092.

Stratton, F. E. (1969). Nitrogen losses from alkaline water impoundments. *J. sanit. Engng Div. Am. Soc. civ. Engrs* **95**: 223–231.

Sylvester, R. O. (1961). Nutrient content of drainage water from forested, urban and agricultural areas. In *Algae and Metropolitan Wastes.* Trans. 1960 Seminar U.S. Dept. of Health, Education and Welfare. Public. Health Service, Robert A. Taft Sanitary Engineering Center, Tech. Rep. SEC TR W61-3: 80–87.

Sylvester, R. O. & Anderson, G. C. (1964). A lake's response to its environment. *J. sanit. Engng Div. Am. Soc. civ. Engrs* **90**: 1–22.

Sylvester, R. O. & Seabloom, R. W. (1963). Quality and significance of irrigation return flow. *J. Irrig. Drain. Div. Am. Soc. civ. Engrs* **89**: 1–27.

Task Group Report 2610P (1967). Sources of nitrogen and phosphorus in water supplies. *J. Am. Wat. Wks Ass.* **59**: 344–366.

Tomlinson, T. E. (1970). Trends in nitrate concentrations in English rivers in relation to fertilizer use. *Wat. Treat. Exam.* **19**: 277–295.

Van Denburgh, A. S. & Feth, J. H. (1965). Solute erosion and chloride balance in selected river basins of the western conterminous United States. *Wat. Resour. Res.* **1**: 537–541.

Vollenweider, R. A. (1968). *Scientific fundamentals of the eutrophication of lakes and flowing waters with particular reference to nitrogen and phosphorus as factors in eutrophication.* O.E.C.D. Water Management Research Group.

Symp. zool. Soc. Lond. (1972) No. 29, 41–67.

# THE APPLICATION OF FUNDAMENTAL LIMNOLOGICAL RESEARCH IN WATER SUPPLY SYSTEM DESIGN AND MANAGEMENT

## J. A. STEEL

*Metropolitan Water Board, Queen Elizabeth II Reservoir, West Molesey, Surrey, England*

SYNOPSIS

Consideration is given to a potable water treatment system which includes an impoundment stage, particular emphasis being accorded to this unit. If such impoundments thermally stratify, then difficulties may be occasioned for water supply by de-oxygenation of the hypolimnion, and the phytoplankton population of the epilimnion. Of primary importance is the loss of available volume caused by the hypolimnetic anaerobism. It is briefly indicated that this may be solved by preventing thermal stratification and supplying sufficient oxygen to the mud surface so as to maintain an oxidized microzone. In the basins considered, the energy requirement to effect this is about 40 g-cm/cm$^2$ day, and the oxygen demand per unit mud surface is assessed as $4 \cdot 0$ g $O_2$/m$^2$ day. Systems are now available which can, economically, supply energy at many times this rate. These energetic capabilities can alter the impounded water's characteristics so as to affect the biota. A "limiting" circulation depth for "Spring" diatoms is, in these waters, suggested to be almost 30 m. Some adverse effects of turbulence are indicated. Grazing by herbivorous zooplankton is suggested to be an important factor in reducing summer phytoplankton crops. The level of this grazing load, taken as twice the daphnid daily assimilation rate, is approximately $0 \cdot 05$–$0 \cdot 10$ g C/m$^2$ day during winter, and can become $1 \cdot 0$–$2 \cdot 0$ g C/m$^2$ day during summer. It is suggested that husbandry of such zooplankton would be desirable, and some means to effect this are discussed. It is possible that, with regard to phytoplankton, one of these means might allow a degree of "negative feedback" to be incorporated in the system. Such design and/or management would allow some system optimization, in which unit outputs are more closely suited to succeeding units.

## INTRODUCTION

In the context of this symposium, I propose to consider only those potable water treatment systems which include an impoundment stage, and are attempting to purify river water subjected to considerable, fluctuating nutrient and bacterial enrichment from sewage and/or land drainage.

A generalized scheme of the most usual layouts of the treatment units is given in Fig. 1. The "waste" products of the processes are also indicated. It is usual to pump water up from the river into the reservoir and then allow the superior head of the reservoir to cause the flow from the reservoir to treatment works.

It is clear that in so far as succeeding units of a treatment process place requirements upon those preceding them, the most effective design or operational regime will be that in which the various units are

viewed as a whole, a system, rather than as a series of units. This is
not the occasion to discuss in any detail the full system, so I shall
consider the treatment works as a single unit.

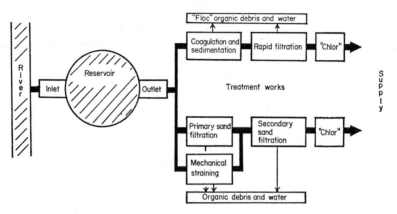

Fig. 1. General scheme of alternative water treatment systems. "Chlor" denotes
chlorination.

The "treatment works" unit imposes the requirement on the outlet
that it supplies a water containing as few suspended particles as practicable and no amount of any undesirable dissolved chemical that could
not be removed by the treatment processes. If the suspended particles
and dissolved chemical concentrations within the reservoir are hori-
zontally and vertically uniform, then that imposition is transferred, by
the outlet, to the reservoir. If however, that is not the situation, then
the patterns of distributions within the reservoir dictate, to a considerable extent, the optimum outlet design.

Within the reservoir, processes both advantageous and disadvan-
tageous to water supply are taking place. Suspended silt may be removed
in large quantities by settlement, whereas the productivity of the basin
may be such that even greater amounts of phytoplankton are produced.
An obvious requirement of the inlet is therefore, having regard to the
quality of the river water, that injection of water into the basin should
ideally not lessen the advantages nor increase the disadvantages. There
are times when the injection of river water causes chemical and/or
biological deterioration of the reservoir water, and it may seem that
the obvious solution is not to pump in any water. The primary reason,
however, for the existence of the impoundment is storage, and it may
only be significantly reduced in volume when the allowable abstraction
from the river does not meet the supply requirement. It is fortuitous
when such situations coincide.

Where the drought river flows and allowable river abstraction fall far short of the required supply volume during that drought period, large volume storage is required with all its attendant complications due to biological productivity and chemical enrichment. Lund (1966a; 1970) has reviewed some of these problems and indicated their importance to water supply. Further, generalized, examples of the difficulties he quotes are given in Windle Taylor (1963–64). Figure 2 is an illustration of the summer "deterioration" of the King George VI Reservoir of the Metropolitan Water Board, during April–September 1963. This rectangular basin, with its long axis orientated north–south, has its outlet in the centre of the southern bank. Figure 2 also indicates the draw-off depths available at that outlet, and, with seiche ranges of 3–4 m, gives some indication of the problems which may occur in such impoundments should a prolonged dry spell require supply from storage

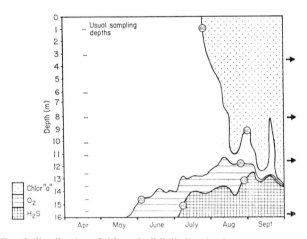

FIG. 2. Depth distribution of chlorophyll "a", dissolved oxygen percentage saturation and hydrogen sulphide in the King George VI Reservoir, April–Sept., 1963.

during late summer. The hatchings indicate the extent of water containing more than 60 $\mu$g chlorophyll "a"/l, less than 20% saturation of dissolved oxygen and more than 1·0 mg $H_2S$/l. The chlorophyll concentrations have been calculated from the chlorophyll/volume and volumes of the dominant alga, *Aphanizomenon flos-acquae*, applied to the count data of S. Biswas & R. L. Colling (unpublished).

Although an acceptable greatest phytoplankton concentration is indicated, it is not an absolute limit, and water containing even greater concentrations could, if at a considerable cost, be treated. Such flexibility does not exist with regard to the dissolved oxygen and even water containing 20% saturation of dissolved oxygen would be viewed with some trepidation. This is because the reduced substances associated with low oxygen tensions will directly interfere with the biochemical aspects of the water treatment process. Of great importance is the potential interference in chlorination, as a public health hazard may thereby arise. The production of considerable quantities of very persistent taste producing substances, occasionally aggravated by necessary chlorination, may also make the water unpalatable.

The lower strata of water must therefore be considered in these circumstances as unusable. As such, some 25% of the available storage becomes more apparent than real. This loss of volume during critical periods is of first priority in any attempt to modify this behaviour artificially, and should generally be reduced even if a consequential increase in the phytoplankton biomass occurs. How great that increase may be before the exercise becomes pointless will naturally depend upon the extant phytoplankton problem and the treatment capabilities. Clearly, if the provision of a 25% increase in usable volume results in a 25% increase in phytoplankton biomass, and the phytoplankton is distributed through the entire depth, then the phytoplankton concentration is unchanged. If the treatment works could cope with the original concentration then the project would be well worth while.

It may be asserted then that the general requirement of the inlet, reservoir and outlet is that they produce from the source, a well oxygenated water which is as nearly as possible free from particles and colour. If an attempt is to be made to design such a capability into this part of the system, there must be some understanding of the biological, chemical and physical processes taking place within the reservoir.

## DISSOLVED OXYGEN AND ENERGY REQUIREMENTS FOR DE-STRATIFIED RESERVOIRS

### Dissolved oxygen demands

In water bodies which thermally stratify with limited hypolimnetic volumes, deoxygenation of that hypolimnion is an eventual outcome of the suppression, at or near the thermocline, of effective transport between deep oxygen sinks and superficial sources. This anaerobism near the mud inevitably allows the train of events so classically detailed by Mortimer (1941) to occur, with all the consequences to chemicals of fundamental importance to both biological production and water treatment. The mud oxygen demand may be reduced to some extent by attempting to produce near meromictic conditions (Lund,

1966a) or by modifying the stratification (Ridley, 1964), however it would be preferable to isolate effectively the oxygen demand of the mud from the free water. This would be achieved by maintaining the oxidized microzone within the superficial mud. Such a microzone forces the anaerobic processes of the mud to be confined beneath it. In order to maintain such a microzone it would be necessary to prevent the stratification of the basin. Any solution to such a problem must therefore have the energetic capability to prevent thermal stratification and allow sufficient oxygen absorption and transport to satisfy the column oxygen demand including that of the mud.

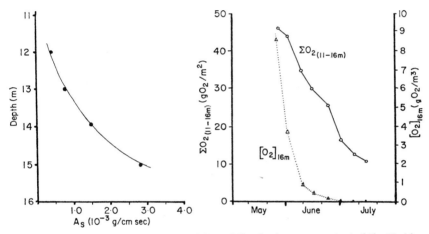

Fig. 3. Coefficient of eddy diffusivity ($A_s$) and dissolved oxygen content of the 11–16 m stratum, and the dissolved oxygen concentration at 16 m in the King George VI Reservoir, May–July, 1966.

The process of such a de-oxygenation in the 11–16 m stratum of the King George VI Reservoir during 1966 is illustrated in Fig. 3. Also shown is the dissolved oxygen concentration of the water in contact with the mud at 16 m, and the mean values of the coefficient of eddy diffusivity within the 11–16 m stratum. This turbulent transport coefficient was estimated from ammoniacal nitrogen and dissolved silica fluxes and concentration gradients within the 11–16 m stratum during the period 26th May–10th July 1966. Although the values of the eddy diffusivity are probably not absolutely correct, the relative magnitudes may be a reasonably true indication of a very significant depression of vertical turbulent transport near 11 m. If vertical turbulent transport of dissolved oxygen is assumed to be completely suppressed at 11 m, then from Fig. 3 a daily maximum consumption rate of 1·0–1·2 g $O_2/m^2$ day may be calculated at a mean oxygen concentration of 2·0 mg/l.  Light and Dark bottle production measurements on water taken at a depth of 10 m indicated no significant oxygen production, but a consumption rate of $\sim 50$ mg $O_2/m^3$ day. This rate, applied to the 11–16 m column, suggests that the oxygen in that column should reduce at a rate of $0 \cdot 25$ g $O_2/m^2$ day. The difference from actuality ($1 \cdot 0$ g $O_2/m^2$ day) we must assume to be due to the consumption of the bottom mud. This rate would be very similar to mud consumption rates that Mortimer (1941) reported for Esthwaite Water and Schliensee, and by Ahlgren (1967) for Lake Narrviken. Observation of the oxygen concentration at the mud/water interface (dissolved oxygen concentration at 16 m, Fig. 3) indicates that this is the mud consumption at oxygen concentrations within the range of $4 \cdot 0$–$0 \cdot 0$ g $O_2/m^3$ at the observed temperature of 11°C. It is clearly the consumption which would exist at approximately $8 \cdot 0$ g $O_2/m^3$ and 18–20°C that is required. That this value should be different from that computed from Fig. 3 is suggested by the oxygen consumption of river muds reported by Edwards & Rolley (1965). Mud oxygen consumption at higher dissolved oxygen concentrations cannot be assessed from the King George VI data, as those higher concentrations at 16 m are associated with the indifferent stability of the water column. In such circumstances zero oxygen flux into the 11–16 m column cannot reasonably be assumed. Resort will therefore be made to Edwards and Rolley's data, for, at the given oxygen concentration and temperature the King George VI mud consumption falls within the range of consumptions exhibited by the muds from rivers Ivel, Gade and Hiz studied by these authors. An empirically fitted equation for these data, encompassing both oxygen concentration and temperature is:

$$\frac{do}{dt} = 1 \cdot 44 \, e^{0 \cdot 07\theta}(1 - e^{-0 \cdot 2[O_2]}) \text{ g } O_2/m^2 \text{ day}. \tag{1}$$

This gives, for a dissolved oxygen concentration of $2 \cdot 0$ g $O_2/m^3$ and a temperature of 11°C, an oxygen consumption rate of almost exactly $1 \cdot 0$ g $O_2/m^2$ day, reasonably near that found in King George VI under similar conditions. Using Equation (1) then, at $8 \cdot 0$ g $O_2/m^3$ and 20°C, the mud consumption will be $4 \cdot 0$ g $O_2/m^2$ day. This rate plus a column demand obtained by summating the volume consumption rate over the full depth, suggests a requirement of about $6 \cdot 0$ g $O_2/m^2$ day.

### Energetics of mixing

It has been assumed that the basin being considered has had little or no flow through it. When, however, the storage volume is determined by the need to deliver the daily supply volume for some forty days, then

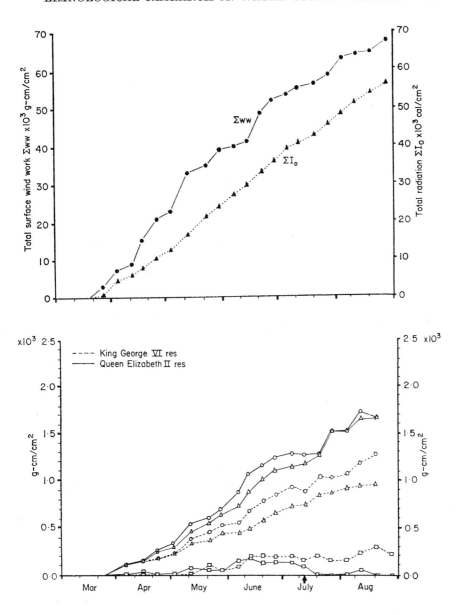

FIG. 4. Summer energetics of King George VI and Queen Elizabeth II Reservoirs during March–August, 1965.

there is a daily output of 2·0–2·5% of the basin's total volume. This advection plus some increase in the intensity of the turbulence it may induce, modify the physical behaviour of the water mass so as to produce stratifications, thermal and chemical, somewhat less stable than would otherwise be the case in the absence of flow. In shallower reservoirs this may well result in a number of complete de-stratifications each year, generally to the detriment of the reservoir quality. Such modification must be allowed for in any estimate of the energetic requirements of the destratifying systems.

Figure 4 illustrates the total "surface work" of the wind, total incident radiation, the "mixing wind work" and the stratification stability in the King George VI and Queen Elizabeth II reservoirs from March to mid-August 1965. These reservoirs are 16 m and 17·2 m deep and 1·3 and 1·4 km$^2$ in area respectively. During the period illustrated Queen Elizabeth II reservoir had 0·80% daily output.

The work required to produce the observed distribution of the summer heat income was evaluated by the "wind work" integral of Birge (1916), on the assumption that all the heat had entered the reservoirs by warming of the water surface, from which it has been carried by mixing processes. The work required to produce isothermal conditions in a stratified water mass was computed by the stability integral of Schmidt (1928). The total amount of work necessary to maintain isothermal conditions during any part of the heating period is then approximately the sum of these two requirements.

The surface wind work was evaluated by using the relationship of Van Dorn (1953) between the wind speed and surface stress, and a surface drift/wind speed factor of 0·03 (Keulgen, 1951; Bye, 1965). Total incident radiation at this time was obtained from Kew.

It may be seen that 91% of all the surface wind work took place during six periods totalling 55 days (30% of total time) and at work rates of $0·9 \times 10^3$ g-cm/cm$^2$ day. During the rest of the time the work rates were about 150 g-cm/cm$^2$ day. The overall average rate was $0·5 \times 10^3$ g-cm/cm$^2$ day. Radiation was incident on the surface at a mean rate of 360 cal/cm$^2$ day.

In King George VI the energy used to distribute the summer heat income was fairly constant at 7·0 g-cm/cm$^2$ day. That is only 1·4% of the surface work rate. In Queen Elizabeth II the distributive work rate is 14·0 g-cm/cm$^2$ day, 2·8% of the surface work. At the same time, both reservoirs were stratifying, the stability increasing about 4·0 g-cm/cm$^2$ day. The flow through Queen Elizabeth II seems to have allowed some greater amount of the surface wind work to have been used in mixing, the very small flow itself seeming not to have been directly responsible.

The result of this extra mixing is that more heat is taken up. In King George VI, during the early part of the heating period, heat was being absorbed at a rate of 192 cal/cm$^2$ day, whereas in Queen Elizabeth II the rate was 274 cal/cm$^2$ day; 53% and 76% respectively of the incident radiation rate. In Queen Elizabeth II therefore, the extra distributive work is offset by greater heat absorption so that the stratification stabilizes at the same rate as in King George VI, although with a differing density distribution. The summer heat budgets of the two reservoirs were 21 × 10$^3$ cal/cm$^2$ (Queen Elizabeth II) and 18 × 10$^3$ cal/cm$^2$ (King George VI).

The work needed to maintain isothermal conditions in Queen Elizabeth II is, therefore, 18 g-cm/cm$^2$ day, only 3–4% of the surface wind work. In fact this work rate figure would presumably be slightly higher as maintaining complete homogeneity would probably result in an even greater net heat absorption rate. This could not be greater than 100% of the incident radiation or about 400 cal/cm$^2$ day. Taking the main heating period as the first 75 days, 30 × 10$^3$ cal/cm$^2$ would be delivered. Distributed through a 17 m column, 1 cm$^2$ in area, this would result in a temperature at that time of $17 \cdot 6 + 4 \cdot 0 = 21 \cdot 6$°C. This would require $2 \cdot 4 \times 10^3$ g-cm/cm$^2$ for complete distribution, a power requirement of 32 g-cm/cm$^2$ day.

The problem of the thermal stratification of Queen Elizabeth II reservoir was considered, during the design stage, by the Chief Engineer's Department of the Metropolitan Water Board, in association with Professor C. M. White of Imperial College. Professor White proposed a solution based upon the action of submerged, turbulent jets, diagrammatically illustrated in Fig. 5.

White, Harris & Cooley (1955, unpublished) decided the inlet requirements for Queen Elizabeth II reservoir by simulating density layering by salt solutions in models and then dispersing the layers with scaled jets. The densities, and some estimates of natural mixing, were obtained

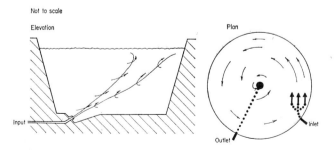

FIG. 5. Diagrammatic representation of action of "inlet" jets.

C

from a few observed thermal patterns in reservoirs in the lower Thames Valley. They found three jets each of 1 m diam. and carrying 1·5 m³/sec to be a sufficient combination.

When operating at the rated capacity, the total daily energy input into Queen Elizabeth II is 1395 g-cm/cm² day, far in excess of the required mixing energy for destratifying this particular reservoir (32 g-cm/cm² day). Not all the jet energy may be devoted to mixing, but three such jets seem quite capable of doing about 500 g-cm/cm² day of direct mixing work. This work rate is of the order of mixing capability to be expected from a continuous wind of 14 m/sec (31·4 mph) assuming previous relationships hold at such high velocities. The residual energy is dissipated against viscosity, satisfying the shear stresses of the driven velocity gradients and attempting to lift the jet stream out of the surface.

There is some evidence (Ridley, Cooley & Steel, 1966) that much less energy input is sufficient to maintain circulation in Queen Elizabeth II. The water mass can be kept in an isothermal condition by a single 22·5° jet operating at 1·85 m³/sec. It seems a possibility that the circulating currents produced by the jet stream's momentum and entrainment demand, the former carrying water from the mixing zone, the latter bringing it to that zone, play some part in this. Cooley & Harris (1954) showed that such currents in a model were ineffective in mixing; it may be, however, that in the natural situation they allow more of the wind work to be used in mixing.

The action of inlet jets will naturally be restricted on those occasions when there is insufficient river water available for abstraction, and some provision for internal circulation would seem desirable. A variety of suggested schemes has been published (Laurie, 1961; Koberg & Ford, 1965; Irwin, Symons & Robeck, 1966; Symons, Irwin, Robinson & Robeck, 1967), the diffused air system of Symons *et al.* being particularly effective in its simplicity, flexibility and cheapness. This method is capable of removing some 3·1 m³/sec of water from the lower depths. An alternative system is the "internal jet" mentioned by Lupton in the discussion to Cooley & Harris (1954). Such a device would need to be capable of accommodating a varying water depth.

### A mixing experiment

During the early part of the heating processes illustrated in Fig. 3, the input to Queen Elizabeth II was via two large, submerged inlets which allow the water to travel vertically to the surface. The input energy imparted by this arrangement at the time was 7·1 g-cm/cm² day. This work rate is, fortuitously, exactly the difference between that of

Queen Elizabeth II (14·0 g-cm/cm² day) and King George VI (7·0 g-cm/cm² day). On 12th July the inlet arrangements were altered to three 22·5° jets, which with an input flow of 0·9 m³/sec through each jet, would impart 185·3 g-cm/cm² day to the basin. After two days the input was once again altered to two 22·5° jets with individual inflows of 1·25 m³/sec. Such an arrangement produces 331·1 g-cm/cm² day of work on the basin. During the destratification process the input had to be stopped for a few days because of river abstraction restrictions, however the water mass was completely isothermal by 26th July. During this period the total mixing work done on the basin was 340 g-cm/cm². During the same period, $2·0 \times 10^3$ g-cm/cm² and $1·358 \times 10^3$ g-cm/cm² were contributed by the wind and the input jets respectively. In King George VI at this time subsurface transfer pumps were operated and the mixing work performed was 110 g-cm/cm². Of this total, 100 g-cm/cm² were presumed to be due to wind work as they were unaccounted for by direct transfer. Assuming a similar amount of work to have been done on Queen Elizabeth II by the wind, then 240 g-cm/cm² was contributed by the jets. This represents 17·3% of the jet energy. Greater efficiencies may be achieved, for the proportion of the jet energy used in mixing is to some extent dependent upon the thermal structure and in this instance the jet was having to transfer water from the deeper strata. Following the destratification, the oxygen percentage saturation became uniform at 81%, an overall increase in dissolved oxygen content of 15·0 g $O_2$/m². The destratified basin, when free of phytoplankton, remained oxygenated at or about 85% of saturation.

From such exercises we find, *a posteriori*, that systems may be devised having the energetic capability to effect destratification and maintain oxygenation. Submerged jets seem to have a dual capability, a direct mixing action and possibly, an agency effect relative to the wind. The very large amount of work they perform consumes only some 3% of the pumping costs, and this relatively cheap availability makes them an extremely attractive input system. Some input flexibility is desirable, as excessive energy inputs may, in certain circumstances, be detrimental. Optimum management requires the ability to choose the input energy to suit requirement and circumstance.

### EFFECTS OF MIXING ON THE BIOCOENOSIS

#### Phytoplankton production

The phytoplankton of a turbulent body of water may be affected either directly, by redistribution for instance, or indirectly, by changes in the environment occasioned by the turbulence. Thus higher suspended silt contents increase the optical density of the water and so decrease the depth of the euphotic zone. In order to assess the relative importance of such inter-relationships it is necessary to start from fundamental models of the energy flows associated with the phytoplankton.

The forms of the light relationships of the diatoms of the King George VI, Queen Mary and Queen Elizabeth II reservoirs during March 1969 are such as to suggest that the hourly gross production within these reservoirs would be reasonably specified by functions amongst those considered by Vollenweider (1965). Assuming a symmetrical day rate to apply to both light and photosynthesis, it is possible to derive from these formulae reasonably simple day rate equations by a slight simplification of the daily course of incident light. Such an operation leads to:

$$\sum GP = \frac{n \cdot P_{\text{opt}} \cdot \Delta}{\bar{\epsilon}_v} \, 0 \cdot 6 \left\{ 1 \cdot 333 \sinh^{-1} \phi - \frac{1}{\phi} [\sqrt{(1+\phi^2)} - 1] \right\} \text{gC/m}^2 \text{ day} (2)^*$$

and

$$\sum GP = \frac{n \cdot P_{\text{opt}} \cdot \Delta}{\bar{\epsilon}_v} \, 1 \cdot 2 \left\{ 1 \cdot 333 \tan^{-1} 0 \cdot 5 \phi - \frac{1}{\phi} \ln[1 + (0 \cdot 5 \phi)^2] \right\} \text{gC/m}^2 \text{ day} (3)$$

where

$$\phi = \frac{I'_{0,\text{max}}}{I_k} \quad \text{and} \quad \bar{\epsilon}_v = 1 \cdot 25 (\epsilon_{530} + b_{530} n). \tag{4}$$

Equation 3 makes some allowance for superficial light inhibition. Such formulations have been found by Steel (in prep.) to give a reasonable description of the gross production during clear days or days of reasonably constant cloud behaviour. Equations 2 and 3 may be reduced somewhat to:

$$\sum GP = \frac{n \cdot P_{\text{opt}} \cdot \Delta}{\bar{\epsilon}_v} \cdot 0 \cdot 6 f_1(\phi) \tag{5}$$

and

$$\sum GP = \frac{n \cdot P_{\text{opt}} \cdot \Delta}{\bar{\epsilon}_v} \cdot 1 \cdot 2 f_2(\phi). \tag{6}$$

The values of $0 \cdot 6 f_1 (\phi)$ and $1 \cdot 2 f_2 (\phi)$ for various values of $\phi$ are shown in Fig. 6.

* A key to symbols is given on p. 65.

Combining Equation 6 with a column respiration estimate (Talling, 1957) and allowing for sedimentation and flow through effects measured

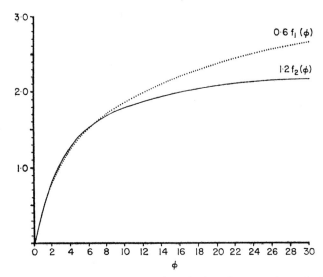

FIG. 6. Values of the light functions $f_1(\phi)$ and $f_2(\phi)$ relative to the ratio $I'_{0,\mathrm{max}}/I_k$.

in these reservoirs, some measure of rates of change of standing crops of phytoplankton may be obtained. During early months of the year relatively little grazing seems to be taking place (Steel, Duncan & Andrew, 1970) and no great error should result by ignoring its effects during early Spring. This "crop production" equation allows an estimate of the maximum realizable mean standing crop of phytoplankton, under a given set of circumstances, in a reservoir. This maximum will be characterized by the rate of change of crop being equal to zero, the most advantageous growth parameter for Spring months being chosen for the solution. In a supply reservoir with 2% output these manipulations result in:

$$\bar{n}_{\mathrm{max}} = \frac{1}{b_{530} \cdot z_{\mathrm{m}}} \left\{ \frac{P_{\mathrm{opt}} \cdot \Delta \cdot f_2(\phi)}{r \cdot P_{\mathrm{opt}} 24 + 0 \cdot 02} - z_{\mathrm{m}} \epsilon_{530} \right\}. \tag{7}$$

Similar procedure for an enclosed reservoir gives:

$$\bar{n}_{\mathrm{max}} = \frac{1}{b_{530} \cdot z_{\mathrm{m}}} \left\{ \frac{P_{\mathrm{opt}} \cdot \Delta \cdot f_2(\phi)}{r \cdot P_{\mathrm{opt}} \cdot 24 + 0 \cdot 0075} - z_{\mathrm{m}} \cdot \epsilon_{530} \right\}. \tag{8}$$

Then for King George VI, $z = 16$ m; $\epsilon_{530} = 0 \cdot 40$; daily flow is zero:

$$\bar{n}_{\mathrm{max}} = 116 \text{ mg chlor ``a''/m}^3$$

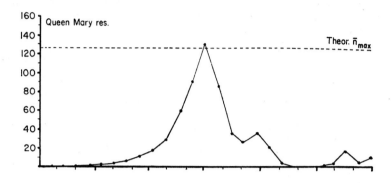

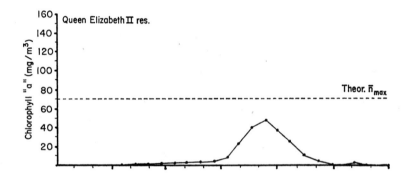

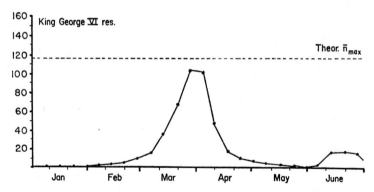

FIG. 7. Mean chlorophyll "a" concentrations in Queen Mary, Queen Elizabeth II and King George VI Reservoirs, January–June, 1969.

for Queen Mary, $z_m = 12$ m; $\epsilon_{530} = 0.65$; daily flow is 2%:

$$\bar{n}_{max} = 126 \text{ mg chlor ``a''}/\text{m}^3$$

for Queen Elizabeth II, $z_m = 17.2$ m; $\epsilon_{530} = 0.75$; daily flow is 2%:

$$\bar{n}_{max} = 58 \text{ mg chlor ``a''}/\text{m}^3$$

if $P_{opt} = 2.1$; $\Delta = 13$; $f_2(\phi) = 1.7$; $r = 0.04$ and $b_{530} = 0.01$ are taken as the growth parameters for early April.

Figure 7 illustrates the mean chlorophyll concentrations in King George VI, Queen Elizabeth II and Queen Mary Reservoirs during early 1969, their respective theoretical maxima being indicated.

It may be seen that algal crops in Queen Mary and King George VI Reservoirs come to within 105% and 85% of their respective theoretical maxima and in Queen Elizabeth II they attained 84%. This degree of agreement in Queen Elizabeth II is fortunate, as the growth in this reservoir begins much later than that in King George VI and Queen Mary. The result is that the growth in Queen Elizabeth II takes place during a period of large environmental change and the assumed constancy in the parameters of Equation 7 is no longer valid. Modifying Equation 7 to allow for changed circumstances, including the input from the river of any algae similar to those within the reservoir, leads to

$$\bar{n}_{max} = 70 \text{ mg chlor ``a''}/\text{m}^3$$

The maximum biomass in Queen Elizabeth II is 70% of this. The relative poorness of this prediction is a reflection of the over-simplification of the energy relationships which exist at this time. For instance, increasing sedimentation rates associated with the higher temperatures have been ignored, and no attempt has been made to accommodate the seemingly very complex behaviour of the relative respiration, to which such a formulation can be very sensitive. The value of the relative respiration used is the mean taken over a spring diatom growth, but not including the values associated with silica depletion. This value is somewhat lower than those generally reported, however fairly close to some of the values originally given by Talling (1957); which values he now considers somewhat low, possibly due to overnight storage of the samples. In view of the importance of this parameter further investigation is being undertaken. The value of $b_{530}$ used here is lower than previously reported by Talling (1960) and Ganf (1970), possibly because of the relatively large cell size of the *Stephanodiscus astraea* which forms 90–95% by volume of these Spring populations.

As such formulations, even when so simplified, do seem to have some validity in estimating the various energy flows within these populations, a possibility that they suggest will be briefly considered. The difference between Equation 6 as a measure of daily gross production in a unit area column and the column respiration, is some estimate of the daily net production in that column. From this may be derived the requirement that:

$$r . P_{opt} . 24 < \frac{P_{opt} . \Delta . f_2(\phi)}{z_m \epsilon_{530}}$$

for the population anabolism to exceed its katabolism. In order, therefore, to restrict the production it is clear that:

$$r . P_{opt} . 24 \geqslant \frac{P_{opt} . \Delta f_2(\phi)}{z_m \epsilon_{530}}.$$

Rearrangement of terms leads to the requirement that:

$$z_m . \epsilon_{530} . \frac{24 . r}{\Delta . f_2(\phi)} \geqslant 1. \tag{9}$$

This is basically Talling's "Column Compensation". The group $(24 . r)/(\Delta . f_2(\phi))$ had a mean minimum of 0.049 during early March of 1967, 1968 and 1969. This value indicates that for limitation of spring diatom crops:

$$z_m . \epsilon_{530} \geqslant 20 \cdot 4. \tag{10}$$

If $\epsilon_{530} = 0 \cdot 69$ be taken as representative of the waters dealt with then the phytoplankton must be circulated through $29 \cdot 6$ m. It is of great interest that Murphy (1962) essentially following Sverdrup (1953) arrived, for column compensation, at almost exactly this value via a different set of formulations, and assuming that "$k_q$" $\cong 1 \cdot 5 \epsilon_{530}$.

All such analysis is based on at least one fundamental premise: that the phytoplankton is homogenously distributed throughout the available depth. Under natural conditions this state may not be realized because net production exceeds turbulent and sinking redistribution or the fluid density distribution allows homogeneity only within restricted and superficial depths. In both instances "stirring" mechanisms, such as jets, may provide some sort of solution. It is clear that whatever the system, it must be capable of generating sufficient turbulence not only to equalize temperature and oxygen vertically, but also to homogenously distribute either buoyant or very nearly buoyant particles. Some care must however be exercised, in that indiscriminate use of the energetic capabilities of such systems may produce undesired secondary effects. The most obvious of these is the maintenance in suspension of a particle population which would otherwise subside. In this respect, the observations of Lund (1966b) with regard to *Melosira* spp. are of particular pertinence. The ideal conditions stipulated by Equation 9 may not thus be possible in any given circumstances, but circulation through as great a depth as possible can still confer great benefits. Thus the greater the $z_m . \epsilon_{530}$ product, the greater must be the $\Delta . f_2(\phi)$ product to allow a net production, in essence, the growth will only begin later in the year. The growth rate in the deeper body of water would be less than that in the shallower due to the generally less efficient conversion of captured energy into organic material. This fact will also tend to produce lower overwintering crops. The consequence of these factors means that the potential maximum would only be approached later in the year. Should that be during the summer months, then the population is inevitably exposed to much greater grazing pressure (Steel *et al.*, 1970). The warmth of the water during summer, and the associated viscosity decrease, results in greater sedimentation losses in diatoms. There seems, as well, a possibility that some of the most common planktonic freshwater diatoms have a lesser physiological capability of withstanding the warmer and brighter conditions of early summer because of relative change in their photosynthetic and respiratory activities. The combination of such circumstances reduces the attainable maximum far below that computed for the very early part of the year.

### Herbivorous zooplankton

Steel *et al.* (1970) included some attempt to assess the load on the production in Queen Mary Reservoir imposed by the herbivorous zooplankton during 1968. In that paper, even with a conservative assessment of "grazing", it was implied that from late spring/early summer onwards the herbivores, in that instance almost exclusively *Daphnia hyalina*, necessarily removed considerable amounts of the phytoplankton. Subsequent to that work, a comprehensive study principally by A. Duncan, has produced some evidence of actual grazing, either from gut contents or by direct viewing of the ingestion of the phytoplankton and/or detritus in a compressorium. The zooplankton of reservoirs described in this paper is characterized by relatively low overwintering standing crops which increase to a very large maximum in late April or early May to be followed, during summer and early autumn, by a series of lesser biomass peaks before being reduced to overwintering levels in late autumn. Of particular interest is the very large increase in the zooplankton biomass during April/May, such that the biomass at that time may be 5–10 times as great as that of the overwintering population. With this change in standing crop, a change in the metabolic activity

per unit weight also occurs (Cremer & Duncan, 1968; Andrew, in prep.).
Andrew (in prep.) suggests this to be largely due to change in the size-
class frequency within the population, for the increase is predominantly
due to very large numbers of *D. hyalina* less than 2·0 mm in length.
The higher respiratory activity per unit weight of these animals causes
the metabolic activity to increase from about 150 $\mu$g $O_2$/mg C day
during late winter and early spring to some 800 $\mu$g $O_2$/mg C day.
Although the water temperatures during April and May are 8–10°C,
warmer than during February or March, it seems that temperature
dependent respiratory changes may not be very important, and have
therefore been ignored. It is clear that whilst respiratory activity of
such animals is complex (see Duncan, Andrew & Cremer, 1970), there
is a distinct change in the metabolic rate per unit weight coincident with
the late spring biomasses. The result of this change, and the increase in
biomass, is that whereas during the early part of the year the zooplankton imposed but 0·05–0·10 g C/m² day grazing load on the basin,
from late April onwards this load can be at least as much as 1·0–2·0 g C/
m² day, assuming that grazing can be represented as twice the daphnid
assimilation (Kibby, 1969).

*Inter-relation between phytoplankton, zooplankton and "input" energy in
a "jetted" reservoir*

Some observations on the phytoplankton, zooplankton and input
energy of Queen Elizabeth II Reservoir during the earlier months of
1968, 1969 and 1970 are shown in Fig. 8. The phytoplankton concentration in the River Thames at Walton is also shown.

Space forbids all but the most salient features of these diagrams to
be discussed. Firstly, and generally, the reservoir temperatures were at
or about 4°C in early March and attained 10°C during the first week in
May. The silica concentration within the basin at the diatom maximum
was sufficient for further growth, always being 3·0 mg/l or more. The
reservoir population consisted of *Stephanodiscus astraea, Stephanodiscus
hantzschii* and *Asterionella formosa*. These algae were amongst the constituents of the river populations, which also contained many acicular
and smaller centric diatoms.

There is clearly indication of support of the reservoir population by
the input energy and, presumably, wind work, such that the reservoir
population becomes a reflection of the river growths. Thus, with
reference to Fig. 8 (a) and (c), a reduction in river population to one-
fifth reduces the reservoir populations to an almost exactly similar
degree, the input energies and zooplankton crops being relatively
similar. It is not as yet known whether it is possible to reduce suffi-

ciently the input energy so as to withdraw that support whilst maintaining the circulation through the full depth. It is possible that some

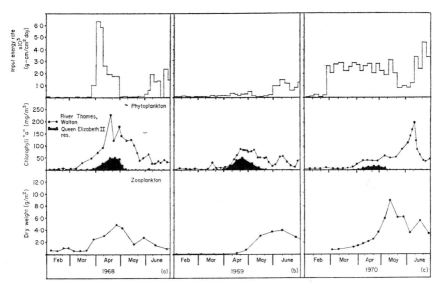

Fig. 8. Chlorophyll "a" concentration and zooplankton biomass in Queen Elizabeth II Reservoir during February–June, 1968–1970, shown with the reservoir "input energy" and chlorophyll "a" concentration in the River Thames at Walton.

compromise will have to be accepted. During May and June however, although high input energies are being used, even very high concentrations of river chlorophyll have no effect on the reservoir. Clearly this must be in part due to greater sedimentation rates, a possibly lessened physiological capability and increased grazing. That the latter must be particularly important is suggested by a number of observations, the first of which is the behaviour depicted in Fig. 8 (b). In 1969, with a low input energy, there was a greater relative reservoir population which attained the same maximum as in 1968 although the river concentration was more than halved. It is possible that this may be due to the input energy in 1969 being insufficient to circulate the phytoplankton through the full depth. However the vertical phytoplankton distribution at the time suggests that it is more probably concerned with the noticeably low zooplankton concentration then in the reservoir. The zooplankton biomass during April 1969 was only about one-tenth of the biomasses during April 1968 and 1970. This very low biomass seems to have been a result of the basin having been closed for a month during part of

December/January 1968/69. During that closure the suspended carbon was reduced to very low concentrations, about 100 $\mu$g C/l, one-fifth of the usual concentration at this time. When the output was resumed, it was via low energy inlet arrangements and at a time when the river particulate carbon was very moderate for that time of year. The result of these circumstances seems to have been a decimation of the overwintering zooplankton population and the time taken for subsequent recovery prevented the early summer maximum occurring until June, a month later than usual. The removal of grazing pressure would seem a plausible explanation of the survival of a greater proportion of the input algae.

A further factor is that the large summer river phytoplankton crops are generally composed of small organisms and include classes of algae other than diatoms. In June 1968 and 1969, for instance, *Scenedesmus quadricauda* and *Stephanodiscus hantzschii* were the dominants, with occasionally, very many extremely small centric diatoms (2–4 $\mu$m). It is probable that the sedimentation and physiology of these algae cannot be assumed to be as disabling in the reservoir during the summer as might be by applying data derived from much larger organisms.

It would seem from preliminary calculations that the energetic requirements of the zooplankton standing crops can only be satisfied by assuming consumption of the input carbon and the reservoir phytoplankton crops.

### Some qualitative observations on buoyant algae, mixing and grazing

In the second half of the year the factors controlling phytoplankton populations are less easily discerned, broadly because of a general change in the dominant flora from Bacillariophyta to Chlorophyta, Xanthophyta and particularly Cyanophyta. The relatively complex interaction between buoyant blue–green algae, turbulence and zooplankton does not allow realistic simplification and interaction will only be very briefly and qualitatively described. In the case of the blue–green algae, if allowed to accumulate at the surface, relatively little primary production is achieved; the more superficial phytoplankton being photoinhibited, the deeper being light limited due to the shading effects of the accumulation, and the algae within the aggregation being limited by the diffusion of metabolites and nutrients. Redistribution within the basin, by increased turbulence, may result in more individuals of the population realizing their gross productive capabilities with a consequent higher growth rate. This results directly from both lessening the cell density and increasing nutrient diffusion rates by turbulent mixing (Munk & Riley, 1952). Such redistribution may not only allow more production but will also bring the alga closer to the deeper outlet valves normally chosen when blue–green algae are present in any quantity. Even these simple observations are complicated by the presence or absence of wind, for at some wind speeds blue–green algae seem to be "driven" sufficiently into the body of water so that for instance, jet distribution will maintain them in the full depth circulation. When herbivorous daphnids are present in considerable quantities, then such redistribution may well bring these buoyant algae from their relatively protected, superficial aggregation into the orbit of the grazing zooplankton. Should these algae exhibit buoyancy variation then their passage from, or to, the surface will take longer the greater the turbulence and so expose them to increased grazing pressures.

The zooplankton must also be to some extent redistributed by the turbulence, probably to a differing degree to non-motile algae. It is impossible to generalize as to whether any such differential redistribution would be beneficial to either phytoplankton or zooplankton. That such differential distribution may not be to the zooplankton's advantage follows if the energetic cost of food capture is increased. The relative distributions which produce such a situation are easily envisaged but how frequently they occur is not yet known.

CONCLUSION

It is becoming increasingly clear that the herbivorous zooplankton of reservoirs like those described in the present paper play a very large part in determining their floristic behaviour. This is particularly true from late April onwards. The importance of this grazing is such that it seems that the maintenance of quite modest herbivore biomasses can preclude enormous crops of any edible alga. In natural situations, however, overgrazing by the zooplankton so reduces the available food that a great consequential decline in that zooplankton occurs. This decline may be further aided by predation. The resultant release of the summer algae from the pressures of grazing, in association with the replicative capability of algae in a productive basin probably accounts for the high summer algal concentrations in those basins. A lessened feeding capability in late autumn and winter (Burns & Rigler, 1967), coupled with the low concentrations of relatively poor quality food, also seems to reduce the zooplankton to no more than the overwintering population and so determines, to some extent, the early zooplankton crops of the following year. The obvious solution is to consider attempts to maintain the herbivore crop artificially, in essence, zooplankton husbandry.

Any such attempts at maintenance may be directed toward the provision of food and/or the removal of pressures on the herbivorous zooplankton. The reduction of predation on the herbivores is clearly in the latter group, and may well be effected in part by the removal of fish (Hrbacek & Novotna-Dvorakova, 1965). The observations of Sorokin (1968) indicate however that young roach (*Rutilus rutilus*) may consume considerable quantities of planktonic algae, *Aphanizomenon* sp. being particularly well utilized. Sorokin also found that young bream (*Abramis brama*) hardly used phytoplankton. It is to be assumed that the perch (*Perca fluviatilis*), the other most commonly caught large fish from the reservoirs studied in this paper, do not consume significant quantities of algae for R. W. White (pers. comm.) during his work on fish, zoo-, and phyto-plankton populations in three lagoons of the Rye Meads Sewage Works, has evidence of this fish actually selecting larger daphnids. In so far as it is practicable it would seem desirable to considerably reduce at least the bream and perch populations. This seems to have been naturally effected, although much of the evidence is relatively circumstantial or subjective (Windle Taylor, 1967–68; Discussion to Collins, 1970). Duncan *et al.* (1970) contains the available evidence, and discussion, of the changes in the biota of these reservoirs during the 1960's over the latter part of which period the summer phytoplankton "cover" has been very considerably reduced. It will be suggested therein that such biotic inter-relationships may well be the principal cause of the decline of the summer and autumn phytoplankton. Summer phytoplankton cover in Queen Mary has been almost as low, during 1968, 1969 and 1970 as in Queen Elizabeth II and King George VI, without any artificial energy input and, latterly, virtually no copper sulphate. To abandon the use of this chemical as an algicide, except perhaps as an extreme measure, is another less obvious means of removing a restriction on the herbivores. This follows from the observation that subsequent to even a very light dose of copper sulphate the number of eggs per female of *Daphnia hyalina* is reduced from 10–12 eggs per female to less than four eggs per female (Andrew, in prep.). Any larger doses may well be directly toxic to *Daphnia*. The effect of copper dosing could therefore prove detrimental both in the short and the long term. It may be, for instance, that the frequently reported "green aftergrowth" of coppering may result from the reduction in severe grazing pressure. In situations where the use of algicides is desirable it would be preferable to use chemicals which interfere solely with botanical processes, attempting to offset the extra cost by greater efficiency. The unreliability of low dose copper sulphate is notorious, particularly in cold water (Windle Taylor, 1963–64).

The provision of food for the grazing zooplankton may be achieved by two means, the first being to arrange the phytoplankton and zooplankton distribution so as to effect removal of the former and sustenance of the latter, and the second to maintain increased concentrations of silt in suspension. It is not, at present, obvious whether imposing a favourable balance between phyto- and zoo-plankton is practicable. Maintaining silt in suspension is quite feasible, particularly in association with the energetic capabilities of inlet jets. The provision of this extra food seems to be particularly important, for the overwintering stock seems to use detritus as its staple diet during late autumn and winter. The relative paucity and nutritional poorness of this food must play some part in determining the level of that overwintering stock. It is quite possible that by increasing the food availability some increase in overwintering capacity may be achieved. An increase in suspended silt may be obtained either by maintaining a greater proportion of the existing silt income in suspension, or by maintaining the same proportion of a greater silt input. This latter is possible only when the treatment works is close to the reservoir. Both of the general treatment systems produce waste products (Fig. 1), that from the sand filtration works being organic matter and the suspending wash water. The wash water volume will normally comprise 1–2% of the works output and is therefore a fairly considerable volume from a large treatment works. This waste is an obvious source of the required extra silt and its use would alleviate to some extent the waste disposal problems of filtration and furthermore, would conserve the washwater. Some indication of the possible effects on the reservoir by returning that waste may be attempted by a consideration of the carbon fluxes within the reservoir during winter. If such an analysis is made on the assumption that mixing can be taken as reasonably instantaneous, that the wash water carbon suffers the same fate as the input carbon derived from the river and that the observed zooplankton winter relationships are maintained, then it seems that the return of 70% of the "waste" carbon may double both the suspended particulate carbon and the zooplankton crop.

This calculated waste return assumes that nearly 80% of the particulate carbon returned to the reservoir plays no further part in metabolic processes. At worst it might be assumed that all that "lost" fraction falls to the bottom, which, allowing for winter and summer conditions, would result in a deposition rate of 363 g $C/m^2$ year, in a reservoir the size of Queen Elizabeth II. This will be equivalent to a dry weight deposit of about 2 $kg/m^2$ year. Assuming a density of 1·5 $g/cm^3$, this weight would represent a packed volume of $1·3 \times 10^3$ $cm^3$. If this volume settles with a relative void volume of 60%, the resulting deposition rate would be $4 \times 10^3$ cm$^3$/m$^2$ year, equivalent to a loss of depth of 0·4 cm/year. This would seem of no great consequence, even if considered over very long periods. Any benthic production would presumably tend to reduce this accumulation.

Such an attempt to produce much larger overwintering zooplankton crops has to take account of the time lags involved in such systems and the possibility of much lower river silt concentrations. For instance, the late autumn river silts may be as low as 1·0 mg C/l consistently. In order, then, to produce a reservoir silt of 1·0 mg C/l with 70% filtered carbon return, more of the input carbon must be retained in suspension. The control of input energy with regard to conditions and the effect required, is obviously necessary for such operations.

A further consequence of this carbon return is an increase in the turbidity of the reservoir. The river silt (River Thames, Walton) during the winter of 1968 had a 530 m$\mu$ "incremental" extinction coefficient of 0·66/m/mg C/l and assuming all the returned carbon to have similar optical properties, $\epsilon_{530}$ in Queen Elizabeth II would increase from the norm of 0·69 to 1·0. If this value of $\epsilon_{530}$ is inserted into Equation 10, then the required circulation depth for limitation becomes 20·4 m instead of the 29·6 m associated with 0·69. This consequence is exactly that proposed by Murphy (1962) in considering the inter-relation between non-productive turbidity and production. In the scheme suggested above there is also an inherent feedback, that should any algal production occur, then the filter washings being returned will contain greater amounts of carbon, treated if necessary so as to render it non-productive. This will raise the reservoir turbidity somewhat and so tend to depress the production. By suitable management it seems very possible that such feedback could always be negative.

The phytoplankton in such systems would have to stand some extreme pressures, both from grazing and competition for light energy, and it seems possible that the pressures may be made so great that extreme limitations will occur. Where circumstances make such schemes possible, and they are used, then the water from the impoundments will be of a quite different character from that normally derived from large volume storage. It will be characterized by containing few or no algae, but instead, suspended silt. By making the basin depth as near to the limiting depth as possible for the water to be stored, then the "limiting silt" concentration would always be a very much lesser weight of material than the weight of algae it was limiting. The supply from such an impoundment would then impose an even, non-algal load on the treatment works. Such water is particularly suited to chemical treatment, which is in turn highly automatable and compact. As such it could offer some alleviation of labour problems. Sand filtration, on the other hand, has the attractions of stability and the production of bio-degradable wastes. When the particles being filtered are non-replicative then mechanized, *in situ* cleaning becomes a possibility. Present experience of such a system in the Metropolitan Water Board suggests that the cleaning device has some difficulty overcoming the mechanical strength of the biological mat which forms on the surface of secondary filters. Changing the character of the reservoir water may possibly allow some reassessment of the filtration process.

I hope these sketchy comments suffice to point the possibilities, technical and economic, which might result from viewing the water treatment process as a single system for design and/or operational purposes. It will, however, require some considerable insight into the interactions within that system for optimization to be achieved. The complexity of those interactions allows so many possible combinations that the empirical approach must necessarily be abandoned for funda-mentalism.

## LIST OF SYMBOLS USED

| | |
|---|---|
| $\theta$ | Temperature |
| $[O_2]$ | Concentration of dissolved oxygen |
| $z$ | Depth |
| $z_m$ | Mixed depth |
| $GP$ | Gross Production |
| $n$ | Phytoplankton concentration |
| $P_{opt}$ | Photosynthetic rate per unit population per unit time at light optimum |
| $\bar{\epsilon}_v$ | Mean vertical extinction coefficient |
| $\epsilon_{530}$ | Vertical extinction coefficient to light of wavelength 530 m$\mu$ |
| $b_{530}$ | "Incremental" vertical extinction coefficient per unit of popu-lation to light of wavelength 530 m$\mu$ |
| $I'_0$ | Incident intensity of photosynthetically active radiation |
| $I'_{0,max}$ | Maximum incident intensity of photosynthetically active radia-tion |
| $I_k$ | The intensity of photosynthetically active radiation at which a photosynthetic rate numerically equal to $P_{opt}$ would be reached in the absence of light saturation |
| $\Delta$ | Day length |
| $r$ | "Relative" respiration $= R/P_{opt}$ |
| $C$ | Particulate carbon concentration |
| $R$ | Respiration per unit of population per unit time |

66    J. A. STEEL

ACKNOWLEDGEMENTS

This contribution is published by kind permission of Dr. E. Windle Taylor, CBE, Director of Water Examination. Such permission, however, in no way implies that the views expressed necessarily coincide with those of the Metropolitan Water Board. My thanks are due to Mr. P. Cooley for reading the manuscript, to Mr. T. Andrew for the use of some of his Queen Elizabeth II reservoir zooplankton data from 1968 and 1969, and to Mr. R. Colling for considerable assistance in the laboratory work.

REFERENCES

Ahlgren, I. (1967). Limnological studies in Lake Narrviken, a eutrophicated Swedish lake. 1. *Schweiz. Z. Hydrol.* **29**: 53–90.
Andrew, T. (In preparation). The production and respiration of reservoir populations of zooplankton, with special reference to Daphnids. PhD thesis, University of London.
Birge, E. A. (1916). The work of the wind in warming a lake. *Trans. Wisc. Acad. Sci. Arts Lett.* **18**: 341–391.
Burns, C. W. & Rigler, F. H. (1967). Comparison of filtering rates of *Daphnia rosea* in lake water and suspensions of yeast. *Limnol. Oceanogr.* **12**: 492–502.
Bye, J. A. T. (1965). Wind-driven circulation in unstratified lakes. *Limnol. Oceanogr.* **10**: 451–458.
Collins, V. G. (1970). Recent studies of bacterial pathogens of freshwater fish. *J. Soc. Wat. Treat. Exam.* **19**: 3–31.
Cooley, P. & Harris, S. L. (1954). The prevention of stratification in reservoirs. *J. Inst. Wat. Eng.* **8**: 517–537.
Cremer, G. A. & Duncan, A. (1968). A seasonal study of zooplankton respiration under field conditions. *Verh. int. Ver. Limnol.* **17**: 181–190.
Duncan, A., Andrew, T. & Cremer, G. A. (1970). The measurement of respiratory rates under field and laboratory conditions during an ecological study on zooplankton. *Polskie Archwm Hydrobiol.* **17** (30): 149–160.
Edwards, R. W. & Rolley, H. L. J. (1965). Oxygen consumption of river muds. *J. Ecol.* **53**: 1–19.
Ganf, G. G. (1970). The regulation of net production in Lake George, Uganda, E. Africa. UNESCO–IBP *Symposium on productivity problems of freshwaters*. Kazimierz-Dolny, Poland.
Hrbacek, J. & Novotna-Dvorakova, M. (1965). Plankton of four backwaters related to their size and fish stock. *Rozpr. čsl. Akad.Věd. (Mpv).* **75** (13): 1–65.
Irwin, W. H., Symons, J. M. & Robeck, G. G. (1966). Impoundment destratification by mechanical pumping. *J. sanit. Engng Div. Am. Soc. civ. Engrs* **92**: SA-6: 21.
Keulgen, G. H. (1951). Wind tides in small closed channels. *J. Res. natn. Bur. Stand.* **46**: 358–381.
Kibby, H. V. (1969). Energy transformations by a population of *Diaptomus gracilis*. PhD thesis, University of London, Westfield College.
Koberg, G. E. & Ford, M. E. Jr. (1965). Elimination of thermal stratification in reservoirs and the resulting benefits. Geological Survey Water Supply Paper 1809-M, U.S. Government Printing Office, Washington D.C. 28pp.

Laurie, A. H. (1961). The application of the "Bubble-gun" low lift pump. *Wat. Waste Treatm.* **8**: 363.

Lund, J. W. G. (1966a). Limnology and its application to potable water supplies. *J. Br. WatWks. Ass.* **49**: 14–26.

Lund, J. W. G. (1966b). The importance of turbulence in the periodicity of certain freshwater species of the genus *Melosira*. (Translation.) *Bot. Zh.*, *Kyyiv* **51**: 176–187.

Lund, J. W. G. (1970). Primary production. *J. Soc. Wat. Treat. Exam.* **19**: 332–358.

Mortimer, C. H. (1941). The exchange of dissolved substances between mud and water in lakes; I & II. *J. Ecol.* **29**: 280–329; III & IV. **30**: 147–201.

Munk, W. H. & Riley, G. A. (1952). Absorption of nutrients by aquatic plants. *J. Mar. Res.* **11**: 215–240.

Murphy, G. I. (1962). Effect of mixing depth on the productivity of freshwater impoundments. *Trans. Am. Fish. Soc.* **91**: 69–76.

Ridley, J. E. A. (1964). Thermal stratification and thermocline control in storage reservoirs. *Proc. Soc. Wat. Treat. Exam.* **13**: 275.

Ridley, J. E. A., Cooley, P. & Steel, J. A. (1966). Control of thermal stratification in Thames valley reservoirs. *Proc. Soc. Wat. Treat. Exam.* **15**: 225–244.

Schmidt, W. (1928). Uber Temperatur und Stabilitatsverhaltnisse von Seen. *Geogr. Annlr* **10**: 145–177.

Sorokin, J. J. (1968). The use of C¹⁴ in the study of nutrition of aquatic animals. *Mitt. int. Ver. Limnol.* **16**.

Steel, J. A., Duncan, A. & Andrew, T. (1970). The daily carbon gains and losses in the seston of Queen Mary reservoir, England, during 1968. UNESCO-IBP *Symposium on productivity problems of freshwaters.* Kazimierz-Dolny, Poland.

Steel, J. A. (In preparation). Production ecology in eutrophic reservoirs. PhD thesis, University of London.

Sverdrup, H. U. (1953). On conditions for vernal blooming of phytoplankton. **18**: 287–295.

Symons, J. M., Irwin, W. H., Robinson, E. L. & Robeck, G. G. (1967). Impoundment destratification for raw-water quality control using either mechanical or diffused-air pumping. *J. Am. WatWks Ass.* **59**: 1268–1291.

Talling, J. F. (1957). The phytoplankton population as a compound photosynthetic system. *New Phytol.* **56**: 133–149.

Talling, J. F. (1960). Self-shading effects in natural populations of a planktonic diatom. *Wett. Leben.* **12**: 235–242.

Van Dorn, W. G. (1953). Wind stress on an artificial pond. *J. Mar. Res.* **12**: 249–276.

Vollenweider, R. A. (1965). Calculation models of photosynthesis—depth curves and some implications regarding day rate estimates in primary production measurements. *Memorie Ist. ital. Idrobiol.* **18**: 425–457.

White, C. M., Harris, S. L. & Cooley, P. (1955, unpublished). *The hydraulic aspect of stagnation in reservoirs.*

Windle Taylor, E. (1963–64). *Res. bact. chem. biol. Exam. Lond. Waters* 41.

Windle Taylor, E. (1967–1968). *Res. bact. chem. biol. Exam. Lond. Waters* 43.

*Symp. zool. Soc. Lond.* (1972) No. 29, 69–86.

# PRODUCTIVITY OF THE RIVER THAMES AT READING

## A. D. BERRIE

*Department of Zoology, University of Reading, Reading, England*

### SYNOPSIS

The ecology of this reach has been studied at all trophic levels as part of the International Biological Programme. The river carries considerable quantities of nutrients and suspended organic matter but is well oxygenated. A rich phytoplankton develops in spring and summer and there is usually a spring bloom of centric diatoms. Over the year, primary production of phytoplankton greatly exceeds respiration in the water column. Benthic algae, aquatic macrophytes and trees adjacent to the river contribute much less material to the system. The macrobenthos is dominated by filter feeding organisms, principally unionid mussels which are not suitable food for fish. The fish populations are dense and have slow growth rates. The annual production of fish is quite high but much of this is attributable to young fish in the first few months of life during which high mortality occurs. The surviving fish depend heavily on allochthonous materials and organic detritus to meet their energy requirements. Young fish consume large quantities of rotifers and cladocerans. The River Kennet joins the Thames within the reach being studied. It has a less well-developed phytoplankton and respiration exceeds photosynthesis in the water column. Aquatic macrophytes provide an important habitat for the invertebrate fauna and care should be taken to ensure their preservation. The quality of the fish for angling is poor and management techniques must be developed if this is to be improved.

## INTRODUCTION

The River Thames is over 300 km long and has a catchment area of almost one million hectares. For most of its length it is dredged for navigation to a minimum depth of 2 m and the flow is regulated by locks and weirs at intervals of about 5 km. At Reading it is a eutrophic lowland river, 40 to 80 m wide with a mean depth of about 3 m in the centre. The water is turbid and no rooted plants grow in the main channel. The area under investigation extends from Caversham Lock to Sonning Lock, a distance of 4·2 km (Fig. 1a). The River Kennet joins the Thames 1·3 km below Caversham Lock and has a considerable effect on the ecology of the Thames below the confluence. The river is also affected by a warm water effluent from Earley Power Station which enters it 1 km above Sonning Lock. This causes a thermal stratification (Mann, 1965a) and the ecological complications are such that the section below the effluent has been excluded from the recent investigations.

The cross section of the river in Fig. 1b shows the presence of four main zones. At intervals along the south bank are beds of *Acorus calamus* L. (sweet flag) which are flooded in winter but become more exposed in summer. Beyond this is a zone of *Nuphar lutea* (L.) (yellow

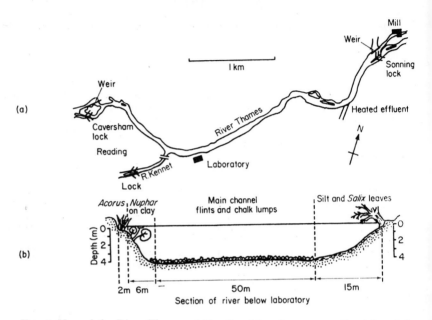

Fig. 1. Map of the River Thames at Reading (a) and a cross section taken below the laboratory (b).

water lily) growing on the slope down to the main channel with the majority of the leaves submerged. The north bank is lined with trees, mainly *Salix* sp. (willow), and on this side the slope to the main channel is formed of roots, leaves, twigs and silt. This last zone is the least studied part of the river since it is difficult to take satisfactory benthic samples or to net fish.

Various aspects of the ecology of this part of the river have been studied during the past twelve years. In the last five years a small team has been attempting to estimate production at all trophic levels as part of the British contribution to the Freshwater Section of the International Biological Programme and this paper attempts to provide a brief survey of the data obtained about the various components of the ecosystem. Detailed accounts of the work will be published elsewhere. Some of the data have already been brought together by Mann, *et al.* (1971).

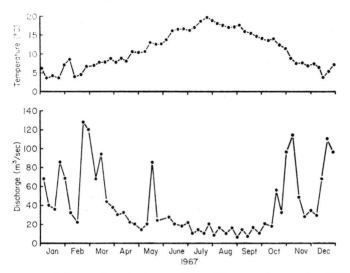

FIG. 2. Seasonal changes in water temperature at the laboratory and in discharge at Caversham Weir.

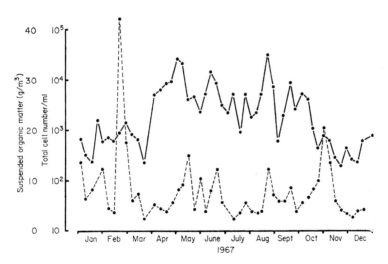

FIG. 3. Seasonal changes in suspended organic matter (broken line) and phytoplankton cell numbers (continuous line) in the River Thames above Kennet Mouth.

The annual changes in water temperature and discharge in 1967 are illustrated in Fig. 2. In very cold winters some ice forms on the river and in summer the temperature usually rises to about 20°C. The temperature is constant from the surface to the bottom of the river. Discharge shows considerable variation and winter floods are about ten times greater than normal summer flow. No continuous records of dissolved oxygen are available but occasional measurements have always given figures around 100% saturation and there is no indication of marked fluctuations. The mean concentration of nitrate is known to be over 4 mg/l and that of phosphate over 2 mg/l. Silica is generally over 10 mg Si/l except when high numbers of diatoms are present.

The total suspended matter in the Thames has a mean value of about 16·5 g/m$^3$ of which about 6·5 g/m$^3$ (40%) is organic matter. The annual variation in suspended organic matter during 1967 is shown in Fig. 3. The highest concentrations were recorded at times of high discharge.

PLANTS

*Phytoplankton*

*Cell numbers*

The numbers of algal cells and their species composition have been recorded weekly (Lack, 1969, 1971) and the changes in total cell numbers during 1967 are shown in Fig. 3. The numbers are low in winter when the discharge is high and are higher from spring to late summer when the flow is lower. Diatoms predominate throughout most of the year and may represent over 90% of the total. Three distinct peaks are present. The first in spring and the third in late summer are made up largely of the centric diatom *Stephanodiscus hantzschii* Grun. while the summer peak is produced by an increase in Chlorophyceae. There is annual variation in the diatom peak which is the greater: in 1967 it was the August peak which reached 32 200 cells/ml. The concentration of silica in the water falls rapidly during diatom peaks but it does not seem to reach a level low enough to limit the growth of diatoms.

*Biomass*

The phytoplankton biomass was estimated by making weekly determinations of chlorophyll "a" and taking this figure as 2% of the dry weight. If the dry weight of phytoplankton is subtracted from the dry weight of suspended organic matter, the difference is the dry weight of tripton present. During summer algae represent up to 75% of the suspended organic matter but in winter they fall to as little as 2% of the total. Taken over a year the mean proportions are about 25% algae and 75% tripton.

The horizontal and vertical distribution of chlorophyll in the river does not vary more than 5% from the mean at any given time and the concentration shows no significant diurnal pattern. This indicates that the water is well mixed and one sampling site may be regarded as representative of that section of the river.

*Production*

Planktonic primary production and total plankton respiration were measured by recording the oxygen changes in light and dark bottles exposed at five depths for 24 h (Kowalczewski & Lack, 1971). Determinations were made about every two weeks for one year and are now being repeated. When the bottles were rotated continuously, to prevent settling, production was 1·38 times higher than in stationary bottles and all results from stationary bottles have been increased by this factor.

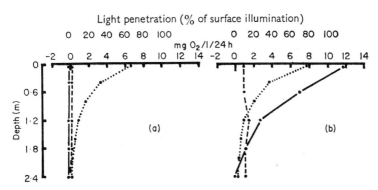

FIG. 4. Vertical profiles showing net oxygen production (continuous line), respiration (broken line) and light penetration (dotted line) in the River Thames above Kennet Mouth in January (a) and April (b) 1968.

Two vertical profiles of net oxygen production are shown in Fig. 4. That of 24 January, 1968 is a typical winter situation with negative net production at all depths and a very low rate of respiration. The level of chlorophyll "a" on that date was 1·6 mg/m³. The profile for 9 April, 1968 shows good spring conditions when the chlorophyll "a" was 63·0 mg/m³. Respiration is much higher and there is a high rate

74 A. D. BERRIE

of production in the uppermost metre of water with euphotic conditions extending down to 2·4 m. The percentage of light penetration was similar at each depth on these occasions but the actual amount of light at the surface was quite different. Respiration is approximately the same at all depths and this provides further evidence of complete vertical mixing of the river water. A series of such profiles has been used in conjunction with data on the shape of the river bed to plot annual curves for total production and respiration. The estimate of annual net production is 4388 kcal/m² and for annual respiration is 2250 kcal/m².

### Benthic algae

Sessile algae are present over the whole bed of the river and some are swept up into the phytoplankton during floods. Considerable growths of *Rhizoclonium* spp. develop in shallow water. An attempt is being made to estimate the production of these algae by enclosing samples of substratum in light and dark perspex domes and recording the oxygen changes. This gives a figure for gross primary production in the domes but the respiration figure includes micro- and macro-benthos which are present on the substratum. Figure 5 shows the results obtained from domes in shallow water during part of 1969. Data from greater depths have nearly always shown community respiration to be greater than gross primary production. The data in Fig. 5 indicate a net production of at least 4·6 g $O_2$/m²/day (16·1 kcal/m²/day) between April and August and 2·5 g $O_2$/m²/day (8·8 kcal/m²/day) over the whole period. Since the winter months were probably negative and

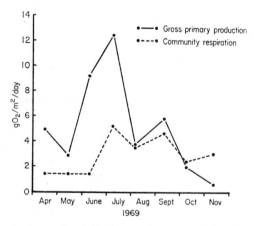

Fig. 5. Gross primary production and community respiration within domes at 0·4 m depth in the River Thames.

since this shallow zone represents only about 10% of the area of river, production by benthic algae must be much lower than that by phytoplankton.

## Aquatic macrophytes

Changes in biomass of *Acorus* and *Nuphar* have been studied and data gathered for shoots, rhizomes and roots separately. It was concluded that a reasonable estimate of net annual production was given by the difference between the maximum and minimum biomass of the shoots plus dead leaf material which accumulated during the growing season. The figures adjusted to show production per square metre of river surface are given in Table I. The differences in the figures above and below Kennet Mouth are due mainly to the differences in the proportion of the river bed occupied by the plants in these two regions.

TABLE I

*Annual net production of aquatic macrophytes per square metre of river surface*

|  | Above Kennet Mouth $kcal/m^2/year$ | Below Kennet Mouth $kcal/m^2/year$ |
|---|---|---|
| *Acorus calamus* | 23·7 | 16·4 |
| *Nuphar lutea* | 0·1 | 27·6 |

## Trees

The leaf fall from the trees lining the north bank of the river has been estimated by Mathews & Kowalczewski (1969). They concluded that the input of leaf litter amounted to $104.4 \ kcal/m^2/year$ if the material fell equally on the bank and in the river. This figure is reduced to $79 \ kcal/m^2/year$ if allowance is made for the higher proportion of the crowns of trees which is over the bank (Mann *et al.*, 1971). Further complications arise if wind action is considered. However, the total contribution is small in comparison with phytoplankton production.

## Leaf decomposition

The rate at which leaf litter was broken down in the river was also studied by Mathews & Kowalczewski (1969). Samples of leaves were placed in bags with a coarse mesh (3·0 mm) which allowed free access of all except the larger members of the invertebrate fauna. Other samples were placed in bags with a fine mesh (0·27 mm) which excluded all but the smallest invertebrates. The results for *Salix* leaves are shown in Fig. 6 and there is very little difference between the data for

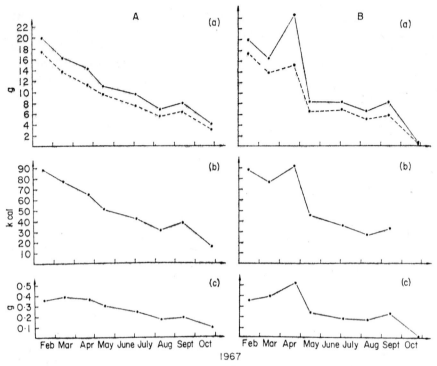

FIG. 6. Changes in bags containing samples of willow leaves submerged in the river: (A) shows data for fine mesh bags and (B) for coarse mesh bags. (a) Dry weight (continuous line) and organic matter (broken line), (b) energy and (c) nitrogen. (Reproduced from *J. Ecol.* by permission of Blackwell Scientific Publications Ltd.)

the two types of bag. It was concluded that the breakdown was effected by microorganisms rather than invertebrates and that the process would be complete within a year. Experiments with leaves of aquatic macrophytes have given similar results but show a more rapid breakdown. Figure 6 shows significant increases in the nitrogen content of the litter during the first three months of the experiment. This is presumably due to absorption from the environment by microbial activity. The amount of nitrogen entering the river in the litter was 0·42 g/m²/year and a further 0·19 g/m²/year accrued after immersion in the river. The nitrogen required for fish production in this area is about 1 g/m²/year and it is possible that this process could be more important in nitrogen cycling in the river than it is as a source of energy.

## INVERTEBRATES

### Macrobenthos

The benthic fauna has been studied along two sets of transects situated above and below Kennet Mouth. Collections taken over the year 1965–66 were examined and annual growth curves and population density curves were constructed for the main species. This gave data on the numbers and mean weights of each cohort which were used to estimate production by the graphical method of Allen (1951). Since no age classes could be recognized in the Tubificidae their production was taken as five times the mean biomass. Chironomidae could not be adequately sampled with the technique used for other groups and an approximate estimate was made.

The data obtained are shown in Table II. There is a great preponderance of filter feeders and most of the biomass consists of the large unionid mussels which were studied by Negus (1966). The only filter feeding organism which is grazed by fish is the bryozoan *Plumatella repens* so that the production by this group of organisms is largely

TABLE II

*Annual production and mean biomass of benthic invertebrates*

|  | Above Kennet Mouth | | Below Kennet Mouth | |
|---|---|---|---|---|
|  | Production kcal/m²/year | Mean biomass kcal/m² | Production kcal/m²/year | Mean biomass kcal/m² |
| **Filter Feeders** | | | | |
| Bivalvia | 61·3 | 214·0 | 25·6 | 80·0 |
| Porifera | 37·8 | 7·9 | 72·3 | 20·5 |
| Bryozoa | 8·1 | 1·5 | 18·4 | 2·5 |
| Total | 107·2 | 223·4 | 116·3 | 103·0 |
| **Browsers and Grazers** | | | | |
| Gastropoda | 13·8 | 13·8 | 8·6 | 11·1 |
| Chironomidae (larvae) | 15·4 | 1·7 | 3·1 | 0·3 |
| Others | 6·1 | 1·4 | 7·3 | 1·7 |
| Total | 35·3 | 16·9 | 19·0 | 13·1 |
| **Predators** | | | | |
| Hirudinea | 2·0 | 1·2 | 1·7 | 1·0 |
| Total | 144·5 | 241·5 | 137·0 | 117·1 |

unavailable to the fish unless they eat decomposing animals which cannot be recognized in the stomach contents.

The pumping activity of *Unio pictorum* (L.) and *Anodonta anatina* (L.) has been investigated and a correlation has been established between the volume of water pumped and the body size. During periods of activity mussels can pump at rates up to 3 l/h but a rate of 1 l/h is more typical. Records of the pumping activity at different times of the year are still incomplete but suggest that pumping may be greatly reduced at low water temperatures. Making allowance for this it is possible to use the data to estimate annual pumping rates and to combine these with the data on size frequency and population density given by Negus (1966). This provides an estimate that the unionid mussels in the Thames pump about 40 m$^3$/m$^2$/year. The energy content of the suspended organic matter in this volume of water would be on average about 1000 kcal which is well in excess of the estimated requirements of the mussels.

## Chironomidae

In collections of benthic invertebrates taken in 1965–66, 80% of the chironomid fauna of each zone was made up of two genera of Chironominae (*Einfeldia* and *Glyptotendipes*) and one of Diamesinae (*Prodiamesa*). Recent collections indicate a serious decrease in the numbers of larvae on the river bed but high densities have been found in the beds of macrophytes. Large species of Chironominae occur in the *Acorus* at densities of over 1000/m$^2$ in early summer. It is unlikely that fish are able to penetrate far into the *Acorus* beds in summer and the insects would only be available as food in the adult stage. On the leaves of *Nuphar*, *Cricotopus* spp. (Orthocladiinae) reach densities of several hundred per leaf and *Rheotanytarsus photophilus* Goet (Chironominae) is also present in considerable numbers. These are detritus feeders which are probably able to exploit organic material which settles on the leaves during summer. The generation time appears to be short at summer temperatures and it seems likely that much of the chironomid production in the river at present is taking place among the macrophytes.

## Zooplankton

The term zooplankton is used here to cover a variety of micro-invertebrates which are capable of swimming freely in the water but may not be truly planktonic. Preliminary investigations carried out in 1970 have shown a considerable range of species with Cladocera, principally Chydoridae and Sididae, being the most important group.

Copepoda and Hydrachnellidae are common but much less numerous while Rotifera appear to be relatively unimportant numerically. The community has a distinct seasonal pattern with one group of species, including planktonic and benthic forms, inhabiting the main channel in winter and spring and reaching a peak of abundance during March and April. A group of littoral species is associated with the *Nuphar* beds from May to October when the plant growth and lower discharge result in almost static conditions in these beds. Since *Chydorus sphaericus* (O. F. Müller) can grow to maturity within a week at 15°C, summer temperatures in the river are suitable for a rapid build up in population densities. The eurytopic species *C. sphaericus* and *Eucyclops agilis* (Koch, Sars) are abundant in the early summer but *Sida crystallina* (O. F. Müller) becomes dominant for most of the period. The main production is clearly in the *Nuphar* beds during summer and a quantitative sampling programme is now in progress. The zooplankton of the Thames includes carnivores, herbivores and detritus feeders but the commonest species are those which feed mainly on detritus.

FISH

### Population estimates

The growth, mortality and population density of bleak (*Alburnus alburnus* (L.)), roach (*Rutilus rutilus* (L.)), dace (*Leuciscus leuciscus* (L.)) and perch (*Perca fluviatilis* L.) over 10 cm long were investigated by Williams (1965, 1967). The fish were sampled with a seine net. A mark-recapture technique was used and checked against estimates based on the area enclosed by the net and the efficiency of the net. Bleak were most numerous with $2 \cdot 53/m^2$, roach came next with $1 \cdot 0/m^2$, and the other two species were each $0 \cdot 1/m^2$. The growth of bleak was relatively fast but that of the other species was poor by comparison with other habitats. The younger fish have now been investigated (Mathews, 1971) using a seine net with a mesh aperture of 3 mm. Marking proved impracticable and population densities were calculated by the method of Seber & LeCren (1967) which involves taking two samples in rapid succession at the same site. During the first few months of life, the fish grow rapidly but the mortality rate is high. The population density at this stage varies from year to year but the estimates are as high as $58/m^2$ for bleak and $19/m^2$ for roach.

### Fecundity

The egg production of bleak and roach was studied quantitatively by Mackay & Mann (1969) and less detailed data were obtained for gudgeon and dace by Mathews (1971). Table III shows the results of combining the data on fecundity of bleak and roach, with an estimate

TABLE III

*Rough estimates of population fecundity of bleak and roach*

| Age | Total no. of fish per 100 m² | No. of females per 100 m² | % mature Apr. 29 | Avg. no. eggs per female | Total egg production per 100 m |
|---|---|---|---|---|---|
| | | Bleak | | | |
| 2 + | 167 | 75·1 | 50 | 4314 | 161 990 |
| 3 + | 84 | 35·3 | 83 | 4912 | 143 916 |
| 4 + | 12 | 5·3 | 91 | 5593 | 26 975 |
| 5 + | 1 | 0·42 | 80 | 6396 | 2149 |
| 6 + | <1 | <0·75 | 67 | 7252 | <3644 |
| 7 + | <1 | <1·00 | 100 | 8258 | <8258 |
| | | | | | <346 932 |
| | | Roach | | | |
| 5 + | 8 | 5·20 | 71 | 4251 | 15 695 |
| 6 + | 6 | 4·86 | 66 | 5185 | 16 631 |
| 7 + | 2 | 1·70 | 75 | 6259 | 7980 |
| 8 + | 1 | 1·00 | 100 | 7597 | 7597 |
| 9 + | <1 | <0·87 | 80 | 9234 | <6427 |
| 10 + | <1 | <1·00 | 100 | 11 180 | <11 180 |
| | | | | | <65 510 |

of the sex ratio, and the population parameters for these species given by Mann (1965b). This indicates a high population fecundity of about 3500 eggs/m² for bleak. Roach have a lower figure of about 650 eggs/m² and the observations indicated that developing eggs may be resorbed before spawning time in this species.

## Production

The population parameters which are available allow production of the main species of fish to be estimated by the graphical method of Allen (1951). A gap exists in the data between spawning and the time at which the fingerlings become vulnerable to netting. Production during this interval is taken as the product of the mean biomass during the interval and the instantaneous growth rate during the interval (Ricker, 1946). An Allen curve for bleak is shown in Fig. 7 and the production of bleak and roach at different stages is given in Table IV.

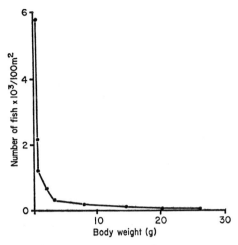

Fig. 7. Allen curve for bleak. Data for small fish collected in 1967 and for large fish in 1959.

The estimated production of the other species of fish is 61 kcal/m²/year. About 70% of the total production is contributed by fish during the first year of life and most of this takes place in the summer months immediately after hatching.

TABLE IV

*Production of bleak and roach at different stages of development (g/m²/year). The period between spawning and fingerling stage is that during which the fish are not vulnerable to the net.*

|  | Bleak | Roach |
| --- | --- | --- |
| Spawning | 6·1 | 0·5 |
| Spawning to fingerlings | 32·6 | 9·8 |
| Fingerlings to 1 year old | 25·9 | 8·2 |
| Fish over 1 year old | 26·9 | 9·6 |
| Total | 91·5 | 28·1 |

### Energy requirements

Mann (1965b) investigated the oxygen consumption of representative species and sizes of fish from the river. With these data and the available population parameters he drew up an estimated total energy budget for the fish. This has now been modified to include the recent

D

data on young fish and on seasonal changes in the calorific value of
fish. The revised figures for the population energy requirements of bleak
and roach are 183 kcal/m²/year during the first year and 877 kcal/m²/
year for fish over one year old.

TABLE V

*Ingestion of food by 0 + fish (kcal/m²/year)*

|                       | Bleak | Roach |
|-----------------------|:-----:|:-----:|
| Diatoms               |   1   |   1   |
| Rotifera              |   0   |  20   |
| Chydoridae            |  56   |   4   |
| *Sida crystallina*    |   9   |   8   |
| Chironomidae (larvae) |  19   |   5   |
| Chironomidae (adults) |  25   |   0   |
| Terrestrial insects   |  23   |   0   |
| Detritus              |   6   |   1   |
| Miscellaneous         |   2   |   3   |
| Total                 |  141  |  42   |

A quantitative study has been made of the diet of bleak and roach
throughout the year (Britton, 1968). The volume of each component
was determined and the figures were corrected to allow for relative
rates of digestion. The energy content of each type of food was determined and the resulting data were used to partition the energy requirements of the fish among the various sources. Table V summarizes the
data for 0 + bleak and roach. Young fish of both species feed mainly on
zooplankton and chironomid larvae but the bleak also consume large
quantities of insects taken at the surface. Table VI provides corresponding data for older bleak and roach. Bleak rely heavily on adult
insects but receive a substantial contribution (13%) in the form of
bait from fishermen. Roach do not derive much energy from animal
food and ingest large quantities of detritus and algae.

DISCUSSION

*Influence of the River Kennet*

The River Kennet is a major tributary of the Thames. Near the
confluence it has a similar annual range of temperature and its minimum
discharge is also similar, being about 5 m³/sec. A typical summer

TABLE VI

*Ingestion of food by fish over 1 year old (kcal/m²/year)*

|  | Bleak | Roach |
|---|---|---|
| Filamentous algae | 0 | 76 |
| Diatoms | 12 | 67 |
| Macrophytes | 4 | 15 |
| *Sida crystallina* | 0 | 18 |
| *Plumatella repens* | 0 | 6 |
| Mollusca | 0 | 13 |
| Chironomidae (larvae) | 1 | 19 |
| Chironomidae (adults) | 123 | 3 |
| Terrestrial insects | 144 | 3 |
| Detritus | 24 | 283 |
| Bread | 38 | 0 |
| *Calliphora* (larvae) | 9 | 1 |
| Miscellaneous | 6 | 13 |
| Total | 361 | 517 |

situation might be represented by a discharge of about 10 m³/sec in the Thames and about 7 m³/sec in the Kennet. During winter floods the Kennet seldom rises much above 20 m³/sec. The river is shallower than the Thames with a mean depth of 1·1 m and extensive beds of *Nuphar* grow in some areas.

The mean concentration of total suspended matter and the organic component of this are almost identical with the figures given for the Thames. However, only 5% of the suspended organic matter in the Kennet is phytoplankton and most of the remainder is probably derived from the effluent of Reading Sewage Works which enters the Kennet about 4 km above the confluence. Limited data on oxygen saturation suggest that it is about 100% during the day but that it may be reduced somewhat at night.

Phytoplankton production is much lower than in the Thames and respiration exceeds photosynthesis in the water column giving a net production of − 275 kcal/m²/year (Kowalczewski & Lack, 1971). Its oxygen concentration is probably maintained by surface diffusion and the photosynthesis of the *Nuphar*.

Below the confluence the phytoplankton of the Thames is diluted and the tripton increased, and the net production in the water column is estimated at 1907 kcal/m²/year. The data in Table II indicate a decrease in the mussel population and a greater development of sponge.

## Fauna of Nuphar beds

The aquatic macrophytes make only a small contribution to the total primary production in the river but they appear to have an important role as a habitat for the fauna. Cladocera and chironomid larvae reach high population densities in the Nuphar beds and large numbers of pulmonate snails occur there also. During summer there is little water movement among the Nuphar leaves and this provides sheltered conditions which suit these animals. The leaves have a large surface for the growth of epiphyton and the deposition of particulate organic matter, and consequently provide good grazing conditions. Large numbers of fish move among the Nuphar and the invertebrate fauna is an important part of their food supply.

Table I shows that there is very little Nuphar above Kennet Mouth. The slope down to the main channel in this area is very steep, sometimes even under-cut, and does not provide a suitable substratum for Nuphar. In other areas the plants are damaged by the propellers of motor launches which continue to increase in number. If the secondary productivity of the river is to be maintained it is important that the Nuphar beds be preserved.

## Fish problems

The fish community is dominated by bleak which are unpopular with anglers. Other fish have poor growth rates and appear to suffer from a shortage of invertebrate food. Although this may affect the fecundity of roach and possibly also other species, there is a high production of young fish. The quantity of fish is large but too few grow to an adequate size for angling.

The growth of fish and the proportion of fish of suitable size for angling should benefit from either an increase in the invertebrate food supply or a decrease in their numbers. No quantitative data are available on predation by pike and perch but it seems doubtful if their numbers are high enough to have much effect on population densities. Fish below certain size limits may not be taken by anglers and the anglers frequently return their catches to the river. The depth and turbidity of the water probably deter piscivorous birds.

In the circumstances, the quality of the fish for angling is only likely to be improved by active management. This could be attempted by encouraging appropriate ecological changes or by direct action on the fish. The former would be difficult to plan on the basis of existing knowledge and might be incompatible with the requirements of navigation and water supply. Direct action, whether by feeding or by removing selected groups, would probably prove too expensive.

## ACKNOWLEDGEMENTS

The data which have been presented are the results of the energy and enthusiasm of the team who have worked in the project. The author wishes to thank the following members of the team for unpublished material included in this paper: Mr. I. McDonald (benthic invertebrates and algae), Mr. T. J. Lack (macrophytes and phytoplankton), Dr. C. P. Mathews (fish), Mr. R. H. Britton (fish diets), Mr. A. Kowalczewski (algae), Mrs. S. McPherson (mussels), Mr. H. H. Bottrell (zooplankton) and Mr. A. P. Mackey (chironomids). Valuable assistance has also been provided by Miss J. Morphey, Mrs. M. Kowalczewski and Mrs. S. White.

The project has been supported by grants from the Science Research Council and the Natural Environment Research Council. The author is indebted to Professor A. Graham for the facilities made available for the project and to the Thames Conservancy for their co-operation in many aspects of the work. The project was initiated by Dr. K. H. Mann and the author has received much advice and encouragement from him and from Professor G. Williams and Mr. E. D. LeCren.

## REFERENCES

Allen, K. R. (1951). The Horokiwi stream. *Bull. mar. Dept. N.Z. Fish.* No. 10:–238.

Britton, R. H. (1968). The diet of roach and bleak in the River Thames in relation to their growth. *J. Anim. Ecol.* **37**: 28P–29P.

Kowalczewski, A. & Lack, T. J. (1971). Primary production and respiration of the phytoplankton of the Rivers Thames and Kennet at Reading. *Freshwat. Biol.* **1**: 197–212.

Lack, T. J. (1969). Changes in the phytoplankton population of the River Thames at Reading (Berkshire). *J. Anim. Ecol.* **38**: 29P–30P.

Lack, T. J. (1971). Quantitative studies on the phytoplankton of the Rivers Thames and Kennet at Reading. *Freshwat. Biol.* **1**: 213–224.

Mackay, I. & Mann, K. H. (1969). Fecundity of two cyprinid fishes in the River Thames, Reading, England. *J. Fish. Res. Bd Can.* **26**: 2795–2805.

Mann, K. H. (1965a). Heated effluents and their effects on the invertebrate fauna of rivers. *Proc. Soc. Wat. Treat. Exam.* **14**: 45–53.

Mann, K. H. (1965b). Energy transformations by a population of fish in the River Thames. *J. Anim. Ecol.* **34**: 253–275.

Mann, K. H., Britton, R. H., Kowalczewski, A., Lack, T. J., Mathews, C. P. & McDonald, I. (1971). Productivity and energy flow at all trophic levels in the River Thames, England. *Proc. U.N.E.S.C.O.–I.B.P. Symp. Productivity Problems of Freshwaters, Poland* 1970: (in press).

Mathews, C. P. (1971). Contribution of young fish to total production of fish in the River Thames near Reading. *J. Fish Biol.* **3**: 157–180.

Mathews, C. P. & Kowalczewski, A. (1969). The disappearance of leaf litter and its contribution to production in the River Thames. *J. Ecol.* **57**: 543–552.

Negus, C. L. (1966). A quantitative study of growth and production of unionid mussels in the River Thames at Reading. *J. Anim. Ecol.* **35**: 513–532.

Ricker, W. E. (1946). Production and utilization of fish populations. *Ecol. Monogr.* **16**: 374–391.

Seber, G. A. F. & LeCren, E. D. (1967). Estimating population parameters from catches large relative to the population. *J. Anim. Ecol.* **36**: 631–643.

Williams, W. P. (1965). The population density of four species of freshwater fish, roach (*Rutilus rutilus* (L.)), bleak (*Alburnus alburnus* (L.)), dace (*Leuciscus leuciscus* (L.)), and perch (*Perca fluviatilis* L.) in the River Thames at Reading. *J. Anim. Ecol.* **34**: 173–185.

Williams, W. P. (1967). The growth and mortality of four species of fish in the River Thames at Reading. *J. Anim. Ecol.* **36**: 695–720.

*Symp. zool. Soc. Lond.* (1972) No. 29, 87–114.

# AN APPROACH TO THE PROBLEM OF POLLUTION AND FISHERIES

J. S. ALABASTER, J. H. N. GARLAND, I. C. HART,
and J. F. DE L. G. SOLBÉ

*Water Pollution Research Laboratory of the Department of the Environment,
Stevenage, Hertfordshire, England*

## SYNOPSIS

Since the main pollution problem for freshwater fisheries in the United Kingdom stems from the combined effect on rivers of sewage and industrial wastes in lowering the concentration of dissolved oxygen and raising that of poisons, principally metals (copper and zinc), cyanides, ammonia, and phenols, work is reviewed to show that the short-term lethal effects of these conditions on trout can be reasonably well defined from laboratory studies. The question remains of predicting the long-term effects on survival and on other responses under the fluctuating conditions characteristic of polluted streams and of determining their ecological importance not only for trout but also for a variety of coarse fisheries, so that realistic water quality criteria for fisheries can be established.

The logical long-term approach would be to develop more elaborate laboratory experiments culminating in work on simulated polluted rivers and partially-controlled natural systems, but an alternative interim approach is described in which empirical relations are sought between short-term estimates of toxicity to fish and the presence or absence of fisheries in polluted rivers. Factors influencing, sometimes perhaps nullifying, straightforward relationships are discussed, including differences in susceptibility between trout and coarse fish. The usefulness of this approach is then illustrated by studies on a polluted stream in Northamptonshire, and also on a major part of the River Trent system where the main poisons are identified and the consequences of changing environmental factors, such as temperature and dissolved oxygen, are considered. Improvements and developments are suggested.

## INTRODUCTION

One of the central issues when considering water pollution and fisheries is to define maximum permissible levels of pollutants. This implies that the causes of pollution should be identified and that their adverse effects on relevant components of the ecosystem should be assessed. Clearly, any practical approach to the problem must be limited, at least initially, not only to those factors that have the greatest impact on fisheries but also to those effects that are most relevant and most easily measured both in the field and in the laboratory. In the United Kingdom the approach during the last decade or so has been to concentrate much of the work on fish themselves, mainly through laboratory studies to assess under various environmental conditions the direct toxicity of the most commonly occurring poisons. The assessment is generally made in terms of concentrations at which times of survival are expected to be relatively long (several months) and at which only a negligibly small proportion of a population of fish would be killed after such a long period of continuous exposure.

No doubt if a reduction to such concentrations were to be attained in rivers now heavily polluted in their upper reaches, there would be some benefit to fisheries if only in the lower reaches where conditions, that are possibly already improved by dilution from unpolluted tributary water, still remain marginal for fisheries. However, it is recognized that there would be no guarantee of a satisfactory improvement throughout such rivers. To arrive at an estimate of "safe" conditions at which a fishery would flourish, additional allowance would perhaps have to be made for sub-lethal ecologically significant adverse effects on fish and other aquatic organisms, including reduced growth and fecundity, avoidance of low concentrations of pollutants, and other alterations in normal behaviour and physiology. These aspects have so far received relatively little attention, partly because of the difficulty in demonstrating their relevance and partly because they would involve the use of considerable resources that might otherwise be deployed on existing lines of enquiry.

An alternative approach recently pursued in the United Kingdom is to seek empirical relations between an assessment of direct toxicity to fish and the status of fisheries in polluted waters. This is described and discussed here, together with a preliminary account of its application in an extensive study of the major part of the River Trent catchment area and a more intensive investigation of the Willow Brook in Northamptonshire.

### EXTENT OF THE PROBLEM IN THE UNITED KINGDOM

The overall position regarding pollution and fisheries in England and Wales was reviewed by the Ministry of Agriculture, Fisheries and Food, with the help of River Boards, in 1955 (Pentelow, 1959), and again in 1964, and it is obvious from a map prepared from data of the earlier survey, but extended to include Scotland, (Clarendon Press, 1963) that the most acute problem—namely in some 800–1000 miles of rivers believed to be fishless—is in the heavily-populated industrialized areas. Here, undoubtedly, wastes of purely domestic origin which constitute the commonest pollutant of rivers are largely responsible since they contain much carbonaceous material, the oxidation of which, in the absence of adequate dilution or aeration, can bring about catastrophic depletion of the dissolved oxygen. Their contribution to direct toxicity of rivers, however, is probably small and almost entirely confined to the presence of ammonia, and is unlikely to be of overriding importance since even undiluted sewage effluent of mainly domestic origin may support coarse fish in the presence of adequate dissolved oxygen (Allan, Herbert & Alabaster, 1958; Alabaster, 1959). In industrial areas, trade wastes are frequently discharged to sewers for treatment with domestic sewage and the sewage effluent therefore may contain many poisonous substances, the most commonly occurring being perhaps ammonia, phenols, cyanide, and metals, especially zinc, copper, cadmium, chromium, and nickel.

Some parts of rivers, particularly those adjacent to fishless areas, may well be marginal for the support of fisheries, but practically no information is available to assess this other than from incidents of mass fish-kills, records of many of which are kept by the River Authorities in England and Wales and the River Purification Boards in Scotland. These show only that of several hundred incidents per annum, involving comparatively small numbers of fish, a substantial proportion are attributable to sewage and industrial wastes; they give no indication of the extent to which the fisheries are affected by such events  or whether less obvious periodic deterioration in water quality also occurs to the detriment of fish populations. Pesticides are blamed for only a small proportion of incidents, often in agricultural areas, and there is little other evidence of damage to fisheries arising from their normal use other than from moth-proofing processes. The main problem therefore arises from the common industrial poisons already mentioned.

FACTORS TO CONSIDER IN ATTEMPTING CORRELATION OF TOXICITY
WITH THE STATUS OF FISHERIES

*Effect of mixtures of poisons*

*Pure substances*

Much of the published information on the toxicity of substances to fish relates to materials tested singly, whereas generally in polluted rivers, and frequently in effluents that are discharged to them, mixtures of poisons are present. A few early workers, for example Southgate (1932), showed that it was possible to determine the effect of a mixture of similar poisons in water by summation of their individual toxic fractions, and others have suggested that synergism may be important, e.g. with heavy metals (Doudoroff, 1952), but in the last decade a considerable amount of more detailed and longer-term work has been carried out.

In general it has been shown that the combined action of several poisons is approximately additive; if, for example, the concentrations of two poisons that kill 50% of the fish in a few days (LC50) are $A_t$ and $Z_t$ respectively, then the concentration of each ($A_s$ and $Z_s$) required in a mixture to give the same toxicity is such that the sum of the fractions $A_s/A_t + Z_s/Z_t$ equals unity. This relation has been found to hold with rainbow trout (*Salmo gairdneri*) for (i) mixtures of zinc and copper in both hard and soft water (Lloyd, 1961), (ii) ammonia and phenol (Herbert, 1962), (iii) ammonia and zinc in both hard and soft water, and also in the presence of reduced dissolved oxygen (Herbert & Shurben, 1964), (iv) copper and ammonia, and zinc and phenol, though there was a tendency to over-predict the toxicity of these two mixtures the lower the percentage response chosen (Herbert & Vandyke, 1964), (v) copper and phenol (Brown & Dalton, 1970), and (vi) phenol and cyanide in saline waters at up to 20% sea water, though at 50 to 70% sea water the observed 48-h LC50 was 1·7 times the predicted value (Ministry of Technology, 1969a).

All the poisons mentioned are comparatively quick acting, in that the 48-h LC50 is very little different from a concentration that would be lethal to 50% of the fish after continuous exposure during a time equal to the normal life span (the median threshold value). Tests with mixtures of zinc and cadmium (a metal lethal to fish at about 1/50 of the 48-h LC50 after prolonged exposure and not normally present in rivers at concentrations likely to contribute significantly to the 48-h LC50) have shown that the 48-h LC50 for zinc was virtually the same in the presence or absence of cadmium at up to 2 mg/l (equivalent to the 96-h LC50) and lower concentrations of zinc, times of survival were accountable by the concentration of cadmium alone (Ministry of Technology, 1971).

Mixtures of three substances have been tested together, including (i) phenol, zinc, and ammonia, in which there was a tendency to over-predict the toxicity where zinc predominated (Brown, Jordan & Tiller, 1969), and equitoxic concentrations of (ii) phenol, zinc, and copper, and (iii) nickel, zinc, and copper (Brown & Dalton, 1970), with which there was good agreement between predicted and observed results.

While the bulk of this work indicates that satisfactory prediction of the toxicity of simple mixtures of the commonly-occurring poisons can be made, there is no theoretical basis for this and no reason to suppose it would be true for other substances or other fish, or for effects other than survival. On the contrary, circumstances can be envisaged when it would not—for example, when complexes are formed between metals and cyanide; certainly there are examples of unpredictable toxicity of complex mixtures, particularly pesticide formulations (Alabaster, 1969).

*Sewage effluent*

The predictive method has been used to estimate the relative importance of the commonly-occurring poisons (ammonia, monohydric phenols, zinc, copper, and free cyanide) in sewage effluents in industrial areas in the United Kingdom, samples being taken from a variety of disposal works covering a range of treatment processes and receiving various types of industrial wastes (Lloyd & Jordan, 1963, 1964); the toxicity of the effluents to rainbow trout was measured under controlled conditions and predicted on the assumption that the toxicity of the mixture of all five poisons could be calculated from chemical analyses in a manner similar to that used in laboratory studies. In 13 out of 18 toxic effluents the predicted toxicities were within $\pm 30\%$ of the observed values, and six effluents were correctly predicted to be non-toxic; only two effluents were more toxic than predicted, probably because of the presence of other unidentified poisons.

*Field studies*

The same empirical approach has been applied in field studies of fishless rivers in the Midlands (Herbert, Jordan & Lloyd, 1965), taking into account the effect of environmental factors on the toxicity of individual poisons in the manner recently summarized by Brown (1968), and in general there was reasonable agreement between predicted and observed toxicity. More recent work has been summarized by Brown, Shurben & Shaw (1970), in which it was shown that there was an overall tendency to under-predict toxicity by about $35\%$ in polluted freshwaters and by about $65\%$ in polluted saline waters.

Thus, all the evidence available suggests that much of the short-term toxicity of the commonly-occurring poisons can be satisfactorily predicted, at least for rainbow trout in freshwater.

*Comparison of susceptibility of trout and coarse fish*

Most of the studies on the effect of pollution on the survival of fish so far referred to have been carried out with the rainbow trout, which is widely used because of its high sensitivity to waters of poor quality, including those containing poisons, its ready availability from trout farms, and its suitability as a laboratory animal. For these reasons and also because of its commercial value in America it has been much used in histological, physiological, biochemical, and behavioural studies, some of which have been concerned with the effect of pollutants. It is

therefore likely to remain for some time the principal test species for
the establishment of water quality criteria to protect fisheries.

However, most of the pollution that affects fisheries in the UK
occurs where coarse fish predominate and, therefore, more attention
will ultimately have to be given to these species, to ensure not merely
that standards of quality for trout waters are also satisfactory for
coarse fish species but also that they are not more restrictive than is
either necessary or practicable.

The moderate amount of information available from the UK on the
comparative sensitivity of coarse fish and trout to pollution has been
reviewed briefly (Alabaster, 1971), and indicates that in general
trout are the most sensitive species to high temperature, low dissolved-
oxygen content, and high pH value, carp (*Cyprinus carpio*) and tench
(*Tinca tinca*) being the most resistant, and the other species being of
intermediate sensitivity. But there are examples of some conditions
under which trout are not the most sensitive; for example perch (*Perca
fluviatilis*) are more sensitive in the presence of high concentrations of
both carbon dioxide and dissolved oxygen, roach (*Rutilus rutilus*) are
slightly more sensitive at pH values of about four, and several species
are more sensitive to high salinity.

*Laboratory studies*

For the commonly-occurring poisons only fragmentary information is available and therefore the details quoted here should not be
used outside this context without first referring to the original papers
and considering the likely effect on toxicity of factors such as the
method of testing, acclimation of fish to environmental variables
before tests are carried out, time of exposure to poisons, variation in
time of survival of individual fish in a population, differences in
environmental factors, including temperature, dissolved-oxygen content, pH value, water hardness, and free carbon dioxide, and also the
presence of complexing agents and other poisons, all of which have
been shown to be important in tests with trout.

*Ammonia.* Experiments with trout, bream (*Abramis brama*), roach,
rudd (*Scardinius erythrophthalmus*), and perch (Ball, 1967a) have
shown that median lethal concentrations of ammonia, for periods of
two or more days are similar for all species. At higher concentrations,
however, trout survive for much shorter periods than coarse fish
(roach, perch, and gudgeon (*Gobio gobio*); Downing & Merkens, 1957).

*Phenol.* Similarly, in recent tests with phenol (Ministry of Technology, 1971), perch, pike, and rainbow trout all responded much more
quickly than common carp, rudd, and eels (*Anguilla anguilla*), but,

except for carp (with a seven-day LC50 of 15 mg/l) all species were of similar susceptibility (seven-day LC50 of 8–11 mg/l). Other tests have suggested that roach are somewhat more resistant than trout (Ministry of Technology, 1969a) and that gudgeon are very much more resistant (unpublished work at the Water Pollution Research Laboratory), their two-day LC50 at 10°C being approximately 25 mg/l compared with 7·5 mg/l for trout. As yet we have no information on the effect of temperature on the toxicity of phenol to coarse fish, though with trout toxicity is highest at low temperatures. Clearly it could be important, because low temperature in winter might increase toxicity as well as exacerbate the situation by causing higher concentrations of poisons in effluents through a reduction in the efficiency of treatment processes.

*Zinc.* The three-day LC50 of zinc for rudd in a hard water is 20–30 mg/l, depending upon temperature and time of year; this is four to six times greater than for trout (Ministry of Technology, 1966). The survival of bream, roach, and perch is similar to that of rudd, while gudgeon are intermediate between these species and trout in their sensitivity (Ball, 1967b).

*Copper.* With copper, extensive tests recently carried out at about 10°C over a ten-day period (Ministry of Technology, 1971) have shown that eels (none of which died during the tests) and pike were more resistant than rainbow trout throughout the period, while rudd and carp were more resistant over only the first few days of exposure, after which time they were more sensitive than trout; perch were consistently the most sensitive species of all. Median threshold values for the concentration of copper were not evident for any of these species of coarse fish within ten days, but it is clear that they would have been no greater than 0·5, 0·25, and 0·2 that of trout for rudd, carp, and perch, respectively.

*Cadmium.* Although cadmium has been found to be very toxic to rainbow trout (seven-day LC50 about 0·01 mg/l), bream were much more resistant, all of a test batch in 5 mg Cd/l surviving for six weeks and all in 0·5 mg/l surviving for ten weeks (Ministry of Technology, 1971).

*Cyanide.* Recent unpublished work at WPRL using juvenile roach at 3–4°C has shown that the 48-h LC50 of cyanide is about half that of rainbow trout, but information on adult roach and other coarse fish species is lacking.

## Field work

The relatively little work that has been carried out with both trout and coarse fish under field conditions has been briefly reviewed

(Alabaster, 1971). In all cases where roach, ruffe (*Acerina cernua*), dace and chub (*Squalius cephalus*) were tested their times of survival were longer than those of trout. With perch, however, in tests in the R. Colne (Allan *et al.*, 1958), survival was shorter than that of trout, possibly because they were more sensitive to the high concentrations of carbon dioxide known to be present in the effluent channel studied.

In general, therefore, while the time of survival of trout is normally shorter than that of the few species of coarse fish that have been exposed to rapidly lethal concentrations of dissolved oxygen or the commonly occurring poisons (ammonia, phenol, zinc, copper (except perch), cadmium, and hydrogen cyanide), they are more resistant, in terms of median threshold concentration than some species of coarse fish to some of these poisons, namely copper (perch, rudd and carp), and hydrogen cyanide (juvenile roach). Much more work, however, is evidently required to establish the relative sensitivity of various species to these poisons.

### Relation between long- and short-term effects of poisons

With the five common poisons, ammonia, phenol, cyanide, copper, and zinc, and mixtures of them, the relation between period of survival of trout and concentration of poison is such that a good indication of the median threshold concentration is obtained within a few days. In these cases, therefore, it would be reasonable to expect to find some general correlation of the 48-h LC50 with long-term survival and also perhaps even with the status of a trout population, though with some of these poisons there may be other relevant effects, such as avoidance reactions induced by copper, and differences in the comparative long-term effects of different poisons on various species, for example on growth. One might also expect a correlation with coarse fish survival since with all these poisons, and all the species of coarse fish that have been tested, the relation between survival and concentration is similar to that of trout, though generally over a rather longer time-scale.

With other metals (cadmium, chromium, and nickel), which are much more toxic to trout after long periods of exposure than the results of short-term tests might suggest, it would not be appropriate to use 48-h LC50 values alongside those for copper and zinc when seeking correlation of toxicity with long-term effects on fish population.

### Fluctuations in toxicity

Most laboratory studies have been carried out with continuous exposure of the fish to constant environmental factors, whereas conditions in rivers are continually changing. This makes it virtually impossible to predict the survival of fish under field conditions.

With some poisons, e.g. cyanide, exposure of the fish for a short time to a concentration that eventually would have proved lethal, has no apparent adverse effect after the fish are transferred to clean water, and also has no effect on their resistance to subsequent exposure to the poison. Such recovery of the fish is not found with all substances. With DDT and an organo-phosphorus pesticide (Abram, 1967), and an effluent containing pesticide residues (Alabaster & Abram, 1965), under conditions in which short (6-h) periods of exposure to the poison alternate with similar periods in clean water, exposure time is approximately additive, the survival time of the fish being approximately equal to the time they would have survived in the mean concentration had it been applied continuously.

Further work with ammonia, zinc and equitoxic mixtures of the two (Brown *et al.*, 1969) has also shown that under conditions in which the concentrations alternated between 1·5 and 0·5 times the 48-h LC50 at intervals of a few hours, survival of trout was close to that of fish kept continuously at the 48-h LC50. More recent tests (Ministry of Technology, 1971) have been made with two poisons, phenol and cyanide, to which trout were exposed for alternate 4-h periods, under continuous-flow conditions, one poison gradually replacing the other, and then over the next period being itself replaced, each having a final concentration equivalent to the 48-h LC50. The results showed that the mixtures were only slightly less toxic than predicted, assuming no recovery of the fish from cyanide, and that the toxicity of the system was reasonably well described by the average conditions.

With other poisons, e.g. the herbicide Reglone (Alabaster & Abram, 1965) and cadmium (Ministry of Technology, 1969a), fish which had been exposed to potentially lethal concentrations for times far shorter than those at which they would have been killed under conditions of continuous exposure, subsequently died after being returned to clean water; for these substances attempts to predict survival from average concentrations would therefore tend to under-estimate toxicity.

Long-term exposure of fish to sub-lethal concentrations of some substances has also been shown to affect their subsequent resistance to poisoning. Trout exposed to ammonia for several months became more resistant to lethal concentrations of ammonia and less resistant to lethal concentrations of zinc (Ministry of Technology, 1968). Somewhat similar results have been reported for rudd exposed to sub-lethal concentrations of zinc; they developed an increased resistance to this poison (Ministry of Technology, 1966). On the other hand trout, after exposure to sub-lethal concentrations of zinc, were of similar sensitivity to a detergent (an alkyl benzene sulphonate) as control fish that had not been exposed to zinc, but were slightly more sensitive than the controls to a mixture of detergent and zinc (Brown, Mitrovic & Stark, 1968).

These examples serve to illustrate some of the possible effects on direct toxicity of fluctuations in chemical conditions in polluted rivers. More information is required on both the nature of variations in quality that occur in rivers, and of their effects on the survival of fish of all kinds before reliable prediction of toxicity can be made.

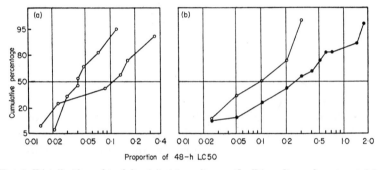

Fig. 1. Distribution of toxicity (a) at two sites on the River Cam where trout fisheries were present (Alabaster, 1970) and (b) for 100 spot samples from the River Trent system; solid symbols, fishless stations; open symbols, stations where fish are present (data replotted from Edwards & Brown, 1967).

INVESTIGATIONS RELATING THE PRESENCE AND ABSENCE OF FISHERIES
TO WATER TOXICITY

### Direct measurements of toxicity (River Cam)

At two sample sites studied by the Ministry of Agriculture, Fisheries and Food over a period of a few months in 1963 (Alabaster, 1970), effluent samples were sufficiently toxic (i.e. killing fish within two days) to be of use for predictive purposes. Additional checks on toxicity were made at each site using batches of trout kept in cages in undiluted effluent as discharged. Maximum concentrations of effluent in each of the rivers, based on the minimum dilution observed during the study, were calculated and expressed as a fraction of the 48-h LC50 for harlequin fish (*Rasbora heteromorpha*), measured under standard conditions (Alabaster & Abram, 1965). The median value for this fraction was 0·1 at one site where the effluent contained high proportions of chlorine and formaldehyde, and 0·04 at the other where the effluent contained a complex mixture of organo-chlorine compounds as well as other substances. The distributions of toxicity are shown in Fig. 1a and serve to illustrate the wide variation that can occur in effluents. Results of other tests carried out with trout and harlequins using the standard procedure, including a soft dilution water, were comparable with those obtained with a natural hard water having a hardness close to that of the receiving streams. At both sites there was sufficient dissolved oxygen in the river to support fish, and trout were known to thrive above and below the points of discharge.

Whether these fisheries would still have flourished had the average toxicity in the rivers and the fluctuations in quality been higher than observed during the field surveys is not known. Nevertheless the results provide some guide to the fractions of the 48-h LC50 that are not inimical to a trout fishery.

### Predicted toxicity

#### River Trent catchment

*Initial survey.* The results of examination of spot samples from 100 sites in the Trent River Authority area have been published (Edwards & Brown, 1967). The predicted sum of estimated fractions of the 48-h LC50 for trout was based on concentrations of the soluble poisons copper, zinc, phenol, ammonia, and cyanide, and excluded detergents and other substances not assayed, such as chlorinated hydrocarbons and suspended solids; the effect of low dissolved-oxygen concentration at the time the sample was taken was also neglected. The data have been re-examined and are shown in Fig. 1b; there is considerable variation and, not unexpectedly, a large overlap between the predicted toxicity associated with the presence of fish and that found in fishless rivers. Where trout and coarse fish were said to be present the sum of the 48-h LC50 was always less than about 0·3, and the median value was about 0·1, but at over 55% of the sites which were fishless the sum of the 48-h LC50 was 0·3 or less, the median being about 0·25.

This analysis provides a useful pointer to the toxicity that might be tolerated by a fishery, though it neglects the effect of some factors which are undoubtedly of importance in predicting toxicity, such as the dissolved-oxygen concentration, and, particularly, the variation in quality that must occur at each of the sites from which a sample was collected.

*Current investigation.* A more intensive study of the area has since been initiated in close collaboration with the Trent River Authority which has provided data on the chemical quality of the water at a large number of sampling stations and has also made an assessment of the status of the fisheries at each. In addition to the five poisons included in predictions made in the initial survey, other toxic metals (nickel, chromium, and cadmium) have been considered as well as the effects on toxicity of environmental factors, including temperature,

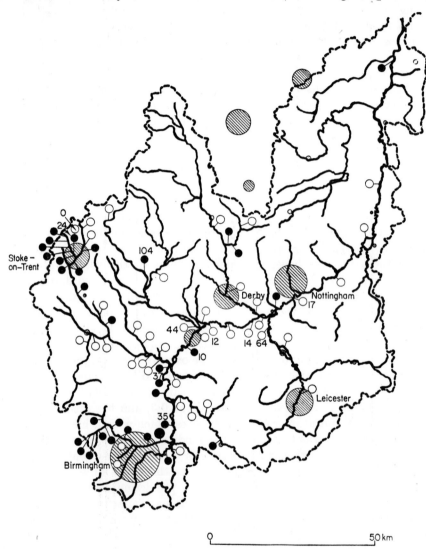

FIG. 2. Map of area administered by the Trent River Authority showing sampling stations for which toxicity has been estimated in 1968 and 1969. Numbers refer to stations mentioned in the text; solid symbols, fishless stations; open symbols, stations where fish are present.

dissolved-oxygen concentration, pH value, and water alkalinity. No allowance has been made for solids in suspension which are also present at many stations, since their concentration is generally well below the level of inert inorganic solids (approximately 80 mg/l) considered marginal for fisheries in the absence of poisons. It is true that much of the suspended matter is derived from storm sewage overflows and sewage effluents and that it also contains metal ions, but recent preliminary experiments (Ministry of Technology, 1971) with effluent solids from an activated-sludge plant to which metal ions (copper, zinc, nickel, or cadmium) had been added suggest that such solids would not be markedly toxic to rainbow trout.

Of 73 stations that have been examined 21 are on the River Trent itself, 35 on its main tributaries, and the remainder on subsidiary water-courses, comprising in all 23 rivers and streams (Fig. 2). Equations representing the graphs relating 48-h LC50 to environmental factors, summarized by Brown (1968), were derived and incorporated in a programme for an ICL 1905 computer to calculate, for each occasion on which the water was sampled and analysed, the proportion of the 48-h LC50 for each poison, the sum of these proportions, and the probability distribution of these sums for each station.

The most comprehensive data are available for 1968 and 1969, but some stations have not yielded usable information because too few samples were taken or too few analyses were made during the year to provide sufficient results to produce a probability distribution. The calculations have been completed for all 73 stations for 1968 and for 36 of them for 1969.

Of the stations for 1968, 49 had sufficient data for ammonia toxicity distributions (10–78 samples in the year), including 26 for which it was also possible to construct distributions for metals (copper, nickel, zinc and cadmium; 10–47 samples), of which seven had sufficient additional information to include cyanide distributions (10–33 samples). Phenols were generally reported as zero (241 out of 252 samples), and even when present were insufficient to alter markedly the shape or position of the distributions.

All but two of the 36 stations for 1969 had sufficient data (10–76 samples) for ammonia toxicity distributions. Metals could be included for 22 of these (10–54 samples), and cyanide for four of them; three stations on the Tame had sufficient data to include phenols (30–34 samples) and again they added little to the total toxicity.

*Results.* A selection of the probability distributions of the sum of the proportions of the 48-h LC50 are compared in Fig. 3a. These include two stations at which fish are absent—Lea Marston on the River Tame,

a point at which the river has been highly polluted by the discharge
of domestic and industrial sewage and effluent from the Birmingham

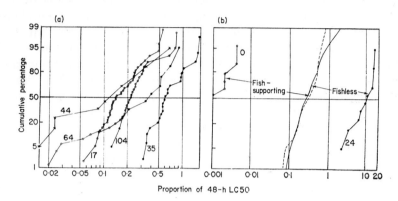

FIG. 3. Distributions of toxicity in the River Trent system in 1968 for (a) five selected
stations and (b) all stations. Crosses, game fish; open circles, coarse fish; closed circles,
fishless. Numbers refer to stations shown in Fig. 2.

conurbation (Station 35), and Rocester on the River Churnet downstream of an industrial discharge containing high concentrations of
toxic metals (Station 104), two stations at which coarse fisheries
exist—Kegworth on the River Soar (Station 64) and Trent Bridge,
Nottingham, on the River Trent (Station 17), and one station at which
game fish, trout and grayling, flourish—Monks Bridge, River Dove
(Station 44).

When all the available distributions for 1968 are plotted on a single
log-probability diagram overlapping of those for coarse and game
fisheries occurs, though the average of the median toxicity is about
0·1 for stations where the fisheries are predominantly trout and grayling,
and 0·2 where there are coarse fisheries. The corresponding figures for
1969 are 0·03 and 0·12 respectively. Some overlapping also occurs at
low and high probability levels (below about 10% and above about
90%) between distributions for sampling stations at which fish are
present (regardless of type), and those at which fish are absent, though
it is still possible to determine an approximate boundary distribution
between the two. This is illustrated in Fig. 3b for the 1968 data, in
which the upper limit of distributions for fish-supporting locations
(dashed line) and the lower limit for those that are fishless is shown
(solid line) together with the two extreme distributions having the
highest and lowest sums of the proportions of the 48-h LC50, namely

Eleanora Street, Stoke (fishless) on the Fowlea Brook near its confluence with the Trent (Station 24) and Norton Green near the source
of the River Trent (Station 0), respectively. The coordinates of the
approximate boundary distribution of 48-h LC50 between fishless and
fish-supporting waters are given in Table I.

TABLE I

*Coordinates of approximate boundary distribution of* 48-*h LC*50 *between fishless
and fish-supporting waters*

| Per cent probability | 1 | 5 | 10 | 25 | 50 | 75 | 90 | 95 | 99 |
|---|---|---|---|---|---|---|---|---|---|
| Sum of proportions of 48-h LC50 | 0·07 | 0·10 | 0·13 | 0·18 | 0·28 | 0·41 | 0·60 | 0·73 | 1·1 |

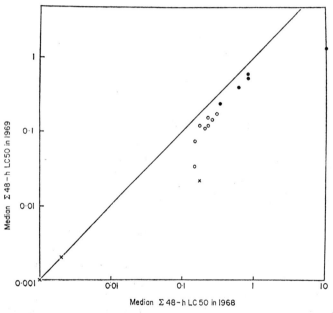

Fɪɢ. 4. Difference in toxicity in the River Trent system between 1968 and 1969.
Symbols as in Fig. 3.

Somewhat similar results are found for the 1969 data that have
been processed so far, though there is evidently a marked reduction in
estimated toxicity at many stations. This is illustrated in Fig. 4, in

which the median toxicity in 1969 is plotted against that at corresponding stations in the previous year. However, despite this reduction in toxicity, in 1969 fish were not reported at any station where they were absent previously. Possibly insufficient time has elapsed since the improvement for new fisheries to become established and, therefore, an assessment of the toxicity associated with fishless rivers, based on the 1969 data, may be unduly low. It will be of interest to see whether the improvement is maintained and whether new fisheries eventually appear.

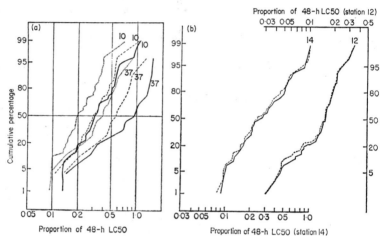

FIG. 5. Effect on toxicity of (a) dissolved oxygen (continuous lines, actual values; dotted lines, assumed values at 100% saturation; broken lines, assumed values at 40% saturation) and (b) temperature (continuous lines, actual values; broken lines, calculated values). Station numbers shown against curves.

*Effect of dissolved oxygen.* To assess the importance of dissolved oxygen on the predicted distributions of toxicity, calculations have been repeated at constant levels of 40, 70, and 100% saturation, other chemical and physical properties being assumed to remain at the observed values. The resulting distributions for 40 and 100% saturation at two fishless stations, Walton-on-Trent (Station 10) and Chetwynd Bridge, River Tame (Station 37), in 1968 are shown in Fig. 5a, together with those calculated using the observed dissolved-oxygen values, of which the means were 38% and 22% for the two stations respectively. The existing distribution of toxicities at Walton lies so close to the boundary thought to be necessary for the existence of fish that a modest increase in dissolved-oxygen concentration at this point might be expected to result in the re-establishment of a fishery. In the case of the Tame at Chetwynd Bridge, however, even if saturation concentrations of dissolved oxygen were to be achieved it seems probable that, unless further action were taken to remove pollutants, a fishery could not exist.

*Effect of temperature.* The effect on the calculated distributions of toxicity of increases in temperature of the Trent arising from the discharge of heated effluents from power stations has been examined by recalculating the distributions of the 48-h LC50 for Willington (Station 12) and Shardlow (Station 14) using the observed temperatures upstream at Walton (Station 10) and Willington respectively (see Fig. 2). For 1968, the average rise in temperature in the Walton to Willington reach, resulting from heated discharges from Drakelow and Burton Power Stations, was 1·4 deg. C, and in the Willington to Shardlow reach, from Willington and Castle Donnington Power Stations, 4·8 deg. C; for 1969 the values were 1·2 deg. C and 3·6 deg. C respectively. The effect of these increases in temperature however, as illustrated in Fig. 5b for the distribution at Shardlow in 1968 and Willington in 1969, is to increase the toxicity only very slightly.

It could be argued that the increases in temperature resulting from the discharge of cooling water might be much higher than those already indicated and, therefore, further calculations have been carried out on the data for Shardlow, assuming a temperature (a) equal to that at Walton, and (b) equal to that at Walton plus 8 deg. C during the summer months May-September and 10 deg. C for the rest of the year. Even with these constraints on the system the effect of temperature was small, the median values for the extreme conditions being within about $3\frac{1}{2}\%$ of those calculated using the observed temperature at Shardlow.

The importance of temperature will, however, depend upon the relative contributions made by the different poisons, since the toxicity of some is increased and that of others decreased by an increase in temperature. It will also depend upon the importance of dissolved-oxygen concentration, which in turn is affected by temperature and, where ammonia is important, upon the extent to which any increases in overall toxicity are offset by reductions in concentration of ammonia and increases in dissolved oxygen as the water passes through cooling towers.

*Relative importance of different poisons.* By calculating for each station separate distributions for toxicity attributable to one or more poisons, the contribution of each to the total can be easily demonstrated as shown in Fig. 6 for Lea Marston on the River Tame for 1969.

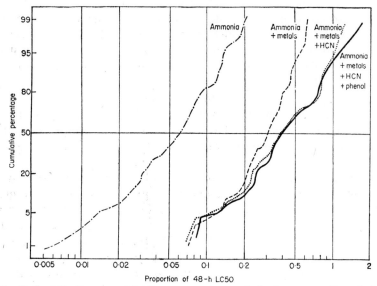

FIG. 6. Contribution to toxicity from ammonia, metals, hydrogen cyanide and phenols at Lea Marston (Station 35) on the River Tame, 1969.

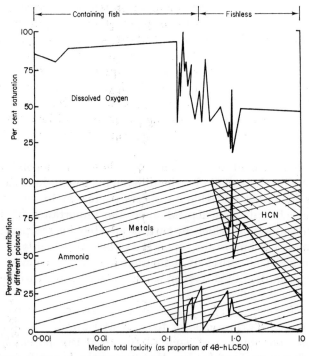

FIG. 7. Contribution to toxicity from ammonia, metals, and hydrogen cyanide and relation between toxicity and dissolved oxygen at stations in the River Trent system in 1968.

Here ammonia contributes only a small proportion of the total toxicity; metals are of overriding importance, and cyanide, and phenol especially, play only a minor rôle. The position for most of the area for 1968 is summarized in Fig. 7 by plotting against the median total toxicity at the various stations the percentages given by the medians for ammonia, metals, and cyanide. Included in the diagram are the two ranges of toxicity associated with the presence and absence of fish and the median concentration of dissolved oxygen (per cent saturation). This underlines the importance of both dissolved oxygen and of metals in determining toxicity over the range where conditions appear to be marginal for fisheries (around 0·28 of the 48-h LC50) and the added importance of cyanide where they are worst.

The relative contributions made by the metals have not yet been analysed in detail, but a preliminary indication of their respective importance can be provided from the unweighted mean of the average concentration of each for all stations, together with estimates of the toxicity of the unweighted mean for each metal under arbitrary standard environmental conditions of some relevance to the catchment area. These are summarized in Table II for 27 stations in 1968 and 23 of the stations in 1969. Zinc makes up more than half the metal concen-

TABLE II

*Contribution by heavy metals to aqueous concentrations and 48-h LC50 in the Trent River Authority area (percentage of total metal-ion)*

|  |  | Zinc | Copper | Nickel | Chromium | Cadmium |
|---|---|---|---|---|---|---|
| Unweighted mean | 1968 | 66 | 12 | 21 | 1 | <1 |
| concentration | 1969 | 63 | 9 | 27 | <1 | 2 |
| Approx 48-h LC50 | 1968 | 44 | 56 | <1 | <1 | <1 |
|  | 1969 | 48 | 51 | <1 | <1 | <1 |

tration, and copper only about ten per cent, but the two contribute almost equally to toxicity and together account for practically all of the 48-h LC50 for all metal ions. Nickel, which comprises more than 20% of the total metal concentration, is much less toxic and accounts for less than one per cent of the total toxicity, as do chromium and cadmium, both of which are present at very much lower concentrations. Since nickel, chromium, and cadmium are all demonstrably toxic to fish at concentrations much lower than the 48-h LC50, a more realistic estimate of their impact on estimated toxicity would be obtained by calculating their contribution as a proportion of their respective median threshold concentrations, determined from toxicity tests of up to two months duration. This has been done in an approximate way in Table III, which shows that cadmium, nickel, zinc, and copper are about equal in importance, while chromium still contributes less than 1%; as a result of the new calculation the total toxicity attributable to metals has about doubled, from 0·25 to 0·45 for 1968 and from 0·13 to 0·29 for 1969.

TABLE III

*Contribution by heavy metals to the approximate median threshold concentration in the Trent River Authority area (percentage of total metal-ion toxicity)*

|      | Zinc | Copper | Nickel | Chromium | Cadmium |
|------|------|--------|--------|----------|---------|
| 1968 | 25   | 31     | 22     | <1       | 21      |
| 1969 | 22   | 24     | 27     | <1       | 27      |

*Mass flow of metals.* Having illustrated the general importance of nickel and cadmium as well as copper and zinc in contributing to the toxicity of the water in the Trent river system, it is of some moment to seek the sources from which they are derived.

Analyses that have already been carried out on the mass flow of pollutants in the Trent (Ministry of Technology, 1969a, 1971) have shown that the largest single contribution is made by the River Tame. This tributary has now been examined in more detail using data collected by the River Authority in 1969. Mass flows have been calculated for the river close to its confluence with the Trent, using observed water quality data and river discharge rates, and have been compared with loads discharged upstream by all known effluents in daily operation.

The results are summarized in Table IV, from which tentative conclusions may be drawn. Since inorganic nitrogen flow in the river is largely accounted for by inputs from sewage effluent and there are substantial losses of non-conservative substances (ammonia and BOD) the balance can probably be regarded as reasonably realistic. Suspended solids and non-ferrous metal ion mass flows are, however, only partially accounted for in terms of normal waste discharges. It is not known what the other sources are, but deposition from the polluted atmosphere may be important, the route to the river being perhaps by intermittent storm discharges. To account for the extra 100 tonnes of solids per day in the Tame catchment the rate of deposition from the atmosphere

TABLE IV

*Mass flow in the River Tame, 1969*

|  | Calculated (tonnes/day) | Observed (tonnes/day) | Calculated (percentage of observed) |
|---|---|---|---|
| Ammoniacal nitrogen | 11·8 | 8·8 | 133 |
| Inorganic nitrogen | 21·0 | 23·3 | 90 |
| BOD | 53·2 | 32·0 | 167 |
| Suspended solids | 51·9 | 152 | 35 |
| Zinc | 0·55 | 1·33 | 42 |
| Copper | 0·16 | 0·35 | 44 |
| Nickel | 0·31 | 0·57 | 55 |
| Chromium | 0·35 | 0·34 | 101 |
| Cadmium | 0·01 | 0·06 | 19 |

would have to be assumed to be of the order of 68 kg/km² day for the whole area, or 180 kg/km² day for the urbanized area only, while the range that has been observed over the catchment as a whole varies from 60 kg/km² day in rural areas to 250 kg/km² day in the most urbanized (Ministry of Technology, 1969b). The metal ion transport capacity of 100 tonnes/day of suspended solids (from sources other than effluent) would be about 0·5 tonnes/day of each metal ion, assuming them to comprise about 0·5% w/w of the solids (the metal content of suspended solids in the Tame varies between 0·05 and 1·5% w/w). This would be sufficient to account for the metal ion mass flow observed in the river.

It also seems that the removal of significant quantities of metal ion from the Tame, where it is now present at a concentration toxic to fish, would not be achieved by further conventional sewage treatment unless steps were taken to intercept a large proportion of the flow of solids in suspension. This in turn would necessitate the construction of a plant capable of treating the whole river, or all storm discharges, during the initial critical phase of storm run-off. Separation of storm run-off by dual sewers might not achieve the desired pollution control in a heavily industrialized urban region such as the one considered.

These conclusions are speculative and remain to be verified. It would however be of interest to know whether similar conclusions are suggested by results elsewhere.

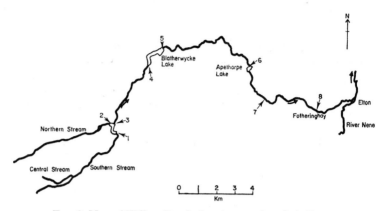

Fig. 8. Map of Willow Brook showing numbered stations.

## Willow Brook

Another, more intensive, ecological investigation of fisheries in a polluted river system is currently being undertaken by WPRL in the Willow Brook, in Northamptonshire, which receives the wastes from a large steel works (Fig. 8). The headwaters, three small, fairly heavily polluted streams, run into a small lake and from thence the river flows for a distance of about 20 km, passing through two further lakes before joining the River Nene.

Preliminary results from routine sampling between November 1969 and May 1970 indicate that ammonia and zinc are the only two poisons continually present at concentrations high enough to contribute significantly to the 48-h LC50, but fish have been killed in the upper reaches on two occasions by discharges of phenol. Low concentrations of cadmium, copper, lead, and nickel have also been found occasionally. Although the lakes in the system, particularly the uppermost one, tend to balance out the fluctuations in flow and in concentration of poisons in the incoming streams, the quality of the water leaving the highest lake shows daily variations in the concentrations of ammonia and zinc, as well as a marked seasonal rhythm in zinc concentration (high in winter, low in summer). A decrease in the concentrations of these two poisons occurs in passing downstream, the total (expressed as the proportion of their 48-h LC50 for trout) falling from a median value of about 0·3 at the outlet from the upper lake to a median of 0·15 some 16 km (ten miles) downstream (Fig. 9). While a good mixed fish population of eight to ten species is present in the lower reaches of the system, netting of the upper lake on a number of occasions has revealed only small numbers of roach, and a few three-spined stickleback

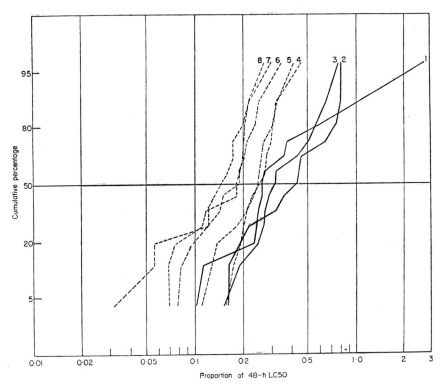

Fig. 9. Distributions of toxicity in the Willow Brook between November 1969 and May 1970. Broken lines, good fisheries; solid lines, fisheries marginal. Numbers refer to stations shown in Fig. 8.

(*Gasterosteus aculeatus* L.). The age-class structure of the sample of roach appeared abnormal, in that apart from two six-year-old, and one five-year-old fish, they were all in their second year. All were in good condition, apart from showing a certain pallor of the liver. Comparison of their sizes with that of roach of equivalent ages from downstream, and from other waters, indicates that they achieved a better-than-average growth rate; this is perhaps attributable to their apparent low population density in the lake. The unusual age-structure of the population possibly reflects some historically catastrophic event, or even the inability of the fish to breed in a water which was previously more heavily polluted.

It may be noted that the median value for the boundary distribution of the estimated 48-h LC50 between those parts of the system supporting a good fishery and those that are virtually fishless or supporting abnormal populations is between 0·32 and 0·25, which is close to the value already described for the River Trent area (0·28).

None of the non-ferrous metals, except zinc, contributes much to the 48-h LC50 in this system but, as in the Trent, some appear to be much more important when their possible long-term effects on trout are considered. Appropriate estimates of median threshold values are not available for the unusually hard water in the Willow Brook (500 mg/l as calcium carbonate), but an approximate assessment of the rôle of these metals is obtained by choosing values found for trout in water having a hardness of about 350 mg/l as calcium carbonate. This shows that of the total toxicity contributed by non-ferrous metals cadmium would account for 68 to 84%, zinc for 11 to 27% and copper, nickel, and chromium together, 6 to 9%.

## DISCUSSION

There is now considerable evidence from the studies in the Trent area, supported by those on the Cam and the Willow Brook, of a general empirical relation between the estimated toxicity (48-h LC50) to trout of polluted water and the presence or absence of fish; the boundary condition corresponds to an annual median of about 0·28 and to a 99 percentile value of about 1·1. This does not necessarily imply that in fishless rivers the toxicity is in excess of 1·1 for a continuous period of at least 1% of the year (3·5 days) and that therefore fish are killed by one adverse period of this length, though this might well happen in some situations. Nevertheless it is of interest to note that the toxicity at a percentile frequency (0·55) equivalent to 48 h out of one year is close to a 48-h LC50 of 1·0. However, it seems more likely, especially in fishless rivers in which the distribution of toxicity is close to those of rivers containing fish, that any immigrant fish trying to remain would be killed over fairly long periods. At present insufficient information is available to say whether any particular fraction of toxicity or any particular pattern of occurrence over a long period would be the limiting factor, or how its adverse effects might be integrated by the fish. More attention must be given to this aspect in future studies.

For the present it may be sufficient to note the general occurrence of a wide overall range of quality having an approximately log-normal distribution that spans approximately one order of magnitude between the 5 and 95 percentile frequency and to recognize this phenomenon when considering standards of quality for fisheries; these should be defined as values not to be exceeded for a given frequency of say 50% or 95% rather than for 100% of the time.

Whether or not the empirical relation found in these studies has any validity elsewhere is not known. It is quite possible that in attempting to sum small fractions of the 48-h LC50 of several poisons, the toxicity of some is under-estimated, for example because of unknown long-term effects, while that of others is over-estimated, for example because of adaptation by the fish. The resulting errors might tend to cancel each other and the same could happen with the relationship derived between toxicity to trout and the presence or absence of coarse fish where the relative sensitivity of two species may be reversed for two different poisons. For this reason alone it would be surprising if the relationships already found were universally applicable, though their chance of failure might be low, except where the nature of both the pollution and the fisheries was markedly different and less diverse than in the present studies.

There is also some uncertainty about the reliability of the actual values that have been used for toxicity as well as of their relationship to the fisheries. One criticism would be that no direct measurement of toxicity was made in either the Trent or the Willow Brook, so that no account can be taken of unknown poisons that might be present. In the rare cases where a single effluent is responsible for polluting a river, an assessment of the toxicity of the river can be made from a direct test with fish in the effluent and dilutions made up with river water, but where, as is more usual, the situation is more complex and the river itself is not demonstrably toxic within a few days or weeks, it may be necessary in a test to make the river water more toxic by adding known poisons.

Clearly, it would also be better to use the species appropriate to the fishery of interest instead of trout only, and also to take as a criterion of toxicity the median threshold or five percentile threshold for survival or inhibition of growth rather than the 48-h LC50.

. Another criticism is that studies of the fisheries in the Trent area were rather limited. The consequence is that improvements in quality such as occurred between 1968 and 1969 could result in an under-estimate of the toxicity that is associated with fishlessness, while a deterioration if it occurred might cause the toxicity associated with the presence of fish to be over-estimated. Clearly much more intensive population studies are desirable to examine in detail the relationship of population structures to fluctuations in water quality.

SUMMARY

1. Work is reviewed to show (i) that the short-term toxicity (48-h LC50) to rainbow trout of mixtures of ammonia, phenol, hydrogen cyanide, copper, zinc, cadmium, and nickel, is largely but not entirely calculable knowing the toxicity of the individual poisons, (ii) that these poisons, excluding cadmium and nickel, account for much of the short-term toxicity of sewage effluents and polluted rivers containing industrial wastes, especially in the Midlands, and (iii) that coarse fish are generally more resistant to these poisons than trout, though there are some exceptions.

2. Studies in the Trent River Authority area and in a stream in Northamptonshire show that there is a wide variation of water quality at any given sampling point and that there is a difference between the calculated 48-h LC50 to trout of waters devoid of fish and of those containing fisheries, the boundary occurring at a median value of about 0·28. Medians based on direct measurements of toxicity at two other polluted sites on the River Cam where trout fisheries exist also lie just below this value.

3. To illustrate the potential usefulness of the empirical relationships that have been found, predictions are made about the effect of temperature and dissolved oxygen on the 48-h LC50, and, more tentatively, on the consequent status of fisheries.

4. The general importance in the Trent area of non-ferrous metals, particularly copper and zinc, together with hydrogen cyanide and also ammonia, in contributing to the estimated 48-h LC50 is underlined alongside the almost equal impact of cadmium and nickel when the long-term survival of fish is considered. In the Willow Brook zinc contributes predominantly to the short-term toxicity and cadmium seems to be most important in the long-term.

5. Possible explanations for empirical relations between toxicity and the presence or absence of fish are discussed. Direct estimates of toxicity using relevant coarse fish species would be preferable to predictions made for trout simply from chemical analyses and quantitative methods of assessing fish populations should be used wherever possible.

ACKNOWLEDGEMENTS

The authors wish to acknowledge the considerable help obtained from the Trent River Authority and the Welland and Nene River Authority in providing data on the quality of water in their areas, and the access to Deene Lake on the Willow Brook, which was kindly given by Stewarts and Lloyds of Corby and Mr. E. Brundell. Miss T. McCullagh assisted in the processing of the data from the Trent area, and many colleagues took part in the field studies on the Willow Brook; their contributions are gratefully acknowledged.

Crown copyright. Reproduced by permission of the Controller of Her Majesty's Stationery Office.

## REFERENCES

Abram, F. S. H. (1967). The definition and measurement of fish toxicity thresholds. *Proc. int. Conf. Wat. Pollut. Res., Munich*, 1966 No. 3. **1**: 75–95.

Alabaster, J. S. (1959). The effect of a sewage effluent on the distribution of dissolved oxygen and fish in a stream. *J. Anim. Ecol.* **28**: 283–291.

Alabaster, J. S. (1969). Survival of fish in 164 herbicides, insecticides, fungicides, wetting agents and miscellaneous substances. *Int. Pest Control* **1969** Mar.–Apr.: 29–35.

Alabaster, J. S. (1970). Testing the toxicity of effluents to fish. *Chemy Ind.* **1970**: 759–764.

Alabaster, J. S. (1971). The comparative sensitivity of coarse fish and trout to pollution. *Proc. 4th Br. Coarse Fish Conf., Liverpool, March* 1969.

Alabaster, J. S. & Abram, F. S. H. (1965). Development and use of a direct method of evaluating toxicity to fish. *Proc. int. Conf. Wat. Pollut. Res., Tokyo*, 1964 No. 2. **1**: 41–60.

Allan, I. R. H., Herbert, D. W. M. & Alabaster, J. S. (1958). A field and laboratory investigation of fish in a sewage effluent. *Fishery Invest., Lond.* (1) **6**: (2): 1–76.

Ball, I. R. (1967a). The relative susceptibilities of some species of freshwater fish to poisons. I. Ammonia. *Wat. Res.* **1**: 767–775.

Ball, I. R. (1967b). The relative susceptibilities of some species of freshwater fish to poisons. II. Zinc. *Wat. Res.* **1**: 777–783.

Brown, V. M. (1968). The calculation of the acute toxicity of mixtures of poisons to rainbow trout. *Wat. Res.* **2**: 723–733.

Brown, V. M. & Dalton, R. A. (1970). The acute lethal toxicity to rainbow trout of mixtures of copper, phenol, zinc, and nickel. *J. Fish Biol.* **2**: 211–216.

Brown, V. M., Jordan, D. H. M. & Tiller, B. A. (1969). The acute toxicity to rainbow trout of fluctuating concentrations and mixtures of ammonia, phenol, and zinc. *J. Fish Biol.* **1**: 1–9.

Brown, V. M., Mitrovic, V. V. & Stark, G. T. C. (1968). Effects of chronic exposure to zinc on toxicity of a mixture of detergent and zinc. *Wat. Res.* **2**: 255–263.

Brown, V. M., Shurben, D. G. & Shaw, D. (1970). Studies on water quality and the absence of fish from some polluted English rivers. *Wat. Res.* **4**: 363–382.

Clarendon Press (1963). *Atlas of Britain and Northern Ireland*. Oxford; Clarendon Press.

Doudoroff, P. (1952). Some recent developments in the study of toxic industrial wastes. *Proc. Conf. ind. Waste Pacif. NW.* No. 4 (1952): 21.

Downing, K. M. & Merkens, J. C. (1957). The influence of temperature on the survival of several species of fish in low tensions of dissolved oxygen. *Ann. appl. Biol.* **45**: 261–267.

E

Edwards, R. W. & Brown, V. M. (1967). Pollution and fisheries: a progress report. *Wat. Pollut. Control* **66**: 3–18.

Herbert, D. W. M. (1962). The toxicity to rainbow trout of spent still liquors from the distillation of coal. *Ann. appl. Biol.* **50**: 755–777.

Herbert, D. W. M., Jordan, D. H. M. & Lloyd, R. (1965). A study of some fishless rivers in the industrial Midlands. *J. Proc. Inst. Sew. Purif.* **1965**: 569–582.

Herbert, D. W. M. & Shurben, D. S. (1964). The toxicity to fish of mixtures of poisons. I. Salts of ammonia and zinc, *Ann. appl. Biol.* **53**: 33–41.

Herbert, D. W. M. & Vandyke, Jennifer M. (1964). The toxicity to fish of mixtures of poisons. II. Copper-ammonia and zinc-phenol mixtures. *Ann. appl. Biol.* **53**: 415–421.

Lloyd, R. (1961). The toxicity of mixtures of zinc and copper sulphates to rainbow trout (*Salmo gairdnerii* Richardson). *Ann. appl. Biol.* **49**: 535–538.

Lloyd, R. & Jordan, D. H. M. (1963). Predicted and observed toxicities of several sewage effluents to rainbow trout. *J. Proc. Inst. Sew. Purif.* **1963**: 167–173.

Lloyd, R. & Jordan, D. H. M. (1964). Predicted and observed toxicities of several sewage effluents to rainbow trout: A further study. *J. Proc. Inst. Sew. Purif.* **1964**: 3–6.

Ministry of Technology (1966). *Water Pollution Research* 1965. London: H.M. Stationery Office.

Ministry of Technology (1968). *Water Pollution Research* 1967. London: H.M. Stationery Office.

Ministry of Technology (1969a). *Water Pollution Research* 1968. London: H.M. Stationery Office.

Ministry of Technology (1969b). *The investigation of air pollution; deposit gauge and lead dioxide observation. April–September* 1969. London: H.M. Stationery Office.

Ministry of Technology (1971). *Water Pollution Research* 1970. London: H.M. Stationery Office.

Pentelow, F. T. K. (1959). The general condition of the rivers of Britain. *Symf. Inst. Biol.* No. 8: 1–10.

Southgate, B. A. (1932). The toxicity of mixtures of poisons. *Q. Jl Pharm. Pharmac.* **5**: 639–648.

Symp. zool. Soc. Lond. (1972) No. 29, 115–133

# FISH PRODUCTION IN FRESHWATERS

## E. D. LE CREN

*Freshwater Biological Association, The River Laboratory,*
*East Stoke, Wareham, Dorset, England*

SYNOPSIS

Production in the ecological (and IBP) sense, is a basic parameter in population dynamics and the ecology of ecosystems linking population density, growth rate and survival rate. For freshwater fish it can best be estimated from data on population abundance and mean size throughout the lives of cohorts. Several estimates are now available from a variety of waters ranging from less than 1 g/m² year to over 60 g/m² year. Few multi-specific estimates have been made; those that have have emphasize the importance of young stages and small species. Freshwater fish production depends upon the basic productivity of the water; high correlations have been shown between primary production and fish production in experimental ponds. Eutrophication may increase overall fish production. Some effects of density on production have been shown; it may act more through mortality in the young stages and growth in later life. Angling may have conflicting requirements and much more will need to be known about freshwater fish production and population dynamics before conservation can be soundly based.

## INTRODUCTION

Research into production, in its ecological sense, has received considerable stimulus in recent years, especially under the auspices of the International Biological Programme. In this paper I review some developments in this field and especially such estimates of fish production in freshwaters as have been made. I also discuss the value of production as one of the central parameters of population dynamics and how it may be affected by various environmental factors. Finally I suggest some ways in which studies of production might aid conservation.

Production as here discussed may be defined as the total elaboration of fish flesh in a given time regardless of its ultimate fate and whether it survives to the end of that time. It is thus a different measure from the yield, though in a well managed fish pond nearly all the production may be harvested as yield and the latter may be used as an approximate measure of production. Ricker (1968) gives a good discussion of the definitions and relationships between various production concepts with particular reference to fish.

Although it is only in recent years that any large numbers of production estimates have been made, the concepts have been thought about for a long time, especially in the context of fish and aquatic ecosystems in general. It will suffice here merely to mention firstly the

Danish marine biologists, originating with Petersen, who were attempting a quantitative description of the trophic structure of the ecosystem in inshore waters between 1900 and 1930. Secondly there was the Russian school led by Ivlev, and thirdly, in North America, Hutchinson, Lindeman, Clarke and Ricker were developing their ideas in the 1940's. The best review of the development of aquatic production biology is probably that of Ivlev (1966). More recent work has been reviewed by Mann (1969). The first published attempt at estimating the production of a freshwater fish was probably Allen's preliminary account of trout production in the Horokiwi River in 1946, followed by Ricker and Foerster's classic account of sockeye salmon production in Cultus Lake (Ricker & Foerster, 1948). There were 20 years of gestation before production then became fashionable and IBP got underway, though throughout that period some of us were thinking about production and making the first attempts at further estimates (Tables I and II) (Le Cren, 1949).

### THE RELATIONSHIPS OF PRODUCTION TO OTHER PARAMETERS

It is important to realize that production is only one of a whole series of related parameters of the population dynamics or "production ecology" of a species. Figure 1 is an attempt to relate these diagrammatically.

The source of all organic energy is the light fixed by photosynthesis (see the bottom of Fig. 1). The inorganic nutrients and carbon dioxide are derived from the physical environment and from the recirculation of nutrients mineralized from organic matter previously produced in the system. The lower levels of secondary production also depend upon allochthonous organic matter and detritus from previous production.

Some freshwater fish feed directly on primary production and some on organic detritus but the majority of the food of most British species

---

Fig. 1. Diagrammatic representation of the inter-relationships between production and other components in the part of the trophic system occupied by a fish population. The items in CAPITALS are matter and/or energy and the flow between them is indicated by solid lines. The items in lower case are processes while the items in *italics* (on the left hand side) are factors influencing these processes; their effects being shown by dotted lines.

There is a loop to the right from PRODUCTION back to POPULATION NUMBER representing production and recruitment and a second loop to the left indicating the special "feed-back" influence of population density, which is indicated by a dot-dash line.

ENERGY lost to the system is shown by oblique dashed lines to J (for joules).

For further explanation see text (elaborated from Backiel & Le Cren, 1967).

*INFLUENCING FACTORS*

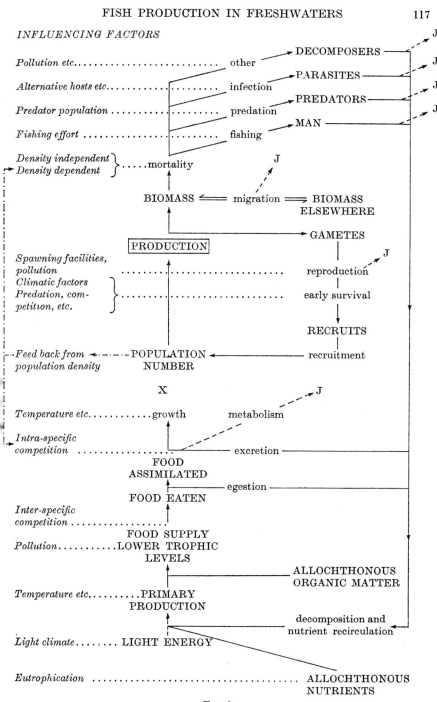

FIG. 1.

consists of invertebrate animals. Some of the available food will be eaten by competitors: fish and other animals. The food that is eaten will mostly be assimilated but some will be egested. Of the assimilated food much of the energy will be lost in metabolism, a little of the matter in excretion; the rest will be used in growth. The product of the average individual growth times the number of individuals in the population is the production.

The population number is decreased by the various forms of mortality but increased by the recruitment of young fish through reproduction. The production of gametes is part of the production process and strictly so is the rearing of recruits, but it is often convenient to consider reproduction, juvenile production and recruitment as a separate system (which has been represented as a loop in Fig. 1).

The production goes to form gametes but also to increase the biomass of the population (stock) of fish present. There is also frequently emigration to and immigration from a stock of fish elsewhere and the effects of this are sometimes difficult to dissociate from those of mortality and recruitment; sometimes the two are linked as, for example, in the salmon.

The biomass is decreased by mortality; which is the fate of most of the somatic production. In Fig. 1 four common causes of mortality are shown: fishing leading to the production of men, predation leading to the production of predators, infection leading to the production of parasites and death through disease, pollution etc. which can provide dead fish for scavengers and decomposers. In each case the matter and some of the energy in the fish is passed onto a succeeding trophic level.

Energy is lost as heat at various points in the system, especially through the metabolism of the fish both in basic physiological activity and that required for food seeking, movement, migration, reproduction, etc.

Some of the factors influencing the various processes are listed on the left of Fig. 1. These are discussed in a later section but it will be noticed that population number has a special influence through density effects at several points in the system. It would be possible to elaborate the various influencing factors much further but the diagram would then become even more complex. It is important to remember that it is already simplified and represents only part of only one trophic level. Nevertheless the kernel of the system for any one population is the production as a sum of the growth of all the individuals present and growth, mortality and recruitment (or natality) are the three key processes.

## METHODS OF ESTIMATING FISH PRODUCTION

As described above the production of a fish stock is the product of the population number of fish in the area being studied and the growth of the individuals. Numbers and individual size are thus the basic data for production calculation. It is convenient and indeed really essential to consider a cohort or year-class of fish through its life, though the various age groups present at any one time can be used to construct a "composite" year-class (with adjustment for differences in year-class strength).

Normally data on abundance and size are available at discrete intervals of time and these can be integrated into production estimates in three ways.

1. Models of population dynamics may be used, the relevant parameters determined and the necessary calculations made, e.g. Beverton & Holt (1957).

2. The instantaneous coefficients of growth and mortality are estimated for successive time intervals together with the numerical abundance on at least one occasion and Ricker's (1958) formula used to calculate production for each period, which is then summed.

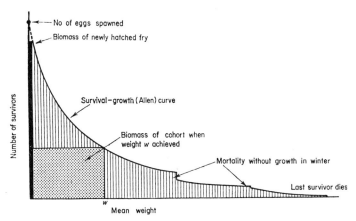

FIG. 2. Diagrammatic survival-growth ("Allen") curve for a hypothetical cohort of fish. The number of fish surviving from the eggs laid until the death of the last survivor is plotted against the mean weight achieved. The biomasses on hatching and at one point later in life are shown together with mortality without growth in winter.

3. The most popular technique is to plot numbers surviving in the cohort against mean weight achieved (Fig. 2) and then measure the

area beneath the resultant curve as an estimate of production. This graphical method is due to Allen (1951) and is colloquially known as the "Allen curve".

The two mathematical methods can be programmed on a computer and thus be quite expeditiously calculated. The Allen curve, however, has the great advantage of providing a visual check on what is happening and an easy way to adjust for suspected errors or bias. Provided the same basic data are used all three methods should produce results that differ only insignificantly. Chapman (1968) discusses the estimation of production.

Total fish production can be divided into two; the production of somatic tissue and that of gonads. In some situations it may be relevant to distinguish between the two; the gonad production can sometimes represent a considerable share of the total production (Le Cren, 1962) or have practical relevance (e.g. in studying sturgeon!).

Allen curves can demonstrate an apparent "negative" production on spawning or over winter. The detail of an hypothetical example of

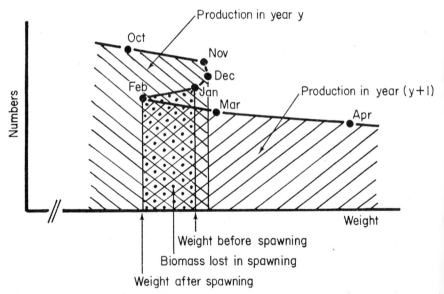

Fig. 3. Enlargement of the detail of a survival-growth ("Allen") curve for an hypothetical cohort of fish over a winter followed by spawning between January and February. The points represent values for survivors and mean weight at successive monthly intervals. The area hatched one way represents the production in year $y$, the area hatched the other way the production in year $(y+1)$. The cross hatched area is the winter and spawning loss in production ("negative production") that has to be made up at the beginning of year $(y+1)$. The dotted area is the loss of production on spawning. The mortality is approximately constant throughout. (See also Chapman, 1968: 190).

a fish spawning in late January is shown in Fig. 3, the regression of the line towards the left between December and January is due to loss in weight in winter, while the much larger loss between January and February is largely caused by the deposition of eggs and milt. Recovery in average weight is fairly rapid but not until March does it exceed the maximum weight achieved the previous autumn. The monthly mortality rate remains roughly constant throughout. The interpretation of such phenomena will depend upon what is to be made of the production data. If they are being used in models of the relationships between trophic levels, i.e. to estimate food consumption, then all production, including the recovery from winter and spawning loss, must be taken into account. Thus in Fig. 3 the cross-hatched area produced originally in year $y$ then lost and produced again at the beginning of year $y+1$ would be counted twice in the total estimate.

Another complication can arise with the movement of fish in and out of the area. If a particular area is being studied for its capability to produce then changes in population numbers due to immigration or emigration can easily be accepted on the Allen curve which will then take account of the production of the migrants while they are in the area.

It is usual to measure fish production on an annual basis but at times it may be instructive to use shorter periods. In temperate regions most production will take place during the summer growing season. It is important to realize that the Allen curve has no time scale, though time divisions can be marked on it if it is wished; they will not be evenly spaced.

Again, it is usual to describe production on an area basis, as most freshwater primary and thus secondary production depend on area In situations where the primary source of energy is largely allochthonous, as in many rivers and small water bodies, an area basis for production may not be so relevant, but often some other aspect of area, such as territorial behaviour (Le Cren, 1965) may be a factor limiting production.

## ESTIMATES OF PRODUCTION

Information on production in freshwater fish now appears to be available for some forty or more natural species-situations. (A great many more data could be found in the fish-culture literature but few of these would be relevant to natural situations.) Table I lists most of these that are readily available. It is probable that there are others, and basic data suitable for making estimates of production may have been collected on a number of other occasions.

Many of the estimates are for salmonids in small streams. This is partly because of the general interest in salmonids but also because electric fishing makes population estimates in small streams easier

TABLE I

*Estimates of production for freshwater fish in natural rivers. All data have been converted to g (fresh weight)/m² year, and rounded to two digits. The range is given where available*

| River | Species | Production | Author |
|---|---|---|---|
| Horokiwi | *Salmo trutta* | 55 | Allen, 1951 |
| Walla | *S. trutta* | 10–18 | Horton, 1961 |
| Lawrence | *Salvelinus fontinalis* | 9–11 | Hunt, 1966 |
| Loucka | *Salmo trutta* | 1·7–8·6 | Libosvarsky, 1968 |
| Black Brows | *Salmo trutta* | 10 | |
| Kingswell | *S. trutta* | 7·4 | |
| Hall | *S. trutta* | 5·2 | Le Cren, 1969 |
| Appletreeworth | *S. trutta* | 3·0 | |
| Nether Hearth | *S. trutta* | 5·0 | |
| | *Cottus gobio* | 1·0 | |
| Shelligan | *Salmo salar* | 5·7–12·3 | Egglishaw, 1970 |
| | *S. trutta* | 6·7–12·7 | |
| Bere | *Salmo trutta* | 2·6–13 | |
| | *S. salar* | 7·2 | |
| | *Cottus gobio* | 6·2–30 | Mann, 1971 |
| | *Phoxinus phonixus* | 2·0 | |
| | *Gasterosteus aculeatus* | 1·8 | |
| Tarrant | *Salmo trutta* | 12 | |
| | *Cottus gobio* | 43 | Mann, 1971 |
| | *Phoxinus phoxinus* | 3·9 | |
| | *Gasterosteus aculeatus* | 0·6 | |
| | Total | 60 | |
| Devil's | *Salmo trutta* | 4·8 | |
| | *Cottus gobio* | 14 | Mann, 1971 |
| | *Gasterosteus aculeatus* | 0·6 | |
| | Total | 30 | |
| Docken's | *Salmo trutta* | 12 | Mann, 1971 |
| | *Phoxinus phoxinus* | 1·9 | |
| | Total | 14 | |

TABLE I—contd.

| River | Species | Production | Author |
|-------|---------|------------|--------|
| Thames | *Rutilus rutilus* | 9·0 | } Mann, 1965 |
|  | *Alburnus alburnus* | 29 |  |
|  | *Leuciscus leuciscus* | 1·3 |  |
|  | *Perca fluviatilis* | 1·5 |  |
|  | *Gobio gobio* | 2·3 |  |
|  | Total | 43 |  |
| Manistee | *Icthyomyzon castaneus* | 0·15 | Hall, 1963 |

*Notes:* In several of these rivers species other than those mentioned occur and may have significant production. Some of the estimates (e.g. Le Cren, 1969) are approximate only. More recent estimates which include the production of younger fish substantially increase the total fish production in the Thames (Mathews, 1971 and pers. comm.). *Icthyomyzon castaneus* is a lamprey and not a fish.

than in most other waters. It will be seen that these range from 2 to about $18 \text{ g/m}^2$ year and there may be some significance in the maximum of between 12 g and 18 g (Le Cren, 1969). One estimate in Table I stands out as much higher than the others; that for the Horokiwi River. There is little doubt that this is an overestimate because early mortality could not be adequately studied. It may also be significant that the brown trout is an introduced species in this river. However, the Horokiwi also holds a good population of eels and a few other fish so the total production must be even larger. Some preliminary experiments with young trout in channels gave some rates of production of the order of $50 \text{ g/m}^2$ year and it is probable that the usual maximum of about $18 \text{ g/m}^2$ year for salmonids is more apparent than real.

It is interesting to compare the trout production and population structure in the English streams listed by Le Cren (1969). These streams ranged from Pennine and Lake District becks with soft water and a low general productivity to small chalk streams in the south with a high calcium content famous for their high productivity and good trout fishing. The production of trout is similar in all but the very poor upland becks, but the population structure is quite different. One beck, Black Brows, had a dense population of young fish, most of which migrated downstream in their second year; about 1 g was the average weight at the end of the first summer. Hall Beck, also in the Lake District, had a dense isolated population, composed of fish of all ages up to at least seven. No fish over 20 g was ever found and growth was therefore exceedingly slow.

In the River Tarrant, in Dorset, the trout population was much sparser but the fish usually achieved 20 g by the end of the first year; a few young salmon were also present. In some reaches of the similar Bere Stream habitats were available for larger trout and occasional fish of up to 1 kg could be found; growth is very rapid. In the soft-water New Forest Docken's Water an intermediate situation exists. The trout production is 12 g/m$^2$ year resulting from moderate growth of a moderate population. Preliminary experiments in channels at East Stoke have shown that high production (up to 50 g/m$^2$ year) can be obtained with artificially high populations of young trout but that there is a negative correlation between population density and growth.

TABLE II

*Estimates of production for freshwater fish in natural ponds and lakes. All data have been converted to g (fresh weight)/m$^2$ year and rounded to two digits. The range is given where available*

| Lake | Species | Production | Author |
|---|---|---|---|
| Cultus | *Oncorhynchus nerka* | 5·9 | Ricker & Foerster, 1948 |
| Five in Michigan | *Salmo gairdneri* | 1·9–8·4 | Johnson & Hasler, 1954 |
| Five in New York | *Salvelinus fontinalis* | 3·3–6·5 | Hatch & Webster, 1961 |
| Three Dubs | *Salmo trutta* | 0·75 | Le Cren, 1962 |
| Reservoir in Oregon | *Oncorhynchus tshawytscha* | 16 | Higley, 1963 |
| Reservoir in Oregon | *Salmo gairdneri* | 5·3 | Coche, 1964 |
| Wyland | *Lepomis macrochirus* | 9·1 | Gerking, 1962 |
| Pond in Pennsylvania | *Micropterus salmoides* | 5–8 | Cooper et al., 1963 |
| Windermere | *Perca fluviatilis* | approx. 20 | Le Cren, 1958a |
| Windermere | *Perca fluviatilis* | approx. 16 | Le Cren, 1962 |
| Windermere | *Esox lucius* | 0·24–0·67 | Kipling & Frost, 1970 |

*Notes:* In no known case has the production of all the species present been estimated. The estimates for *Perca fluviatilis* in Windermere and *Salmo trutta* in Three Dubs are very approximate.

Data for salmonids and centrarchids in small lakes give production rates of a similar order of magnitude to salmonids in streams. (Table II.) The data for pike in Windermere (Kipling & Frost, 1970) are of a lower order of magnitude which may be a reflection of the position of this species at a higher trophic level in the food pyramid.

For very few water bodies are there production data for all the species of fish; in most of the cases discussed above only one or two species have been studied. K. H. Mann and his co-workers however, have studied the production of all the abundant species of fish in the Thames (Mann, 1965; Berrie—this Symposium, pp. 69–86) and have found some very high levels of production—perhaps up to 100 g/m² year. R. H. K. Mann has studied most of the species in four smaller streams in southern England (Mann, 1971) and found total production rates of up to 60 g/m² year. In this latter situation it is interesting to note that (as described above) the salmonid production was no more than in "poor" northern streams, but in the chalk streams there is a large added component of production by non-salmonid species, particularly the bullhead (*Cottus gobio*).

A feature of all these estimates, and particularly the situations of higher production, is the large contribution made by small and/or young fish. In terms of production the dominant species in the Thames is the bleak, in the chalk streams the bullhead (neither species of interest to fishermen). A large share of the production goes to the rearing of recruits to the stock of other species too, and it may not be generally realized that not only are the early stages of the life of a cohort crucial in determining its survival but they may also make major demands on the productive capacity of the environment to provide food for the species (Le Cren, 1962; Cushing—this Symposium, pp. 213–232).

FACTORS AFFECTING FISH PRODUCTION

Estimates of production are not ends in themselves; they will enlarge our understanding of the ecology of fish only if they can be compared with one another and the differences between them related to factors in the environment.

It is convenient to group those factors influencing production into three broad groups: (a) those relating to general productivity and other trophic levels, (b) those relating to species composition, inter-specific competition and inter-active segregation, and (c) those relating to population abundance and growth within the species and especially the effects of population density. I will discuss these in turn.

### General productivity

The data of Table I illustrate the influence of general productivity. If calcium content is used as a measure of the general fertility of a water (albeit an arbitrary one), then there is a clear correlation between it and total fish production (Le Cren, 1969). There are obviously other factors at work, such as temperature and the variance of discharge, but the general concept of increase in total fish production with an increase in general productivity must be accepted, even if the details and the reasons have yet to be found.

This concept, of course also finds support from fish cultural practice. There are vast numbers of empirical data relating the chemical fertilization of ponds to fish yield. Wolny & Grygierek (1970) however, have made more sophisticated investigations and shown strong positive correlations between primary production and fish production in experimental ponds. (It is perhaps reassuring to production ecologists to have such direct experimental verification that the food chain works!)

## Species composition

The data of Table I also show (as discussed above) that some of the differences in the series of streams of increasing productivity were due to an increase in the number of species involved. Most of the northern streams contain only one or two species whereas the chalk streams and the Thames have five or more species contributing significantly to the total production.

This concept is also well known in fish culture, where many of the more sophisticated and productive practices involve multi-specific stocking (Hickling, 1962).

The phenomenon of interactive segregation has been discussed by Nilsson (1967) and others but there are few data on the exact effect on both total production and the production of each species of changing the number of species involved. It would seem likely that adding another species will increase the total production but also reduce the production of the species already present. Many British freshwater fish seem to eat a broadly similar range of invertebrate food, but their feeding habits do differ in detail and quantitative balance over the spectrum of diet, and these differences are doubtless enhanced by competition and interactive segregation.

## Intra-specific factors

Although the direct effect of population density on production is not well known the general relationship between density and growth rate has been studied in a number of species. Sometimes no relationship has been found but usually there is a negative correlation; crowded fish do not grow as well. This is well known for pond culture (Walter, 1934; Hepher, 1967) and there is usually considered to be an optimum stocking density, the "carrying capacity", for maximum yield (which may be equated to production). Hepher (1967) shows that there is a constant negative log log relationship between growth rate and population density with a coefficient of about 0·7 for densities below the carrying capacity. This means that the population density can be increased faster than the growth rate declines and so production increased up to the "carrying capacity" point where the growth rate then declines much more sharply with further increases in population.

Experiments with trout fry during the early weeks of growth showed that the instantaneous growth rate was negatively proportional to the logarithm of population density (Backiel & Le Cren, 1967). At the same time territorial behaviour led to the instantaneous mortality rate being proportional to the logarithm of population density (Le Cren, 1965; Backiel & Le Cren, 1967; Le Cren, 1972). The result of these density effects on growth and mortality is that the production increases rapidly but not proportionally with increase in initial population density until a maximum is reached which is then maintained regardless of density.

In discussing these relationships Backiel & Le Cren (1967) postulated that the effects of population density were mostly on mortality early in life and mostly on growth later in life though this is not always so; nor is there enough evidence to make more than tentative generalizations.

Over and above density-dependent effects on mortality (and growth) are those mainly abiotic factors in the environment which can affect production. These include year to year temperature variations, which can frequently affect growth (Le Cren, 1958; Kipling & Frost, 1970) and also those factors that affect the early survival of cohorts (year classes) and thus their production throughout their life. One of the best documental examples of this is the pike population in Windermere. Over a period of 19 years Kipling & Frost (1970) found considerable variation in year-class strength and thus in the contribution of each year class to production which varied from 1·0 mg to 6·7 mg. Though the situation was influenced by an intensive experimental fishery most of the large variations were caused by climatic factors. Another example of the effects of cohort strength on production is the classic study of young sockeye salmon in Cultus Lake by Ricker & Foerster (1948). There can be seen the effects on both production and yield of different rates of egg deposition, experimental variation in the type of breeding allowed, density-dependent effects on growth and survival and the effect of an experimental reduction in predators (Le Cren, 1962).

It is clear that a great many factors can affect production, some, but not all, of which can be influenced by Man.

## CONCLUSIONS FOR CONSERVATION AND MANAGEMENT

Estimates of production are of limited value in themselves, but, as shown above, can be compared one with another and with other factors to yield a better understanding of the production processes in the ecosystem. Moreover, it is clear that production is but one population parameter; and it is linked to population numbers or density and rates of growth, mortality, recruitment and migration. Production does, however, embody the essence of these other parameters and if one measure has to be chosen is probably the best as an epitome of both the quantitative role and the performance of the taxon concerned in the ecosystem being studied.

The word "conservation" has been used for the management of rivers since mediaeval times so it is particularly appropriate to use it now in a discussion of the relevance of production to the conservation of fishery resources.

Traditionally the prime effect of Man on fish has been that caused by fishing; by his cropping of fish production to yield food for himself. The effects of fishing on the population dynamics of fish are now relatively well understood (Gulland, 1967). The immediate effect of a significant fishing effort is to reduce the population density, increase the total mortality rate, and lower the average age of the population. This will tend both to reduce the production and increase the effects upon the total population and production of variations in cohort strength. In many situations, provided the fishing is not too intense, there will be compensatory increases in growth rate and the survival of young fish that will partially restore the situation. For example the pike in Windermere responded to an intensive fishery with increased average juvenile survival so that the population density returned to its original level (Kipling & Frost, 1970).

One of the effects of increasing the intensity of fishing is to increase the proportion of the production that is harvested (the yield) in relation to the production. One of the prime aims of fishery management is to ensure that the fishing effort is just right to provide a long-term yield that is optimum in biological and economic terms. The immediate aim of an optimum fishing rate (and selection of the optimum size and age of capture) is to avoid catching the fish of each cohort before it has had a chance to reach its maximum cohort biomass, or too early in its production history.

The second aim must be to ensure adequate recruitment for subsequent cohorts (Parrish, 1972). Density-dependent mortality will usually ensure that a considerable reduction in the number of spawners can take place before there is any reduction in recruits. Indeed there may even be an increase in recruitment with a reduction in spawners, as appears to have happened with the pike in Windermere. Where fishing is particularly intense, however, and climatic factors cause great variation in the survival of young, then fishing can cause a reduction in recruitment. Unfortunately the operation of these density-independent variables makes the elucidation of the factors controlling recruitment very difficult and time consuming, though for many freshwater fish the experimental approach could be helpful (Le Cren, 1972).

In British salmon fisheries great efforts have been made to protect the spawning escapement by law and management. The size of a cohort of salmon when it returns to the coast (and is subject to capture) may depend upon the size of the cohort when it migrated as smolts. The number of smolts, however, appear not to bear a simple or immediate relationship to the number of their spawning parents and until this relationship is established and the factors influencing it understood the management of salmon fisheries will remain empirical. The experiments with trout indicate that the total production of young salmon and yield of smolts may be linked to the area of fry-rearing ground available. Competition from trout for this space may also be important.

Sport fishing for trout and coarse fish is, however, much more important in Britain than commercial fishing for salmon or other species. Most coarse fish that are angled are returned to the water, though not all may survive capture and retention in a keep net. The coarse fish angler appears to desire a dense population of well grown but hungry fish of a variety of chosen species. There are biological conflicts here because densely populated and hungry fish are rarely well grown. The high rates of total production found in some rivers indicate that there may not be much room for improving overall production but that management may be able to direct more of it into useful species and make the recruit rearing process more efficient and reliable. Coarse fisheries occasionally suffer from inexplicable reductions in fish stocks which may partly be due to failures in recruitment.

Eutrophication of inland waters from detergent, sewage and agricultural fertilization is considered a contemporary problem, but it should not be forgotten that the fish culturist takes great trouble to fertilize his ponds so that they become a rich "soup" of phytoplankton (Hickling, 1962). The cyprinids in good fish ponds are both large and numerous. Fishery management should seek ways in which to utilize this eutrophication for production while avoiding the dangers of deoxygenation and the practical difficulties caused by too many macrophytes and filamentous algae.

The third main human effect on inland waters is that of pollution. Very few if any studies have been made of the long-term effects of sub-lethal pollution on fish production, so it is possible to make only conjectures about what these might be. Pollution from domestic sewage will usually kill or discourage the presence of some of the more susceptible species but its fertilizing effect may increase the growth rate and production of other species. Fish ponds have been successfully fertilized with sewage. Many sewage effluents, however, contain toxins which alone or together can have serious effects on the survival of fish. There are also indications of subtle effects from sub-lethal concentrations of substances such as chlorinated hydrocarbons on the survival and reproduction of fish (Macek, 1968, 1969). In summary, then, it would seem that the effects of pollutants on fish production must usually be deleterious except where no toxic substances are involved and deoxygenation is minimal.

### DISCUSSION AND CONCLUSIONS

The study of the production ecology of fish is still in its infancy, but several measures of fish production in natural situations are now available and crude comparisons can be made, for example between salmonid production by different species in different types of stream. Although eventually the number of estimates may allow statistical analyses of correlations between the production measurements of various species in various habitats and lead to some general conclusions, equally valuable progress is likely to result from the detailed investigation of the structure and functioning of the production-dynamic mechanisms (Fig. 1). Model building has been popular among fishery biologists for a long time and has often proved rewarding (Beverton & Holt, 1957). Some of the newer models now being developed involve whole ecosystems and the use of systems analysis and computers (e.g. Krogius, Krokhin & Menshutkin, 1970). Such models will help to build up an intimate understanding of what might be called the "production-metabolism" of the ecosystem and then lead through both computer and field experimentation to the identification of those key points in the system which are likely to be sensitive. Such sensitive points might be those through which human interference could be damaging or those through which beneficial manipulations could be effected.

Before freshwater fish populations can be managed on a really rational basis there will have to be a much greater understanding of population dynamics and production ecology. This can come only as a result of long-term fundamental research, but concurrently with this, and as an aid to the solving of immediate practical problems, there should be a programme of empirical experimentation. Such knowledge as we already have of fish production ecology should be used in the design of these experiments and the basic research and practical experimentation should progress step by step in close liaison with each other.

ACKNOWLEDGEMENTS

I am indebted to my colleagues and especially Mr R. H. K. Mann for assistance in the preparation of this paper.

REFERENCES

Allen, K. R. (1946). The trout population of the Horokiwi River. *Rep. Fish. N.Z.* **1945** Appendix: 33–40.
Allen, K. R. (1951). The Horokiwi Stream: a study of a trout population. *Fish. Bull. N.Z.* **10**, 1–238.
Backiel, T. & Le Cren, E. D. (1967). Some density relationships for fish population parameters. In *The biological basis of freshwater fish production*: 261–293. (Gerking, S. D., ed). Oxford: Blackwell.
Beverton, R. J. H. & Holt, S. J. (1957). On the dynamics of exploited fish populations. *Fish. Invest., Lond.* (2) **19**: 1–533.
Chapman, D. W. (1967). Production in fish populations. In *The biological basis of freshwater fish production*: 3–29. (Gerking, S. D. ed). Oxford: Blackwell.
Chapman, D. W. (1968). Production. In *Methods for the assessment of fish production in fresh waters. IBP Handbook No. 3*: 182–196. (Ricker, W. E., ed). Oxford: Blackwell.
Coche, A. G. (1964). *Net production of juvenile steelhead*, Salmo gairdneri *Richardson, in a freshwater impoundment*. Ph.D. Dissertation, Oregon State University, Corvallis. (Quoted by Chapman, 1967).
Cooper, E. L., Hidu, H. & Andersen, J. K. (1963). Growth and production of largemouth bass in a small pond. *Trans. Am. Fish. Soc.* **92**: 391–400.
Egglishaw, H. J. (1970). Production of salmon and trout in a stream in Scotland. *J. Fish Biol.* **2**: 117–136.
Gerking, S. D. (1962). Production and food utilization in a population of bluegill sunfish. *Ecol. Mongr.* **32**: 31–78.
Gulland, J. A. (1967). The effects of fishing on the production and catches of fish. In *The biological basis of freshwater fish production*: 399–415. (Gerking, S. D., ed). Oxford: Blackwell.
Hall, J. D. (1963). *An ecological study of the chestnut lamprey,* Icthyomyzon castaneus *Zirard, in the Manistee River, Michigan*. Ph.D. Dissertation, University of Michigan, Ann Arbor. (Quoted by Chapman, 1967.)
Hatch, R. W. & Webster, D. A. (1961). Trout production in four central Adirondack mountain lakes. *Fm. Res., Ithaca* No. 373: 3–81. (Quoted by Chapman, 1967.)

Hepher, B. (1967). Some biological aspects of warm-water fish pond management, In *The biological basis of freshwater fish production*: 417–428. (Gerking, S. D.. ed.) Oxford: Blackwell.

Hickling, C. F. (1962). *Fish culture.* London: Faber & Faber.

Higley, D. L. (1963). *Food habits, growth and production of juvenile chinook salmon*, Oncorhychus tshawytscha (*Walbaum*), *in a eutrophic reservoir.* M.S. Thesis, Oregon State University, Corvallis. (Quoted by Chapman, 1967.)

Horton, P. A. (1961). The bionomics of brown trout in a Dartmoor stream. *J. Anim. Ecol.* **30**: 311–338.

Hunt, R. L. (1966). Production and angler harvest of wild brook trout in Lawrence Creek, Wisconsin. *Wisc. Conserv. Bull.* **35**: 1–52.

Ivlev, V. S. (1966). The biological productivity of waters. *J. Fish. Res. Bd Can.* **23**: 1727–1759. (Translation of Ivlev, V. S. (1945). Biologicheskaya productionost' vodoemov. *Usp. sovrem. Biol.* **19**: 98–120.)

Johnson, W. E. & Hasler, A. D. (1954). Rainbow trout production in dystrophic lakes. *J. Wildl. Mgmt* **18**: 113–134.

Kiping, C. & Frost, W. E. (1970). A study of the mortality, population numbers, year class strengths, production and food consumption of pike, *Esox lucius*, in Windermere from 1944 to 1962. *J. Anim. Ecol.* **39**: 115–157.

Krogius, P. V., Krokhin, E. M. & Menshutkin, V. V. (1970). Digital computer simulation of the ecosystem of lake Dal'nee. In *Prelim. Pap. UNESCO-IBP Symposium on productivity problems of freshwaters, Kazimierz-Dolny, Poland.* May 1970, 2,: 227–235. (Kajak, Z., ed.)

Le Cren, E. D. (1949). The interrelationships between population, production and growth-rate in freshwater fish. *Proc. Linn. Soc. Lond.* **161**: 131–140.

Le Cren, E. D. (1958a). The production of fish in fresh waters. In *The biological productivity of Britain*: 67–72. (Yapp, W. B. & Watson, D. J., eds). London: Inst. Biol.

Le Cren, E. D. (1958b). Observations on the growth of perch (*Perca fluviatilis L.*) over twenty-two years with special reference to the effects of temperature and changes in population density. *J. Anim. Ecol.* **27**: 287–334.

Le Cren, E. D. (1962). The efficiency of reproduction and recruitment in freshwater fish. In *The exploitation of natural animal populations*: 283–296. (Le Cren, E. D. & Holdgate, M. W., eds). Oxford: Blackwell.

Le Cren, E. D. (1965). Some factors regulating the size of populations of freshwater fish. *Mitt. int. Verein. theor. angew. Limnol.* **13**: 88–105.

Le Cren, E. D. (1969). Estimates of fish populations and production in small streams in England. In *Symposium on salmon and trout in streams*: 269–280. (Northcote, T. ed.). *Macmillan Lect. Br. Columb. Univ.*

Le Cren, E. D. (1972). The population dynamics of young trout (*Salmo trutta*) in relation to density and territorial behaviour. In *Symposium on stock and recruitment.* Aarhus 1970. (Parrish, B. B., ed.) *Rapp. P.-v. Reun. Cons. perm. int. Explor. Mer.* **164**.

Libosvarsky, J. (1968). A study of brown trout population (*Salmo trutta* morpha *fario* L.) in Loucka creek (Czechoslovakia). *Acta sci. nat. Brno* **2**: 1–56.

Macek, K. J. (1968). Reproduction in brook trout (*Salvelinus fontinalis*) fed sublethal concentrations of DDT. *J. Fish. Res. Bd Can.* **25**: 1787–1796.

Macek, K. J. (1969). Growth and resistance to stress in brook trout fed sublethal levels of DDT. *J. Fish Res. Bd Can.* **25**: 2443–2451.

Mann, K. H. (1965). Energy transformations by a population of fish in the River Thames. *J. Anim. Ecol.* **34**: 253–275.

Mann, K. H. (1969). The dynamics of aquatic ecosystems. *Adv. Ecol. Res.* **6**: 1–81.

Mann, R. H. K. (1971). The populations, growth and production of fish in four small streams in southern England. *J. Anim. Ecol.* **40**: 155–190.

Mathews, C. P. (1971). Contribution of young fish to total production of fish in the River Thames near Reading. *J. Fish. Biol.* **3**: 157–180.

Nilsson, N. A. (1967). Interactive segregation between fish species. In *The biological basis of freshwater fish production*: 295–313. (Gerking, S. D., ed). Oxford: Blackwell.

Parrish, B. B. (ed) (1972). Symposium on stock and recruitment. *Rapp. P.-v. Reun. Cons. perm. int. Explor. Mer.* **164.**

Ricker, W. E. (1958). Handbook of computations for biological statistics of fish populations. *Bull. Fish. Res. Bd Can.* **119**: 1–300.

Ricker, W. E. (ed) (1968). *Methods for assessment of fish production in fresh waters. IBP Handbook No. 3.* Oxford: Blackwell.

Ricker, W. E. and Foerster, R. E. (1948). Computation of fish production. *Bull. Bingham Oceanogr. Coll.* **11**: 173–211.

Walter, E. (1934). Grundlagen der allgemainen fisherielichen Produktionslehre. *Handb. Binnenfisch. Mitteleur.* **4**: 480–662.

Wolny, P. and Grygierek, E. (1970). Increasing of fish ponds production. In *Prelim. Pap. INESCO-IBP Symposium on productivity problems of freshwaters, Kazimierz Dolny, Poland.* May 1970. **2**: 459–460. (Kajak, Z., ed.)

*Symp. zool. Soc. Lond.* (1972) No. 29, 135–154.

# PROBLEMS OF THE CONSERVATION OF FRESHWATER ECOSYSTEMS

## N. C. MORGAN

*Nature Conservancy, Edinburgh, Scotland*

### SYNOPSIS

Conservation of freshwater is defined by the author as the management of water bodies towards specified aims, with the intention of maintaining their scientific interest or rehabilitating their physical, chemical or biological quality. This may be done passively or actively and the paper outlines the major problems in the United Kingdom and some of the steps taken by the Nature Conservancy and other organizations in conserving freshwaters. A survey of open water sites throughout Britain is nearing completion with a view to selecting a series of high quality sites as National Nature Reserves to represent the range of variation of this habitat. Refence is made to the problems of conservation of rare species and measures taken with the Lochmaben vendace. Water abstraction and storage is a major problem with differing effects of varying types of reservoir, irrigation and more recently abstraction of water from chalk aquifers. Increasing pressures to use open water for recreation have caused problems in the conservation of habitat and wildlife particularly near large cities. Quantitative data are needed on effects of different recreational activities. The well known problems of industrial and domestic pollution are mentioned and the effects of various agricultural practices gone into in more detail particularly in relation to nutrient levels in drainage water. The decline in amounts of aquatic vegetation in some water bodies is recorded and possible causes discussed. Herbicides are used extensively in S.E. England for clearing drainage ditches and the side effects on other components of the ecosystem are considered. Difficulties in conserving freshwaters are discussed, particularly the need for control of the use of the whole catchment.

### INTRODUCTION

In this paper, "conservation of freshwater ecosystems" is defined as the management of freshwater in order to maintain quality in an area of special scientific interest or to rehabilitate the physical, chemical or biological quality of an area altered by man's activities. This may be done passively or actively. In the former case it may involve only the protection of an area from the adverse activities of so called "advancing" civilization so as to maintain the *status quo*. In the latter it may involve radical change in factors regulating the ecosystem in order to direct "natural" changes or to hold a particular stage in the evolution of, say, a hydrosere, e.g. a fen. With the increase in man-made water bodies such as reservoirs, barrages and gravel pits, active conservation may consist not only of creating new aquatic habitats, but in directing the changes so as to create different types of aquatic habitat within the same water body, thereby producing a variety of physical and chemical conditions and community structure. Active management also includes applying remedial measures to water bodies which have been biologically degraded by industrial and domestic pollution or affected by the more subtle changes brought about by pesticide and herbicide use, other changes in agricultural practices and other land use.

In the past, freshwater was managed chiefly in the interests of navigation, irrigation, domestic and industrial water supply, disposal of sewage and industrial effluents, power, fisheries or waterfowl. The Nature Conservancy is interested in the much broader implications of the whole ecosystem often for a multiplicity of uses, including amenity. This science is only in embryo, with relatively little knowledge of what techniques to use in many circumstances. Research must be directed at understanding the intricate relationships between animals and plants and their environment if we are to plan better management. This research will range in degree of sophistication from simple empirical manipulatory experiments in which change and effect are recorded, without necessarily understanding the processes involved, to an understanding of the complex inter-relationships within an ecosystem such as that aimed at by the Marion Lake (Efford, 1970) and Loch Leven IBP projects (Morgan, in press). These may result in the production of complex mathematical models which can be tested on computers and used to predict the results of environmental manipulation. Such major studies cannot stop short at the water's edge but must extend into the whole catchment as in the studies at Hubbard Brook, New Hampshire (Likens, Bormann, Johnson & Pierce, 1967; Johnson, Likens, Bormann & Pierce, 1968; Fisher, Gambell, Likens & Bormann, 1968; and Bormann, Likens & Eaton, 1969) and the proposed studies by the Environmental Division of the Department of Scientific and Industrial Research at Wellington, New Zealand.

It is essential that the aims of management are clearly stated before any research or management is carried out. Too often people ask how they should manage a water body without having any clear idea of what they want to manage it for.

In this paper I shall outline the types of conservation problem existing in freshwater, with particular reference to those faced by the Nature Conservancy in Britain.

## SELECTION OF NATURE RESERVES

### The United Kingdom

In order to preserve a representative series of the types of freshwater found in the U.K., the Nature Conservancy is in the course of selecting and setting up a series of Nature Reserves in which the predominant interest is freshwater. Our knowledge of the freshwaters of Great Britain, apart from certain well studied areas such as the Lake District, is scanty, so that this conservation review exercise has involved a great deal of survey work, the field part of which is completed. Only high quality sites, i.e. sites which are not biologically degraded, have been considered, with regard to the degree of representativeness, diversity of habitat and species content. Only sites which can be adequately protected will be selected with the aim of maintaining them in their present condition.

A few primarily research sites may be selected in which management techniques for use in other Reserves will be developed.

## Project Mar

In 1962, at the MAR Conference on the conservation and management of marshes, bogs and other temperate wetlands, it was agreed that a list of European and North African Wetlands of international importance should be compiled as necessary background for an international convention on the conservation of wetlands. A list of sites was published (Olney, 1965). It was intended to be limited to water bodies less than 6 m deep, although a few deeper sites are included, and it is biased towards those sites of high ornithological interest. It was proposed that representative reserves should be established in all the sites listed to guarantee the future of essential wetland habitats and their plant and animal populations.

## Project Aqua

In 1969 a list of internationally important sites was published as a result of ground work carried out by the International Association of Theoretical and Applied Limnology, the Commission on Ecology of IUCN and IBP/PF (Luther & Rzóska, 1969). This consists of a world wide coverage of brackish and freshwater sites of agreed international importance for research, education or training. The list is to be submitted to the United Nations for recognition and the countries concerned will be asked to accept national responsibility for the conservation of the sites.

Much of this is "passive" conservation, seeking protection of the environment from chiefly man made changes and occasionally natural changes such as erosion.

### CONSERVATION OF RARE SPECIES

The case for the safeguarding of rare species of plants and animals depends upon the particular circumstances. Where a species is at the edge of its range and dying out in one country, but widespread and abundant in other parts of the world, the cost and effort of trying to maintain it may not be justified on scientific grounds. This may be particularly so where the decline is related to climatic change. On the other hand speciation is often more active at the edge of a species range and the situation may be of interest to geneticists. If however the species is rare on a world wide basis there may be justification in expending considerable resources on maintaining it. One of the most essential problems is to determine what is a viable population. Duffey (1968) has looked into this for the large copper butterfly *Lycaena dispar* How.

The British race *L. dispar dispar* How. bred in the marsh land around Whittlesea Mere but became extinct after the marsh was drained in 1851. Introductions of the Dutch race *L. dispar batavus* Obth. are artificially maintained at Woodwalton Fen National Nature Reserve. Duffey concludes that about 20 ha of the Reserve could be managed to provide suitable habitat for the butterfly and its food plant but this is probably too small for a viable population to maintain itself without artificial aid.

Another problem is the mobility of the species. With plants, or invertebrate species which do not leave the water, it may be feasible to maintain a satisfactory breeding population in quite a small area. However with aquatic birds, amphibia or emerging insect species the breeding population may actively or passively migrate outside the protected area and be exterminated or be so reduced in numbers that population maintenance is not possible.

Whether the population of a rare species can be conserved depends on the cost of the management required in relation to the money available. Sometimes active conservation measures may be carried out very cheaply as with the Scottish race of the vendace, *Coregonus vandesius* Richardson. This is now confined to one lake—Mill Loch, Lochmaben which is receiving increasing amounts of domestic sewage. It is likely that this fish will eventually die out in Mill Loch and the Nature Conservancy is attempting to introduce it into a number of physically and chemically suitable hill lochs in S.W. Scotland by planting fertilized eggs and unfed fry there.

## WATER ABSTRACTION AND REGULATION

### *Reservoirs*

Various types of water storage and regulating reservoirs are used in Britain and the conservation implications depend upon the type.

*Water supply reservoirs*

*Impounding reservoirs.* These are normally used for water supply for drinking water and industrial purposes. There is often seasonal draw-down of water level which exposes a large area of the littoral zone. As a result such reservoirs often have no macrophytic vegetation and indeed it may be good practice on the part of the water authority to regulate the draw-down in order to prevent the development of macrophytic vegetation which can cause water supply problems when it decays or becomes detached from the bottom in the autumn. Rivers running out of these reservoirs will have low flow rates over most of the year and compensation water must be provided by statute for the fishery interests.

*Regulating reservoirs.* These store water during periods of heavy rainfall and release this into the river, in order to maintain the flow, during dry periods. Recently regulating reservoirs have been installed on the headwaters of the Welsh Dee and its tributaries. The water is not normally abstracted directly from the reservoirs for water supply purposes but the river is used as an aqueduct and abstraction takes place lower down the river. This is good conservation as it has little effect on the river compared with large impoundments. Indeed it may be argued that the river flora and fauna are better off since they are not subjected to such high spate conditions or to such low flows during drought as would be expected under a natural regime. The implications of this scheme are being carefully watched by fisheries interests.

*Pump storage.* These reservoirs are used to hold water pumped from other catchments during periods of high flow. The stored water is utilized subsequently during periods of shortage from other sources. There are now several large pump storage reservoirs particularly in S.E. England and the Midlands, such as Hanningfield, Abberton, Grafham Water and the proposed reservoir at Empingham. The reservoirs themselves suffer from the same problems as impounding reservoirs. Interesting biological problems arise since water is often pumped from different river systems with the consequent mixing of water of different nutrient levels in the reservoir.

*Hydro-electric reservoirs*

*Impoundment reservoirs.* These reservoirs are used to supply water to turbines for the generation of electricity. The water is stored for varying periods depending on the position of the reservoir on the river system and the particular use of that reservoir. They may collect water from other watersheds as for instance from the Spey to the

Tummel-Garry system. Water is often considerably redistributed within
the catchment area and some rivers are dried out completely as in the
Tummel-Garry system. Fluctuations in water level are seasonal in the
header reservoirs of the systems. The degree of draw-down depends on
rainfall and upon the generating programme. In header reservoirs
large areas of the bottom may be exposed for several months and the
number of aquatic species which can exist in such conditions of extreme
draw-down is limited. In "run-of-river" reservoirs, such as at Faskally,
Pitlochry, which is the lowest reservoir on the Tummel-Garry system,
there is only a small diurnal fluctuation in water level and here a
wider range of species can survive.

*Pump storage reservoirs.* Several schemes are either in operation or
construction on some of the larger Scottish lochs such as Loch Awe
and Loch Ness. Electrical power is used during off-peak periods to
pump water into storage reservoirs up the neighbouring hillsides, and
this water is used to generate electricity during peak periods of electricity use. This results in a 24 h cycling of water in the header reservoir
from the full state to the practically empty state and such reservoirs are
virtually of no conservation value. The lower loch becomes tidal because
of this 24 h regime but, since these schemes have only been put into
operation in the larger lochs, the rise and fall in their water level is
only a few centimetres.

## Barrages

Proposals for large estuarine barrages such as in Morecambe Bay,
the River Dee and The Wash have rather exciting implications for
freshwater biologists. Although this is a loss of estuarine environment,
such barrages would create large stretches of relatively shallow
freshwater which could be of high conservation interest. The Nature
Conservancy has put forward proposals for the development of certain
areas of polder to create wildlife refuges comparable with the Norfolk
Broads. By careful design and manipulation a diversity of shallow
freshwater habitat, plants and animals should result.

On the other hand the damming of a large area of freshwater behind
a complete barrage may hazard the passage of migratory fish such as
salmon and sea trout between the river and the sea. Even though a
fish ladder is included in the barrage, the characteristics of the estuary
may be so "abbreviated" as to cause difficulties for ascending adult
fish under the reduced flow of river water entering the sea. Similarly
descending smolts may have difficulty in finding their way out of the
large shallow reservoir, behind the barrage, where they are likely to be
heavily predated by trout, pike and fish-eating birds.

*Estuarine bunds*

Proposals to build bunded reservoirs in some estuaries, such as the alternative proposals for the Dee Estuary, are again of conservation interest since new freshwater areas will be created. They should not be a conservation hazard to anadromous fish since the flow of the river will not be impeded.

The exposure of large areas of the littoral zone of reservoirs during periods of draw-down is unsightly. It also denudes this zone of most macrophytic vegetation, restricting the species of algae and invertebrates that can survive there. If this zone is used for spawning by any of the fish species present, draw-down at the wrong time can eliminate a whole year class. Where the sides of the reservoir are steep sided as in many of the Highland hydro-electric reservoirs, there is probably little that can be done to alleviate the unsightly exposure of large barren areas of stones, gravel or sand. Where the slopes at the side of a new reservoir are slight, steps can be taken in the design of new reservoirs to prevent large shallow bays and inlets from being exposed during periods of draw-down, by the construction of small barriers across the mouths of these bays which will retain a shallow depth of water in them. These bunded areas can be increased in size by bulldozing material from the shoreward side of the shallows into deeper

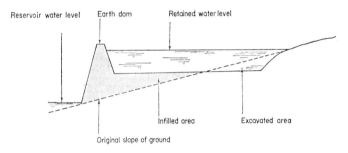

Reservoir water level   Earth dam   Retained water level

Infilled area   Excavated area

Original slope of ground

FIG. 1. Improvement of reservoir littoral zones by bunding.

water to provide large flat bottomed zones with a maximum depth of about 3 m (Fig. 1). This need not seriously affect the total storage capacity of the reservoir, and would greatly increase the amenity and conservation value of the margins of the reservoirs. Such methods are especially practical where small streams flow into the bunded areas and replace losses of water by evaporation and seepage.

Where cost prevents schemes of this sort, planting suitable aquatic plant species may help to alleviate the consequences of draw-down, particularly where the bottom is composed of fine sediments as opposed to eroded stony shores. At a number of such reservoir sites the author has seen the aquatic *Littorella uniflora* (L.) Aschers, *Polygonum amphibium* L., *Myosotis* spp., *Mentha aquatica* L., *Hippuris vulgaris* L., *Glyceria fluitans* (L.) R.Br., *Apium inundatum* (L.) Rchb.f. and *Eleocharis palustris* (L.) Roem. and Schult. growing amongst annual terrestrial vegetation, having survived several weeks of exposure following draw-down of the water level.

## Irrigation

In dry weather there is an increasing demand from farmers and horticulturalists for water for irrigation. In the past the water has mainly been drawn direct from rivers under licence from the River Authorities who consult with the conservation interests. More recently some farmers have constructed ponds to store water. These are filled when the rivers are high and the water is used for irrigation during dry periods. This is good conservation practice.

## Abstraction from chalk aquifers

In the areas of England situated on chalk, Water Authorities are increasingly looking towards the water stored in the chalk aquifers as a supplementary water supply. Schemes put forward so far consist of two types:

(i) Pumping water from the chalk aquifer during periods of low water in order to maintain the flow in rivers above a set minimum level. This type of scheme is proposed for the River Lambourn and a detailed study of the hydrological and biological implications is being financed by the Thames Conservancy and the Water Resources Board. Such schemes are likely to prevent or reduce the duration of extreme high or low water. Preliminary studies suggest that the effects upon the fauna and flora of the river and the chemistry of the water are likely to be negligible.

(ii) Pumping direct from the chalk aquifer into the mains water supply or storage reservoirs. Such schemes have been put forward for the Sydling, in Dorset, the Wylye, in Hampshire, and other places. In some instances such as in the Sydling, pumping from the aquifer will convert a permanent river into a winter-borne and in other cases it will reduce the dry weather flow. In either case this could have serious biological consequences.

The shallow Breckland Meres are of high conservation interest because of the fauna and flora associated with periodic drying out or reduction in water level. A test pumping scheme is being carried out from the chalk aquifer in this area. The Great Ouse River Authority is recording the water level in some of the meres and has sunk a recording-well midway between two of the more important meres so that water levels can be recorded in relation to the pumping. Extensive drying out of these meres could completely destroy their high conservation interests.

Pumping schemes could also have a serious effect upon the water meadows adjacent to chalk streams and the Nature Conservancy is initiating studies on the vegetation of certain water meadows in conjunction with the test pumping schemes.

In view of the potential use of water from the large aquifers in the chalk in southern Britain it is essential that the conservation consequences are well understood.

An important criterion in relation to all abstraction and regulatory schemes is the minimum acceptable flow in rivers affected by them. Considerable attention has been directed to this by the Lancashire River Authority in relation to fisheries interests (Stewart, 1969). It is also of paramount interest to the River Authorities in relation to the dilution factors for sewage and industrial effluents. In the long term it would be desirable to gain knowledge of the wider implications of the amounts of water let down rivers on the ecosystem as a whole.

### MULTIPLE USE OF OPEN WATERS

People are increasingly using lakes, reservoirs, canals and rivers for recreation. Their pursuits include fishing, bird watching, swimming, canoeing, sailing, rowing, picnicking and holiday boating as well as more noisy pursuits such as power boating and water ski-ing. Many of these activities are incompatible with each other and they vary in their impact on the ecosystem. Waterside holiday cottages and caravan sites can also have detrimental effects.

Education authorities and organizations such as Wildlife Trusts, the Royal Society for the Protection of Birds and the Nature Conservancy are setting up education centres, nature trails and so on to satisfy an increasing demand for information about the environment. There is also an increasing awareness of the amenity values of water "landscapes".

The integration of these interests with the conservation of wildlife is becoming increasingly difficult with the build-up in intensity of water use and the development of new pursuits. A problem for the manager is to put a value on amenity and wildlife but some measure of this is given by an estimate (by the Countryside Recreation Research Advisory

Group) of 500 000 bird watchers using open waters and the recent census of anglers for England and Wales which showed that 2 800 000 people fish regularly.

Within the multiple use of our waters must of course be included water abstraction and impoundment.

The impacts of recreation on the ecosystem may be considered under the following headings.

### Disturbance

This applies mainly to nesting waterbirds but wintering birds are also subject to disturbance.

Few quantitative studies have been done in the U.K. on the effects of disturbance. I. Newton (pers. comm.) has shown that disturbance of nesting ducks caused a significant increase in predation on eggs. In a control area with 84 nests, which were not disturbed, 17% were predated and in the disturbed study area with 781 nests, 41% were predated. The disturbance in the disturbed study area was minimal amounting to one or two visits to the nests per week.

Conflicting activities can be segregated. Zones are established as wildlife reserves into which no boats are allowed, and in which there is no bank fishing and picnicking. Hides, with screened walkways, are erected for the use of the public interested in ornithology. Research is needed on the effects and best methods of segregation.

### Pollution

Effects of fuel spillage, and sewage and waste from boats and caravan sites are mentioned elsewhere.

### Mechanical destruction of habitat

The bow wave of power boats can flatten emergent vegetation and erode shorelines. Propellers entangle and cut up submerged vegetation, and can completely eliminate it. They disturb soft mud bottoms, dispersing particles of sediment throughout the water mass. This spoils the amenity value and reduces light penetration causing decline in amounts of algae and rooted vegetation. Intensive picnicking, swimming and fishing from the banks can destroy shoreline vegetation.

Sukopp (1971) reported the effects of intensive recreation on the Havel lakes near Berlin. Between 1962 and 1967, 16% of the length of shoreline made up of reed swamp was denuded at the rate of 1200 m/year. There was a 31% deline in area of reed swamp, the greatest decline being in *Phragmites communis* Trin.

The channelling of boat launching sites into harbour areas with proper jetties will partly relieve the rest of the shoreline. Many people swim at the Berlin Havel lakes and, at weekends, the lakes are accessible to 350 000 people, i.e. 9 persons/m shore. Probably the only answer to this problem is to limit the number of people on the lakes as it would probably be undesirable to route such large numbers of people to swimming platforms or rafts.

## Wildfowl introductions

Canada geese, *Brenta canadensis* (L.), were introduced over 300 years ago into England (Boyd & Matthews, 1963) and large flocks of these have established themselves in a number of places, notably in Lincolnshire and Lancashire. Similarly large stocks of feral greylag geese, *Anser anser* (L.), are breeding in Wigtownshire (Atkinson-Willes, 1963) and in the Norfolk Broads and there are numerous smaller colonies throughout the country. In recent years the activities of individuals and the Wildfowlers' Association of Great Britain and Ireland, in breeding and releasing these species, and mallard, has increased. Also the breeding and release of other species including exotics is being encouraged.

The impact of these rearing programmes on native wildfowl species and on other aquatic organisms should be measured carefully and assessed. Aggressive species, such as Canada geese, could easily drive out other species. Fiala & Kvĕt (in press) have shown that greylag geese can graze young growths of *Phragmites communis* extensively.

Active encouragement of a species by feeding, by the public, can be significant. Sukopp (1971) reports that mute swans, *Cygnus olor* (Gmelin), on the Berlin Havel lakes have increased from none in 1947 to 718 in 1969 because of feeding. This species feeds naturally on plant material, particularly submerged macrophytes, and build-up to these numbers could significantly damage littoral weed beds.

## POLLUTION

The biological degradation of freshwater communities by industrial and domestic pollution (Klein, 1957; Hynes, 1960) is well known in Britain, particularly in rivers in densely populated areas. The recovery of rivers receiving many polluted effluents can only be brought about slowly as industry and local authorities are required to raise the standards of treatment by law. Poorly treated sewage can greatly increase the nutrient levels and cause eutrophication problems (Vollenweider, 1968). Detergents greatly increase the amounts of phosphate which is often a limiting factor in plant growth in freshwater. Fortunately, since sewage is usually discharged at "point sources"

F

it is feasible to reduce the amounts of plant nutrients by known treatment methods although this may be expensive. On the other hand
nitrate from farmland (Section on pp. 146–148) gradually infiltrates
into waterways over the whole catchment area and there is no practical
method known for substantially reducing it.

### EFFECTS OF AGRICULTURE AND FORESTRY

#### Insecticides

Following the classical work on Clear Lake (Hunt & Bischoff, 1960)
a large literature has accumulated on the effects of organo-chlorine
insecticides on aquatic organisms. Build-up of insecticides in the food
chain can lead to the elimination of species at the higher trophic levels
and sensitive species at lower trophic levels. This serious conservation
problem is now well recognized and in more advanced countries the
more persistent insecticides are only allowed limited use. Damage to
freshwater organisms can only be controlled by reducing the input and
legislation exists whereby River Authorities can prevent the discharge
of effluents containing persistent insecticides into freshwaters. Careless
throwing of containers with insecticide in them into ponds and streams
can cause severe local poisoning.

#### Herbicides

The widespread use of herbicides in agriculture and forestry can
cause a local decline in aquatic vegetation when the herbicide acciden-
tally "drifts" on to waterways. Emergent vegetation is more likely
to be affected than submerged vegetation. The conservation hazards
are however far greater when herbicides are used for the control of
water weeds (Section on pp. 150–151).

#### Nutrients from farmland

The increasing levels of plant nutrients in waters can cause intense
growths of phytoplankton and filamentous algae (Lund, 1972)
and may, via the phytoplankton and macrophytes, have more far
reaching effects on the invertebrates, as indicated at Loch Leven
(Morgan, 1970).

Although the phosphate entering lakes from "point" sources of
sewage and industry is controllable, the input of nitrate from the land
is a serious conservation problem in some areas. At Loch Leven, over
90% of nitrate nitrogen entering the lake comes from farmland and the
annual total of nitrate entering has doubled between 1966 and 1969
(Morgan, in press). In the County of Kinross, which is largely made up of
the Loch Leven catchment area, the amounts of nitrogen fertilizer added

to farmland increased three times between 1952 and 1968 (Fig. 2). Rigorous timing of the application of inorganic fertilizers and careful

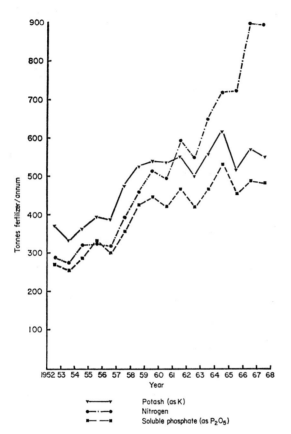

FIG. 2. Changes in fertilizer use for the County of Kinross. (Based on figures issued by the Department of Agriculture and Fisheries for Scotland.)

application of slurries from intensive cattle and pig units (for example not on hard frosted ground when they can be washed away in high concentrations by surface run-off) will go a considerable way to reducing the nitrate losses, but these measures are dependent on the individual farmer. Woldendorp, Dilz & Kolenbrander (1966), working on the losses of nitrogen fertilizer from grass-land by leaching, found scarcely any losses with spring and summer application of ammonium nitrate, except when heavy rainfall followed application. However, from 30–60%

of the nitrogen applied during the autumn and winter was leached. Kolenbrander (1969) obtained similar results, finding a maximum loss of 40% of the nitrogen applied occurred in November. Slow release fertilizers have been suggested, as a means of preventing this loss, but during maximum growth periods the crop requires large quantities of readily available nitrate and this will not be provided by slow release fertilizers. With more intensive agricultural practices, both in amounts of stock kept and increased yield of crops, the losses of nitrates from the land are likely to increase rather than decrease.

The distribution of phosphate fertilizer from the air over forestry plantations is being increasingly practised particularly in regions such as the Scottish Highlands which are nutrient poor. In these areas phosphate is normally the limiting nutrient in the lake water. Application of phosphate, at rates similar to those being applied to the forests, can cause considerable biological changes (Brook & Holden, 1957; Holden, 1959; Morgan, 1966). Regular aerial spreading would cause increased biological productivity in the lakes affected. This may be undesirable in some of our high grade oligotrophic lakes and measures must be taken to regulate application of fertilizer from the air in the proximity of lakes known to be of high conservation value.

### CHANGES IN THE AMOUNTS OF AQUATIC VEGETATION

#### Increases

Substantial increases in the amounts of macrophytic vegetation have been reported from North American and from New Zealand lakes, which are said to be caused by increased amounts of nutrients entering from sewage and agriculture (Fish, 1968).

#### Decreases

In other areas there has been a striking decline in the amounts of rooted vegetation in some lakes (Olsen, 1964; Morgan, 1970).

A similar decline has taken place in submerged and floating attached aquatic vegetation in the Norfolk Broads since World War II. Table I shows the situation in a number of broads surveyed in 1968 and 1969, where it has been possible to obtain data from earlier years for comparison. Most of the broads are less than 2 m deep and aquatic vegetation formerly grew extensively over them. Now, vegetation is absent from, or extremely sparse in, the open water of Barton, Alderfen, Surlingham, Rockland, Ranworth and Filby. This is true of a number of other Broads, such as Bargate, Cockshoot, Malthouse, Ormesby (North), Ormesby (South), Ranworth, Rollesby, Salhouse, South

Walsham and Strumpshaw, which are not included in the table. Although Rockland Broad had a 30% cover of vegetation in 1968, this was virtually entirely *Nuphar lutea*, which has been observed to be the last species to disappear in a number of broads where the vegetation has now gone. *Nymphaea alba* is also very tenacious as is shown at Alderfen and Barton.

The first observed decline in vegetation in the Yare Broads appears to have taken place about 1948–1950 (M. George, pers. comm.), which coincides with the decline at Loch Leven. Lambert (1965) noted that at Hoveton Great Broad, on the Bure system, *Stratiotes* was dominant in 1947, but had completely disappeared by 1953.

The scale of decline is illustrated by such statements as "The great floating masses of hornwort (*Ceratophyllum demersum*) which used to cover the surface of Surlingham, Strumpshaw and Rockland Broads in late summer and effectively excluded all other plants below them" (Lambert, 1965). Similarly when Alderfen was visited in 1963 by M. George (pers. comm.) it was completely choked by *Ceratophyllum*.

At Eglwys Nunydd, a nutrient rich reservoir in South Wales, the amounts of *Polygonum amphibium*, the only aquatic macrophyte present, are declining each year (R. W. Edwards, pers. comm.).

Thorough investigation of the causes of the decline in these submerged and floating attached macrophytes has still to be made. Olsen (1964) records the complete elimination of submerged macrophytes in Lake Lingby Sø which he attributes to a great increase in phytoplankton density resulting from increasing nutrient enrichment from sewage. Reduction in light penetration, associated with dense phytoplankton, may have contributed to the decline of macrophytes at Loch Leven (Morgan, 1970) and in the Norfolk Broads but this is not in itself a completely satisfactory explanation since, in both areas, species which have floating attached leaves have declined or disappeared. Also Secchi disc readings show no relationships to the amount of vegetation, as measured by the proportion of the bottom covered by vegetation (Table I). Nor was there any consistent relationship between phosphate and nitrate levels of the Broads and the quantities of plants.

Bye (1966) in a chemical and botanical investigation of Broadland dykes concluded that the most important factor causing the absence of aquatic vegetation in certain dykes is the presence of a considerable depth of semi-liquid, strongly reducing ooze which creates anaerobic conditions. Casual observations during the survey reported here indicated that macrophytes were seldom present when these fluid muds reached within 25 cm of the water surface. Such a mud surface does not give a secure anchorage for macrophytes but one might have expected that genera such as *Ceratophyllum, Stratiotes, Hydrocharis* and *Lemna* would be able to survive in these conditions.

The increased motor boat traffic on the Broads must have contributed to the decline in plants, due to mechanical damage, stirring of the mud and pollution by sewage and waste discharged overboard. Ellis (1965) records that the water colour of Surlingham Broad is a dirty brown from disturbance by boats. On the other hand there is no public boat traffic on Ranworth and Alderfen where the plants have also disappeared. The restriction of boating to certain buoyed areas and alternative methods of disposal of wastes are necessary conservation measures.

Another factor operating in the Broads was the large population of coypu, *Myocaster coypus* (Molina), which reached its peak in 1960 before large scale trapping was brought into force. Ellis (1963) states "Broads were denuded of water lilies, bullrushes, reed-mace and reeds . . . hundreds of acres of saw-sedge were laid low." Whole plants of the following open water species were eaten: *Elodea canadensis, Hydrocharis morsus-ranae, Myriophyllum spicatum, M. verticillatum, Potamogeton lucens, P. pectinatus* and the turions of *Stratiotes aloides*. It is noticeable how little *E. canadensis, H. morsus-ranae, P. lucens* and *S. aloides* is now present (Table I) but the two *Myriophyllum* spp. and *P. pectinatus* are abundant in some places, particularly Hickling and Horsey now that the coypu population has been very much reduced. The water lilies seem to have partially recovered from the state described by Ellis. Emergent vegetation has totally recovered.

At Loch Leven there has been a considerable decline in emergent vegetation (Morgan, 1970) which has not been paralleled at the Broads. Olsen (1964) records that although the submerged macrophytes have disappeared at Lake Lingby Sø there was no change in the distribution of *Phragmites communis*, and *Typha angustifolium* L. increased.

## HERBICIDES

In the Fens of East Anglia and the Romney Marshes herbicides are now being used extensively to control aquatic vegetation in drainage ditches, and in some areas for the eradication of reed beds. Obviously, where large areas of a particular plant are eliminated the fauna and flora which go with the offending species are also lost. Thus about 260 sq. km of reed in the Fens were destroyed using dalapon and the entire population of the reed warbler, *Acrocephalus scirpaceus* (Hermann), was eliminated (N. W. Moore, pers. comm.). Similarly, if considerable areas of submerged macrophytes are destroyed, the accompanying epiphytic flora, invertebrates, fish and bird species which live or feed on them will be greatly reduced.

Misapplication of herbicides for aquatic weed control can result in rapid uptake of all available oxygen by decaying vegetation, with repercussions on the fauna, dramatic fish kills, and high bacterial populations. For this reason Blok (1968) recommends that herbicides should be applied before 15 March because of the susceptibility of larval pike to deoxygenation. Alternatively only small areas should be treated at a time so that anaerobic conditions are not produced.

Much of the work that has been done on herbicides, as a method of controlling aquatic plants, has dealt with their efficacy rather than the side effects. Blok (1968) and van der Struik (in press) point out that although paraquat and diquat break down quickly and are therefore short-term in effect they allow the development of filamentous algae which often replace the macrophytes and themselves become a serious nuisance. The latter author considers diuron to be more satisfactory. It is effective against filamentous algae, including *Cladophora*, as well as macrophytes. van der Struik records that where plants useless to carp, such as *Elodea*, *Chara* and filamentous algae, were killed by diuron, carp production increased, but in other ponds where *Potamogeton* spp. were killed, carp production decreased. Blok found that mineralization of dead plant material was retarded after application of diuron and that the phytoplankton was affected selectively; only flagellates, and in some cases, a few diatoms survived for a considerable time after application. He considers the long term effects on the biotope as a whole require more study.

Way, Newman, Moore & Knaggs (1971), in experiments where submerged plants, principally *Elodea*, were treated with paraquat, found that one lake remained substantially clear of vegetation for two years after treatment and that filamentous algae did not develop. There did not appear to be any major mortality of invertebrates, fish or breeding birds, although by 16 days after application the population and species diversity of the zooplankton had declined.

It is clear that further research is needed on the conservation implications of the use of these herbicides to control aquatic plants.

CONCLUSIONS

Although I have touched upon some of the more important problems in the conservation of freshwaters it is not possible to be comprehensive since there are probably many other less obvious problems which we do not yet know about and will only detect by careful monitoring of the environment. It is only by biological surveillance that new threats to freshwater fauna and flora may be detected early enough, when they arise, to prevent serious consequences developing.

A difficult problem with the conservation of freshwaters is that a water body can only be conserved effectively with proper control of the whole watershed. On the other hand freshwater ecosystems can be used as delicate sensors of environmental contamination within the catchment.

## ACKNOWLEDGEMENTS

I am most grateful to Dr. Martin George for help in assembling information on the decline of aquatic plants in the Norfolk Broads. My thanks are also due to Dr. D. Jenkins and Dr. P. S. Maitland for helpful comments on the script.

## REFERENCES

Atkinson-Willes, G. L. (1963). *Wildfowl in Great Britain.* London: H.M.S.O.

Bennet, A. (1883). On *Najas marina* L. as a British plant. *J. Bot.* **1883**: 353.

Blok, E. (1968). Herbiciden in Viswater (Experiments with herbicides in fishing waters). *Proc. Symp. Eur. Weed Res. Counc.* **9** (1967): 51–65.

Bormann, F. H., Likens, G. E. & Eaton, J. S. (1969). Biotic regulation of particulate and solution losses from a forest ecosystem. *Biol. Sci.* **19**: 600–610.

Boyd, H. & Matthews, G. V. T. (1963). The control of wildfowl stocks. In *Wildfowl in Great Britain.* 331–333. (Atkinson-Willes, G. L., ed). London: H.M.S.O.

Brook, A. J. & Holden, A. V. (1957). Fertilization experiments in Scottish freshwater lochs I. Loch Kinardochy. *Freshwat. Salm. Fish. Res.* No. 17: 1–30.

Bye, V. (1966). *Chemical analyses of certain dykes and broads in the valleys of the River Bure, Yare and Thurne.* Internal report held at the Nature Conservancy, Bracondale, Norwich.

Duffey, E. (1968). Ecological studies on the large copper butterfly *Lycaena dispar* Haw. *batarus* Obth. at Woodwalton Fen National Nature Reserve, Huntingdonshire. *J. appl. Ecol.* **5**: 69–96.

Efford, I. A. (1970). Marion Lake project 1969–1970. International Biological Programme Canada. *Rep. Inst. Anim. Resource Ecol. Univ. Br. Columbia* **1970**: 1–82.

Ellis, M. B. (1940). The Norfolk sea floods. 11. Detailed observations on the flora at Horset. *Trans. Norfolk Norwich Nat. Soc.* **15**: 34–40.

Ellis, E. A. (1963). Some effects of selective feeding by the Coypu (*Myocastor coypus*) on the vegetation of Broadland. *Trans. Norfolk Norwich Nat. Soc.* **20**: 32–35.

Ellis, E. A. (1965). *The Broads.* London: Collins.

Fiala, K. & Květ, J. (in press). Dynamic balance between plant species in South Moravian reed-swamps. *J. Ecol.*

Fish, G. R. (1968). The oxygen content of some New Zealand lakes. *Verh. int Ver. Limnol.* **17**: 392–403.

Fisher, D. W., Gambell, A. W., Likens, G. E. & Bormann, F. H. (1968). Atmospheric contributions to water quality of streams in the Hubbard Brook Experimental Forest, New Hampshire. *Wat. Resources Res.* **4**: 1115–1126.

Holden, A. V. (1959). Fertilization experiments in Scottish freshwater lochs II. Sutherland 1954. Chemical and botanical observations. *Freshwat. Salm. Fish. Res.* No. 24: 1–42.

Hunt, E. G. & Bischoff, A. I. (1960). Inimical effects on wildlife of periodic DDD applications to Clear Lake. *Calif. Fish Game* **46**: 91–106.

Hynes, H. B. N. (1960). *The biology of polluted waters.* Liverpool: Liverpool University Press.

Jermy, A. C. (1956). *Extract from an annotated list of vascular plants found on Calthorpe Broad in 1956.* Internal report held at Nature Conservancy, Bracondale, Norwich.

Jermy, A. C. (1959). *The vegetation and its ecological status at Alderfen Broad, Norfolk.* Internal report held at Nature Conservancy, Bracondale, Norwich.

Johnson, N. M., Likens, G. E., Bormann, F. H. & Pierce, R. S. (1968). Rate of chemical weathering of silicate minerals in New Hampshire. *Geochim. Cosmochim. Acta* **32**: 531–545.

Klein, L. (1957). *Aspects of river pollution.* London.

Kolenbrander, G. J. (1969). Nitrate content and nitrogen loss in drain water. *Neth. J. agric. Sci.* **17**: 246–255.

Lambert, J. M. (1965). The vegetation of Broadland. In *The Broads*: 69–92. (Ellis, E. A., ed). London: Collins.

Lambert, J. M. & Jennings, J. N. (1951). Alluvial stratigraphy and vegetational succession in the region of the Bure Valley Broads. 11. Detailed vegetational–stratigraphical relationships. *J. Ecol.* **39**: 120–148.

Likens, G. E., Bormann, F. H., Johnson, N. M. & Pierce, R. S. (1967). The calcium, magnesium, potassium, and sodium budgets for a small forested ecosystem. *Ecology* **48**: 772–785.

Lund, J. W. G. (1972). 11*th Symposium of BES.* The scientific management of animal plant communities for conservation (E. Duffey and A. S. Watt, eds). London, Blackwells.

Luther, H. & Rzóska, J. (1969). *Project Aqua.* A list of aquatic sites proposed for conservation on the basis of their scientific value. London: IBP Central Office.

Morgan, N. C. (1966). Fertilization experiments in Scottish freshwater lochs II. Sutherland, 1954. 2 Effects on the bottom fauna. *Freshwat. Salm. Fish. Res.* No. 36: 1–19.

Morgan, N. C. (1970). Changes in the fauna and flora of a nutrient enriched lake. *Hydrobiologia* **35**: 545–553.

Morgan, N. C. (in press). Productivity studies at Loch Leven (a shallow nutrient rich lowland lake). In *Proc. UNESCO-IBP Symp. prod. probl. freshwat. Interim Res. I.B.P./P.F.* Poland, 1970.

Olney, P. S. (1965). Project Mar. The conservation and management of temperate marshes, bogs and other wetlands. List of European and North African wetlands of international importance. *IUCN Publs.* No. 5: 1–102.

Olsen, S. (1964). Vegetation saendringer i Lingby Sø. Bidrag til analyse af kulturpavirkninger pa vand-og Sumpplante vegetationen. *Bot. Tidsskr.* **59**: 273–300.

Pallis, M. (1911). The river-valleys of East Norfolk: their aquatic and fen formations. In *Types of British vegetation*: 214–245. Tansley, A. G. (ed). Cambridge: University Press.

Stewart, L. (1969). Criteria for safeguarding fisheries, fish migration, and angling in rivers. *Ass. River Auth. Yb.* **1968**: 134–149.

Sukopp, H. (1971). Effects of man, especially recreational activities, on littoral macrophytes. In Proceedings of the IBP/UNESCO symposium on aquatic macrophytes. *Hidrobiologia* **12**.

van der Struik, Ir. A. (in press). Control of water plants. *Proc. Br. coarse Fish Conf.* **4**: (1969).

Vollenweider, R. A. (1968). *Scientific fundamentals of the eutrophication of lakes and flowing waters, with particular reference to nitrogen and phosphorus as factors in eutrophication.* Paris: Techn. Rept., DAS/CSI/68.27. Organisation for Economic Cooperation and Development.

Way, J. M., Newman, J. F., Moore, N. W. & Knaggs, F. W. (1971). Some ecological effects of the use of paraquat for the control of weeds in small lakes. *J. appl. Ecol.* **8**: 509–532.

Woldendorp, J. W., Dilz, K. & Kolenbrander, G. J. (1966). The fate of fertilizer nitrogen on permanent grassland soils. *Proc. gen. Meeting Eur. Grassld Fedn* **1**: 53–68. Wageningen 1965.

# Marine

Symp. zool. Soc. Lond. (1972) No. 29, 157-160.

# INTRODUCTION

## H. A. COLE

*Fisheries Laboratory, Lowestoft, Suffolk, England*

The papers included in this section cover varied aspects of the problems of conservation and productivity of marine resources. The contribution from Garrod & Clayden which follows this, broadly ranges over the conservation and management problems of the sea fisheries. I propose to state some general remarks which will, I hope, show the importance of the coastal environment in relation to the conservation of both inshore and offshore species and highlight the opportunities which exist in this environment for productive research within the capabilities of the marine stations and the universities.

Although the value of marine fishery products as landed in the United Kingdom lies somewhere between 60 and 70 million pounds sterling per annum, only a part of this total comes from the seas around Britain. United Kingdom fishermen exploit stocks of fish, cod especially, inhabiting distant waters as far afield as Greenland, Labrador and Newfoundland in the west, in addition to those at Iceland, in the Barents Sea, off the Norwegian coast and Faroe, and in the North Sea, the Irish Sea and other coastal areas around Britain. We are concerned with conservation questions in all these seas, which are covered by two international regulatory bodies to which the United Kingdom belongs—the North-East Atlantic Fisheries Commission (NEAFC) and the International Commission for the Northwest Atlantic Fisheries (ICNAF). There is a substantial framework of international research which supports the work of these regulating commissions and this, understandably enough, is based almost entirely upon the work of the Government fisheries laboratories in the member countries. These laboratories focus their attention in the main on the principal commercial species of fish and shellfish and on the way in which the stocks vary in abundance and are affected by fishing patterns and conservation measures. We are very conscious, however, of the need for increased research on the broader biology of the fish and shellfish themselves, and its inter-relationship with the environment, and with the food on which the fish depend. We have also become more concerned in recent years about the negative side of the question, the possible effects on the stocks of fish and shellfish of pollution, a subject referred to in this and the Freshwater Section.

Although Garrod deals principally with the main deep-sea commercial fish stocks, the subsequent papers are concerned with the young fish and plankton and productivity. I wish to stress particularly the desirability of extending studies of young fish and to describe briefly the opportunities that such studies present for important and original research by both universities and research councils as well as by fisheries laboratories. It does not seem to be sufficiently appreciated that, although the principal fisheries take place offshore in international waters, many of the commercially-important species of fish have their nursery areas in shallow coastal waters where the young fish are particularly exposed to environmental fluctuations and to the effects of pollution. This is true not only of the major kinds of flatfish, e.g. plaice, sole, turbot and brill, but also of herring, saithe, whiting and several others. So the young fish which are the source of recruitment to the commercial stocks fished in common in international waters are found to a large extent in national waters. This question of pollution effects is therefore a matter for international concern. Moreover, it is becoming increasingly certain that the relative strength of a fish year-class is determined at a very early stage in the life-cycle, probably during the planktonic larval phase and in the short period during which the post-larvae take to the bottom (in the case of demersal fish), and this emphasizes again the great importance of studies of this particular phase of the life-cycle.

To dissect the situation a little further, although there may be many environmental factors affecting the survival of young fish at this stage, a few seem to be of overriding importance, for instance, on the physical side, temperature, particularly as affecting the duration of larval stages, but especially, among the biological factors, the presence at the right time of suitable food in sufficient abundance. Clearly, however, there is an interaction between factors, e.g. temperature, rate of growth, development of food species, and predation.

The accessibility of these young fish in shallow waters near the shore, the feasibility of sampling them with quite inexpensive equipment, and their suitability for experimental work in the laboratory, makes this a particularly attractive area of research for workers at universities and marine stations. It is not essential to confine research to commercial species only (although many of these have been imperfectly studied) when attempting to establish basic principles governing, for example, growth, behaviour or survival; there are literally dozens of species of non-commercial fish which are readily available. In these circumstances there is, I contend, no excuse for confining one's attention to goldfish when one can go to the seashore at almost any point around the British coast and find interesting populations of young marine fish, immediately accessible, which can be studied with very simple equipment and which are often highly adaptable to maintenance in experimental aquaria. There is the added incentive that new discoveries may assist very materially in understanding the causes of fluctuations in commercially-valuable species and so point the way to improved conservation.

A further point of some significance is that we are rapidly moving towards a stage where it is possible by means of standard relatively simple techniques to rear some of these fish, such as plaice and sole and even herring, in the laboratory and to set up critical experiments to examine the effects of environmental factors upon them. Such laboratory studies can be compared with ecological studies of the same species in coastal waters and, by combining the two approaches, there is the possibility of making substantial advances in knowledge. It is very important indeed that we should have more integrated work of this kind. Although I have referred especially to possible influences of pollution on the abundance and survival of young fish, there is also a need for quantitative studies of the effects of predation, disease and parasites, both directly upon the young fish and also on the plankton and bottom animals on which they feed. It is appreciated that there may be a problem of continuity, especially in university departments which are heavily dependent upon post-graduate students. However, the normal post-graduate course leading to a Ph.D. provides for two seasons of field work, and the accessibility and seasonal abundance of young fish, and the ease with which many of them may be maintained in laboratory conditions, are strong points in their favour.

In this section we shall also be referring in one contribution to shellfish and these, with a few important exceptions such as *Nephrops* and escallops, are almost confined to coastal and estuarine waters and so are particularly well placed for the application of cultivation or management procedures. They are also especially liable to be damaged by changes in the environment brought about by pollution but are, in general, very accessible to study. In the case of molluscan shellfish, effective field sampling of populations is easily achieved and experimental studies in the laboratory do not present any great difficulty. Moreover, artificial rearing techniques for several important species of both molluscs and crustaceans are well established. Once again the circumstances are favourable for a combined approach to research through experimental work in the laboratory and ecological studies on the shore or at sea. In the shellfish field the marine stations and universities have made and are continuing to make substantial contributions but there is a need for a more adventurous approach; the combination of modern analytical and recording instrumentation and acute observation in the field should provide us with a measure of the ecological effects of pollution and other environmental changes which is so necessary if planning control is to be sensibly related to the preservation of the marine environment and the maintenance of natural resources.

In this brief introduction, the aims have been firstly to emphasize the importance of shallow coastal and estuarine waters in maintaining the abundance and variety of fish and shellfish stocks available for commercial exploitation, and secondly to stress both the need for additional basic work on their biology in support of applied studies and the opportunities which this situation presents for the application of modern techniques of ecological analysis to enthusiastic and skilful scientists at the universities and marine stations.

*Symp. zool. Soc. Lond.* (1972) No. 29, 161–184.

# CURRENT BIOLOGICAL PROBLEMS IN THE
# CONSERVATION OF DEEP-SEA FISHERY RESOURCES

## D. J. GARROD

*Fisheries Laboratory, Lowestoft, Suffolk, England*

and

## A. D. CLAYDEN

*Faculty of Medicine, University of Sheffield, Sheffield, England**

SYNOPSIS

Current problems of the conservation of deep-sea fishery resources show many features in common, regardless of the species involved. The current status of the north Atlantic cod resources is reviewed to illustrate these problems and to show why management is at present concerned to find acceptable methods of regulating the amount of fishing. The development of the cod fisheries is then simulated in a dynamic mathematical model which is used to investigate the long-term effects of different management procedures.

INTRODUCTION

The recent upsurge of public interest in conservation has been stimulated by an increasing awareness that the activity of man may have an irreversible effect on his environment. However, conservation is often regarded as being synonymous with the preservation of a species, and it must be remembered that the changes wrought by man are not necessarily undesirable. In the context of marine fisheries it is certainly true that conservation is most important in so far as it is necessary to secure the maximum benefit to man from the available resources.

The concept of a maximum sustainable protein yield is one objective which has proved part of the rationale for discussions of fishery conservation problems, but these have also involved some appreciation of the wider implications of any proposed management measures. For example, the economic aspects of fishing operations have become increasingly relevant to management policies. Global fishing capacity has expanded, with a consequential decline in the abundance of individual resources and a general reduction of catches per standard unit of fishing time. This trend has sharpened international competition and it has contributed to the adoption of industrial support policies by a number of countries (OECD, 1965). This in turn has led fisheries

* Present address: Glamorgan County Council, Cardiff, Wales.

management and research to consider explicitly the amount of fishing in relation to the physical yield, in order to appraise the economic implication of fishery regulation.

At the biological level, fishery research has been concerned with the response of a resource as a system to increased predation by man. The extent of our present understanding of such systems is a function of the amount of change that has been observed in fishery resources and hence a function of time and the pattern of development of the fisheries. The north Atlantic resources are closest to nations that have had industrialized fleets for the longest time and so our understanding of these resources is as advanced as it is for any fishery resources in the world.

From these studies it has become evident that although every stock and fishery has unique characteristics, their dynamics are based on population mechanisms that are common to all, differing in degree rather than principle. Thus, although the research has its foundations in the studies of individual resources, between-stock comparisons are of increasing importance to identify the underlying general principles (see for example, Beverton, 1963; Cushing, in press). This level of understanding is still essentially restricted to within-stock population mechanisms. As yet there is little understanding of the biological interaction between species of the same tropic level, and still less of the interaction between fish and fisheries exploited at different levels of the same ecosystem. These deficiencies reflect the timescale of fishery research: obviously the response of a stock to its own exploitation can be observed and interpreted more rapidly than the effect of changes that are one or more steps removed from it.

Fishery biologists are aware of these shortcomings and know that present biological concepts of management may require modification, but this does not alter the need to proffer the best advice available within the constraints of present knowledge, because the problem of conserving marine fishery resources exists and is the subject of international discussion. The more exact nature of this problem can be illustrated by a review of the north Atlantic cod resources, remembering that the essence of the problem is inherent in the exploitation of any living wild resource on the high seas.

THE COD FISHERIES OF THE NORTH ATLANTIC 1946–1968

## Distribution

Commercially valuable cod resources occur on the continental shelf throughout the north Atlantic north of 45°N. They are distributed in a number of biologically discrete stocks whose location and isolation is a function of their thermal tolerance and the hydrographic and seabed topography (Fig. 1). Each stock has its own unique characteristics of

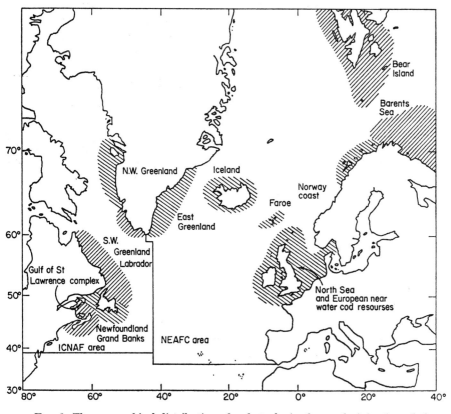

FIG. 1. The geographical distribution of cod stocks in the north Atlantic and the areas of jurisdiction of the North-East Atlantic Fishery Commission (NEAFC) and the International Commission for the Northwest Atlantic Fisheries (ICNAF).

morphological variation, growth rate, fecundity, age at maturity, etc. These stocks are located at varying distances from the nations wishing to exploit them and this has influenced the design of fishing vessels used to work them. Thus the characteristics of range, speed, voyage duration and catch storage necessary for the efficient exploitation of resources in the North Sea differ from those required for the exploitation of stocks in Arctic waters. As a result the cod fisheries of the north Atlantic fall into two groups characterized by the vessels that fish

them. On the one hand are the stocks on the shelf off north-western
Europe currently fished by trawlers up to 130 ft length which store
their catch on ice and are virtually restricted by their size to the one
area; these are termed European *near-water* resources. On the other
hand there are the *distant-water* resources exploited by larger trawlers
up to 230 ft (1500 tons), in addition to the near-water size trawlers
operated on the distant resources by countries with an adjacent coastline. The largest of the distant-water trawlers have the range and voyage
duration to fish anywhere in the north Atlantic basin according to the
short-term fishing prospects, though so far they have not fished the
European near-waters because the fishing intensity of the smaller
vessels of the first group has kept stock abundance in these areas
below the level that could provide attractive fishing for the larger
vessels. Because of the mobility of these vessels there is now reason
to consider the distant-water fish stocks as a single resource from the
point of view of their exploitation, although they remain biologically
discrete. The cod stocks in question are:

1. Arcto-Norwegian: (a) Barents Sea, (b) Norway coast, (c) Bear
   Island/Spitsbergen.
2. Iceland.
3. (a) Faroe plateau⎫Faroe.
   (b) Faroe bank ⎭
4. East Greenland.
5. South-west Greenland.
6. North-west Greenland.
7. Labrador/northern Newfoundland.
8. Newfoundland Grand Bank.

Additional cod resources not listed occur in the Baltic, North Sea
and south and west of Great Britain, all of which constitute the
European near-water resources, and in the Gulf of St Lawrence area
of the north-west Atlantic. The latter are relatively insignificant in the
context of the north Atlantic as a whole and neither group will be
considered further in this paper.

The importance of the distant-water complex can be judged from
the catches of selected north Atlantic marine products in 1968 (ICES,
1969; ICNAF, 1970) summarized in Table I. Cod contribute 30% of
the total yield of all marine fish and 54% of the catch of demersal
species caught principally by trawling: 75% of this cod is taken from
the distant-water stocks. Without going into detail it is clear that the
economy of the distant-water fleets is at present heavily dependent on
the fortunes of the cod fisheries, and in practice for many countries,
including England, the distribution of fishing by the distant-water

fleet to date has been almost completely determined by the availability of cod.

*Marine fish production in the north Atlantic 1968 (thousand tons round fresh)*

| | North-east Atlantic | North-west Atlantic | Total | Group yield (million tons) |
|---|---|---|---|---|
| Pelagic species | | | | |
| Herring | 2334 | 923 | 3257 | 5·3 |
| Others | 1939 | 113 | 2052 | |
| Demersal species | | | | |
| Cod distant-water complex | 1532 | 1444 | 2976 | |
| European near-waters | 533 | — | 533 | 3·9 |
| Other cod | — | 417 | 417 | |
| Other species, for human consumption | 1758 | 834 | 2592 | 3·3 |
| Other species, for reduction | 695 | — | 695 | |
| Elasmobranchs and others unspecified | 380 | 170 | 550 | 0·6 |
| Total | 9171 | 3901 | 13 072 | |

*The development of the distant-water cod fisheries*

One of the authors (Clayden, in press) has recently completed a review of the expansion of fishing in the distant-water sector, as part of a project to construct a dynamic simulation of the fishery as a whole. This involved, *inter alia*, the expression of the fishing effort capacity available in participating countries in terms of a common unit of fishing effort by appropriate conversion factors based on the recorded performance of the vessels. The development of fishing effort expressed in this unit (the English ton-hours of fishing time) is shown in Fig. 2. As regards the division of effort between major fishing areas (Fig. 2A), in the north-east Atlantic fishing effort expanded steadily to a peak in 1961 and then appears to have become more stable, but in the north-west Atlantic there has been a continuing increase since comprehensive statistics first became available in 1955. Overall there remains a slight upward trend in total effort.

The breakdown of this total effort between four major components is shown in Fig. 2B. The greater proportion of the available capacity is generated by the mobile distant-water fleets. The two largest individual national components of this fleet, England and USSR, have been

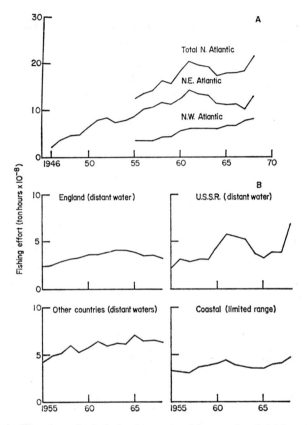

FIG. 2. A. The chronological development of international fishing effort in the north Atlantic. B. The chronological development of fishing effort by main components of the international fleet.

separated from a balance contributed by other countries.* The fishing effort by this other-country group shows a slightly increasing trend. Between England and the USSR, however, there is an interesting contrast; the activity of the English fleet increased up to 1963 but since then it has declined slightly. This reflects the modernization of the fleet from side trawlers, which were effectively restricted to distant waters of the north-east Atlantic, to numerically fewer but larger

* Belgium, Federal Republic of West Germany, Faroes, France, German Democratic Republic, Iceland, Norway, Poland, Portugal, Spain.

freezer trawlers which can also fish the north-west Atlantic. The USSR
north Atlantic fleet fishing for cod expanded to a peak in 1961 but
then, as cod yields in the north-east Atlantic fell away, part of the
fleet was redeployed on to other species in the north-west Atlantic,
notably silver hake, redfish and herring. This redeployment is reflected
as an apparent drop in capacity in the cod fisheries in the mid-1960s,
but a reversion appears to have occurred in the most recent years.

The fourth component, the coastal fishery group, is comprised by
nations with a coastline adjacent to a fishery, and is comparable to
the near-water group noted earlier. The Norwegian, Greenland and
North American components are specially important within this group,
but it should be noted that the fishing by Iceland has been excluded
because it is centred on a particular fishery which takes place mainly
within the exclusive fishery limit at Iceland and so can be considered
to be outside the present context. The fishery capacity of these coastal
fleets appears to be increasing slightly but this may be an artefact

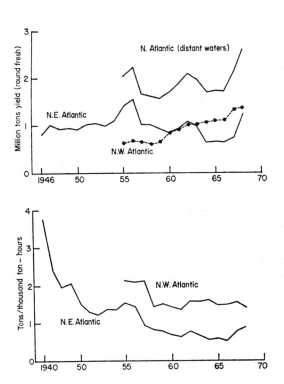

Fig. 3. The total catch and catch per unit effort of cod in the north Atlantic distant-
water resources 1946–1968.

created by the technical difficulty of expressing the fishing effort of extremely diverse inshore fishing gears in terms of the standard unit.

The economic problems facing the industry are reflected in the chronological series of catches and catch per unit effort shown in Fig. 3, the latter being expressed as the number of tons landed per 1000 ton-hours of fishing which approximates to one hour's fishing by a modern freezer trawler.

The north-east Atlantic data show clearly that cod catches have been remarkably stable throughout the period; increased fishing has distributed the yield over an increasing number of units with decreasing catch to each. By the late 1950s the catch per unit effort in the north-west Atlantic was sufficiently advantageous to outweigh the increased steaming time involved for the northern European nations, and a gradual redistribution of fishing effort took place. This expansion of fishing in the north-west has been accompanied by increasing catch, implying stable catch per unit effort, but in fact the grouped data conceal the movement of the European effort first to West Greenland, and then to Labrador and Newfoundland as successive stocks showed symptoms of depletion.

The extension of the range of fishing operations to the north-west Atlantic stimulated northern European nations to design vessels to process their catch at sea so that, having arrived on the fishing grounds, they can remain in the area until the total catch is adequate. These designs have been taken up by other countries and the trend has now culminated in an international fleet of freezer factory trawlers which is extremely mobile, fishing with an increasing variety of types of trawler and able to move from one region to another according to information which is often more freely exchanged between fishermen of competing nations than between fishermen competing for the same national market. The position has now been reached in which the abundance of all the cod stocks is broadly comparable, except at Iceland and Faroe where the stock abundance is lower. This trend to increased technological sophistication , with its implied increase in investment and operating costs, has taken place since 1963; but there is no evidence that it has been accompanied by any long-term increase in catches (see Fig. 3).

THE MANAGEMENT PROBLEM

The catch level discussed above has been maintained up to 1970 by expansion on to new grounds, and by removal of a part of the standing stock in those areas. To that extent catches have exceeded production. The generation time of the Arctic cod stocks is of the order of ten years, so that only now are the north-west Atlantic stocks beginning to approach an equilibrium level related to recent levels of fishing. A reduction in catch is therefore to be expected which cannot now be offset by the development of relatively lightly fished cod resources: this situation will intensify the problems facing national fleets. But at the same time relatively recent entrants to these fisheries may seek to increase their share of the catch for reasons which are economically sound to them (see Gulland, 1968a) and in so doing commit other countries to increase their own fleet capacity if they wish to maintain their own share of production from the resource. Thus, the diverse motives of the participants make the multi-nation fishery inherently vulnerable to an expansion of fishing effort, to the detriment of the collective position. In addition fishermen operating fleets with limited range have a strong interest in the influence of increasing fishing activity by larger vessels on their traditional resources.

The problems of the north Atlantic cod fisheries in 1970 are not new, but there is now an increasing urgency to find the solutions within the near future because the limit of expansion on to less fully exploited cod resources has now been reached.

The most important biological problem to be solved is whether or not these stocks are capable of sustaining the recent yields in the long term. Hitherto, stock assessments have assumed that fishing will not have a significant influence on the capacity of the stock to reproduce itself and therefore that any particular level of yield defined by the interaction between fishing, growth and natural mortality can be sustained. This concept is fundamental to the *yield-per-recruit* assessment approach (Beverton & Holt, 1957) as it has been applied, but it is becoming less certain as the longer-term effects of prolonged intensive fishing upon spawning stock size and its possible effect upon subsequent recruitment become apparent (ICES, in press).

For the north Atlantic the options at present enabling management to regulate the fisheries are defined in the terms of reference of the fishery Commissions (see Section, pp. 173–178). We may note here that the regulation of the amount of fishing is a main concern at present, for reasons which will be evident from the foregoing description of the fishery. The complexity of the problem has so far necessitated its consideration on a single geographical area/stock basis, but with the existing mobility of the fleets it is also worthwhile to consider the broader implications should regulation of the amount of fishing in one area lead to the redeployment of fishing on to adjacent resources. To do this Dr Clayden has constructed a time-varied model of the cod stocks listed earlier, to simulate their historical development and to provide a basis for investigating the implications of various management strategies.

The deterministic yield model currently used for fishery assessments has many derivatives, but in essence it predicts the yield per recruit from the characteristics of growth and natural mortality in relation to fishing mortality over a specified range of age. This usage has the important limitation that yield is derived as the equilibrium yield per recruit. In reality unregulated fisheries are seldom sufficiently stable to obtain a true equilibrium level, if only because recruitment varies from year to year, with a consequential effect on the distribution of fishing mortality. The deterministic model does not attempt to predict a true yield (although it may be derived quite easily) but rather a proportionate difference that might be achieved under a different set of fishing circumstances. By incorporating both fishing mortality and recruitment as explicit variables the time-varied model can take into account seasonal and annual variations in the fisheries and generate its own distribution of fishing effort, thus giving access to the yield of fisheries in transitional states.

The model is initiated by a matrix of the absolute number of cod of each age group in each stock in an initial year. Each stock is then subjected to a unit of fishing effort on a speculative basis to see what catch per unit effort it would yield per month. The available fishing capacity is then distributed in proportion to the relative catch per unit effort of each stock, catching a certain number of fish which, when added to losses through natural mortality, leaves a number of survivors in each stock at the beginning of the next month. The computation is then repeated, with appropriate modification of the seasonality factor. The numbers caught are raised to the weight yield by the growth characteristics of the stock in question: recruits are added to the stock in the September-November period, and at the end of the calendar year all age groups are updated one year.

The constant parameters of the model are thus:

(i) the initial stock numbers;

(ii) the selection characteristics of the gear, expressed as partial recruitment factors per age group;

(iii) weight at age;

(iv) natural mortality;

(v) the seasonal pattern of the catchability coefficient.

Variable parameters are the absolute number of young cod recruiting to each stock each year and the amount of fishing effort.

The fishing effort input permits the model to be used either with a fixed amount of fishing directed to each stock, or with fishing effort taking up a distribution varying in relation to the abundance of each stock. The *fixed effort* model has been used to establish the validity of the biological parameters by using the chronological record of fishing effort on each stock to generate the equivalent record of yield. This same criterion has then been used to assess the accuracy of the *mobile effort* model, in which there is no constraint on the distribution of fishing. This requires the fishing effort input in terms of the available fishing effort capacity per country per month and an additional weighting factor incorporating other factors that influence the distribution of fishing. This weighting factor is in a sense an economic variable and could be extremely complex: to date it has been compounded of the distance of the stock from a home port in each country (to take account of the fishing time/steaming time ratio), the prevalence of other species of commercial importance on the same ground, and the relative value of cod from different grounds.

A comparison between the historic record and the simulation incorporating the mobility feature is summarized for the north-east and north-west Atlantic areas in Fig. 4. It is immediately obvious that the correspondence of the model to actuality is best for the north-east Atlantic stocks, and in fact the simulation for the north-west Atlantic area excludes the Grand Bank, Newfoundland, stock because the model failed to provide a realistic representation of that fishery. The different level of success in simulation is a reflection of the adequacy of the basic data available and some of the constraints in the model. For example, for simplicity growth rates have been assumed to be stable at the recently observed levels, whereas in fact they are known to have increased during the period. In the model this causes an overestimate of yield in the earlier years. More seriously, the north-west Atlantic grounds attract too high a proportion of the available effort. This is especially obvious when the north-west Atlantic grounds are first included in 1955; it implies some inadequacy in the assumption of the model governing the distribution of effort with respect to relative catch rates, or in the degree of mobility of national fleets.

Even so, the correlation between observed and simulated levels of effort, which is a dependent variable in the mobile effort model, is

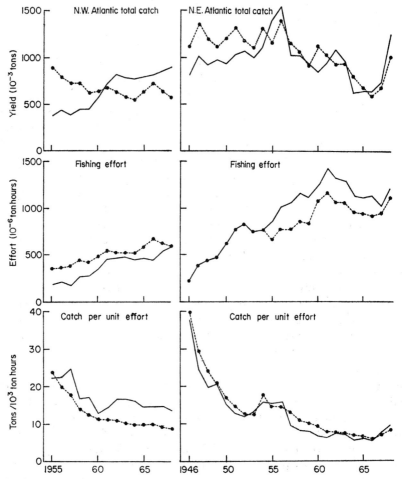

Fig. 4. Comparison of the actual record of the north Atlantic distant-water cod fisheries (full line) with the record simulated in a time-varied mathematical model (broken line).

reasonable, being significant at the 99·9% level for four of the five north-east Atlantic stocks and at between 95% and 99·9% in four of the five north-west Atlantic stocks. The correlation was non-significant only for the Grand Bank stock. The fishing effort on the Arcto-Norwegian stock as a whole, at Faroe, and on the north-west and east Greenland stocks was simulated within 15% of the actual level.

It is reasonable to conclude from this that the model does incorporate the main determinants of fish population size and of the distribution of fishing with respect to them. Even though there remain obvious imperfections in the results it is therefore of interest to use the model to investigate the implications of different management strategies.

## APPLICATION OF THE MODEL TO INVESTIGATE MANAGEMENT STRATEGIES

Management of the north Atlantic fisheries is vested in the North-East Atlantic Fisheries Commission (NEAFC) and the International Commission for the Northwest Atlantic Fisheries (ICNAF). The areas over which they have jurisdiction are shown in Fig. 1. Both are empowered to regulate fishing to obtain the maximum sustainable yield, and measures that may be considered to achieve this are:

1. (a) minimum size limits of fish caught; (b) regulation of fishing gear, e.g. the mesh size of cod-ends of trawls;
2. (a) prescription of overall catch limits; (b) closed seasons or areas.

Although there is some overlap in function they have been grouped into two categories because the first group is intended to delay the age at first capture of the fish and so maximize the yield that can be achieved at a specified level of fishing, whereas the second group can be used to regulate the amount of fishing itself and so offers more direct economic benefits (Gulland, 1968b; Gulland & Carroz, 1968).

Since their inception the Commissions have been mainly concerned with Group 1 measures to ensure a size at first capture consistent with the increasing level of fishing effort. For the cod fisheries under discussion the minimum mesh sizes for the cod-ends of trawls have been gradually adjusted upward to the minimum of 130 mm (manila) which is at present in force, or proposed for all the named distant-water cod stocks except Faroe (110 mm manila). In the north-east Atlantic this regulation has been supported by minimum landing sizes of fish.

In recent years the Commissions' discussions have centred on the further benefits that could follow limitation of the amount of fishing, particularly with regard to the Arcto-Norwegian cod, North Sea herring, north-west Atlantic haddock and salmon. The last three of these are sufficiently isolated, from both the biological and exploitation points of view, that they can be regulated individually. For the cod stock however it is evident that the regulation of the amount of fishing in particular areas of the north Atlantic will have implications for the cod fisheries elsewhere.

The implication of further unlimited expansion of cod fishing, or of limitation in part of the resource complex, can be examined using the model. The effects of further adjustment in mesh size can also be

D. J. GARROD AND A. D. CLAYDEN

*Summary of simulated effects of fishery management*

| | Simulation series | Stock | | | |
|---|---|---|---|---|---|
| | | 1 Barents Sea | 2 Norway coast | 3 Bear Island | 4 Iceland |

A. Recruitment pattern as observed 1960–1970
  1 Cod fisheries as they have developed
  2 Total fishing capacity = fishing mortality $F = 0.6$;
  3 (and 6 in B) Total fishing capacity = fishing mortality $F = 0.6$;
  4 (and 7 in B) Total fishing capacity = fishing mortality $F = 0.8$;
  5 As 3, with age at recruitment to the fisheries delayed one year

| | | 1 | 2 | 3 | 4 |
|---|---|---|---|---|---|
| Total catch | 1 | 433 | 58 | 216 | 158 |
| (tons $\times 10^{-3}$) | 2 | 356 | 138 | 173 | 144 |
| | 3 | 322 | 165 | 174 | 156 |
| | 4 | 330 | 120 | 172 | 152 |
| | 5 | 275 | 337 | 160 | 175 |
| Total effort | 1* | 603 | 288 | 160 | 169 |
| (ton-hours $\times 10^{-6}$) | 2 | 374 | 170 | 120 | 270 |
| | 3 | 328 | 264 | 211 | 162 |
| | 4 | 447 | 336 | 281 | 218 |
| | 5 | 292 | 293 | 197 | 162 |
| Catch per unit effort | 1 | 1·20 | 0·28 | 0·98 | 0·82 |
| (tons/$10^{-3}$ ton-hours) | 2 | 0·94 | 0·81 | 1·44 | 0·52 |
| | 3 | 0·97 | 0·62 | 0·82 | 0·95 |
| | 4 | 0·73 | 0·36 | 0·60 | 0·68 |
| | 5 | 0·92 | 1·14 | 0·81 | 1·18 |

B. Recruitment reduced in stocks 1–3 to the estimated level of the 1965–1969

| | | 1 | 2 | 3 | 4 |
|---|---|---|---|---|---|
| Total catch | 6 | 142 | 97 | 67 | 156 |
| | 7 | 148 | 72 | 68 | 149 |
| Total effort | 6 | 266 | 256 | 161 | 182 |
| | 7 | 368 | 328 | 217 | 242 |
| Catch per unit effort | 6 | 0·53 | 0·38 | 0·42 | 0·84 |
| | 7 | 0·40 | 0·22 | 0·31 | 0·60 |

*Fishing effort in 1969 only.

II

*options in the north Atlantic cod fisheries, 1960–1970*

| | | | | | | Total | Mean |
|---|---|---|---|---|---|---|---|
| 5<br>Faroe | 6<br>North-<br>west | 7<br>Greenland<br>South-<br>west | 8<br>East | 9<br>Labrador<br>+3 K L | 10<br>Grand<br>Banks | | |

distribution of effort fixed to this level per stock
distribution of effort mobile
distribution of effort mobile

| 5 | 6 | 7 | 8 | 9 | 10 | Total | Mean |
|---|---|---|---|---|---|---|---|
| 29 | 226 | 74 | 20 | 312 | 257 | 1783 | |
| 35 | 217 | 71 | 18 | 295 | 234 | 1681 | |
| 34 | 209 | 71 | 18 | 284 | 237 | 1670 | |
| 32 | 210 | 69 | 19 | 276 | 220 | 1600 | |
| 42 | 214 | 79 | 18 | 312 | 295 | 1907 | |
| 63 | 169 | 50 | 40 | 331 | 244 | 2118 | |
| 60 | 200 | 60 | 40 | 300 | 300 | 1894 | |
| 65 | 159 | 85 | 32 | 307 | 280 | 1894 | |
| 85 | 218 | 114 | 44 | 412 | 364 | 2519 | |
| 67 | 153 | 85 | 31 | 313 | 301 | 1894 | |
| 0·41 | 1·31 | 0·78 | 0·64 | 1·15 | 0·91 | | 0·85 |
| 0·58 | 1·08 | 1·18 | 0·46 | 0·98 | 0·78 | | 0·88 |
| 0·53 | 1·31 | 0·82 | 0·57 | 0·91 | 0·83 | | 0·83 |
| 0·38 | 0·96 | 0·60 | 0·42 | 0·67 | 0·59 | | 0·60 |
| 0·61 | 1·39 | 0·91 | 0·57 | 1·00 | 0·95 | | 0·95 |

year-classes

| 5 | 6 | 7 | 8 | 9 | 10 | Total | Mean |
|---|---|---|---|---|---|---|---|
| 34 | 210 | 71 | 19 | 282 | 231 | 1309 | |
| 31 | 210 | 68 | 19 | 272 | 212 | 1249 | |
| 71 | 174 | 93 | 35 | 344 | 312 | 1894 | |
| 93 | 237 | 124 | 48 | 458 | 404 | 2519 | |
| 0·47 | 1·21 | 0·75 | 0·52 | 0·82 | 0·72 | | 0·67 |
| 0·34 | 0·83 | 0·52 | 0·39 | 0·60 | 0·48 | | 0·47 |

simulated by incorporating an appropriate adjustment of the partial recruitment per age group matrix. Such simulations cannot yet be projected into the future with any confidence because of assumptions concerning future recruitment, but the principal effects can be illustrated by running the model using the biological parameters that have been observed but with varied conditions for exploitation of the stocks.

The results of a series of simulations are summarized in Table IIA as the mean catch, fishing effort and catch per unit effort that would have been achieved in the period 1960–1969 under the conditions described. These are compared with the actual simulated performance in the expanding fishery, but it is important to remember that these are not exact simulations; they can only be taken to represent a resource complex with biological characteristics that remain the same as those of the cod stocks in recent years.

Series 1 summarizes the simulation of the expanding fishery over the period 1960–1969 on which Figs 2 and 3 are based, but the effort data relate only to 1969 to show the total fishing capacity then available (2118 × 10⁶ ton-hours). Deterministic assessments of individual stocks indicate that a fishing mortality ($F$) of 0·6 on fully recruited age groups will give a yield close to the yield/effort optimum (see for example ICES, 1970; Horsted & Garrod, 1969). The sum of the fishing effort required to generate this level of fishing mortality on all the stocks considered amounts to 1894 × 10⁶ ton-hours, and Series 2 allocates this level of effort to each stock in such a way that it cannot be redeployed. This represents the situation where limitation of fishing effort is applied to limited areas and the stocks are in equilibrium with respect to that effort. The comparison between 1 and 2 shows a small advantage in total catch to the developing fishery (Series 1) which stems from the depletion of the standing crop of the north-west Atlantic stocks during the early years of the series and from high yields in Stocks 1 and 3 at the end of the period. These last are temporary features associated with the distribution of fishing effort at the end of the decade. Comparison of the effort shows that Series 1 carries a 12% excess over Series 2 in terms of total capacity required and a marked imbalance towards the north-east Atlantic, with the fishing in that area in 1969 being much greater than that required to generate the optimum level. This gave catches above the long-term sustainable average at that time, but will be offset by lower than average catches in the following years.

The third series permits the total fishing capacity generating $F = 0·6$ to distribute itself according to the varying abundance of the different stocks. Comparison of the effort summary for Series 1, 2 and 3 shows how this distribution might differ from the distribution in 1969 on the fixed effort situation. Comparison of total catch and catch per unit effort of these three simulations in fact shows very little change. The differences between individual stocks would have varying significance for difference countries, but as a broad generalization the production from the total resource would be virtually the same.

Series 4 illustrates the effect if fishing effort continued to expand to a capacity that could generate $F = 0.8$ per stock, this being a linear projection of the trend in total effort in Fig. 2 through 1975. This fishing effort is again deployed in relation to relative stock abundance, showing clearly that the total yield is slightly lower than when $F = 0.6$, but also that there is a fall in catch per unit effort.

The fifth series shows the possible effect of a further increase in age of recruitment to the fishery, a Type 1(b) regulation corresponding to a further increase in the minimum mesh size of cod-ends of trawls. This simulation confirms other methods of assessments in predicting an overall improvement in yield and catch per unit effort. But the increase in catch per unit effort is not uniform and one of the difficulties of further regulation along this line can be seen in the comparison of catch per unit effort in the three interlinked units of the Arcto-Norwegian stock (the Barents Sea, Bear Island and Norway coast groups) in Series 2 and 5. The increase in age at recruitment would give an overall 10% increase in yield from the stock as a whole, but a greater proportion of it would be derived from the fishery for older larger fish, much of which occurs within Norwegian exclusive fishery limits and so is not accessible to all nations. Likewise the predicted improvement in the Iceland fishery would involve some redistribution of the catch between differing parts of the fishery. Regulation along these lines thus reaches a point where the overall benefits are not equal for all participants.

In addition, though it is not evident in this series of simulations, many of these fisheries include catches of other important species, notably haddock and redfish, which would be significantly impaired by further mesh size regulation with respect to cod alone.

The series as a whole oversimplify reality because the effect of any one situation will vary between countries, as described, but they serve to show that the yield of cod from the north Atlantic stocks is close to the maximum that can be achieved. The total fishing effort currently available is not greatly in excess of the optimum $F = 0.6$ defined here, although the pattern of its geographical expansion has led to an imbalance in its distribution between the north-east and north-west Atlantic. At the same time comparison of simulations 2 and 3 suggest that given some regulation of the amount of fishing capacity any distributional imbalance of fishing effort should correct itself over a period of years, without loss of yield. The truth of that supposition really depends on the state of the resources and the level of fishing effort when a regulation became effective: it could be that the fisheries will have become so heavily dependent on the year-classes just recruiting to the exploited stock that a large proportion of the fishing effort would move from one stock to another in successive years according to the relative year-class size. This would create an oscillating distribution or pulse fishing, symptoms of which are already evident in the present imbalance which has been generated by the recruitment of two very strong year-classes in the Arcto-Norwegian stock. This system could still produce comparable yields, but it is more sensitive to the chronological distribution of good year-classes in the different stocks.

The conclusion is that there is no increase in catch to be gained by further increase in fishing effort in the north Atlantic cod fisheries, and fishing effort could be stabilized at its present level, or reduced slightly, without loss of catch. The application of this on a limited area basis would imply a reduction in fishing on some stocks which could be expected to influence the operational flexibility of some vessels. If it could be done on an Atlantic-wide basis distributional imbalance would correct itself and there would be operational advantages in retaining the mobility of effort. On the other hand if a further increase in fishing effort were to take place, total catch and catch per unit effort would be decreased, and the fleet mobility would lead to oscillation and vulnerability in the stocks and yields.

The conclusions illustrated by the simulations provide the biological justification for the present policy of the Commissions in searching for an internationally agreed system of regulating the amount of fishing.

THE RISK OF BIOLOGICAL OVERFISHING IN THE NORTH ATLANTIC COD
STOCKS

In addition to the potential economic benefits of a regulation of the amount of fishing, this would also reduce the existing risk that very intensive exploitation of particular resources might lead to biological overfishing in the sense of a fishery-induced reduction in the recruitment of young fish to the stocks. The simulations summarized in Table IIA, and indeed all yield-per-recruit assessments, assume that recruitment is not influenced by the fishery. To date this exclusion has been one of necessity because of the technical difficulty of demonstrating and quantifying the relationship between recruitment and spawning stock size. It can reasonably be argued that if the effect cannot be demonstrated then it is not likely to be significant in relation to other factors influencing recruitment. The difficulty here lies in the retrospective nature of population analyses as they apply to actual fisheries; the full implications to the spawning stock and subsequent recruitment of the high levels of fishing observed in recent years are not yet apparent in the available data, but evidence is accumulating that this is a factor which should be taken into account (ICES, in press).

The Artic cod is particularly vulnerable to depletion of the spawning stock because fish first recruit to the fishery at 3 years of age, and 50% maturity is not achieved until much later (9–10 years in Arcto-Norwegian cod (Ponomarenko, in press)). At the present level of fishing mortality the spawning potential may be reduced to less than 10% of its original level. Of the cod stocks considered here, the progressive decline in spawning fish with increased fishing is best documented for the Arcto-Norwegian (Garrod, 1968, in press).

Figure 5 is a scatter diagram of the number of recruits per spawning stock size in this stock (biomass being used as an index of fecundity), with the points joined in a time series. The form of the relationship is obscured by the obviously high variance, and the only certain relationship between the two variables is that it must pass through the origin.

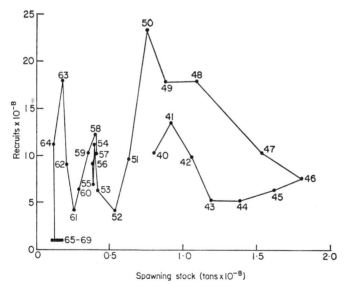

Fig. 5. Scatter diagram of the recruitment in relation to spawning stock size in named years for Arcto-Norwegian cod.

It is clear from Fig. 5 that the spawning stock of Arcto-Norwegian cod is now relatively very small indeed. A very productive fishery on the stock as a whole in 1968–1969 has been based upon the immature phase of two very good year-classes spawned in years of demonstrably favourable environmental conditions, 1963 and 1964. Surveys have shown that the subsequent year-classes of 1965–1969 are extremely poor, suggesting that recruitment is now being influenced by lack of egg production, and when these five year-classes grow to maturity in the mid-1970s the spawning stock could be fished down to an even lower level than the present one. It is therefore relevant to evaluate the possibility that the Arcto-Norwegian cod stock is entering a more prolonged period of below average recruitment.

The effects of this eventuality can be simulated in the model by reducing the recruitment to the stock in the Barents Sea, Norway coast and Bear Island fisheries to a lower level corresponding to that estimated for the 1965–1969 year-classes. The results are summarized in Table IIB for the two projected levels of overall fishing effort ($F = 0·6$ and $F = 0·8$). Comparing Series 3 and 6, at the lower level of effort, fishing would divert from the Arcto-Norwegian to other stocks, but the element of coastal fishing by vessels of restricted range would remain. Overall catches would fall substantially owing to the reduction of yield from the Arcto-Norwegian stock, and catch per unit effort would fall owing to the reduction in the abundance of these and other stocks to which fishing effort would be diverted. At the higher level of effort, obtained by projecting the 1955–1969 trend through to 1975 (Series 7), the increased intensity of fishing caused by diversion to the north-west Atlantic would reduce the catch per unit effort in those stocks so that even in its depleted condition the Arcto-Norwegian stock would regain some of its attraction, and effort there would return towards the level which may have led to the initial decline in recruitment. Thus, in principle, at higher levels of effort accompanied by limited recruitment failure, the relative abundance between stocks can be re-established at a lower level of stock abundance and yield. These simulations illustrate the interaction between biologically separate stocks that follows from the degree of mobility of international fishing fleets, and emphasize the importance of research to determine the significance or otherwise of the stock/recruitment relationship.

### CONCLUDING REMARKS

Although the final simulations described imply a possible deterioration of the cod fisheries this should not be interpreted as a prediction for the coming decade. The model is not exact and can only illustrate principles and the implications of continued increase in the amount of fishing. It is perhaps a hopeful sign that the fishing effort data illustrated in Fig. 2 suggest a reduction in the rate of expansion in recent years.

This, however, does not negate the implications of the existing situation in the Arcto-Norwegian stock to the productivity of the north Atlantic cod fisheries as a whole, as implied by Simulation Series 6.

One obvious alternative to regulation of the amount of fishing is the voluntary diversion of existing fleet capacity to other resources within and beyond the north Atlantic basin. Prospects for this are not good although there are other resources in the north Atlantic, both at the same depth (particularly coalfish), and on the deepening edge of the continental shelf. The USSR has carried out the most intensive exploratory research in this field, with results which encouraged them to divert a part of their north-west Atlantic fleet to fish for silver hake, haddock and herring during the mid-1960s. It was this change in fishery objective that is presumed to have led to the reduction in USSR fishing effort in the cod fisheries in the period 1963–1968 (Fig. 2). However, it appears that these alternative resources have become rapidly depleted, with a consequent reversion of some USSR effort back into the cod fishery. Beyond the north Atlantic basin other countries, including some fishing in the north Atlantic, are already exploiting comparable resources in the south Atlantic to a significant level. This does not augur well for the alternative resource solution to the problem.

From the biologist's point of view, the desirability of finding some acceptable means of regulating fishing effort remains paramount. International research of recent years has shown that almost every major resource of fish for direct human consumption in the north Atlantic besides cod is also being fully exploited. Though the sustainable yield and the amount of fishing associated with it may vary between resources, the fishing capacity necessary to secure this maximum already exists, and if one or more resources suffer severe depletion, then the fleets must necessarily intensify their activity on new resources, or others that are already fully exploited.

Redeployment between stocks of the same or different species can sustain total production for a time, but in the longer term it aggravates the situation in the area to which effort is diverted, especially when, as now, this is already fully exploited. Sustained production in the mobile effort situation depends on the recovery of the resource that has been temporarily abandoned. This may take place rapidly if adequate protection is given to prevent the premature return of effort but, as has been shown for cod, if the available effort is greater than the total required to generate the optimum level of effort on every stock, a proportion of fishing may return before recovery is complete. Economic conditions could eventually dictate the final level of fishing effort but it is doubtful if this could result in production as efficient as could be achieved by management.

Even given a solution to the management problems it is evident that U.K. supplies of fish for human consumption from traditional distant-water resources are unlikely to increase in the long term. We must therefore look to the efficient use of our own near-water and coastal resources to help ensure the present level of self-sufficiency of fish production against any increase in demand that might be anticipated. So far as the biological aspects of resource management are concerned, present techniques provide guidance to manipulate a given level of recruitment to the best advantage. But, as implied by the simulations described, recruitment itself is potentially a much greater source of variation, yet our understanding of the processes governing recruitment is in its infancy. The mechanisms determining the growth and survival of larval and very young fish, and of other marine resources, appear to provide the most direct link between primary production and the biological production currently utilized by man. These vulnerable stages of the life history of both offshore and inshore stocks of marine invertebrates, as well as vertebrates, frequently occur in coastal waters. There they are susceptible to pollution and competition with alternative uses of the coastal environment. At the same time their location may render them more amenable to positive management designed to augment the resources.

SUMMARY

The problems of conservation and management of fishery resources show many features in common, regardless of the species involved. These are illustrated by a review of the current status of the north Atlantic cod resources which largely determine the amount and distribution of international fishing in the area. The north Atlantic cod fisheries have gradually intensified since 1946, with a geographical progression from the north-east to the north-west Atlantic accompanied by increasing technological sophistication and mobility of the fleets involved. This development has reduced the abundance of the resources and management responsible for both these and other resources is now concerned to find a method of controlling the amount of fishing.

The development of the fisheries has been simulated in a dynamic mathematical model which was then used to investigate the implications of different management strategies. It is shown that the existing level of fishing effort is slightly above an Atlantic-wide optimum but that there is a geographical imbalance which has caused some north-east Atlantic stocks to be severely over-exploited in recent years. It is also shown that even at the present level of fishing the resources may be vulnerable to biological overfishing.

It is concluded that, irrespective of likely future management measures, U.K. supplies of fish from traditional distant-water resources are unlikely to be increased in the long term, and it is therefore important to investigate closely the population mechanisms, particularly recruitment, that govern the size and potential production of U.K. near-water and coastal resources.

## REFERENCES

Beverton, R. J. H. (1963). Maturation, growth and mortality of clupeid and engraulid stocks in relation to fishing. *Rapp. P.-v. Réun. Cons. perm. int. Explor. Mer* **154**: 44–67.

Beverton, R. J. H. & Holt, S. J. (1957). On the dynamics of exploited fish populations. *Fishery Invest., Lond.* (2), **19**, 533 pp.

Clayden, A. D. (in press). Simulation of the changes in abundance of the cod (*Gadus morhua* L.) and the distribution of fishing effort in the north Atlantic. *Fishery Invest., Lond.* (2), **27**.

Cushing, D. H. (in press). Stock and recruitment and the problem of density dependence. *Rapp. P.-v. Réun. Cons. perm. int. Explor. Mer.*

Garrod, D. J. (1968). Stock and recruitment relationships in four north Atlantic cod stocks. *ICES C.M.* 1968/F: 14 6 pp. (mimeo).

Garrod, D. J. (in press). The variation of replacement and survival in some fish stocks. *Rapp. P.-v. Réun. Cons. perm. int. Explor. Mer.*

Gulland, J. A. (1968a). The concept of marginal yield from exploited fish stocks *J. Cons. perm. int. Explor. Mer* **32**: 256–261.

Gulland, J. A. (1968b). The concept of maximum sustainable yield and fishery management. *FAO Fish. tech. Pap.*, No. 70, 13 pp.

Gulland, J. A. & Carroz, J. E. (1968). Management of fishery resources. *Adv. mar. Biol.* **6**: 1–71.

Horsted, Sv. A. & Garrod, D. J. (1969). A yield per recruit function for Subarea 1. Cod. *ICNAF Res. Doc.* 69/85, 5 pp. (mimeo).

ICES (1969). Northeast Atlantic: Nominal catches 1968. *ICES C.M.* 1969/D:7 45 pp. (mimeo).

ICES (1970). Report of the North-East Arctic Fisheries Working Group. *Coop. Res. Rep., Cons. perm. int. Explor. Mer*, Series A No. 16, 60 pp.

ICES (in press). Symposium on Stock and Recruitment. Univ. Aarhus, Denmark, 7–10 July 1970. *Rapp. P.-v. Réun. Cons. perm. int. Explor. Mer.*

ICNAF (1970). Statist. Bull. int. Commn NW. Atlant. Fish, Vol. 18, for the year 1968, 141 pp.

Organization for Economic Cooperation and Development (1965). Subsidies and other financial support to the fishing industries of OECD member countries. OECD, Paris, 252 pp.

Ponomarenko, V. P. (in press). On the probable relation between age composition of the spawning stock and abundance of cod year-classes in the Barents Sea. *Rapp. P.-v. Réun. Cons. perm. int. Explor. Mer.*

*Symp. zool. Soc. Lond.* (1972) No. 29, 185–201.

# LABORATORY STUDIES RELATED TO ZOOPLANKTON PRODUCTION IN THE SEA

## E. D. S. CORNER

*Marine Biological Association Laboratory, Plymouth, Devon, England*

SYNOPSIS

The question of how much particulate food has to be captured by zooplankton in order to provide a known amount of animal tissue is an important aspect of the general problem of zooplankton production in the sea and one that has given rise to numerous studies in the laboratory. The nature of these laboratory investigations is illustrated in the present account by examples drawn mainly from recent work with the Calanoid copepods. Particular emphasis is given to topics such as: possible food sources and the assimilation of food by the animals; factors affecting metabolic rates (measured in terms of oxygen uptake and the levels of nitrogen and phosphorus excreted); efficiencies with which different dietary materials are used by copepods for growth and egg-production; and total rations needed daily by the animals for growth and maintenance. Note is made of the relevance of the various laboratory findings to certain field studies and some attention given to possible ways in which zooplankton production in the sea could be affected by pollutants.

## INTRODUCTION

Innumerable studies have been made in the laboratory of topics such as the feeding and metabolism of zooplankton. But to illustrate the general lines of approach and some of the difficulties encountered, the present paper is mainly concerned with a particular group of animals— the Calanoid copepods—which are of central importance to the marine food web in many sea areas. One use of these laboratory studies has been to provide physiological data for use in mathematical models predicting zooplankton production in the sea; another has been to emphasize the danger of selecting "average" values for certain of these data (e.g. daily ration, respiration rate), which are now known to vary considerably in response to several different factors.

In dealing with these topics I shall try not to lose sight of the fact that the present Symposium is also concerned with the question of conservation, and will occasionally refer to the use of pollutants in laboratory studies which, preliminary as most of them are, seem relevant to certain aspects of zooplankton production.

## FOOD AND FEEDING

That various species of marine zooplankton feed on unicellular algae has been demonstrated in many laboratory studies (summarized by Corner & Cowey, 1968): in addition, an inverse relationship between the levels of zooplankton and phytoplankton has been observed in several sea areas where grazing by the animals seems to be the main factor reducing the plant population (Harvey, Cooper, Lebour & Russell, 1935; Riley, 1946; Curl, 1962; Cushing & Vućetić, 1963; Martin, 1965). However, laboratory studies have shown that the relationship between zooplankton and phytoplankton, in terms of grazing, is by no means straightforward.

Calanoid copepods can act as filter-feeders, passing a current of sea water through a sieve that retains particulate materials. However, the animals do not ingest these materials at a constant rate. For example, Mullin (1963), in laboratory studies of grazing by *Calanus hyperboreus*, found that the rate decreased with time up to 24 h. In addition, the daily volume of sea water swept clear varied inversely with the food level; and the number of plant cells ingested (or ration) increased at

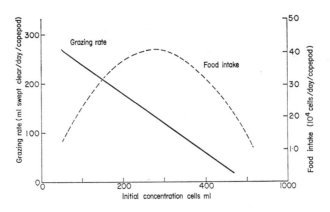

FIG. 1. Grazing by female *Calanus hyperboreus* on various concentrations of *Ditylum brightwellii*. (After Mullin, 1963.)

first with cell concentration but, after reaching a maximum, continuously decreased as progressively higher levels of food were used (Fig. 1). Similar results have been obtained with other species (Haq, 1967). However, although Mullin found that grazing rates increased as food concentrations diminished (the maximum value in experiments with *Ditylum brightwellii* as the food was found with a concentration of 50 cells/ml), others have observed that when the concentration of plant food falls below a certain threshold value, grazing stops (see Parsons, Le Brasseur, Fulton & Kennedy, 1969). This finding (which illustrates one difference between the feeding behaviour of zooplankton and that of

fish) is regarded by Adams & Steele (1966) as having important ecological significance in reducing the grazing mortality of the phytoplankton.

A further aspect of zooplankton behaviour that affects phytoplankton production is that of vertical migration: thus, the animals, by
feeding near the surface of the sea mainly at night, are thought to
allow the phytoplankton sufficient time by day to increase the standing
stock (Petipa & Makarova, 1969). McAllister (1970) has recently
described some interesting laboratory findings which show that estimates of secondary production from field data are markedly different
depending on which period of grazing is assumed, the growth rate of
animals feeding only at night being over twice that of continuous
feeders.

Laboratory studies have shown that when phytoplankton is absent,
or present in only small amounts, copepods can make use of alternative
sources of food, eating other copepods for example (Anraku & Omori,
1963). Indeed, Mullin (1966), investigating 19 species of Calanoid
copepod from the Indian Ocean, found that all consumed animal food
at least as readily as they fed on phytoplankton, and several ate animal
food only.

A third possible source of food for zooplankton is marine detritus.
The fact that animals are able to capture this material has long been
known from examination of the gut contents and from the finding that
faecal pellets are produced by animals feeding on intractable materials
such as Indian ink (Marshall & Orr, 1952), polystyrene pellets (Paffenhöfer & Strickland, 1970) and emulsified droplets of fuel oil (M. F.
Spooner, pers. comm.). In some coastal areas, detritus includes very
fine particles of sand and mica released into the sea from china-clay
works. No study seems to have been made of the effect of this unnatural
detritus on zooplankton production in these areas, but there is little
doubt that it would interfere with the process of filter-feeding.

Compared with the large body of evidence showing that many plant
and animal diets are valuable as foods for zooplankton, the nutritive
value of detrital diets has yet to be adequately demonstrated. True,
Baylor & Sutcliffe (1963) have shown that detritus obtained from sea
water by the action of rising bubbles has some nutritive value for
nauplii of *Artemia salina*; but the animals did not develop as well as did
controls fed on yeast or marine algae, and no attempt was made to see
whether the detritus contained dietary factors needed to support
reproduction. Recently, E. I. Butler, E. D. S. Corner, S. M. Marshall
and A. P. Orr (unpublished observations) have used several forms of
particulate material, including detritus, as foods for *C. finmarchicus*;

but the only diets of nutritive value in terms of supporting egg production and maintaining body weight were microzooplankton and the faecal pellets released by *Calanus* when feeding on diatoms.

The various laboratory studies so far outlined are relevant to investigations of the phytoplankton/zooplankton relationship in the sea. For example, because grazing rates vary with concentration and type of food, zooplankton cannot be assumed to ingest a constant daily ration when feeding on changing levels and mixtures of plant food in the sea: to which extent, some mathematical models incorporating this assumption have been in error (see Mullin, 1963). Again, laboratory experiments demonstrating that zooplankton can feed on different kinds of particulate material emphasize that estimates of secondary production should not be based on the assumption that all the animals are herbivorous. Thus, after a spring diatom flowering, the population of animals may have increased and that of the plants may have decreased to a point where omnivorous or even carnivorous feeding is predominant. In addition, laboratory findings indicating that microzooplankton are of much greater nutritive value than detritus as food for copepods suggest that carnivorous feeding may help these animals to survive the winter in sea areas where plant food is virtually absent at that time of year. However, other factors are involved, among which are the utilization of body reserves and a reduction in metabolic rate (Butler, Corner & Marshall, 1970).

## METABOLIC RATE

Calculations of the food requirements of copepods in the sea have frequently incorporated data obtained in laboratory studies of respiration rate (see review by Mullin, 1969), and the value selected can greatly influence estimates of secondary production (McAllister, 1970). It is therefore important to recognize that respiration rates can vary considerably in response to many different factors. For example, work by Petipa (1966) illustrates how these values change with the development of a particular species—in this case, the planktonic copepod *Acartia clausi* (Table I). In terms of body weight, heavier animals respire at rates lower than those of lighter animals of the same species, the relationship for *A. clausi* being $Q = 0.437\ W^{0.811}$, where $Q$ is respiration rate and $W$ is body weight. Estimating the effect of body weight on the respiration rate of a mixed population of zooplankton would be more straightforward if, for example, the value of 0.811 applied to all species; but Conover (1968) quotes values ranging from 0.66 to 1.14 and Haq (1967), studying respiration by *Metridia* spp., obtained values of only 0.37 to 0.48.

Metabolic rates are not always determined in terms of oxygen uptake: in some studies, rates of nitrogen and phosphorus excretion

TABLE I

*Changes in metabolic rate with stage of development. Data for oxygen consumption from Petipa (1966); for nitrogen excretion from Corner et al., 1967; for phosphorus excretion from Hargrave & Geen (1968). Oxygen consumption by A.* clausi *is related to body weight by the expression* $Q = 0.437 \ W^{0.811}$

| Species | Stage | | |
|---|---|---|---|
| (a) Oxygen uptake ($\mu$l/mg dry weight/h) | | | |
| *Acartia clausi* | NI–CIII | CIV–CV | Adults |
| | 6·0 | 5·3 | 2·6 |
| (b) Nitrogen excretion ($\mu$g/mg body N/h) | | | |
| *Calanus finmarchicus* | NI–CIII | CIV–CV | Adults |
| | 14·6 | 2·4 | 2·0 |
| (c) Phosphorus excretion ($\mu$g/mg body weight/day) | | | |
| *Acartia tonsa* | NI–NVI | CII–CIV | CV–CVI |
| | 13·9 | 12·7 | 10·2 |

have been used. It might be argued that whereas oxygen uptake is a true measure of metabolic rate, the amounts of nitrogen and phosphorus excreted by the animals could include soluble substances released with faecal material. However, recent evidence (see review by Corner & Davies, 1971) indicates that this is not so: the nitrogen and phosphorus excretions represent end-products of metabolism. Certainly, rates of nitrogen and phosphorus excretion are related to body weight in the same way as oxygen uptake, heavier animals excreting less nitrogen and phosphorus in terms of body weight than lighter animals of the same species (Corner, Cowey & Marshall, 1965, 1967; Hargrave & Geen, 1968).

There is some evidence that small, pelagic copepods with high metabolic rates are particularly sensitive to toxic agents in the sea (Corner & Sparrow, 1956; Marine Biological Association Report, 1968). If this proves to be generally true, then conceivably the introduction of small concentrations of harmful substances into a particular sea area may, by selectively eliminating the small and active members of the population, change the whole nature of secondary production. More detailed toxicity work using zooplankton animals of different body weights and metabolic rates may shed further light on this aspect of pollution.

Other factors influencing zooplankton metabolism that have been studied in the laboratory are temperature, pressure, food level and season of year. Work by Marshall, Nicholls & Orr (1935) has shown that the respiration rate of *C. finmarchicus* roughly doubles with a 10°

TABLE II

*Respiration rates of* Calanus finmarchicus *at different temperatures. (Data from Marshall* et al., *1935)*

| Temp. (°C) | Respiration rate (ml $O_2$/1000 animals/h) | | |
|---|---|---|---|
| | Stage V | ♀♀ | ♂♂ |
| 5 | 0·17 | 0·31 | 0·26 |
| 10 | 0·25 | 0·40 | 0·38 |
| 15 | 0·46 | 0·57 | 0·61 |
| 20 | 0·61 | 0·83 | 0·99 |

rise in temperature within the range normally found in the sea (see Table II); and in a study by Corner *et al.* (1965) a similar trend was found in terms of nitrogen excretion. On the other hand, as far as the effects of hydrostatic pressure are concerned, studies seem to have been made only with euphausiids (Teal & Carey, 1967; Pearcy & Small, 1968) and the results in general support the view that respiration rates do not markedly vary throughout the range of pressures normally encountered by these animals in the sea.

Concerning food level, experiments carried out with *C. hyperboreus* in spring showed that the respiration rates of actively feeding animals were nearly 40% higher than those of starved controls (Conover & Corner, 1968); similarly, the rate of nitrogen excretion by *C. finmarchicus* was found to increase when the animals fed on greater concentrations of various unicellular algae (Fig. 2: Corner *et al.*, 1965). The respiration rate of these animals varies considerably with the season of the year (Cowey & Corner, 1963) and recently it has been shown that seasonal variations in their nitrogen and phosphorus excretion roughly correspond to changes in levels of plant food in the sea (Fig. 3: Butler *et al.*, 1970).

The release of considerable amounts of organic nitrogen as amino acids by zooplankton has been reported (Webb & Johannes, 1967);

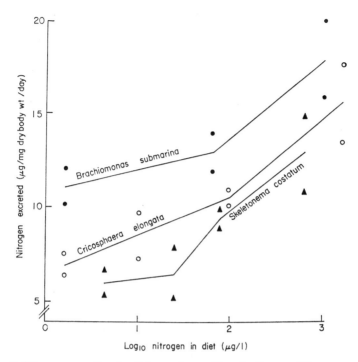

Fig. 2. Nitrogen excretion by *Calanus finmarchicus* feeding on different concentrations of three algae. (From Corner *et al.*, 1965.)

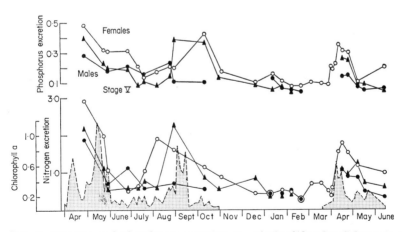

Fig. 3. Nitrogen and phosphorus excretion as μg/animal/day by *Calanus* in the Clyde sea area between April, 1968 and June, 1969. Stippled areas show chlorophyll "a" in 5 litres of sea water as $E^{005}_{1cm}$ in a 10 ml acetone extract. (From Butler *et al.*, 1070.)

and, in a study using *C. finmarchicus*, it was observed that high levels of amino-nitrogen, in addition to ammonia, were released by these animals in response to overcrowding (Corner & Newell, 1967). Relevant here, perhaps, is the fact that another form of stress, heavy-metal poisoning, can also cause an increased loss of nitrogen as amino acids by larger crustacea (Corner, 1959). True, this particular problem has not yet been studied with zooplankton; but an increased loss of important body constituents, such as amino acids, in response to toxic substances is certainly a possible way in which small concentrations of heavy metals could influence zooplankton production in the sea.

For zooplankton, the atomic ratio oxygen consumed : nitrogen excreted (O : N ratio) shows considerable variation with season (Conover & Corner, 1968), values changing with the type of material being oxidized by the animals. Thus, Harris (1959) found an average value of 7·7 for mixed zooplankton in Long Island Sound at a time of year when the animals—mainly *Acartia* spp.—were having to compete for plant food (Conover, 1956). This low value implied that protein was the material being utilized when food was scarce, and similar findings have been made with other species of zooplankton (Cowey & Corner, 1963; Linford, 1965). On the other hand, when food is plentiful in the sea, O : N ratios can rise considerably, an average value of 31·1 being found for *C. hyperboreus* during spring (Conover & Corner, 1968), probably reflecting the fact that lipid was being used as a substrate.

The fact that the metabolic rates of zooplankton vary with body weight, stage of development, species, food level and temperature (and the further fact that there are seasonal variations in the materials oxidized—moreover, seasonal variations that are more marked with some species than with others) increases the difficulty of selecting a realistic value for the respiration rate of a mixed population of the animals in order, say, to calculate their daily rations of food in the sea. There is also the process of vertical migration by zooplankton which, according to Petipa (1967), can increase the energy expended in metabolism by animals in the sea to more than 30 times that of those kept in the laboratory. Petipa's (1967) conclusions were based on changes in lipid content, estimated from the difference in volume of the oil-sacs of animals captured at the surface just before the downward migration at dawn, and those caught at depths just after this migration had been completed. While the ingenuity of the method has been praised, there are reservations about its precision (Mullin, 1969). Possibly, chemical analyses of vertically migrating zooplankton might help to shed light on this important aspect of the general problem.

## ASSIMILATION OF FOOD

Apart from losses associated with metabolism, the quantity of captured food finally invested in growth by zooplankton depends upon the percentage that is digested and assimilated (i.e. the assimilation efficiency). The first laboratory measurements of this were those of Marshall & Orr (1955a) using *C. finmarchicus* fed numerous algal diets labelled with radioactive phosphorus. The values found were notably high, always being greater than 50% and usually more than 80%. Later experiments (Marshall & Orr, 1955b) using $^{14}C$ instead of $^{32}P$ as a label also gave high values, as did studies of assimilation efficiency in terms of dietary nitrogen (Corner et al., 1967) as well as natural particulate material (Corner, 1961). Average values of 70% or more have also been obtained for other species, notably *Temora longicornis* (Berner, 1962), *C. hyperboreus* (Conover, 1966) and *Metridia lucens* (Haq, 1967).

In general, these studies have shown that, within the range of food concentrations normally encountered in the sea, the assimilation efficiencies of copepods are high. Further evidence of this has recently been obtained in studies using *Calanus* spp. taken from the Clyde sea area during the spring diatom flowering (Butler et al., 1970). Metabolic rates, in terms of the quantities of nitrogen and phosphorus excreted, rose to nearly three times the average winter level (Fig. 3), yet the percentage of dietary nitrogen assimilated was calculated to be 60% and that of dietary phosphorus nearly 80%.

## GROWTH EFFICIENCY

Of particular relevance to studies of secondary productivity in the sea is the recent development of methods by which several species of Calanoid copepod have been successfully reared in the laboratory (Zillioux & Wilson, 1966; Corkett, 1967; Mullin & Brooks, 1967) and direct measurements made of growth rates under different environmental conditions. For example, it has now been shown how growth rates increase with temperature (Mullin & Brooks, 1967) and vary with both quality and quantity of algal diet (Paffenhöfer, 1969; Mullin & Brooks, 1970). The availability of certain zooplankton organisms in culture also facilitates investigation of how very low concentrations of various pollutants affect the growth of the animals, a study that so far seems to have been confined to nauplii of the barnacle *Elminius modestus* (Corner, Southward and Southward, 1968) but could now be extended to include several zooplankton species.

The percentage of captured food invested in growth is defined as the gross growth efficiency and is usually given the symbol $K_1$ (see Conover, 1968). In laboratory studies with copepods, this value has been expressed in terms of a particular dietary constituent such as nitrogen (Corner *et al.*, 1967) or phosphorus (Butler *et al.*, 1969, 1970); or as calories (Petipa, 1967). The data obtained, summarized in Table III, show that gross growth efficiency in terms of egg production is lower than that calculated for growth from egg to adult; but possibly this is because the number of eggs laid may have been seriously underestimated. It is also clear that gross growth efficiency in terms of one dietary constituent can be different from that in terms of another: for example, $K_1$ values for phosphorus are less than those for nitrogen (Butler *et al.*, 1969, 1970), reflecting the fact that although the assimilation efficiency of dietary phosphorus is greater than that of dietary nitrogen, higher proportions of body phosphorus are metabolized daily. It follows that high values for gross growth efficiency will be obtained for dietary constituents that are easily assimilated but not readily metabolized by the animals. A natural product that comes within this category is the plant compound phytol, which accumulates as pristane in the animals in proportion to the quantity of phytoplankton ingested (Blumer, Mullin & Thomas, 1963a,b): "unnatural" products are pesticides such as DDT and certain mercury compounds (see review by Korringa, 1968), although it should be noted that mercury is, in fact, slowly excreted by at least one species of zooplankton with a high metabolic rate (Corner & Rigler, 1958). Mammals are known to metabolize a wide variety of toxic substances—including certain polycyclic hydrocarbons and phenols found in fuel oil (see, for example, Corner & Young, 1955) and it would be interesting to know to what extent, if any, zooplankton may share this ability.

### DAILY RATION

The quantity of food ingested daily by a copepod, as percentage body weight, has been determined in laboratory experiments as the sum of the amounts used for growth (or egg production) and metabolism, together with the quantity unassimilated. If these daily rations were fairly standard for all the animals in a natural population, calculations of the total plant food consumed daily by the population would be straightforward. However, laboratory studies indicate that even within one group of zooplankton animals daily rations can change in response to a number of factors. For example, the data in Table IV show how the daily rations vary with stage of development for two species of

## TABLE III

### Gross growth efficiencies ($K_1$ values) for Calanoid copepods

| Stage | A. clausi (calories) | C. helgolandicus (calories) | C. finmarchicus (nitrogen) | C. finmarchicus (phosphorus) | R. nasutus (carbon) |
|---|---|---|---|---|---|
| Nauplius → adult | 16·1 | 29·5 | 33·1 | 28·3 | 35 |
| Egg production | 1·8 | 2·0 | 14 | — | — |
| Spring weight increase (V's and adults) | — | — | 26·8 | 17·2 | — |

Data for A. clausi and C. helgolandicus from Petipa, 1967: average values. Data for C. finmarchicus from Corner et al., 1967 and Butler et al., 1969, 1970. Data for R. nasutus from Mullin & Brooks (1970): average values.

## TABLE IV

### Daily rations as percentage body calories for the different stages of two species of copepod (data from Petipa, 1967)

| | N2 | C1 | C2 | Stage C3 | C4 | C5 | ♀♀ (eggs) |
|---|---|---|---|---|---|---|---|
| Acartia clausi | 148·1 | 125·5 | 110·4 | 106·1 | 85·9 | 72·6 | 66·0 |
| Calanus helgolandicus | 18·5 | 42·2 | 57·1 | 78·0 | 103·2 | 115·6 | 138·4 |

copepod (Petipa, 1967). In these experiments, growth was estimated from the weights and durations of the various stages; but, whereas the respiration of *Acartia* was measured directly, that of *Calanus* was calculated from the quantity of lipid utilized by animals vertically migrating in the sea (see page 192). The difference between the two sets of data is striking; but may to some extent reflect the unreliability of the second method.

TABLE V

*Daily rations as percentage body carbon of* Rhincalanus nasutus *feeding at two different temperatures*

| Food | Temp. (°C) | Rations of different stages | | |
|------|------------|------------|------------|------------|
| | | (Nl → Cl) | (Cl → C4) | (C4 → Adult) |
| *Thalassiosira* | 10 | 59·0 | 27·2 | 24·0 |
| | 15 | 71·4 | 68·7 | 45·0 |
| *Ditylum* | 10 | 46·1 | 45·1 | 23·5 |
| | 15 | 164·0 | 68·7 | 35·4 |

(Calculated from data of Mullin & Brooks, 1970.)

Further examples of laboratory estimates of daily rations (Table V), calculated from the data of Mullin & Brooks (1970), illustrate how the ration is greater at higher temperatures (reflecting increased rates of growth and metabolism) and varies with diet. Further data, obtained by Butler *et al.* (1970), are summarized in Table VI and show how the

TABLE VI

*Daily rations (as percentage body N and percentage body P) of* Calanus finmarchicus *feeding on natural particulate material in the Clyde sea area*

| Time of year | Sea tempera-ture (°C) | Stage | Daily ration | |
|------|------|------|------|------|
| | | | % Body N | % Body P |
| Spring | 6·7 | V's and young adults | 13·4 | 17·6 |
| Winter | 8·3 | V's | 4·5 | 8·0 |
| Winter | 8·3 | ♀♀ | 3·1 | 9·4 |

(Data from Butler *et al.*, 1970.)

daily ration varies with different dietary constituents (the phosphorus requirement is higher than the nitrogen) and seasons of year. Similar values have been found by Parsons *et al.* (1969) for the daily rations (in terms of body weight) used by several species of zooplankton feeding on natural populations of phytoplankton from the Strait of Georgia. In six of the experiments the daily ration was in the range 4·0 to 20·2% body weight, although in two further instances higher values (45% and 60%) were found.

Compared with these laboratory findings, daily rations estimated in certain field studies have sometimes been very large. For example, Cushing (1964) quotes a value of 370% body weight per day for Stage V *Calanus* during a spring diatom flowering in the North Sea, a value so much in excess of the daily requirements for growth and metabolism as to imply that much of the algal food was being uselessly destroyed. The idea that zooplankton feed "superfluously" was put forward by Beklemishev (1957, 1962), who claimed that during a spring diatom increase the animals would assimilate only a relatively small fraction of the food they captured. This view has not been upheld by the results of numerous laboratory studies of food assimilation using Calanoid copepods (see p. 193). However, an alternative view, expressed by Cushing & Vućetić (1963), holds that destruction of algae takes place outside the animal. Zooplankton that can make use of both plant and animal diets must be able to capture food material covering a wide range of sizes, and Marshall & Orr (1962) have described seeing frustules of very large cells of *Biddulphia sinensis* in the guts and faecal pellets of *C. finmarchicus* feeding on this species. On the other hand, examples of copepods breaking up large plant cells and ingesting only smaller fragments have also been reported (Cushing, 1955; Petipa, 1960: cited by Marshall & Orr, 1962). It is possible that the extent to which the animals feed in this way varies with both the level and type of food available; but, so far, laboratory studies have not provided any quantitative information.

CONCLUSIONS

In this brief account I have tried to outline laboratory studies that have supplied information relevant to field investigations of zooplankton production in the sea; and to show how great is the variation in the data in response to a number of different factors. Not least among these factors, of course, is the taxonomic composition of the zooplankton populations, and future work in this field should recognize the need to widen the range of representative zooplanktonic species for which physiological data are obtained. There also seems to be a case for further studies of vertical migration and algal spoliation in order to see whether these processes cause a very high daily ration to be needed by zooplankton in certain sea areas.

Although the various laboratory studies described in this paper are not directly related to the question of conservation, at least by complementing field investigations they may help towards a better understanding of the general principles of zooplankton production in the sea, and so provide a more reliable background for use in assessing the possible changes caused by pollution.

## REFERENCES

Adams, J. A. & Steele, J. H. (1966). Shipboard experiments on the feeding of *Calanus finmarchicus* (Gunnerus). In *Some contemporary studies in marine science:* 19–35. (Barnes, H., ed). George Allen & Unwin Ltd., London.

Anraku, M. & Omori, M. (1963). Preliminary survey of the relationship between the feeding habit and the structure of the mouth parts of marine copepods. *Limnol. Oceanogr.* 8: 116–126.

Baylor, E. R. & Sutcliffe, W. H. Jr. (1963). Dissolved organic matter in seawater as a source of particulate food. *Limnol. Oceanogr.* 8: 369–371.

Beklemishev, C. W. (1957). Superfluous feeding of the zooplankton and the problem of sources of food for bottom animals. *Trud. vsesoyuz. gidrobiol. Obshch.* 8: 354–358.

Beklemishev, C. W. (1962). Superfluous feeding of marine herbivorous zooplankton. *Rapp. P.-v. Réun. Cons. perm. int. Explor. Mer* 153: 108–113.

Berner, A. (1962). Feeding and respiration in the copepod *Temora longicornis* (Muller). *J. mar. biol. Ass. U.K.* 42: 625–640.

Blumer, M., Mullin, M. M. & Thomas, D. W. (1963a). Pristane in zooplankton. *Science, N.Y.* 140: 974.

Blumer, M., Mullin, M. M. & Thomas, D. W. (1963b). Pristane in the marine environment. *Helgoländer wiss. Meeresunters.* 10: 187–201.

Butler, E. I., Corner, E. D. S. & Marshall, S. M. (1969). On the nutrition and metabolism of zooplankton. VI. Feeding efficiency of *Calanus* in terms of nitrogen and phosphorus. *J. Mar. biol. Ass. U.K.* 49: 977–1001.

Butler, E. I., Corner, E. D. S. & Marshall, S. M. (1970). On the nutrition and metabolism of zooplankton. VII. Seasonal survey of nitrogen and phosphorus excretion by *Calanus* in the Clyde sea area. *J. mar. biol. Ass. U.K.* 50: 525–560.

Conover, R. J. (1966). Factors affecting the assimilation of organic matter by zooplankton and the question of superfluous feeding. *Limnol. Oceanogr.* 11: 346–354.

Conover, R. J. (1968). Zooplankton – life in a nutritionally dilute environment. *Am. Zool.* 8: 107–118.

Conover, R. J. & Corner, E. D. S. (1968). Respiration and nitrogen excretion by some marine zooplankton in relation to their life cycles. *J. mar. biol. Ass. U.K.* 48: 49–75.

Conover, S. A. M. (1956). Oceanography of Long Island Sound, 1952-1954. IV. Phytoplankton. *Bull. Bingham Oceanogr. Coll.* **15**: 62–112.

Corkett, C. J. (1967). Technique for rearing marine calanoid copepods in laboratory conditions. *Nature, Lond.* **216**: 58–59.

Corner, E. D. S. (1959). The poisoning of *Maia squinado* (Herbst) by certain compounds of mercury. *Biochem. Pharmac.* **2**: 121–132.

Corner, E. D. S. (1961). On the nutrition and metabolism of zooplankton. I. Preliminary observations on the feeding of the marine copepod, *Calanus helgolandicus* (Claus). *J. mar. biol. Ass. U.K.* **41**: 5–16.

Corner, E. D. S. & Young, L. (1955). Biochemical studies of toxic agents. 8. 1:2-Dihydronaphthalene-1:2-Diol and its role in the metabolism of naphthalene. *Biochem. J.* **61**: 132–141.

Corner, E. D. S. & Sparrow, B. W. P. (1956). The modes of action of toxic agents. I. Observations on the poisoning of certain crustaceans by copper and mercury. *J. mar. biol. Ass. U.K.* **35**: 531–548.

Corner, E. D. S. & Rigler, F. H. (1958). The modes of action of toxic agents. III. Mercuric chloride and *N*-Amylmercuric chloride on crustaceans. *J. mar. biol. Ass. U.K.* **37**: 85–96.

Corner, E. D. S. & Newell, B. S. (1967). On the nutrition and metabolism of zooplankton. IV. The forms of nitrogen excreted by *Calanus*. *J. mar. biol. Ass. U.K.* **47**: 113–120.

Corner, E. D. S. & Cowey, C. B. (1968). Biochemical studies on the production of marine zooplankton. *Biol. Rev.* **43**: 393–426.

Corner, E. D. S. & Davies, A. G. (1971). Plankton as a factor in the nitrogen and phosphorus cycles in the sea. *Adv. mar. Biol.* **9**: 101–204.

Corner, E. D. S., Cowey, C. B. & Marshall, S. M. (1965). On the nutrition and metabolism of zooplankton. III. Nitrogen excretion by *Calanus*. *J. mar. biol. Ass. U.K.* **45**: 429–442.

Corner, E. D. S., Cowey, C. B. & Marshall, S. M. (1967). On the nutrition and metabolism of zooplankton. V. Feeding efficiency of *Calanus finmarchicus*. *J. mar. biol. Ass. U.K.* **47**: 259–270.

Corner, E. D. S., Southward, A. J. & Southward, E. C. (1968). Toxicity of oil-spill removers ("detergents") to marine life: an assessment using the intertidal barnacle *Elminius modestus*. *J. mar. biol. Ass. U.K.* **48**: 29–47.

Cowey, C. B. & Corner, E. D. S. (1963). On the nutrition and metabolism of zooplankton. II. The relationship between the marine copepod *Calanus helgolandicus* and particulate material in Plymouth sea water, in terms of amino acid composition. *J. mar. biol. Ass. U.K.* **43**: 495–511.

Curl, H. Jr. (1962). Standing crops of carbon, nitrogen, and phosphorus and transfer between trophic levels in Continental Shelf waters south of New York. *Rapp. P.-v. Réun. Cons. perm. int. Explor. Mer.* **153**: 183–189.

Cushing, D. H. (1955). Production and pelagic fishery. *Fish. Invest., Lond.*, (2) **18**, No. 7, 104 pp.

Cushing, D. H. (1964). The work of grazing in the sea. In *Grazing in terrestrial and marine environments*: 207–225. (Crisp, D. J., ed.). London: Blackwells Scientific Publications.

Cushing, D. H. & Vućetić, T. (1963). Studies on a *Calanus* patch. III. The quantity of food eaten by *Calanus finmarchicus*. *J. mar. biol. Ass. U.K.* **43**: 349–371.

Haq, S. M. (1967). Nutritional physiology of *Metridia lucens* and *Metridia longa* from the Gulf of Maine. *Limnol. Oceanogr.* **12**: 40–51.

Hargrave, B. T. & Geen, G. H. (1968). Phosphorous excretion by zooplankton. *Limnol. Oceanogr.* **13**: 332–342.

Harris, E. (1959). The nitrogen cycle in Long Island Sound. *Bull. Bingham oceanogr. Coll.* **17**: 31–65.

Harvey, H. W., Cooper, L. H. N., Lebour, M. V. & Russell, F. S. (1935). Plankton production and its control. *J. mar. biol. Ass. U.K.* **20**: 407–442.

Korringa, P. (1968). Biological consequences of marine pollution with special reference to the North Sea fisheries. *Helgoländer wiss. Meersunters.* **17**: 126–140.

Linford, E. (1965). Biochemical studies on marine zooplankton. II. Variations in the lipid content of some Mysidacea. *J. Cons. perm. int. Explor. Mer* **30**: 16–27.

Marine Biological Association (1968). *"Torrey Canyon" pollution and marine life.* (Smith, J. E. ed.). Cambridge: University Press.

Marshall, S. M. & Orr, A. P. (1952). On the biology of *Calanus finmarchicus*. VII. Factors affecting egg production. *J. mar. biol. Ass. U.K.* **30**: 527–548.

Marshall, S. M. & Orr, A. P. (1955a). On the biology of *Calanus finmarchicus*. VIII. Food uptake, assimilation and excretion in adult and stage V. *Calanus. J. mar. biol. Ass. U.K.* **34**: 495–529.

Marshall, S. M. & Orr, A. P. (1955b). Experimental feeding of the copepod *Calanus finmarchicus* (Gunner) on phytoplankton cultures labelled with radioactive carbon. *Pap. mar. Biol. and Oceanogr., Deep-Sea Res., Suppl. to Vol.* **3**: 110–114.

Marshall, S. M. & Orr, A. P. (1962). Food and feeding in copepods. *Rapp. P.-v. Réun. Cons. perm. int. Explor. Mer* **153**: 92–98.

Marshall, S. M., Nicholls, A. G. & Orr, A. P. (1935). On the biology of *Calanus finmarchicus*. VI. Oxygen consumption in relation to environmental conditions. *J. mar. biol. Ass. U.K.* **20**: 1–28.

Martin, J. H. (1965). Phytoplankton-zooplankton relationships in Narragansett Bay, *Limnol. Oceanogr.* **10**: 185–191.

McAllister, C. D. (1970). Zooplankton rations, phytoplankton mortality and the estimation of marine production. In *Marine food chains:* 419–457. (Steele, J. H., ed.). Edinburgh: Oliver and Boyd.

Mullin, M. M. (1963). Some factors affecting the feeding of marine copepods of the genus *Calanus. Limnol. Oceanogr.* **8**: 239–250.

Mullin, M. M. (1966). Selective feeding by calanoid copepods from the Indian Ocean. In *Some contemporary studies in marine science:* 543–554. (Barnes, H., ed.). London: George Allen and Unwin Ltd.

Mullin, M. M. (1969). Production of zooplankton in the ocean: the present status and problems. *Oceanogr. mar. Biol.* **7**: 293–314.

Mullin, M. M. & Brooks, E. R. (1967). Laboratory culture, growth rate and feeding behaviour of a planktonic marine copepod. *Limnol. Oceanogr.* **12**: 657–666.

Mullin, M. M. & Brooks, E. R. (1970). Growth and metabolism of two planktonic marine copepods, as influenced by temperature and type of food. In *Marine food chains:* 74–95. (Steele, J. H., ed.). Edinburgh: Oliver and Boyd.

Paffenhöfer, G-A. (1969). The cultivation of *Calanus helgolandicus* under controlled conditions. *Helgoländer wiss. Meersunters.* **20**: 346–359.

Paffenhöfer, G.-A. & Strickland, J. D. H. (1970). A note on the feeding of *Calanus helgolandicus* on detritus. *Mar. Biol.* **5**: 97–99.

Parsons, T. R., Le Brasseur, R. T., Fulton, J. D. & Kennedy, O. D. (1969). Production studies in the Strait of Georgia. Part II. Secondary production under the Fraser River Plume, February to May 1967. *J. exp. mar. biol. Ecol.* **3**: 39–50.

Pearcy, W. G. & Small, L. F. (1968). Effects of pressure on the respiration of vertically migrating crustaceans. *J. Fish. Res. Bd Can.* **25**: 1311–1316.

Petipa, T. S. (1966). Oxygen consumption and food requirements in the copepods *Acartia clausi* (Giesbrecht) and *A. latisebosa* (Kritcz). *Zool. Zh.* **45**: 363–370 (Min. of Ag., Fish. and Food Trans. No. NS.90).

Petipa, T. S. (1967). On the efficiency of utilization of energy in pelagic ecosystems of the Black Sea. In *Struktura i dinamika vodnykh soobshchestv i populyatsii*: 44–64 (Ser. Biologiya Morya) Acad. Sci. Ukraine, Naukova Dumka, Kiev (Fish. Res. Bd Can. Trans. No. 973).

Petipa, T. S. & Makarova, N. P. (1969). Dependence of phytoplanton production on rhythm and rate of elimination. *Mar. Biol.* **3**: 191–195.

Riley, G. A. (1946). Factors controlling phytoplankton populations of Georges Bank. *J. mar. Res.* **6**: 54–73.

Teal, J. M. & Carey, F. G. (1967). Effects of pressure and temperature on the respiration of euphausiids. *Deep-Sea Res.* **14**: 725–733.

Webb, K. L. & Johannes, R. E. (1967). Studies of the release of dissolved free amino acids by marine zooplankton. *Limnol. Oceanogr.* **12**: 376–382.

Zillioux, E. J. & Wilson, D. F. (1966). Culture of a planktonic copepod through multiple generations. *Science, N.Y.* **151**: 996–997.

*Symp. zool. Soc. Lond.* (1972) No. 29, 203–212.

# CHANGES IN THE DISTRIBUTION AND ABUNDANCE OF ZOOPLANKTON IN THE NORTH SEA, 1948–1969

## J. M. COLEBROOK

*Oceanographic Laboratory, Edinburgh, Scotland*

### SYNOPSIS

Data from the Continuous Plankton Recorder Survey have been used to provide information about the year-to-year fluctuations in the standing crops of the zooplankton of the North Sea for the period 1948–1969. A marked feature of the fluctuations has been a progressive change affecting the abundance, the timing of the seasonal cycle, and the pattern of the geographical distribution of a number of species. A number of examples are given.

There is some similarity between the form of this change and recent changes in climate. It is difficult, however, to establish any clear relationship because of the lack of ecologically orientated monitoring of the environment. The change is similar in form to changes likely to be produced in the plankton by increased pollution of the area. The need is stressed for detailed examination of year-to-year fluctuations in the plankton in order to differentiate between natural and man-induced effects.

The observed changes can also be used to estimate the time-lag involved in the detection of any future change induced by increased pollution. It is estimated that at least three years' data would be required to detect a change, and at least ten years' data would be needed to give any quantitative assessment of the magnitude of the change.

It is suggested that in view of these unsatisfactory long delays, the survey requirements needed to improve on them should be investigated and if possible implemented in those areas considered to be most at risk.

### INTRODUCTION AND MATERIAL

The plankton provides the first links in the food chain of the marine ecosystem. Studies of the long-term fluctuations in the abundance of plankton organisms are, therefore, important in relation to the conservation of marine resources. They can assist in the interpretation of fluctuations in the success of commercial fisheries, providing indications, for example, of whether those fluctuations are due to natural causes or to over-intensive exploitation. Studies on long-term fluctuations in the plankton can also provide information about some aspects of pollution, particularly eutrophication.

The Continuous Plankton Recorder (Hardy, 1939) has been used in a survey of the plankton of the North Sea in which samples have been collected in every single month since January, 1948 (Glover, 1962). The data derived from this survey provide excellent material for the study of long-term variations (Colebrook, 1966; Colebrook & Robinson, 1964).

In order to demonstrate the magnitude of year-to-year fluctuations in relation to geographical and seasonal variation and to differences between species, a four-factor analysis of variance has been carried out involving 13 species of zooplankton in 4 areas for 12 months and

TABLE I

*Variance ratios for the four main factors of an analysis of variance involving 13 species of zooplankton in 4 areas for 12 months and 22 years*

|  | Species | Months | Areas | Years |
|---|---|---|---|---|
| Variance ratio | 278·4 | 66·3 | 45·1 | 17·3 |

22 years. Table I shows the variance ratios, relative to the residual variance, for each of the four main factors, in each case summing the variances for all the sources of variation involving the factors. As

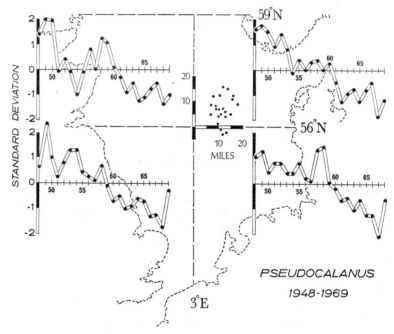

FIG. 1. Annual fluctuations in the abundance and distribution of *Pseudocalanus elongatus* in the North Sea, 1948–1969.

might be expected, differences between species provide the largest variance ratio; next come seasonal fluctuations, then geographical, and lastly year-to-year variations, with a ratio not much greater than one third of that for geographical variation.

This highlights one of the main problems of dealing with year-to-year variations, in that they are small in magnitude in relation to other sources of variability, and this leads to difficulties in the detection and identification of meaningful forms of variation.

Any plankton variable considered over a period of years can remain stable, or it can fluctuate in a random manner about a static mean, or it can change in a systematic way showing a clear pattern of variation in time. From many points of view change is the most interesting form of variation, and some examples of change are available from studies of the plankton data for the North Sea.

RESULTS

By far the most spectacular change has been a progressive reduction in the abundance of the copepod *Pseudocalanus elongatus,* which is illustrated in Fig. 1. The graphs show the fluctuations in the annual means, based on log-transformed data, for each quarter of the central and southern North Sea. The graphs are presented on a standardized scale, each having a mean of zero. In all four areas there has been an approximately linear decline in abundance, and in each area numbers are now about a quarter of what they were in the late forties. This represents a considerable change in what is numerically the most abundant copepod in the North Sea.

The scatter diagram shown in the centre of Fig. 1 indicates the location of the centre of gravity of the geographical distribution of *Pseudocalanus* in each year from 1948–1969. The scale of the graph is four times the scale of the chart, and it is obvious that in spite of the marked change in abundance, the geographical pattern has remained remarkably stable.

Figure 2 shows two diagrams demonstrating both seasonal and annual variations in abundance. To construct these diagrams the mean abundance for each month from January, 1948 to December, 1969 was entered in a month/year array, and contours were drawn around the values. In the original versions, four contours were drawn with the levels selected to give equal spacings between the contours. In these diagrams only the middle two contours are given, in order to emphasize the changes taking place during times of high rates of increase and decrease in abundance at the beginning and end of each season.

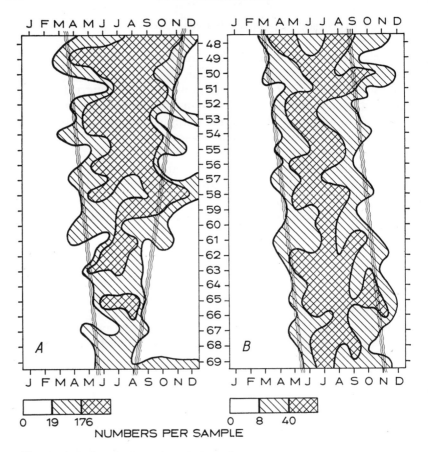

FIG. 2. Annual and seasonal variations in the abundance of (A) *Pseudocalanus elongatus* and (B) *Temora longicornis* in the south-west North Sea.

Figure 2*A* is for *Pseudocalanus* for the south-west area. It shows very clearly a progressive reduction in the length of the season, presumably associated with the reduction in abundance; at the same time, there is little or no indication of any marked change in the timing of the seasonal cycle. In contrast to this *Temora longicornis* (Fig. 2*B*) shows a progressive change in the timing of its occurrence, getting later by about six weeks over the 22 year period. There is, however, little or no change in its season duration. The annual fluctuations in abundance for *Temora* are given in Fig. 3. There is some indication of a reduction in abundance in the northern areas but not in the south. The scatter diagram in the centre of Fig. 3, showing the locations of the centres of gravity of the geographical distribution, indicates a southward and eastward shift in the sixties (indicated by 6's) compared with the late forties and fifties (indicated by 4's and 5's).

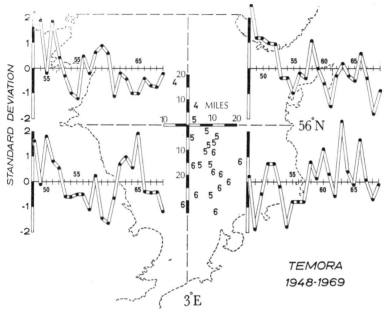

Fig. 3. Annual fluctuations in the abundance and distribution of *Temora longicornis* in the North Sea, 1948–1969.

There are other species which exhibit similar changes. Figure 4 shows changes in the seasonal cycle for the thecosome *Spiratella retroversa* and the copepod *Acartia clausii*. *Spiratella* shows a decline in abundance and a shortening of season duration similar to that of *Pseudocalanus*, while the main summer peak of *Acartia* shows a progressive change in timing similar to that for *Temora*. Figure 5 shows the annual fluctuations in abundance for *Acartia* in each quarter of the North Sea. The western quarters show some indication of a progressive increase in abundance, and the centre of gravity plot shows signs of a northward and westward shift in the centre of the geographical distribution. These are both opposite to the trends shown by *Temora*, in contrast to the similarity of change in the seasonal distribution of *Temora* and *Acartia*, demonstrated in Figs 2 and 4.

These are selected examples from a considerable mass of evidence supporting the conclusion that in the North Sea over the last 22 years

an approximately linear change has taken place, affecting abundance
and/or timing and/or distribution for a number of species.

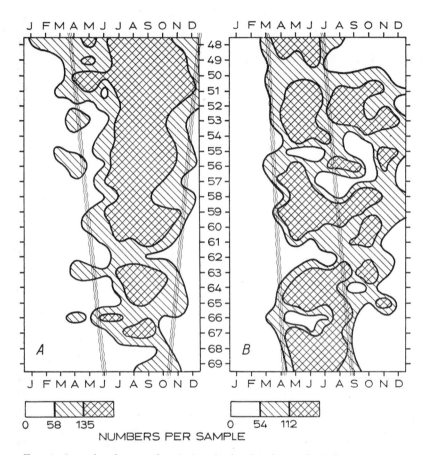

Fig. 4. Annual and seasonal variations in the abundance of (A) *Spiratella retroversa*
in the north-west North Sea and (B) *Acartia clausii* in the south-east North Sea.

Not all species show the change. Figure 6 shows the monthly fluctuations of the copepod *Calanus* in the two western quarters of the
North Sea. In the north, the timing of the spring increase shows a
remarkable degree of stability, in the south the variation is much
greater but there is no convincing indication of any progressive change.
This geographical differentiation is closely paralleled by the phytoplankton and is almost certainly due to the fact that in the northern

area a clear thermocline is formed during the summer, whereas in the south there is little or no thermal stratification at any time during the year.

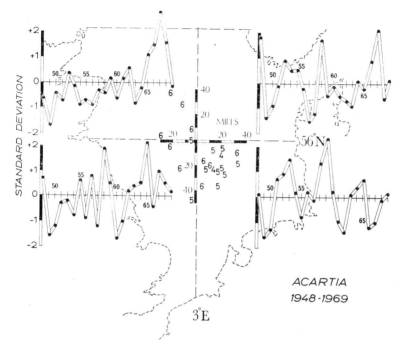

Fig. 5. Annual fluctuations in the abundance and distribution of *Acartia clausii* in the North Sea, 1948–1969.

## DISCUSSION

The general situation with regard to year-to-year variations in the zooplankton of the North Sea is obviously rather confusing, but a dominant pattern of linear change with time can be detected in a number of species. This, however, appears to be distributed in an apparently haphazard way, showing marked differences between species with regard to the form and distribution of the change. As was pointed out earlier, year-to-year variation accounts for a relatively small proportion of the total variability, and it is very probable that a number of examples of the change are obscured by the background of error variation. This is suggested quite forcefully by the results of Principal Component Analyses (see for example, Colebrook, 1964) applied to the annual fluctuations in abundance for the species occurring in each area.

H

The first components for each of the four areas (Fig. 7) all show the linear change fairly clearly. Of the species included in the analyses only the cladocera *Evadne* and *Podon* had low vector values in all the areas. The remaining 15 species all showed reasonably strong relationships with the components in one or more of the areas.

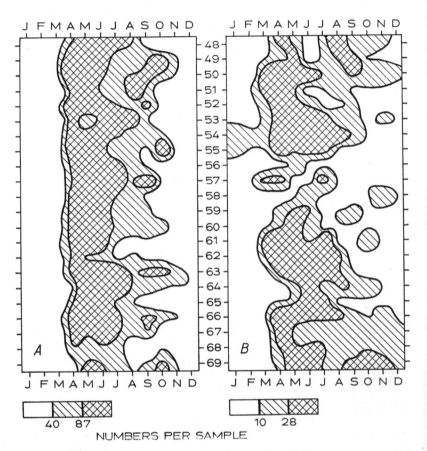

Fig. 6. Annual and seasonal variations in the abundance of *Calanus* spp. in (*A*) the north-west and (*B*) the south-west North Sea.

Attempts have been made to carry out similar analyses on estimates of timing and season duration, but so far they have not been very successful.

The kinds of year-to-year variation shown by the plankton are obviously important from the point of view of conservation, which, as well as relating to fisheries, also involves the detection and identification of the effects of pollution. In the open waters of the North Sea, it seems very likely that some forms of pollution, for example the accumulation of toxic substances or progressive eutrophication, could generate fluctuations similar in nature to the linear change in abundance, timing and distribution of zooplankton which has been taking place over the last 22 years.

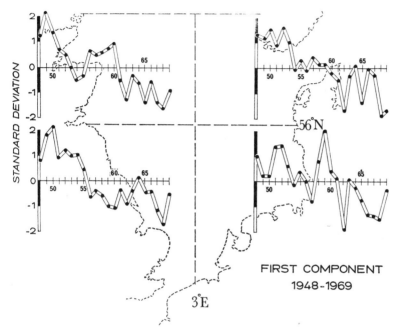

FIRST COMPONENT
1948–1969

FIG. 7. First principal components of annual fluctuations in zooplankton abundance in each quarter of the North Sea, 1948–1969.

This highlights one of the main problems we are likely to be faced with in the identification of changes induced by pollution. The zooplankton changes observed in the North Sea during the last 22 years are believed to be due to a change in climate, although convincing relationships with climatic factors have yet to be established. How is it going to be possible to differentiate between this kind of change and a similar change induced by, say, the progressive accumulation of a toxic substance?

It will, I think, be important to look at year-to-year variations in seasonal cycles and in geographical distribution as well as simple year-to-year fluctuations in abundance. It seems possible that the distribution of the change amongst the different forms of annual variation might provide the means for differentiating between natural and man-induced changes.

The derivation of expressions of year-to-year changes in seasonal and geographical variation requires fairly elaborate surveys, but without this information I am sure that the identification of man-induced changes is going to be very difficult.

It is also possible to use the observed linear change in the North Sea to provide an estimate of the inevitable time-lag involved in the detection of a change. It is estimated that, if the linear change were to stop or move in the opposite direction, it would take at least three years to get a clear indication of the alteration. Five or six years' data would be required to provide reasonable confirmation, and at least ten years would be needed to give any quantitative estimate of the magnitude of the change.

In relation to man-induced changes, time-lags of this extent do not seem to be very satisfactory. Improvements can only be achieved by better surveys. For fairly obvious reasons, very little is known about the effects, on estimates of long-term changes, of variations in sampling intensity, sampling pattern, counting effort and so on. In view of the importance of the rapid detection of changes in the plankton in relation to pollution studies, the necessary survey requirements should be investigated and, if economically feasible, implemented in those areas considered to be most at risk.

## References

Colebrook, J. M. (1964). Continuous plankton records: a principal component analysis of the geographical distribution of zooplankton. *Bull. mar. Ecol.* **6**: 78–100.

Colebrood, J. M. (1966). Continuous plankton records: geographical patterns in the annual fluctuations of abundance of some copepods in the North Sea. In *Some contemporary studies in marine science:* 155–161 (Barnes, H., ed). London: George Allen and Unwin.

Colebrook, J. M. & Robinson, G. A. (1964). Continuous plankton records: annual variations of abundance of plankton, 1948–1960. *Bull. mar. Ecol.* **6**: 52–69.

Glover, R. S. (1962). The Continuous Plankton Recorder. *Rapp. P.-v. Réun. Cons. perm. int. Explor. Mer* **153**: 8–15.

Hardy, A. C. (1939). Ecological investigations with the Continuous Plankton Recorder: object, plan and methods. *Hull Bull. mar. Ecol.* **1**: 1–57.

*Symp. zool. Soc. Lond.* (1972) No. 29, 213–232.

# THE PRODUCTION CYCLE
# AND THE NUMBERS OF MARINE FISH

## D. H. CUSHING

*Fisheries Laboratory, Lowestoft, Suffolk, England*

### SYNOPSIS

The general thesis was put forward that the three processes governing numbers in marine fish populations, which generate losses due to density-independent, density-dependent and competitive causes, occur during the larval drift from spawning ground to nursery ground. All three were linked to a single process, the match or mismatch of the production of larvae and that of their food. This general thesis was applied to the particular problem of the recruitment of plaice in the southern North Sea; it was found that recruitment was inversely dependent upon the wind strength in March, as was expected from the way in which the production cycle develops.

## INTRODUCTION

The recruitment to fish stocks is variable, and in herring stocks the variability is greater in deeper water (Cushing, 1967). It has been shown that good periods of catches to the Norwegian and Swedish herring stocks varied with the degree of ice cover north of Iceland (Beverton & Lee, 1965). Certain year-classes of cod are abundant in many stocks in the North Atlantic, and, further, the strong 1950 year-class was common to a number of species. These associations are so widespread in the geographical sense that only changes in climate can be responsible for them. Cushing (1966) put forward the thesis that differences in recruitment in fish stocks are generated by changes in wind strength and direction and in radiation which, between them, affect the timing and variability of the production cycle; in other words, recruitment is a function of the food available to the larval fish. In this paper, this thesis is generalized to the problem of the natural regulation of numbers in a fish population and applied in particular to the plaice stock in the Southern Bight of the North Sea. The more general thesis is put forward which suggests that not only the generation of recruits, but also the control of numbers in marine fishes, and its modification by stock density and by competition, is governed by the match or mismatch of the timing of production of larvae to that of their food.

## THE SINGLE PROCESS GOVERNING THE NUMBERS OF MARINE FISH

As part of the development of a later equation, Ricker (1958) expressed the control of numbers in a fish population in the equation

$R = \alpha P\,\mathrm{e}^{-\beta P}$, where $P$ is stock in eggs, $R$ is recruitment, $\alpha$ is the coefficient of density-independent mortality, and $\beta$ is the coefficient of density-dependent mortality. The first of the three processes is represented by $\alpha P$, the effect of density-independent factors upon the product of stock and fecundity, that is, the number of eggs laid. The second process is the variation of recruitment by density-dependent factors, i.e. $\beta P$. The third is represented by the stock, the magnitude of which is the result of competition throughout evolutionary periods. It is possible that, in marine fishes, all three are effected by a single process in their planktonic lives during the larval drift from spawning ground to nursery ground. The main evidence for this view is in three parts.

The first process is the determination of year-classes by density-independent causes; these appear to be related to climatic changes, with which differences in recruitment can be conveniently correlated. Ottestad (1942) showed a clear correlation for 55 years between cod catches on their spawning ground off the Lofoten Islands in northern Norway and the periodicities in the widths of annual rings in pine trees in the same region (Fig. 1). From the material on the growth rings on pine trees, four periodicities were calculated, each with different phases in any given year. The average proportion of a year-class in the age distribution at any age is known for the period of 55 years. Each fraction was raised by the appropriate sine value and then the four curves were added. The summed curve was fitted by least squares to the data on catches ($r = 0\cdot84$) as shown in Fig. 1. The data and the fitted curve are independently derived. Differences in catches over the long time period of examination were mainly due to recruitment, which were themselves correlated with the effects of climatic change

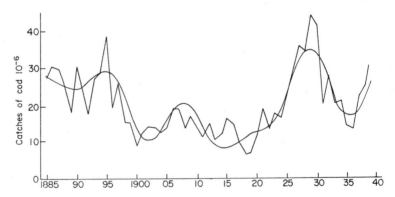

Fig. 1. Catches of cod in the Vestfjord fitted by a curve based on the periodicities in the annual rings of pine trees in the same area (Ottestad, 1942).

deduced from the rings on pine trees. This successful correlation with
the results of climatic change rather than any specified one shows that
a proper index of climatic change, for this purpose, had not been
evolved at that time. Many other attempts have been made to relate
forms of climatic change to recruitment, but nearly all of them have
failed. However, my colleagues, Garrod & Dickson (in press), have
successfully related the true recruitments (obtained from virtual
population estimates) of the Arcto-Norwegian cod stock to differences
in surface salinity in the German Bight (and to temperature differences
along the Kola meridian) (Fig. 2). Either index estimates the variation
of the wind direction in the eastern north Atlantic; a peak in either

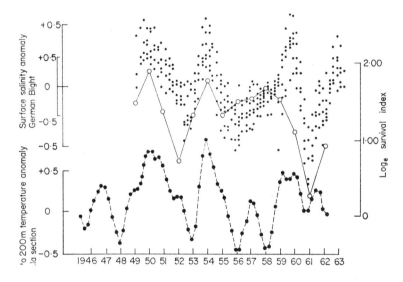

Fig. 2. Relationship between survival indices (recruitment as proportion of parent
stock) of the Arcto-Norwegian stock of cod and anomalies of surface salinity in the
German Bight and anomalies of temperature along the Kola meridian (north from
North Cape) (Garrod and Dickson, in press).

index registers a change from the average westerly flow to increasing
southerliness. The oceanographic changes are induced both by advection
and by changes in the loss of sensible and latent heat to the atmosphere
(Dickson, in press), themselves associated with changes in wind strength
between the Iceland low and the Azores high. Effectively, the recruitment to the Arcto-Norwegian cod stock varies with differences in
wind strength and direction. The link between recruitment and the

periodicities in the pine trees in the Lofoten area may be established in the variation of wind strength and direction.

In the sea, climatic changes affect production cycles in their timing, amplitude and spread. The start of any temperate production cycle is controlled by the critical depth; this is the depth at which photosynthesis exceeds respiration when both are integrated in depth. Production starts when the critical depth exceeds the depth of mixing. The subsequent progress of production is governed by the ratio of compensation depth (where respiration rate equals photosynthetic rate) to depth of mixing, the production ratio. Hence the cycle in spring is controlled partly by the increasing radiation and partly by the decreasing wind strength, which itself depends upon its direction. Cushing (1970) has suggested that, in the temperate spring, fishes tend to spawn at fixed seasons; the standard deviation of the peak spawning date of four common fish was shown to be as low as a week. The two correlations for the Arcto-Norwegian cod stock suggest that differences in recruitment are correlated with variations in wind strength and direction. Hence it is likely that such differences are generated by the

TABLE I

*Differences between the three groups of herring*

|  | Winter | Autumn | Spring | |
|---|---|---|---|---|
| $T_{max}$ (years) | 12 | 16 | 23 | ⎤ |
| $L_m$ (cm) | 21–23 | 23–25 | 25–28 | |
| $L_\infty$ (cm) | 28·5–29·5 | 30·5–31·5 | 35·0–37·0 | |
| $K$ | 0·35–0·50 | 0·35–0·43 | 0·17–0·25 | Growth |
| Gonad weight at $T_{max}$ (g) | 44 | 55 | 88 | ⎤ |
| Fecundity at mean length ($n$. $10^3$) | 38 | 80 | 51 | ⎦ |
| Egg diameter (mm) | 1·4–1·5 | 1·1–1·2 | 1·5–1·7 | Reproduction |
| Duration of maturity stages IV, V | long | short | long | ⎦ |
| Depth of water on larval drift (m) | 40 | 40–80 | 80+ | |
| Variability in timing of production cycle | low | moderate | high | |
| Growth | fast | moderate | slow | |

Notes: $T_{max}$ is age attained at 95% $L_\infty$.
$L_m$ is the length at which half the population has attained maturity.
$L_\infty$ is the asymptotic length in the von Bertalanffy growth equation.
$K$ is the rate at which $L_\infty$ is attained in the von Bertalanffy growth equation.

match or mismatch of the production of fish larvae in time to the production of their food, for example, copepod nauplii, which depend upon the timing of the production cycle. So the first factor in the control of numbers, the determination of year-class strength, probably takes place during the larval drift from spawning ground to nursery ground and is probably mediated by the supply of food to the larval fish. However, it must be pointed out that other environmental effects can play their part.

The second process in the control of numbers is that effected by density-dependent mortality. In the north-east Atlantic there are nine herring stocks, in three groups of autumn, winter and spring spawners. The three groups differ considerably, as seen in Table I (Cushing, 1967). Spring spawners are twice as heavy (at maximum weight), live twice as long and grow at about half the rate of winter spawners; a consequence is that the gonads of spring spawners are twice as heavy as those of winter spawners. But the fecundity is only a little greater because the eggs are one-third larger by volume. Because the depth of water over which the larvae drift is much greater for the spring spawners than for the winter spawners, the variability in the timing of the production cycle is much greater. Then the spring spawners live longer and damp the higher variability of their recruitment by stabilizing the spawning stock through a greater number of year-classes. The spring and winter spawners have big eggs and retain them in the gonads for long periods; presumably the parents divert protein to the gonads in the summer and the eggs are kept until the best time to spawn in the following winter or spring. Then the large eggs provide yolk to sustain the larvae if the production cycle is late; in the autumn, this problem is less important because food is likely to be abundant. The main conclusion is that the profound differences in growth and in reproduction between the three groups are adaptations to match the three forms of production cycle.

The differences between the three groups are considerable and they could well be genetically distinct, although this has not been shown. In a long-term sense, the size of any population is controlled by the pressure of selection. But at any one point of time, this pressure is expressed by the magnitude of density-dependent mortality. Not only are the differences between the groups seen to be adaptations to the three forms of production cycle, as shown in Table I, but each of the three is linked specifically to a particular form of cycle—North Sea, shelf or oceanic. The production cycle is that which occurs during the larval drift and if the selection within and between stocks, favouring particular cycles, occurred then, the regulation of numbers would take place during the larval drift. The generality of this mechanism is confirmed by the successful use of the numbers of O-group fish to predict incoming year-classes (plaice, Wimpenny, 1960; herring, Dragesund & Nakken, in press; cod, Nizovtsev, 1966, 1967, 1968, 1969). Any prediction of recruitment at an early stage in the life history means that the density-dependent processes have been completed. Further, many of the metamorphosed fish, plaice or cod, feed on animals, such as worms or bivalves, the numbers of which are only indirectly related to the production cycle on the nursery ground—let alone that along the larval drift.

The third process controlling numbers in the population is competition. In the area of larval drift of plaice in the Southern Bight of the North Sea, larvae of other fish species are also present—cod, sandeels, whiting, dabs and herring. The larvae of all the species are about the same size and in general share the same food, for example, copepod nauplii, copepodite stages and *Oikopleura*. At this stage in the common life cycle, the shared food provides the greatest opportunity for competition, expressed as the difference between growth and mortality; it is this difference which generates the competitive differences in numbers and biomass between species. At later stages in the life cycle, when individuals live far apart on specialized foods, the chances of competition are infrequent.

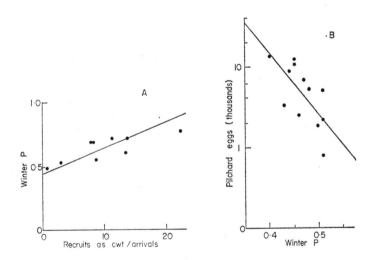

Fig. 3. A. Dependence of winter phosphorus, sampled one year after the herring were hatched, upon recruitment to the stock of Plymouth herring (Cushing, 1961). B. Dependence of numbers of pilchard eggs (or stock) upon the winter phosphorus, six months after they were hatched (Cushing, 1961).

During the thirties, a stock of pilchards succeeded one of herring in the western Channel (Cushing, 1961). Figure 3A shows the dependence of winter phosphorus, a year after the herring were hatched, upon recruitment to the herring stock, during the twenties; Fig. 3B shows the dependence of pilchard eggs, or stock, upon the winter phosphorus, six months after the eggs were hatched, during the period from the thirties to the fifties. Recruitment to the herring stock failed in 1930, so the stock disappeared in the late thirties. The stock of pilchards reached high levels in 1936, about a generation after the failure of the herring recruitment. Let up to one-third of the winter phosphorus represent larval pilchards, which need not be six months old, so long as the phosphorus is transferred to animals which survive the winter. Further, let us suppose that four-month-old herring eat larval pilchards, then the two regressions and the sequence of events can be explained in the simplest manner. That is, during the twenties, herring ate the relatively younger pilchards during the summer, and when the herring died out the pilchards increased; so with high herring stock more free phosphorus was available in the winter, but in later years, with high pilchard stock, one-third of it was locked in living material. Whether true or not, it represents a likely mechanism of events in the plankton; the important point is that the process of competition may have occurred along the larval drift in the plankton. When the stock of Californian sardines collapsed in the late forties, it was succeeded by a stock of anchovies. It is possible that the competition in this case also occurred in the planktonic phase of the life cycle.

The argument has been presented that during the larval drift of many fish recruitment is determined, numbers regulated and competition established. If all three do occur at the same time, they may be mediated by a single process. Variations in recruitment appear to be correlated with the match or mismatch of the production of fish larvae to the production of their food; variations of density within stocks or between stocks can generate the control of numbers within a stock or competition between stocks. So the single process is the use made of the food available by the larval population.

THE PLAICE OF THE SOUTHERN NORTH SEA

*Larval drift*

In the previous section, the general principles governing the numbers of some marine fish were expounded. Any particular exposition may diverge in detail for a number of reasons; for example, the depth of

mixing is sometimes difficult to estimate, partly because the dependence
of the wind-mixed layer upon the strength of the wind is not always
well described, and partly because profound mixing can occur quite
independently of any effect of the wind.

The spawning ground of the plaice in the Southern Bight of the
North Sea lies in the centre in the main stream of Channel water between

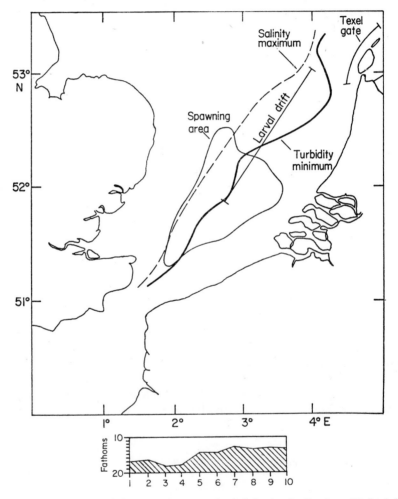

Fɪɢ. 4. The centre of the spawning ground of plaice in the Southern Bight (after
Simpson, 1959), the larval drift in the water of maximum salinity and minimum
turbidity and the Texel gate to the inshore region (Dietrich, 1954). Inset below is
shown the average depth along the larval drift, with fifteen miles on either side.

the northern part of the Thames Estuary and the Hook of Holland. Simpson (1959) has published contoured distributions of the newly-spawned eggs (Stage Ia) for 11 years. The average centre of the spawning ground from these distributions lies at 51° 45′N, 2° 45′E. From the distribution of larvae (Harding & Talbot, in press) it can be shown that the larval drift, from spawning ground to nursery ground, lies along the zone of minimum turbidity and maximum salinity (Lee & Folkard, 1969) to a point at about 53° 00′N, 4° 00′E. This position is not so firmly established as the centre of the spawning ground because fewer cruises sampling plaice larvae are available and because inevitably they spread and drift in directions which are variable within a limited arc. Figure 4 shows the average direction of larval drift, which means that the metamorphosed plaice end up on the northern Dutch coast or amongst the islands of the Wadden-sea.

Dietrich (1953) has shown that 10 miles off Texel Island in 28 m there is an inshore movement of water towards the south-east at the bottom, as distinct from a surface movement towards the north-west. So a rough mechanism is available to carry the metamorphosed fish inshore. The mechanism depends on the boundary between the English Channel water, which lies in the centre of the Southern Bight, and the stratified Dutch coastal water, which extends outwards about 10 miles from the Dutch coast. When the tides flow parallel to the coast, the English Channel water in the upper water column turns to the left during the tidal cycle and, below it, the Dutch coastal water turns to the right; then at a particular state of tide, the surface water moves offshore and the bottom water moves inshore, at about 20 cm/sec, i.e. as much as $\frac{1}{3}$ knot. This particular period lasts for about an hour, but the total residual is about 7 cm/sec ($\frac{1}{8}$ knot), due easterly. So, at Dietrich's anchor station off Texel Island, metamorphosing plaice could move inshore at 3 miles/day. Dietrich makes the important observation that six necessary conditions (e.g. with the axis of tidal streams parallel to the coast and an intense horizontal density boundary) occur only in two places in the North Sea, north-west of Texel and Vlieland and seaward of the North Friesian Islands off the coasts of southern Denmark and northern Germany. So, there are two "gates" through which the metamorphosing plaice can come inshore, one for the Southern Bight stocklet and one for the German Bight stocklet. It is possible that animals which fail to reach the gates, for one reason or another, are lost to either stock. Figure 4 shows the position of the Texel gate (from Dietrich's Fig. 12) and it will be seen that the track of the larval drift ends close to this position.

## Timing of the primary production cycle

The depth of water along the larval drift ranges from 20 to 40 m and it tends to be deeper in the south (Fig. 4). The bottom consists of fine and medium sand in varying proportions. It is a region of the least tidal streams in the Southern Bight, but the average tide flows at about 1·5 knots and a thermocline never develops there. A full description of the distribution of turbidity in relation to the bottom sediments and tidal streams is given in Lee & Folkard (1969). Joseph (1957) has published a vertical section of the particle content of the water for 24 h in 28 m west of Texel Island, i.e. at Dietrich's anchor station. Joseph's figure is reproduced here as Fig. 5. The concentration at slack water just off the bottom may be as low as 5–6 mg/l, but at

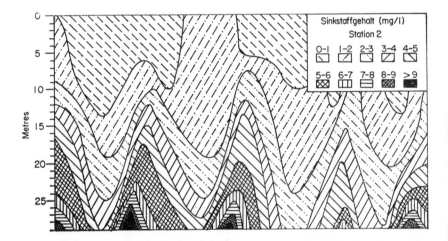

Fig. 5. The concentration of particles at different depths in the water during tidal cycles off Texel Island (Joseph, 1957).

high water just off the bottom the concentration increased to $> 9$ mg/l, whereas that of 5–6 mg/l was found at about 12 m; so, during a tidal cycle, the particles were swept from the bottom where the tidal streams are slower to more than halfway up the water column. The specific gravity of the sand particles originating from the bottom is high and so neutrally buoyant (or nearly so) algal cells would be expected to be mixed from surface to bottom during a tidal cycle.

The maximum tidal streams in Joseph's observations ranged from 40–80 cm/sec (about 0·75–1·50 knots), which are less than the average tidal streams along the larval drift. So the algal cells are probably spread up and down the water column by tidal forces alone and the depth of mixing is effectively the depth of water. Further, the wind strength would not modify it. A production cycle starts when the depth of mixing becomes less than the critical depth; so in the Southern Bight, production will start when the critical depth exceeds the depth of water. The rate at which production proceeds depends upon the development of the ratio $D_c/D_m$, where $D_c$ is the compensation depth and $D_m$ the depth of mixing; if the latter is the depth of water, $Z$, then it depends upon $D_c/Z$ and the change in this ratio is change in the compensation depth only.

Lee & Folkard (1969) published distributions of turbidity in the Southern Bight as measured with a hydrophotometer at 5 m. There are two contrasting distributions; in one, the percentage transmission varied (along the larval drift) from 20–60% and in the other from 60–80%. In the first, the wind was north-westerly and north-easterly at 10·0–12·5 m/sec (18–23 knots) and, in the second, it was easterly, $< 5$ m/sec ($< 9$ knots). Thus, there is an association between wind strength and turbidity. So the compensation depth may be modified directly by the strength of the wind and the production ratio, $D_c/Z$, is also modified by it.

The compensation depth and critical depth can be calculated for an average condition with a method developed by Dickson & Cushing (in press), based on formulae of Laevastu (1960) and Lumb (1964). Laevastu gives:

$$Q_c = 135 \sin \delta(a + b \sin \delta) mwh/cm^2, \tag{1}$$

where $Q_c$ is the total incoming radiation, $\delta$ is the altitude of the sun, and $a$ and $b$ are constants.

Taking

$$Q'_s = (Q_c/69\cdot6) ly/min \tag{2}$$

then

$$Q'_{ss} = 0\cdot5 Q_s - (3.Q_s'/\delta_N) ly/min, \tag{3}$$

where $\delta_N$ is the sun's altitude at noon, and $Q_{ss}'$ is the photosynthetic energy reaching the surface at noon in the band $0\cdot380$–$0\cdot720$ m$\mu$.

Strickland (1960) suggests that total energy is reduced by half in the photosynthetic band; Laevastu recommends the expression ($3/\delta$; as a percentage) to describe the losses due to reflection at a given altitude of the sun. Strickland (1960) produces some evidence to show that the energy reaching the compensation depth is $3 \cdot 5.10^{-3}$ ly/min, so the noon compensation depth $(_N D_c)$ is:

$$_N D_c = \frac{1}{k} \ln \frac{3 \cdot 5.10^{-3}}{Q'_{ss}}, \qquad (4)$$

where $k$ is the extinction coefficient.

Lumb (1964) published a number of values for the constants $a$ and $b$ in Equation 1; the average cloudiness in the Southern Bight ranges from 70% in January to 56% in May (Lumb, 1965). I have calculated with two sets of constants, $(A)$ low cloud of 3–5 oktas; well-broken low cloud with little or no medium or high cloud, $(B)$ medium cloud of 6–8 oktas; thick layers of medium cloud. As a very rough approximation, I have assumed that the 70% cloud in January approximated to $B$ and that the 56% cloud in May approximated to $A$; so the following calculations have been carried out in $B$ for January and February and in $A$ for March, April and May.

Jerlov (1951) gives the trend of absorption of *total* energy by coastal water types 1, 3, 5, 7 and 9. The total energy is given by $2Q'_{ss}$ and so the percentage energy reaching the compensation depth can be obtained from $(3 \cdot 5.10^{-3}/2Q'_{ss}).100$. Then from Jerlov's Fig. 50, the noon compensation depth can be read off. The average compensation depth over the day is given by $0 \cdot 64 \; _N D_c$. Figure 6A shows the trend of average compensation depth for the five water types from January

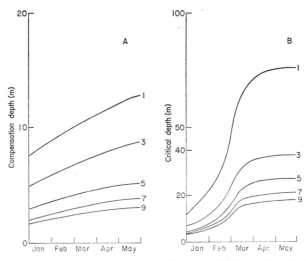

Fig. 6. A. Compensation depths in the Southern Bight of the North Sea from January to May in coastal water types 1, 3, 5, 7 and 9. B. Critical depths in the Southern Bight of the North Sea from January to May in coastal water types 1, 3, 5, 7 and 9.

to May. Table II shows the ratio of compensation depth to depth of
water, for depths of 20 m and of 40 m.

TABLE II

*The production ratio, $D_c/Z$, in 20 m and 40 m*

| | Water type | Jan | Feb | March | April | May |
|---|---|---|---|---|---|---|
| $Z = 20$ m | 1 | 0·41 | 0·52 | 0·50 | 0·58 | 0·63 |
| | 3 | 0·27 | 0·34 | 0·32 | 0·39 | 0·42 |
| | 5 | 0·16 | 0·20 | 0·22 | 0·23 | 0·25 |
| | 7 | 0·11 | 0·16 | 0·16 | 0·17 | 0·19 |
| | 9 | 0·10 | 0·10 | 0·13 | 0·14 | 0·15 |
| $Z = 40$ m | 1 | 0·20 | 0·26 | 0·25 | 0·29 | 0·32 |
| | 3 | 0·13 | 0·17 | 0·16 | 0·20 | 0·21 |
| | 5 | 0·08 | 0·10 | 0·11 | 0·11 | 0·13 |
| | 7 | 0·05 | 0·08 | 0·08 | 0·08 | 0·09 |
| | 9 | 0·05 | 0·06 | 0·07 | 0·07 | 0·08 |

Steele (1965) has developed a curve which describes the trend of
photosynthesis with depth and the following formula is given for
determining the critical depth:

$$D_{cr} = \frac{p_m}{r} \cdot \frac{e}{k}\left[1 - \exp\left(-\frac{I_o}{I_m}\right)\right],$$

where $p_m$ is the maximum rate of photosynthesis, $r$ is rate of respiration,
$0·1p_m$ (and in a day $p_m/r = 5$), $k$ is the extinction coefficient of the
water, $I_o$ is the photosynthetic energy reaching the surface in $ly/d$, and
$I_m$ is the photosynthetic energy which generates $p_m$, 90 $ly/d$.

Jerlov (1951) tabulates extinction coefficients (his Table 33) by
depth intervals 0–1 m, 1–2 m, 2–5 m, 5–10 m; an average coefficient,
weighted by depth, was calculated. The critical depth was calculated
for the coastal water types 1, 3, 5, 7 and 9 in the months January to
May; the results are given in Fig. 6B. The mean energy extinction
coefficient (from Jerlov's Table 33) at 5 m was calculated for each
water type and then the transmission coefficient was calculated:

| | Water type | | | | |
|---|---|---|---|---|---|
| | 1 | 3 | 5 | 7 | 9 |
| Transmission coefficient | 82% | 76% | 67% | 59% | 53% |

Lee & Folkard (1969) used a hydrophotometer at 5 m which has a selenium rectifier cell. Jerlov used the same type of cell with filters, but with approximately the same spectral response; his energy curves were constructed from the measurements through the filters. The peak for coastal water 7 is at 560 m$\mu$, which is not far from that of the common selenium rectifier cell, so the transmission coefficients for the more turbid waters would correspond quite well to the hydrophotometer measurements. Then the clearer water types are underestimated. The measurements by Lee and Folkard range from 20–80% along the larval drift, 60–80% in calm weather and 40–60% in rough weather; provisionally, let us assign coastal water type 1 to calm weather and water type 9 to rough weather.

Figure 6B, showing the estimated critical depths, suggests first that production must start in the shallow water before the deeper waters, i.e. from the Dutch coast outwards and, secondly, that it starts in late January and in early February in 40 m in calm weather. Then, in fairly rough weather, production is restricted to the shallow water and, in very rough weather, there will be no production. The progress of production, based on Fig. 6A, can be estimated from the productive ratio $D_c/Z$ given in Table II. In calm weather (water type 1), the reproductive rate of the algae ($R . D_c/Z$) is roughly halved in shallow water; in 40 m, it is reduced to $\frac{1}{5}-\frac{1}{3}$. In rough weather, the productive ratio is reduced to $\frac{1}{10}$ or less in 40 or 20 m. So, production must increase more rapidly in shallow water off the Dutch coast. But the most important conclusion is that production is cut back and progresses slowly. This rate of progress presumably depends upon the depth of water and upon the frequency of wind strengths. If the wind strength declines sharply in time, production should increase quickly; if it declines slowly, it should increase slowly. Then if recruitment to the plaice stock, the average date of peak spawning of which is 19 January, depends upon the match of the production of larvae to that of their food, an inverse correlation would be expected between year-class strength and wind strength.

The steps in calculating compensation depths and critical depths are based on average cloud covers, a very rough estimate of the energy at the compensation depth and an estimate of $p_m$. The magnitude of any estimate may be wrong, but the conclusions are based on the trend of estimates. In particular, it is difficult to believe that the full potential of the algal reproductive rate is never reached; but if each productive ratio should be raised by $1 \cdot 0/0 \cdot 63$, then the range remains from $0 \cdot 08$ in January in rough weather to $1 \cdot 00$ in May in calm weather. It is possible that the compensation energy in the southern North Sea is less than $3 \cdot 5.10^{-3}$ ly/min.

*The timing of spawning and the production cycle in relation to subsequent recruitment*

The first and general part of this paper presents an argument that numbers in marine fish populations are often controlled during the period of larval drift. Evidence was presented that year-classes were determined, that density-dependent mortality was in the main completed, and that the main force of competition occurred during the larval drift from spawning ground to nursery ground. It is possible that such processes are predominantly completed during this early phase of the life history, but it is also likely that they may continue at later stages. If density-dependent growth and density-dependent mortality are linked, as one might expect, the persistence of density-dependent growth to later stages might indicate the continuance of processes which control numbers. Recruitment may well be determined mainly during the planktonic phase of the life cycle, but a fine control may occur at later stages; as demersal fish settle at metamorphosis from the volume of the sea to the surface of their nursery grounds the density-dependent effects may be intensified. But because the little fish have migrated into a profoundly different ecosystem, the control of the numbers that remain will not be affected by the processes in the plankton. So, relationships established on the basis of planktonic processes might contain a component of residual variance associated with processes at a later stage in the life cycle.

The second and particular part of the paper describes the biology of the plaice in the Southern Bight of the North Sea. The larval drift has been described in terms of spawning ground, the timing of spawning, the distribution of larvae and the relevant hydrographic structures. The mechanisms which determine the shape of the production cycle have been described. In general, it starts in February or March during the period at which the larvae hatch (i.e. three weeks or so after 19 January, the mean date of peak spawning). The month of March is likely to be critical when on average the yolk supply starts to run out. But the development of the production rate is sensitive to the effect of wind strength upon the turbidity. Hence I would expect the reproductive rate of the algae to develop rather slowly and the production cycle itself to build up rather slowly, but more quickly in the shallow water. It has been known for a long time that production builds up from the Dutch coast and that it starts earlier in the shallow water in the northern part of the larval drift (T. Wyatt, pers. comm.). Shelbourne (1957) has shown convincingly that the plaice larvae feed on appendicularians, which in turn feed on algae. Most fish larvae depend upon the larvae of secondary producers, copepod nauplii or, for plaice, growing appendicularians. It is likely that the start of secondary production is linked to a minimum level of algal food and hence to the timing processes. So recruitment should be related inversely to wind strength. The relationship might well be a "noisy" one, for the general reasons given in the previous paragraph and for particular ones associated with the as yet undescribed population dynamics of the appendicularians.

The plaice population in the southern North Sea can probably be divided into three stocklets, with spawning grounds in the Southern Bight, in the German Bight and off Flamborough Head. Adult fish have been tagged on these grounds and all the tags recovered during subsequent spawning seasons came from the spawning ground on which the fish were tagged (de Veen, 1961). There are differences in the otolith structure between the German Bight stock and the Southern Bight stock which imply that they grow up in different nurseries (de Veen & Boerema, 1959). The positions of the Texel and the North Friesian gates suggest that there is a hydrographic mechanism by which the stocks remain isolated. Lastly, in the late fifties the stock of eggs in the German Bight stock increased by up to ten times, when the Southern Bight stock of eggs up to 1961 remained at the same level as in the early fifties (Buckmann, 1961). This implies that recruitment to the two stocklets was not changing in the same way during this time period.

The catch statistics have not yet been analysed by stocklets because the fish appear to mix on their feeding grounds and individuals cannot be separated there into the three putative groups. The population in the southern North Sea was originally treated as a single stock and for many purposes this is valid. During the thirties and forties, Lowestoft trawlers worked in the Southern Bight and beyond the Norfolk Banks and it is likely that samples of their catches predominantly represented the Southern Bight stocklet. By the late fifties and early sixties, Lowestoft trawlers worked far away on the Fisher Bank on the biggest fish which they could find. They were fish of the German Bight stocklet; so not only were the Lowestoft fishermen using the growth of the fish to the best advantage, they had also exploited the increase in numbers in the German Bight. In order to understand the processes, the two stocklets must now be separated because the increase in numbers occurred in only one of them.

Figure 7 shows the dependence of the stock density, in numbers of 4-year-old plaice sampled at Lowestoft from 1929–1950 (excluding the war years) upon the mean wind strength for March in the years when the fish were hatched; this inverse relationship is significantly different from zero at $P$ 0·05 ($n = 16$). The error about the regression is high, but the relationship is perhaps not expressed in the best possible way. First, it should eventually be possible to use about forty years of observations rather than sixteen. Secondly, the observations of

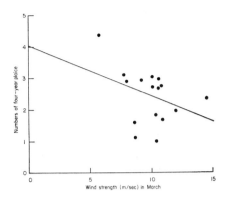

FIG. 7. Dependence of year-class strength of the plaice in the Southern Bight of the North Sea (in stock density in thousands of four-year-olds per 100 hours fishing) upon the mean wind strength for March in the year in which they were hatched.

recruitment should be expressed as deviations from the stock/recruitment curve; the present curve (Cushing & Harris, in press) is based on data for the southern North Sea as a whole. However, there is a sufficient relationship in the limited amount of data used to suggest an inverse dependence of recruitment upon wind strength as suggested earlier.

There is obvious value in being able to forecast recruitment some years ahead, at least to identify the good and bad year-classes as distinct from the average ones. To do so we need the positions of spawning and nursery ground and the track of the larval drift between them. Although they are well known for some stocks of some species, there are many stocks for which information is lacking. However, it can be readily obtained now that fish larvae can be adequately sampled with high-speed nets up to the age of metamorphosis. Then information on the critical depth, compensation depth and depth of mixing can be collected at the right place and time.

SUMMARY

Numbers in animal populations are controlled by density-independent, or environmental, factors, by density-dependent factors and by competition. In marine fish, it is suggested that the main effects of all three are completed during the period of the larval drift from spawning ground to nursery ground. The availability of food for the larvae is considered as a single process governing all three factors. Recruitment to the Arctic cod population was shown to depend upon differences in three disparate climatic factors; common to these are differences in wind strength, so they might affect recruitment by changing the timing of the production cycle. The replacement of herring by pilchard in the Channel during the thirties may have taken place during the planktonic phase of the life cycle and so competition may take place then. Today, fisheries biologists can predict the future year-classes by sampling the little O-group fish on the nursery grounds; this can only mean that the density-dependent processes were completed before the fish metamorphosed.

A particular study was made of the plaice population in the Southern Bight of the North Sea. The larval drift was shown to lie in the water of maximum salinity and minimum turbidity. Dietrich has shown that where the tidal streams run parallel to the coast near a water mass boundary, the water near the bottom flows inshore at 3 knots/day; such a position is found off the islands of Texel and Vlieland. Evidence is presented that the tidal streams alone mix the water completely and so the depth of water is the depth of mixing. It is possible that turbidity increases with wind strength, and compensation depths and critical depths have been calculated on this basis. The nature of the production cycle in the Southern Bight is described. It is likely that the year-class strengths of the plaice sub-population in the Southern Bight of the North Sea are affected by wind strengths, which affect the turbidity of the water.

REFERENCES

Beverton, R. J. H. & Lee, A. J. (1965). Hydrographic fluctuations in the North Atlantic Ocean and some biological consequences. In *The biological significance of climatic changes in Britain:* 79–107. (Johnson, C. G. & Smith, L. P., eds), (Inst. of Biol., Symposia, No. 14.) London and New York: Academic Press.

Bückmann, A. (1961). Über die Bedeutung des Schollenlaichens in der südöstlichen Nordsee. *Kurze Mitt. Inst. FischBiol. Univ. Hamb.* No. 11: 1–40.

Cushing, D. H. (1961). On the failure of the Plymouth herring fishery. *J. mar. biol. Ass. U.K.* 41: 799–816.

Cushing, D. H. (1966). Biological and hydrographic changes in British Seas during the last thirty years. *Biol. Rev.* 41: 221–258.

Cushing, D. H. (1967). The grouping of herring populations. *J. mar. biol. Ass. U.K.* 47: 193–208.

Cushing, D. H. (1970). The regularity of the spawning season of some fishes. *J. Cons. perm. int. Explor. Mer* 33, 1: 81–92.

Cushing, D. H. & Harris, J. G. K. (in press). Stock and recruitment and the problem of density dependence. *Rapp. P.-v. Réun. Cons. perm. int. Explor. Mer.*

Dickson, R. & Cushing, D. H. (in press). *The distribution of compensation depths in the North Atlantic.*

Dickson, R. R. (in press). Climatic deterioration and the Atlantic fishery. In *Sea Fisheries Research.* (Harden Jones, F. R., ed.).

Dietrich, G. (1954). Verteilung, Ausbreitung und Vermischung der Wasserkörper in der südwestlichen Nordsee auf Grund der Ergebnisse des "Gauss"-Fahrt im Februar/März 1952. *Ber. dt. wiss. Kommn. Meeresforsch.* **13**: 104–129.

Dragesund, O. & Nakken, O. (in press). Relationship of parent stock size and year-class strength in Norwegian spring spawning herring. *Rapp. P.-v. Réun. Cons. perm. int. Explor. Mer.*

Garrod, D. J. & Dickson, R. (in press). The influence of environmental factors on recruitment of the Arcto-Norwegian cod stock. Appx I to Garrod, in: *Sea Fisheries Research,* (Harden Jones, F. R., ed.).

Harding, D. & Talbot, J. W. (in press). Recent studies on the eggs and larvae of the plaice (*Pleuronectes platessa* L.) in the Southern Bight. *Rapp. P.-v. Réun. Cons. perm. int. Explor. Mer.*

Jerlov, N. (1951). Optical studies of ocean waters. *Rep. Swed. deep Sea Exped.* 1947–1948, **III**, 1: 1–59.

Joseph, J. (1957). Extinction measurements to indicate distribution and transport of watermasses. *Proc. UNESCO Symp. Physical Oceanography,* Tokyo, 1955: 59–75.

Laevastu, T. (1960). Factors affecting the temperature of the surface layer of the sea. *Commentat. physico-math.* **25** (1): 136 pp.

Lee, A. J. & Folkard, A. R. (1969). Factors affecting turbidity in the southern North Sea. *J. Cons. perm. int. Explor. Mer,* **32** (3), 291–302.

Lumb, F. E. (1964). The influence of cloud on hourly amounts of total solar radiation at the sea surface. *Q. Jl R. met. Soc.* **90**: 43–56.

Lumb, F. E. (1965). Meteorology of the North Sea. Ser. Atlas of the Marine Environment. *Amer. Geogr. Soc.* Folio 9: 3 pp.

Nizovtsev, G. P. (1966). Soviet researches on the O, I, II, and III age-groups of young cod in the Barents Sea. *Annls biol., Copenh.* **21**: 78–79.

Nizovtsev, G. P. (1967). Soviet investigations on young cod of O, I, II and III age-groups in the fishing areas I and IIa. *Annls biol., Copenh.* **22**: 76–77.

Nizovtsev, G. P. (1968). Soviet investigations of young cod of the O, I, II and III age-groups in the Barents Sea in 1966. *Annls biol., Copenh.* **23**: 102–104.

Nizovtsev, G. P. (1969). Soviet investigations on young cod of the O, I, II, and III age-groups in the Barents Sea. *Annls. biol. Copenh.* **25**: 112–114.

Ottestad, P. (1942). On periodical variations in the yield of the great sea fisheries and the possibility of establishing yield prognoses. *FiskDir. Skr.,* (Ser. Havunders.) **7**, 5: 11 pp.

Ricker, W. E. (1958). Handbook of computations for biological statistics of fish populations. *Bull. Fish. Res. Bd Can.* No. 119: 300 pp.

Shelbourne, J. E. (1957). The feeding and condition of plaice larvae in good and bad plankton patches. *J. mar. biol. Ass. U.K.* **36**: 539–552.

Simpson, A. C. (1959). The spawning of the plaice (*Pleuronectes platessa*) in the North Sea. *Fishery Invest. Lond.* (2), **22**, 7: 111 pp.

Steele, J. H. (1965). Notes on some theoretical problems in production ecology. *Mem. Ist. ital. Idrobiol.* **18**, Supp: 383–398.

Strickland, J. D. H. (1960). Measuring the production of marine phytoplankton. *Bull. Fish. Res. Bd Can.* No. 122: 172 pp.

de Veen, J. F. (1961). The 1961 tagging experiments of mature plaice in different spawning areas in the southern North Sea. *ICES C.M.* 1961, Near Northern Seas Committee, No. 44: 7 pp. (mimeo).

de Veen, J. F. & Boerema, L. K. (1959). Distinguishing southern North Sea spawning populations of plaice by means of otolith characteristics. *ICES C.M.* 1959, Near Northern Seas Committee, No. 91: 5 pp. (mimeo).

Wimpenny, R. S. (1960). Young plaice hauls off the English east coast. *Fishery Invest., Lond.* (2), **23**, No. 1: 20 pp.

*Symp. zool. Soc. Lond.* (1972) No. 29, 233–258.

# ON THE IMPORTANCE OF THE WADDENSEA AS A NURSERY AREA IN RELATION TO THE CONSERVATION OF THE SOUTHERN NORTH SEA FISHERY RESOURCES

J. J. ZIJLSTRA

*Rijksinstituut voor Visserijonderzoek, IJmuiden,
Netherlands*

### SYNOPSIS

The Waddensea, a tidal area in the northern part of the Netherlands, will possibly be closed off from the North Sea by the construction of dykes between the belt of isles. The paper considers the importance of this extremely rich tidal area as nursery ground for two economically important demersal fish species, plaice and sole. It gives preliminary results of a study to assess the relative contribution of the Dutch part of the Waddensea to the coastal nurseries of the two species.

### THE PROBLEM

The Waddensea is a large estuarine area lying off the coast of the northern part of the Netherlands (Fig. 1). The area is partly separated

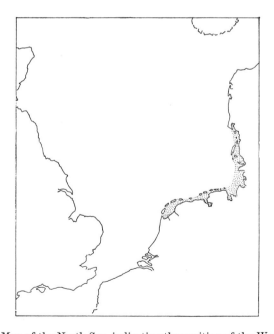

Fig. 1. Map of the North Sea, indicating the position of the Waddensea.

from the North Sea by a belt of sandy isles, remnants of a once closed dune-coast, through which the sea broke in pre-historic times. Between the isles are tidal inlets, which form the connection with the North Sea. The Dutch Waddensea is part of a much larger Wadden area, extending to the east along the German and Danish North Sea coasts over a distance of several hundred kilometres. The Dutch Waddensea covers about 35% of the total Wadden area.

Recently the future destiny of the Dutch part of the Waddensea has come under discussion. With modern methods of dyke construction a closure of the Waddensea by the construction of dams through the tidal inlets and over the mostly shallow Wadden area is likely to be possible, and use of the enclosed area for recreation, forestry, agriculture, industry and as a freshwater basin has been mentioned.

The Netherlands has a long history of dyke-building which has been largely determined by the position of the country in the delta of large continental rivers (the Rhine, the Meuse, and the Scheldt), and the consequential low level of the land in relation to the bordering North Sea. The fact that the country tends to sink relative to the sea level with an approximate speed of 20 cm per century has made the construction of sea defences imperative. After a long period in which dyke-building on the sea-side was mainly restricted to the defence of the land and to the reclamation of areas which were only occasionally flooded, a new era started when in the early 1930s the Zuidersea was closed off by a heavy dyke of about 30 km long, separating the Zuidersea from the Waddensea and turning it into a freshwater lake. The size of this lake has since been reduced by the creation of several "polders" within the lake, which are mainly used for agricultural purposes.

In 1953 a flood around the southern inlets of Holland, in the province of Zeeland, initiated another large-scale operation, aimed at closing off all the inlets in the south with the exception of the southernmost one (Westerschelde), which forms the approach to Antwerp. The old inlets will be used mainly for freshwater basins. This work is now under construction and is scheduled to be finished in the late 1970s. At that time large reserves of experience, research facilities, material and manpower will become available for new objects, hence the discussions in recent years about the future of the Waddensea.

With the two large projects—the closure of the Zuidersea and the closure of the southern inlets—the interests of the local fisheries have been considered and assessed so far as possible. In both cases the local fishing industries have received or will receive some compensation for their losses. In the Zuidersea the local fishery was based mainly on a herring and an anchovy tribe which visited the area for spawning. Both fish tribes have disappeared completely since the closure. In the southern inlets local fishing is mainly for shrimps (*Crangon crangon* L.), but in this area there are also important oyster and mussel cultures. When the operation in the southern inlets is completed the oyster culture will disappear, but the mussel culture can be continued on a reduced scale in the Waddensea.

As in the case of the Zuidersea and the southern inlets, the discussions around the Waddensea are considering the interests of the fisheries, together with many other interests, e.g. nature conservation (the area is of major importance as overwintering ground for many birds), recreation, safety, industry, etc. The interests of the local fishery can be assessed relatively easily, the most important fisheries in the area being the already mentioned mussel culture and a shrimp fishery. In the case of the Waddensea, however, a new aspect has emerged which was not previously considered, namely the function of the area as a nursery for a number of species which are of great economic importance for the fisheries in the southern and central North Sea.

Many investigations in the past have indicated that the nurseries of plaice (*Pleuronectes platessa* L.), sole (*Solea solea* L.) and herring (*Clupea harengus* L.) are located in coastal and inshore areas. For North Sea plaice it has been suggested that the Waddensea would be the major nursery area (Bückmann, 1934a; Tåning, 1943). Bückmann (1934b) expressed the view that the Waddensea acts as the main nursery ground for sole also. For both species, however, observations of young fish in coastal areas outside the Waddensea show that the nurseries are not restricted to the Waddensea itself (Johansen, 1922; Bückmann, 1934a,b). The probable importance of the Waddensea as a nursery area for plaice and sole is also reflected in the large by-catches of immature fish of these species in the shrimp fisheries of the Waddensea, as reported in recent years by Meyer-Waarden & Tiews (1965) for the German Wadden area and by Boddeke (1963, 1967) for the Dutch Waddensea.

The position of the Waddensea as a nursery for herring is less well documented but reports on the immigration of herring larvae into the German Wadden area by Bückmann (1950) and into the Dutch Waddensea by Postuma (1969) in spring, just prior to the start of the main growth season, suggest an important nursery function.

Investigations on the by-catches of the shrimp fisheries suggest that the Waddensea could also be a nursery of some importance for whiting (*Odontogadus merlangus* L.) and cod (*Gadus morhua* L.) (Meyer-Waarden & Tiews, 1965).

When only plaice, sole and herring are considered it appears that
these species have contributed about a third of the total North Sea
catches in recent years (1966–1968), mainly because of the large landings of herring. Considering only the Dutch catches, which can be
appreciated in terms of both weight and value, the three species again
cover about a third of the total landings in weight, but over 60% in
terms of value in the years 1966–1968. Here the expensive sole is the
most important species. The value of the landings of the three species
in Dutch ports (about Hfl. 135 million annually in 1966–1968) is such
that the interests of the local fisheries in the Waddensea of about Hfl.
20 million annually in 1966–1968 are small in comparison. Therefore,
if the Waddensea should act as a major nursery for the three species
so that the loss of part of the area could cause a significant reduction
in recruitment to the adult stocks, it seems highly likely that the losses
of the open sea fisheries would exceed those of the local fisheries in the
Waddensea, even when only the Dutch fisheries are considered.

It is for this reason that a special research programme involving
several scientists of our Institute was started to determine the importance of the Waddensea nursery. Earlier observations have indicated
that younger stages of the three species are found in most coastal
areas so the study could not be restricted to the Waddensea. The
programme is therefore aimed at establishing the distribution of the
young stages of demersal species in coastal waters, and though the
area investigated is limited to the Dutch coast for reasons of manpower
and ship facilities, it is hoped that additional information will also be
obtained from other areas. Our wishes in this respect were already
formulated by Tåning in 1951, when he asked for "international
cooperation in studying the distribution and abundance of young
plaice in all Wadden areas from Holland to the Horns Reef area and
England as well".

The study includes only demersal species. This is partly because
no single gear will sample adequately both demersal and pelagic
species. Moreover most pelagic species show strong shoaling behaviour
which in combination with the great hydrographic and topographic
diversity of the coastal nurseries, especially in the Waddensea, makes
sampling very difficult. Even with the non-shoaling demersal species
adequate quantitative sampling raises major problems (Bückmann,
1934a).

This paper will only report on young plaice and sole. For these
species earlier studies of Bückmann (1934a,b) and Smidt (1951) have
shown that the young fish enter the coastal area in May–June, when
they are 3–4 months old in the case of plaice and 0–1 month old in the

case of sole. A proportion of the young soles is probably also born in the coastal nursery (J. F. de Veen, pers. comm.). In the coastal zone the O-group fish grow quickly in their first summer, reaching a length between 6 and 11 cm by autumn. At that time most of the fish leave the coastal region and move to deeper areas off the coast. In spring of the next year the now 1 year-old fish (I-group) return to the coast. Larger individuals tend to leave the coastal area in their second summer, and in autumn most fish leave the coastal nursery on their migration to deeper water, few returning for a third summer. The migration towards the coast in spring has to be considered as a feeding migration (Johansen, 1913). Growth occurs mainly in summer, when the young fish are in the coastal nursery (Bückmann, 1934a). The autumn migration is probably to evade the low temperatures occurring in the coastal area in winter which are lethal for small soles (Woodhead, 1964).

Our study was primarily started against the background of an imminent closing of the Dutch part of the Waddensea. Its results can, however, also be applied to improve existing methods for forecasting future recruitment to the fisheries, which was the object of a similar study for plaice in Denmark (Johansen, 1922; Tåning, 1943, 1951). Moreover, it may have applications in pollution problems. The salinity distribution along the continental coast of the North Sea indicates that the often heavily polluted freshwater discharges from the large rivers move along the coast in a north-easterly direction and tend to stay in the coastal zone (Goedecke, Smed & Tomczak, 1967). In a special case of a copper-nitrate poisoning Roskam (1965) showed this transport along the Dutch coast into the Waddensea. This means that in the North Sea in particular coastal nursery areas will be affected by pollution as mentioned by Korringa (1968).

SIZE AND CONDITIONS OF THE WADDENSEA IN RELATION TO OTHER
COASTAL AREAS

*Physical characteristics*

The continental coastal zone of the North Sea, up to 15 km off the coast, taken from Cape Grisnez to Hanstholm, covers some 15 000 sq. km. The Waddensea from Den Helder in the Netherlands to Esbjerg in Denmark covers an area of about 8000 sq. km, of which nearly 3000 sq. km lies in Dutch territory. The southern inlets of Holland, a third area of possible importance as a nursery, have a size of about 1500 sq. km. The Waddensea thus covers about 33% of the potential nurseries along the continental coasts of the North Sea, the Dutch part being about 12%

238 J. J. ZIJLSTRA

Fig. 2. Aerial view of the eastern part of the Dutch Waddensea at low tide, showing the tidal flats and the canals

The Waddensea itself is a shallow area in which tidal currents have formed a complicated system of tidal canals and creeks. Inlets of up to 40 m depth between the isles branch into canals and creeks and become shallower until they gradually merge into large tidal flats. These tidal flats, dry at low tide, cover about 60% of the Waddensea area. The belt of isles on the outside of the Waddensea, which is well developed along the Dutch coast, protects the Wadden area from heavy wave action. Figure 2 gives an aerial view of part of the Waddensea at low tide. In the open coastal zone outside the isles and off the Dutch west coast the bottom usually slopes gently from the sandy beaches and even at a distance of 15 km from the coast the depth does not generally exceed 15 m. Only a small portion of this open coastal area is exposed at low tide but its position and shallow depth make the zone particularly vulnerable to wave action.

The influence of freshwater discharges on the coastal zone has already been mentioned in the first section. Salinity is usually low in the whole area $(29–32^0/_{00})$, and particularly so in the Waddensea $(16–31^0/_{00})$ indicating a high admixture of river water. Temperatures in the coastal zone are relatively high in summer and low in winter. Again, the Waddensea temperatures are more extreme than in the open coastal zone and zero temperatures often occur in winter.

Mainly because of the large freshwater discharges the coastal area is rich in nutrients, as is shown by Johnston & Jones (1965) and by Tijssen (1968, 1969). Phosphate and nitrite-nitrate values are evidently higher in the coastal zone than in the open sea and studies by Postma (1954, 1966) in the western part of the Dutch Waddensea have indicated that this area is itself richer in nutrients than the open coastal zone. Kühl & Mann (1953, 1954, 1957), studying the discharge areas of the rivers Ems, Weser and Elbe in the Waddensea, have also found a decrease in nutrients in the direction of the open sea. However, Postma also found that whereas nitrogen constituents are carried into the Waddensea from the IJsel Lake (the former Zuidersea), phosphorus constituents enter the Waddensea from the coastal waters.

The inward transport of small suspended material of partly organic origin is also very important for the Waddensea. This transport, described by Postma (1961) for the western part of the Dutch Waddensea, is caused by an asymmetrical shape of the ebb and flood curves in the small tidal channels. The process leads to a high level of suspended material in the Waddensea in summer which consists of about 17% (dry weight) of organic matter (mostly detritus), derived mainly from the coastal area. Moreover, by the same process, a large amount of silt accumulates in the water and on the bottom of the Waddensea. Postma

& Rommets (1970) estimate the transport of organic carbon into the Waddensea to be about equal to the primary production of organic carbon in the area, the latter being hampered by the great turbidity. From the studies of Postma the Waddensea appears as an area rich in nutrients and in suspended organic material, and in which the process of accumulation of suspended material plays an important rôle.

### The benthic fauna

The situation described above, with a high amount of suspended matter partly deposited in the tidal creeks and on the flats, is extremely favourable for the development of a rich bottom fauna. Some of these organisms, e.g. mussels, cockles, filter particulate food from the passing tidal water; others, e.g. worms, live on and in the deposited material. There is an extensive literature on the bottom fauna, in particular from the Danish and German Waddensea and from the open German Bight, but because of different measures used by the various authors it is not easy to compare their figures. Gessner (1957) has summarized data on the standing crop of bottom organisms, using material of Linke and Hagmeier. Despite a high degree of variability the material indicates that in the Waddensea (Jade) the standing crop of bottom organisms varies between 5–5000 g/sq. m, whereas in the open sea region of the German Bight the averages for several stations varied from about 30–300 g/sq. m. (The data given refer to wet weight.) Investigations by Smidt (1951) in the Danish Waddensea give an average figure of 174 g/sq. m in the southern part of the Danish Waddensea and 497 g/sq. m in the northern part. These figures, also referring to wet weight, are high when compared with similar data from the German Bight, Kattegat, Ringkøbing Fjord and other regions. Data from Ziegelmeier (1960) for the bottom fauna of the open German Bight in years 1949–1958 varied between 27–88 cm³/sq. m. Accepting a specific gravity of one it appears that this bottom fauna is considerably less than that of the Waddensea measured by Smidt and Gessner. It appears from these data that the bottom fauna of the Waddensea has a biomass of the order 3–9 times higher than in the other areas considered. Finally, data from Eisma (1966) on molluscs in an area off the Dutch coast, excluding the Waddensea, show the highest numbers of individuals per square metre close to the coast, in areas with much silt in the bottom.

As this paper deals with the nursery ground aspect of the Waddensea the interest in the bottom fauna is only in so far as it serves as food for young fish. Several studies have been made on the food of young plaice, showing that worms, smaller crustaceans and small thin-shelled molluscs are of main importance. This is for instance mentioned by Smidt (1951), citing Blegvad. Smidt shows that about half the weight of the bottom fauna in the Danish Waddensea can be considered as "first class plaice food". The figures he gives for some open sea areas such as the German Bight (data from Hagmeier) and the Kattegat (data from Blegvad) show far lower proportions. Smidt's material therefore suggests that in these open sea areas the standing crop of bottom organisms is not only lower than in the Waddensea but also contains a lower proportion of food suitable for young plaice.

In this section it has been shown that the Waddensea is more fertile in many respects than the open coastal area, the latter being richer again than the offshore areas. Freshwater discharges have been mentioned as a source of this fertility. Now, freshwater resources generally are becoming progressively more polluted by discharge from human communities, agriculture and industries, and amongst other side effects these may result in still higher nutrient concentrations. In the river Rhine, the largest single freshwater source to the southern North Sea, the phosphate-ion concentration increased from $0 \cdot 19$ mg/l in the years 1954–1956 to $0 \cdot 54$ mg/l in 1965–1967, whereas in the same period the nitrate-ion concentration increased from $8 \cdot 0$ to $11 \cdot 0$ mg/l. It therefore seems reasonable to suppose that the fertility of the coastal waters will have increased and is still increasing with a consequent effect on marine organisms in the area. In the years since 1946 the plaice and possibly also the sole stocks have increased in size, and the growth rate of herring has also increased, particularly in the first year of life. Such changes may themselves be related to the influence of changing fertility of the coastal waters on the growth and survival of young fish on the nursery grounds.

THE RESEARCH PROGRAMME

The area investigated along the Dutch coast is indicated in Figs 3–5. It includes the Waddensea, the southern inlets, the coastal zone and some lines of stations up to 40 miles off the coast. This area is fished twice a year during a two week period. Four ships have been employed because the techniques for sampling the inlets, the coastal area and the open sea are quite different. Two small flat-bottomed vessels fish the inlets in the north (Waddensea) and in the south (Zeeland); a larger vessel (35 m) fishes the coastal zone up to a distance of 12 miles off the shore line; and the largest ship (60 m) takes the open sea stations, which overlap partly with stations in the coastal zone. The largest vessel also fishes a number of stations in the German

K

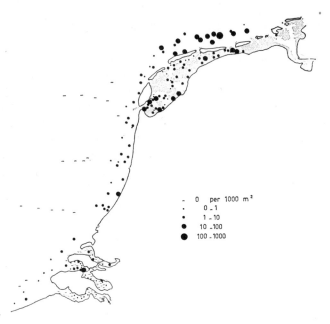

Fig. 3. Distribution of hauls in the Dutch coastal area in September–October 1969. The size of the dots indicates the numbers of O-group sole (under 13 cm) per thousand square metres fished.

Fig. 4. Distribution of hauls in the Dutch coastal area in May 1970. The size of the dots shows the numbers of I-group sole (under 13 cm) per thousand square metres fished.

Bight, off the German and Danish coast, up to Esbjerg. These stations
have not been included in Figs 3–5, because information on the coastal
region was not available for that area.

In determining number and duration of the hauls, an important
consideration was the expectation that the variance on a haul would
be high, especially in the inlets. Bückmann (1934a), fishing the German
Waddensea with a young plaice trawl, concluded that no reliable estimates of the abundance of young plaice could be obtained for the area

- 0 per 1000 m²
- 0-1
- 1-10
- 10-100
- 100-1000

Fig. 5. Distribution of hauls in the Dutch coastal area in April 1969. The numbers of
I-group plaice (under 13 cm) caught per thousand square metres fished are indicated by
the size of the dots.

due to this high variance. Tåning (1943) also mentions the great
variability in O-group plaice catches in the Waddensea, but shows at
the same time that there is a relation between the strength of a year-
class estimated as O-group in the Waddensea and as adult fish in the
offshore fisheries. It is our intention to carry out a number of experiments to establish the variance on a haul. In one experiment in the
southern inlets in which 40 hauls were made on the same spot during one
week the standard deviation for I-group sole catches was estimated at
about 20% of the mean catch, which seems rather low. However, to
cope with a possible high variance many hauls are made of short duration (15 min).

The nets used are beam trawls, with shrimp nets (mesh size about 2 cm), fitted with a groundrope with bobbins and one tickler chain. The two larger vessels fish with a beam trawl of 6 m, the smaller ones with a 3 m beam trawl. Experiments designed to determine the catch rate of these two trawls indicated that for sole the 6 m beam trawl caught about twice as much as the 3 m beam trawl, whereas for plaice the 6 m beam trawl caught more than twice the amount of the 3 m beam trawl (about 2·7 times). The nets were fished at about 6 k/h but recent experiments have indicated that fishing speed is a very important factor in determining catch rates. For young soles, for instance, the best catches per unit area fished were obtained with low speeds (1–2 k/h).

In order to randomize the sampling as far as possible the positions of the trawl hauls have been varied over the whole area investigated, in so far as the circumstances allow this procedure. However, in the coastal zone no hauls can be made within a distance of one mile off the coast owing to wave action and the shallow depth. Moreover, sampling in the area north of the Waddensea isles is hampered by the presence of old minefields and in the inlets sampling the tidal flats offers major problems, the ships used still having too much draught to fish on the flats at high tide. Fishing, therefore, is mainly done in the permanently covered deeper parts. Bückmann (1934a) and Smidt (1951) give arguments that young plaice migrate up the flats with high water, but R. Boddeke concludes from his material (pers. comm.) that with the exception of flounders very few fish actually go on the flats. If fish do migrate up the tidal flats with rising tide our sampling will underestimate the numbers of fish in the inlets.

The surveys are made between April and October in principle, because the young fish leave the inlets in winter and fishing in the inlets in mid-summer is hampered by the presence of large amounts of free-floating algae (Ulva spp.), which clog the nets. Up till now surveys were made in April, May and in September/October, when clogging does not occur.

Fish caught are sorted into species and separated into different age groups using the Petersen method. A reasonable number of otoliths is collected for sole and plaice to allow a breakdown into age groups at a later stage of the analysis. All numbers are converted to numbers caught per 1000 sq. m fished. This may be used as an index of population size provided we can assume that our sampling instrument, the beam trawl, catches the same proportion of the population in the path of the trawl on each occasion. This important assumption is being tested.

This study was started in 1969. In order to account for annual variations in the distribution and abundance and to adapt the techniques as the study goes along, the exercise was planned for a period of five years. Full results can therefore not be expected, but the first three surveys might be indicative of the final outcome of the study.

The distribution of young soles in Dutch coastal waters is shown in Figs 3 and 4 for the surveys in September/October 1969 and in May 1970. The data relate to soles smaller than 13 cm, which means O-group sole in autumn ($\frac{1}{2}$ year-old) and I-group sole in spring (1 year-old). In the figures all individual hauls are shown by dots, the size of the dots indicating the numbers caught on 1000 sq. m fished, grouped into five categories. All data refer to one year-class, born in the spring of 1969.

The distribution of young plaice is demonstrated in Fig. 5, showing the catches of plaice smaller than 13 cm in the survey of April 1969 (i.e. 1968 year-class). At that time the plaice were about 1 year-old. That survey was less complete than the May survey in 1970 because it only covered the western part of the Dutch Waddensea.

For both I-group sole and plaice the spring surveys gave the largest catches in the Waddensea area. Catches per 1000 sq. m fished were relatively low in the coastal zone, whereas larger catches were found along the closed western coast of Holland. The southern inlets had higher catches than the coastal zone, but much lower than the Waddensea. During the autumn cruise the O-group sole had a more seaward distribution, with high catches in the coastal zone, in particular in the area north of the Waddensea isles.

Interpreting these results with the knowledge gained in older studies of Bückmann (1934) and Smidt (1951), it seems likely that in September/October 1969 the O-group sole had already begun to leave the Waddensea and other inlets on their autumn migration to the open sea. During the spring surveys the, at that time, I-group sole and plaice had returned from their overwintering grounds and had moved into the inlets.

From the data on O- and I-group fish shown in Figs 3–5 and from similar material on plaice and sole (not illustrated here) it is possible to estimate the relative importance of the various nurseries along the Dutch coast. This was done by dividing the coastal area and the inlets into small sub-areas and multiplying the average catch per 1000 sq. m in that area with the size of the area. In the inlets (Waddensea, Zeeland) only the size of the permanently covered areas has been considered. The coastal zone from Belgium to Germany was divided into six areas, the Waddensea into eleven areas and the southern inlets into nine areas. In each area between 5 and 20 hauls have been made, on which the average catch per 1000 sq. m was based. There are of course other methods to determine the relative numbers in each area, for instance by relating the sub-areas to water depth or to distance from the coast, and though these have not been used for the purpose of this paper, they will be tried in future.

TABLE I

*Estimated numbers of soles smaller than 13 cm in the Waddensea, the southern inlets (Zeeland) and the open coastal zone of the Netherlands up to 8 miles from the coast*

| Area | Size of the area (km²) | Catch (numbers) per 1000 m² | Estimated numbers in area (millions) | % of total numbers in Dutch coastal area |
|------|------|------|------|------|
| I-group in April 1969 (year-class 1968) | | | | |
| Waddensea* | 1436·6 | 4·19 | 5·53 | 66 |
| Zeeland | 577·9 | 2·61 | 1·34 | 16 |
| Open coast | 4909·7 | 0·28 | 1·50 | 18 |
| O-group in September/October 1969 (year-class 1969) | | | | |
| Waddensea† | 1436·6 | 7·02 | 10·08 | 8 |
| Zeeland | 577·9 | 1·15 | 0·70 | 1 |
| Open coast | 4909·7 | 20·05 | 109·41 | 91 |
| I-group in May 1970 (year-class 1969) | | | | |
| Waddensea | 1436·6 | 9·36 | 13·71 | 63 |
| Zeeland | 577·9 | 4·82 | 3·31 | 15 |
| Open coast | 4909·7 | 1·41 | 4·80 | 22 |

* Areas not fished in the eastern part of the Waddensea deduced from proportions in May 1970.
† Surveys incomplete in the eastern part of the Waddensea, average catch per 1000 m² used for whole Waddensea area.

The results of the method used here are given in Table I for O- and I-group sole and Table II for O- and I-group plaice. The most important conclusion from the two tables is that during the two spring surveys, when the young sole and plaice have entered the coastal region on their feeding migration, the major part of them is found in the inlets. Only about 20% of the small soles and plaice present along the Dutch coast

TABLE II

*Estimated numbers of plaice smaller than 13 cm in the Waddensea, the southern inlets (Zeeland) and the open coastal zone of the Netherlands up to 8 miles off the coast*

| Area | Size of the area (km²) | Catch (numbers) per 1000 m² | Estimated numbers in area (millions) | % of total numbers in Dutch coastal area |
|---|---|---|---|---|
| I-group in April 1969 (year-class 1968) | | | | |
| Waddensea* | 1436·6 | 29·46 | 44·46 | 82 |
| Zeeland | 577·9 | 7·28 | 3·84 | 7 |
| Open coast | 4909·7 | 1·01 | 5·55 | 10 |
| O-group in September/October 1969 (year-class 1969) | | | | |
| Waddensea† | 1436·6 | 12·92 | 18·56 | 53 |
| Zeeland | 577·9 | 2·26 | 1·25 | 4 |
| Open coast | 4909·7 | 2·83 | 15·36 | 44 |
| I-group in May 1970 (year-class 1969) | | | | |
| Waddensea | 1436·6 | 5·53 | 8·82 | 74 |
| Zeeland | 577·9 | 0·67 | 0·41 | 3 |
| Open coast | 4909·7 | 0·55 | 2·70 | 23 |

* Areas not fished in the eastern part of the Waddensea deduced from proportions in May 1970.
† Surveys incomplete in the eastern part of the Waddensea, average catch per 1000 m² used for whole Waddensea area.

was found in the open coastal zone, despite the fact that the size of the coastal zone is much larger than that of the inlets. Among the inlets the Waddensea appears as the most important one, partly because of its larger space but also because of a higher density of the young fish as indicated by our sampling method. The density in the southern inlets is usually higher than in the open coastal nursery, at least for soles.

The distribution of the young fish in the autumn cruise is quite different from that in the spring surveys. As mentioned before in relation to Figs 3–5, the different distribution is attributed to an autumn migration to the open sea. In this connection the high numbers of young sole, caught just north of the Waddensea isles (Fig. 4) presumably representing emigrants from the Waddensea, are significant in stressing the importance of the Waddensea as a nursery for sole.

It is remarkable that the numbers calculated for the whole nursery area along the Dutch coast are much higher in the autumn of 1969 than in the next spring (May, 1970). Our estimate of the numbers of the

1969 year-class of sole are about 120 million in September/October 1969 and only 22 million in May 1970. The difference for plaice is less striking, being 35 million in September/October 1969 and 12 million in May 1970. A further difference between plaice and sole is that the latter is relatively more numerous in the open coastal zone in September/October, which suggests that the sole is leaving the inlets at an earlier date than the plaice.

One could think of many reasons for the large differences in numbers for the same year-class in autumn and the next spring. A high mortality rate, partly due to the shrimp fisheries, could cause a sharp reduction in numbers during the winter months (R. Boddeke, pers. comm.). On the other hand the autumn figures could be enhanced by an immigration into Dutch waters of young fish, in particular sole, from the German Bight, moving on their autumn migration in a westerly direction. However, since a slight easterly migration of the soles north of the Waddensea isles was noticed at the time of the survey this explanation seems unlikely. Finally, a high availability to the gear at the time of the autumn cruise could be responsible; this might be general throughout the Dutch coastal zone, or, judging from the high catches north of the Wadden isles, it might be restricted to that area alone.

By assuming that the soles which entered the Waddensea in the spring of 1970 were those which left the area in the preceding autumn, one could also argue that the remarkably high catches north of the isles really indicate a low availability of soles in the Waddensea. This interpretation finds some support in the fact that the difference in numbers estimated in the nurseries south of the Waddensea area, along the open west coast and in the southern inlets between autumn 1969 (about 14 million) and spring 1970 (about 8 million) is less than the corresponding difference in the Waddensea area. The implication that the young fish, particularly soles, are underestimated in the Waddensea because of a lower availability to our gear seems not unreasonable considering the complicated topography of the area: pockets of small soles might easily be missed in areas where fishing is impossible, for instance on mussel beds, or on the large tidal flats which were not counted in our calculations. However, this source of error would be compensated to some extent by the absence of sampling within one mile offshore in the coastal zone where young fish could also be numerous.

DISCUSSION

First estimates of the distribution of young sole and plaice in the Dutch coastal waters indicate the Waddensea to be the most important nursery. The two spring surveys suggest that about 65% of the I-group sole and 80% of the I-group plaice present in Dutch coastal waters were concentrated in the Waddensea area. The distribution of young soles during the autumn survey, when the fish had left the inlets and were particularly numerous just north of the Waddensea isles, also points at the importance of the Waddensea nursery. Relatively few fish were found in the open coastal zone.

Our surveys have not yet caught O-group sole and plaice during their first summer, partly because a summer survey in the inlets would be hampered by clogging of the nets. There are, however, reports from former studies indicating the O-group fish of the two species to be even more numerous in the inlets than the I-group (Bückmann, 1934a,b; Smidt, 1951). Bückmann, for instance, states that in plaice only the smaller individuals of the O-group return to the Waddensea in the next spring. Our data suggest something similar for sole, as the larger soles of the I-group are found in the open coastal zone, as shown in Table III for part of the western Waddensea in May 1970.

TABLE III

*Mean length of I-group sole in May 1970 in different parts of the western Waddensea and in the neighbouring coastal area*

| Area | Mean length of I-group soles (cm) |
| --- | --- |
| Outside the inlet (Marsdiep) | 11·8 |
| About 5 km inside the inlet | 10·9 |
| About 15 km inside the inlet | 10·8 |
| About 30 km inside the inlet | 10·3 |

It therefore seems possible that O-group plaice and sole will be found in even greater proportions in the inlets than the I-group. A summer survey is planned in 1971 to verify this point.

An uncertain factor in the assessment is the sampling gear, the beam trawl, which is not ideal. As with any fishing method it cannot be expected to catch all the fish in its path, but as long as the proportion caught of the fish present does not vary between areas within and between surveys our results will be valid. It is, however, difficult to verify this point. Experiments have been started at sea to study the efficiency of the beam trawl by improving gear and fishing technique, e.g. trawling speed. In addition, tank experiments are planned for the future. The first results of these studies seem to indicate that because the six metre nets used in the open sea catch more than twice the amount of young plaice than the three metre nets employed in the inlets, the proportion of young plaice in the open coastal zone is overestimated.

An indirect check of the methods can be made by comparing the numbers of young sole and plaice in the coastal nursery, as deduced by our methods, with estimates of the average numbers of 3 year-old recruits of these species in the North Sea fisheries. Taking the density of the young fish in the German–Danish coastal waters as equal to that in the Dutch nurseries, the numbers in the total nursery area along the continental coast will be about three times those in the Dutch coastal area. The numbers of young sole would then be 45 million, based on the I-group fish in the two spring surveys and 360 million fish, using the data from the one autumn cruise. For plaice the figures for the two spring surveys and the autumn survey are more alike at about 100 million fish. J. F. de Veen (pers. comm.) estimates the numbers of an average year-class of sole at age three in the North Sea at about 140 million fish and of plaice at about 500 million fish. These calculations demonstrate that our estimates of the numbers of young sole and plaice in coastal nurseries are very low. Assuming a natural mortality rate of 0·2 between age 1 and age 3 and neglecting a possible fishing mortality (shrimp fisheries), our estimates for 1 year-old plaice would be about five times too low, and for 1 year-old sole about three to four times, considering only the spring surveys. Only in the case of the O-group sole, met during the autumn cruise, would the numbers be relatively high. Our numbers of O- and I-group sole and plaice are also low when compared with the estimated numbers killed by the shrimp fisheries in the Waddensea. Meyer-Waarden & Tiews (1965) found the numbers of O-group plaice destroyed in the German Waddensea to be about 160 million fish annually in the years 1954–1958 and O-group soles to be 40 million. R. Boddeke (pers. comm.) estimates the numbers of young plaice and sole destroyed in the Dutch part of the Waddensea to be even higher: over a milliard young plaice (all age groups) in 1964 and 150 million soles of the strong 1963 year-class in 1963 and 1964.

It seems most probable that our low estimates of the abundance of young flatfish are mainly caused by a low efficiency of the nets employed. Other explanations are that recruitment to the offshore stocks from the German–Danish coastal areas is much higher than presumed here, though this seems unlikely considering the numbers destroyed in the shrimp fisheries, or that young flatfish occur in large numbers in other regions, e.g. on the English coast. It is also possible that the year-classes considered in the surveys (1968–1969) could be far below average so that the comparison between the survey data and average year-class strength in the commercial fishery is not valid. This point can be verified when the year-classes surveyed do appear in the offshore stock.

Having reached the tentative conclusion that the Waddensea functions as an important nursery area for sole and plaice, one might

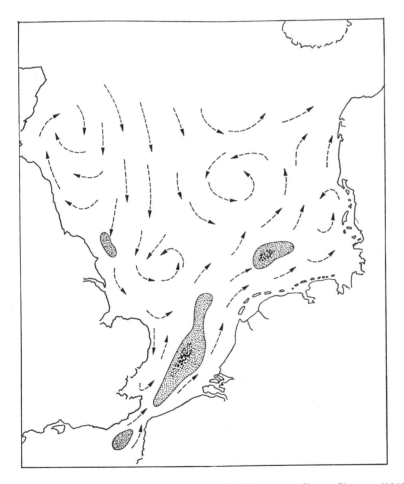

Fig. 6. The distribution of plaice eggs in the North Sea, according to Simpson (1959), showing the position of the main spawning grounds and the residual flow system in the area (Böhnecke, 1922).

consider how the young fish manage to penetrate the area. For sole this question has a relatively simple qualitative answer. Soles are reported to spawn in late spring in areas close to the coast (ICES, 1965); in their spawning migration the adult fish penetrate even into the inlets in Zeeland and in the Waddensea so that sole eggs hatch in or near the nurseries at the start of the growth season. Plaice, on the other hand, are born in the open sea, some 20–60 miles off the coast, in January–March. In Fig. 6 the main spawning grounds of plaice are shown according to Simpson (1959), together with the residual flow system in the area (Böhnecke, 1922). The figure indicates that the pelagic eggs and larvae in the major spawning areas in the southern and south-eastern North Sea will be transported along the continental coast in a north-easterly direction. The transport distance in the pelagic phase before metamorphosis, when a young fish starts its demersal life, is estimated by Simpson at about 140 n. miles. This transport would bring most larvae from the spawning areas in the southern and south-eastern North Sea in a position 20–40 miles off the Waddensea at the time of metamorphosis (Simpson). From that position the young demersal plaice migrates probably actively to the coast, arriving there at the time the growth season starts. The position of the spawning grounds of plaice thus seems to be related to the Waddensea area. The low numbers of young plaice in the southern inlets as compared with the numbers in the Waddensea support this hypothesis. The relatively small spawning area off Flamborough Head along the English north-east coast, situated in a different current system, could be connected with nursery areas in the Humber–Wash region in a similar way.

In herring, mentioned in the first section (p. 235) as another economic important species for which the Waddensea could function as the main nursery, the position of the spawning grounds in the open sea could also indicate a relation to the south-eastern North Sea, as shown in Fig. 7. In addition, the length distribution of the immature herring in the North Sea seems to point at the south-eastern part as an important nursery. In an international study to locate the main nurseries for herring in the North Sea, it appeared that in all year-classes investigated length increased from south-east to north-west with the smallest individuals in the south-eastern corner (ICES, 1969). As the migration of the immature herring, which goes in a general north-westerly direction, seems to be length dependent, this length distribution indicates the south-eastern corner of the North Sea as a major nursery for the small and young herring. In addition, Postuma, Zijlstra & Das (1965) showed that in the Dutch coastal region the smaller herring are found in the inlets. They explained this distribution by an outward

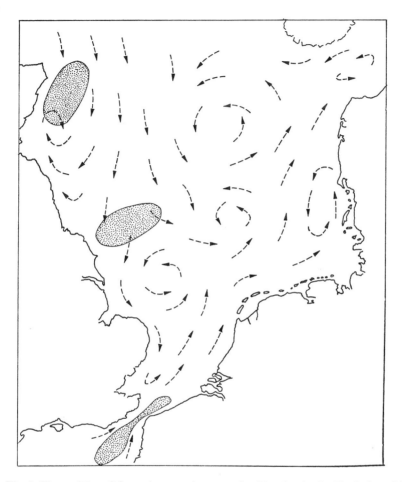

Fig. 7. The position of the main spawning grounds of herring in the North Sea with the residual flow system in the area (Böhnecke, 1922).

migration, related to length. A similar observation was made by Bück-mann (1950) for the German Waddensea. As mentioned in the first section (p. 235), reports of various authors on the immigration of herring larvae into the German and Dutch Waddensea area also suggests an important nursery function of the Waddensea for herring.

Coming back now to the original problem, the effect of a closure—complete or partial—of the Waddensea on the recruitment of plaice, sole and possibly herring to the offshore resources of the southern North Sea, our first results on the distribution of the young fish in the coastal nurseries seem to justify a conclusion that such an operation could have a significant effect, though it cannot be quantified at present. The only objection to this conclusion could be that the nurseries are not fully used at present, so that a loss of part of the area would be compensated by a better use of, i.e., a higher density, in the remaining nurseries.

Little is known about the numbers of young fish which can grow up in a nursery. Bowers (1966), studying the growth of hatchery-reared plaice, reports that under optimal conditions about twelve 1 year-old plaice can be kept per square metre. If the Waddensea would provide these optimal conditions, some 40 milliards of young plaice could be produced by the area. A comparison with the numbers of an average plaice year-class at age three, about one milliard fish, might suggest that there is ample space in the nurseries. It is questionable, however, whether the Waddensea provides the optimal conditions mentioned by Bowers, especially since the experimental approach neglects the presence of numerous other animals in the Waddensea, preying on plaice food. Experience from former large-scale closures of coastal areas, such as the Zuidersea, is also of little assistance in this respect: the former Zuidersea did not serve as a nursery area for many young plaice and sole, probably because of its low salinity (Anon, 1922).

The observations of Bückmann (1944) and Tåning (1947) about a decrease in growth of young plaice with densities during the war years is very relevant to these problems. Bückmann mentions the possibility that the cause is not so much lack of food but lack of space. Both authors show that the effect of crowding on the growth is more pronounced in I–III-group plaice than in O-group plaice. This is in conformity with more recent observations by J. F. de Veen (pers. comm.) that growth in O-group soles shows no relation to density. For the older fish, however, it seems that under certain conditions, such as those generated by the cessation of fishing from 1939–1945, food or space in the nursery do become limiting factors.

The observation of Beverton & Holt (1957) on plaice that no relation seems to be present between the numbers of eggs produced by the parent stock and subsequent recruitment could also be interpreted that space in the nursery is limited. In this interpretation the number of surviving larvae would also be more than sufficient to fill the space in the nurseries, so that the size of the nurseries determine the level of recruitment rather than the size of the parent stock.

From these considerations it seems unlikely that the loss of a large part of the nursery area of plaice and sole, which a closure of the Dutch Waddensea would certainly mean, will be compensated completely by higher density in the remaining nurseries. It seems much more likely that such a loss will result in the disappearance of that part of the stock which uses the lost area as a nursery. In the case of plaice, for instance, a closure of the Dutch Waddensea could lead to the loss of the Southern Bight plaice population, which spawns in the deep water channel in that area.

As yet little research has been carried out in sea fisheries about the importance of nursery areas in determining the size of the adult stocks, although recently studies have been started in connection with pollution problems in some estuarine areas (Clark, Smith, Kendall & Fahay, 1969). An observation of Le Cren (in press) concerning freshwater salmonids, indicating that the size of the adult stock will depend more than anything upon the area of fry rearing ground available, could equally apply to many sea fishes with restricted nursery areas.

SUMMARY

This paper deals with the possible consequences of a closure—complete or partial—of the Dutch section of the Waddensea for some fish species which are of great economic importance for the southern North Sea fisheries. A closure could affect several species, e.g. plaice, sole and herring, which have their nursery grounds in coastal waters such as the Waddensea.

The Waddensea is very rich in nutrients, suspended material and bottom fauna, suitable for fish food, due to an accumulation process of suspended matter of partly organic origin.

A study to evaluate the relative importance of the Waddensea is described. The methods employed, intensive sampling with beam trawls in the Dutch coastal and inshore waters, provide only information on demersal species, such as plaice and sole. The limitations and dangers of the method are discussed.

The first results of this study, which is planned as a long-term project, indicate the Waddensea to be the main nursery in the Dutch coastal area. Estimates from two spring surveys (1969, 1970), covering the start of the growth season, show that of I-group fish about 64% of all soles and about 80% of all plaice present in Dutch coastal waters occur in the Waddensea. Less than 20% of the about 1 year-old fish of these species were found in the open coastal area. The importance of the Waddensea nursery for sole was also suggested by a high concentration of O-group soles just north of the Waddensea during the one autumn survey, when a large part of the young soles had already left the Wadden area.

Moreover, the location of the main spawning grounds of plaice and possibly also of herring, in relation to the current pattern in the North

Sea, conforms with the function of the Waddensea as the major nursery for these species.

The effect of a partial closure of this presumably main nursery is discussed and some arguments put forward which make it unlikely that the loss of part of the Waddensea would be compensated by higher densities in the remaining nurseries.

## ACKNOWLEDGEMENT

The study, on which this paper reports, is carried out by a team of scientists of the Fisheries Laboratory in IJmuiden, Netherlands. The following scientists participate in the study: Messrs R. Boddeke, N. Daan, K. H. Postuma, J. F. de Veen and the author.

## REFERENCES

Anon (1922). *Flora en fauna der Zuiderzee*, (H. C. Redeke, ed.) Helder, De Boer.
Beverton, R. J. H. & Holt, S. J. (1957). On the dynamics of exploited fish populations. *Fishery Invest., Lond.* (2), **19**: 533 pp.
Boddeke, R. (1963). Donkere wolken boven de kustvisserij. *Viss. Nieuws* **16** (8): 194–197.
Boddeke, R. (1967). Visserij-biologische veranderingen in de westelijke Waddenzee. *Visserij* **20** (9): 213–222.
Böhnecke, G. (1922). Salzgehalt und Strömungen der Nordsee. *Veröff. Inst. Meeresk. Univ. Berl., N.F., A. Geogr. Naturwiss. R.H.* No. 10: 1–34.
Bowers, A. B. (1966). Growth in hatchery-reared plaice. *Rep. Challenger Soc.* **3**: 18.
Bückmann, A. (1934a). Ueber die Jungschollenbevölkerung der Deutschen Wattenküste der Nordsee. *Ber. dt. wiss. Kommn Meeresforsch.* N.F. **7** (3): 205–213.
Bückmann, A. (1934b). Untersuchungen über die Naturgeschichte der Seezunge, die Seezungenbevölkerung und die Seezungenfang in der Nordsee. *Ber. dt. wiss. Kommn Meeresforsch.* N.F. **7** (2): 1–114.
Bückmann, A. (1944). Die Schollenbevölkerung der Helgoländer Bucht ünd die Einschränkung der Fischerei während der Kriegsjahre 1914–1918 und 1939–1942. *Rapp. P.-v. Réun. Cons. perm. int. Explor. Mer* **114**: 1–42.
Bückmann, A. (1950). Die Untersuchungen der Biologischen Anstalt über die Oekologie der Heringsbrut in der südlichen Nordsee. *Helgoländer wiss. Meeresunters.* **3**: 171–205.
Clark, J., Smith, W. G., Kendall, A. W. Jr. & Fahay, M. P. (1969). Studies of estuarine dependence of Atlantic coastal fishes. *Tech. Pap. U.S. Fish Wildl. Serv.*, No. 28, 132 pp.
Eisma, D. (1966). The distribution of benthic marine molluscs off the main Dutch coast. *Neth. J. Sea. Res.* **3** (1): 107–163.
Gessner, F. (1957). *Meer und Strand.* Berlin: VEB Deutscher Verlag der Wissenschaften.

Goedecke, E., Smed, J. & Tomczack, G. (1967). Monatskarten des Salzgehaltes der Nordsee. *Dt. hydrogr. Z.* Reihe B (4), No. 9: 1–13.

ICES (1965). Report of the working group on sole. *Coop. Res. Report* No. 5, 126 pp.

ICES (1969). Report of the North Sea young herring working group. *Coop. Res. Report*, Ser. A. No. 14, 87 pp.

Johansen, A. C. (1913). Contributions to the biology of the plaice, with special regard to the Danish plaice-fishery. VI. On the immigration of plaice to the coastal grounds and fiords on the west coast of Jutland. *Meddr Kommn Havunders.* (Serie Fiskeri) **4** (4): 1–26.

Johansen, A. C. (1922). On the density of the young plaice population in the eastern part of the North Sea and the Skagerak in pre war and in post war years. *Meddr Kommn Havunders.* (Serie Fiskeri) **6** (8): 1–31.

Johnston, R. & Jones, P. G. W. (1965). Inorganic nutrients in the North Sea. *Serial atlas of the marine environment*, Folio 11. New York, Am. Geogr. Soc.

Korringa, P. (1968). Biological consequences of marine pollution with special reference to the North Sea fisheries. *Helgoländer wiss Meeresunters.* **17**: 126–140.

Kühl, H. & Mann, H. (1953). Beiträge zur Hydrochemie der Unterelbe. *Veröff. Inst. Meeresforsch. Bremerh.* **2**: 236–268.

Kühl, H. & Mann, H. (1954). Ueber die Hydrochemie der unteren Ems. *Veröff. Inst. Meeresforsch. Bremerh.* **3**: 126–158.

Kühl, H. & Mann, H. (1957). Beiträge zur Hydrochemie der unteren Weser. *Veröff. Inst. Meeresforsch. Bremerh.* **5**: 34–62.

Le Cren, E. D. (in press). The population dynamics of young trout (*Salmo trutta*) in relation to density and territorial behaviour. *Rapp. P.-v. Réun. Cons perm. int. Explor. Mer.*

Meyer-Waarden, P. F. & Tiews, K. (1965). Der Beifang in den Fängen der deutschen Garnelenfischerei in den Jahren 1954–1960. *Ber. dt. wiss. Kommn. Meeresforsch.*, N.F. **18** (1): 13–78.

Postma, H. (1954). Hydrography of the Dutch Waddensea. *Archs néerl. Zool.* **10** (4): 1–106.

Postma, H. (1961). Transport and accumulation of suspended matter in the Dutch Waddensea. *Netherlands J. Sea Res.* **1** (1/2): 148–190.

Postma, H. (1966). The cycle of nitrogen in the Waddensea and adjacent waters *Netherlands J. Sea Res.* **3** (2): 186–221.

Postma, H. & Rommets, J. W. (1970). Primary production in the Waddensea. *Netherlands J. Sea Res.* **4** (4): 470–493.

Postuma, K. H. (1969). On the herring larvae in the Dutch Waddensea 1967–1969. ICES CM/H: 22 7 pp. (mimeo).

Postuma, K. H., Zijlstra, J. J. & Das, N. (1965). On the immature herring of the North Sea. *J. Cons. perm. int. Explor. Mer* **29** (3): 256–276.

Roskam, R. Th. (1965). A case of copper pollution along the Dutch shore. ICES CM/1965, No. 44, 4 pp. (mimeo).

Simpson, A. C. (1959). The spawning of the plaice in the North Sea. *Fishery Invest.*, *Lond.* (2), **22** (7): 1–111.

Smidt, E. L. B. (1951). Animal production in the Danish Waddensea. *Meddr Kommn Danm. Fisk.-og Havunders.* (Serie Fiskeri) **11**, 6: 1–151.

Tåning, A. V. (1943). Fluctuation in the number of O-group plaice fished in the Waddensea. *Annls. biol.*, *Copenh.* **1**: 135–137.

Tåning, A. V. (1947). Observations on young plaice in the Danish Waddensea during the war. *Annls biol. Copenh.* **2**: 53–54.

Tåning, A. V. (1951). Occurrence of O-group plaice in the Danish Waddensea. *Annls biol., Copenh.* **7**: 91–92.

Tijssen, S. B. (1968). Hydrographical and chemical observations in the Southern Bight, August and November 1967. *Annls biol., Copenh.* **24**: 52–56.

Tijssen, S. B. (1969). Hydrographical and chemical observations in the Southern Bight, February, May, August and November 1968. *Annls biol., Copenh.* **25**: 51–59.

Woodhead, P. M. J. (1964). The death of North Sea fish during the winter 1962–63, particularly with reference to the sole, *Solea vulgaris. Helgoländer wiss. Meeresunters.* **10**: 283–300.

Ziegelmeier, E. (1960). Investigations of the bottom fauna in the eastern part of the German Bight, 1958. *Annls biol., Copenh.* **15**: 62–63.

*Symp. zool. Soc. Lond.* (1972) No. 29, 259-269.

# SOME RELATIONSHIPS BETWEEN THE FOOD INTAKE AND GROWTH OF YOUNG FISH

## L. BIRKETT

*Fisheries Laboratory, Lowestoft, Suffolk, England*

### SYNOPSIS

The efficiency of food conversion in fish is a fundamental aspect of the productivity of the ecosystem in which they live and it is especially important to the production and survival of juvenile fish that sustain exploited stocks. In experiments the conversion efficiency of fish is known to vary widely and it is shown that a large part of this variation is related to changes in condition factor of the fish, and hence to the dynamics of materials stored within the body. It is postulated that the form of growth, i.e. growth in length, growth in weight or isometric growth, is determined by different threshold levels of feeding rate, the utilization of food depending upon the condition factor of the fish. The application of experimentally determined estimates of conversion efficiency to natural populations is also discussed.

### INTRODUCTION

This paper is intended as a brief review of experiments of the "growth and maintenance" type, which are performed in order to study the dependence of growth upon food consumption in fish. A comparative evaluation of the increasing amount of data should be of practical use in studies of production, in which this dependence is so often obscured by factors such as mortality, recruitment or other population changes. In tneir recent review paper, Paloheimo & Dickie (1966) were evidently inspired by the need to draw baselines through the many sets of data which have been presented in such different ways as to make direct comparisons rather difficult. Here, some aspects of experimental growth and feeding relationships not already elaborated by these authors are introduced.

The contrast, and relationship, between the immature, fast-growing phase and the mature phase in which growth gradually becomes reduced is well known to fishery biologists; it has provided a crucial test of empirical growth theories (Pütter, 1920), among which the Bertalanffy function (von Bertalanffy, 1938, 1964; Beverton & Holt, 1957) appears to be the one most generally applicable. In young fish, rapid growth must have some survival value, since it presumably removes them from the influence of predators; it also enables young fish to spread to feeding grounds further afield from the nursery grounds, or to exploit larger food-species under less competitive conditions. Such considerations as these emphasize the relevance of growth/feeding studies in conservation also, since the conservation of young fish, the recruits to the fishable stock, is of prime importance.

The food provides the building materials for synthesis, the materials to be stored in the body as reserves, and the substrates for all energy processes. In adult fish, a high proportion of the produced matter is annually shed as eggs or sperm, but this has been little studied as a nutritional problem, and this paper is not concerned with it.

The utilization of food may be stated as follows:

$$\text{Food} = \begin{array}{c} \text{Materials} \\ \text{used for} \\ \text{biosynthesis} \end{array} + \begin{array}{c} \text{Materials} \\ \text{stored as} \\ \text{reserves} \end{array} + \begin{array}{c} \text{Materials} \\ \text{used in} \\ \text{metabolism} \end{array}$$

In this statement, "energy" is virtually synonymous with "materials", but the rigorous concepts of animal energetics have yet to be applied to fish as they have been to mammals (e.g. Brody, 1945; Benedict, 1938; Blaxter, 1967).

The conversion of food to growth introduces the concept of efficiency. In its simplest form, this is the ratio of the gain in weight per unit of total food intake during a given period of time. The transfer is modified by two factors: first, the need to replace matter or energy lost through internal turnover and secondly the diversion of absorbed materials into storage. These requirements provide a threshold in the dependence of growth upon food, which was recognized by various authors who tried to determine maintenance requirements by the direct method of restricted feeding (Dawes, 1930, 1931, in *Pleuronectes platessa* L.; Pentelow, 1939; Brown, 1946, in *Salmo trutta* L.; Elder, 1962, in *Bagrus docmac*; Johnson, 1966, in *Esox lucius* L.).

Food consumed in excess of the maintenance requirements is converted *pro rata* into growth; feeding below the maintenance level leads to loss of weight. According to Dawes (1930, 1931) the plaice in his experiments converted to growth approximately 20% of the food given in excess of maintenance requirements. Similar values were obtained by Pentelow (1939) and Brown (1946) for trout.

The conversion efficiency may be expressed mathematically as follows. The simple or net efficiency, $E$, is $\Delta W/\Delta I$, where $\Delta W$ = net body gain and $\Delta I$ = total food intake. The *pro rata* or gross efficiency, $E^*$, is $\Delta W/\Delta(I - I_m)$, where $\Delta I_m$ = maintenance requirement.

## VARIANCE OF THE NET EFFICIENCY, $E$, IN EXPERIMENTS

When no food is taken $\Delta W$ is negative, since the body loses weight; hence during complete starvation $E$ is always negative, and could reach a very low value. At the maintenance point, $\Delta W = 0$, and hence $E = 0$. The upper limit of $E$ is rather less than $1 \cdot 0$ (or $100\%$), because a substantial proportion of the food energy is converted to metabolic energy. Experimentally determined values of $E$ do not usually exceed $0 \cdot 6$ ($60\%$ conversion). The variance of $E$ has two main components, arising within and between individuals, for any given type of food. Differences in convertibility also exist between foods, which are probably due to differences in their composition. The wide range of $E$ values usually obtained within any set of experimental observations poses the problem of which value represents the true conversion efficiency under ecological conditions.

Undoubtedly the rate of feeding, that is the amount of food consumed by a fish per unit time, influences the value of $E$. Paloheimo & Dickie (1966) found a significant negative correlation between $\log E$ and the rate of intake, for a number of species. The equation by which this relationship was described by these authors is as follows:

$$\log E = -a - b \ . \ \Delta I / \Delta t \qquad (1)$$

in which $a$ and $b$ are two constants. A plot of $\log E$ against $\Delta I / \Delta t$, the feeding rate, yielded straight lines for the published data which these authors employed. However, Rafail (1968, 1969) produced evidence to show that Equation (1) represents a special case of the relationship between $E$ and feeding rate and that $E$ could, and in fact necessarily does, increase with intake at first. Presumably, the special relationship implied by Equation (1) may be dependent on some of the factors governing the actual feeding rate established by experimental fish; these, as stated by Paloheimo & Dickie, quoting Brown (1946), may include competitive or "hierarchical" relationships among fish when fed in groups, temperature differences and the level of food supply. Since $E$ also varies between individuals kept at the same temperature, in isolation, and under surplus food supplies, it is obvious that hierarchies or food-levels are not the only factors involved.

The within-individual variance in $E$ may be largely overcome by comparing the cumulative gains with the cumulative intake, in individuals that have been kept under continuous observation for relatively long periods. Figure 1 shows a few examples of such comparison, and is based on data for three species: plaice, *Pleuronectes platessa* L., cod, *Gadus morhua* L., and *Tilapia mossambica* Peters. During quite long periods in each case, the cumulative gains regressed linearly upon the cumulative intake. The slope in the linear regressions is an estimate of

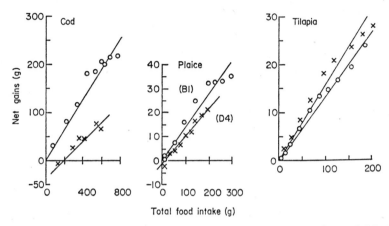

FIG. 1. Cumulative plots of net gain against food intake in individual fish (cod, plaice) or groups of fish (*Tilapia*). Observations at intervals of 10 days (cod, *Tilapia*) from L. Birkett (unpublished data), or 14 days (plaice, Dawes, 1931). The data for plaice and cod are typical of those for other cases in these two experiments.

the mean net efficiency. As an example, the mean value of $E$ obtained by linear regression for one plaice, D4, was $0 \cdot 126 \pm 0 \cdot 006$; this may be compared with the mean of the several fortnightly values of $E$ for the separate periods comprising this curve, which was $0 \cdot 094 \pm 0 \cdot 108$. Comparing the two coefficients of variation, that for the regression slope is $\pm 4 \cdot 7\%$, while that for the separate fortnightly values is $\pm 115\%$. Clearly the estimation of sustained efficiencies offers a substantial reduction of within-individual variance. Similar results are obtained from other examples of cumulative values.

Even this approach, however, does not remove the variance between individuals, and, as shown by the examples in Fig. 1, there remains a considerable range of long-term sustainable efficiency within the individual, between different periods. Birkett, in an experiment with cod, found that there was a correlation between the net efficiency and the rate of change of the condition factor of the fish. The latter is calculated as $q = w/l^3$, where $w$ = weight (in mg), $l$ = length (in cm), and $q$, the condition factor, is thus in units of mg/cm$^3$. According to the concept that growth is normally isometric in fishes, $q$ is independent of age (Beverton & Holt, 1957). However, it is well known that $q$ fluctuates in a seasonal pattern (e.g. Graham, 1924; Hickling, 1930;

Le Cren, 1951); it also varies, and sometimes quite rapidly, in fish held under experimental conditions (e.g. Dawes, 1930, 1931; Brown, 1946; L. Birkett, unpublished data).

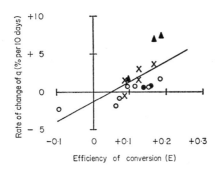

FIG. 2. The efficiency of conversion is correlated with the rate of change of condition factor. These data are for the plaice in the maximum-feeding experiment at Cawsand (Dawes, 1931). Symbols denote the initial condition factor: solid circles, 10–11 mg/cm$^3$; crosses, 9–10 mg/cm$^3$; triangles, 8–9 mg/cm$^3$; open circles, 7–8 mg/cm$^3$.

Figure 2 shows that a correlation exists between the rate of change of $q$, and the mean net efficiency, in Dawes' plaice; those shown here were the maximum-fed plaice of the Cawsand, 1930, experiment. The data are arranged according to the value of $q_0$, the initial condition factor; the values represent periods of between 28 and 99 days, during which there were approximately linear trends in the condition factor, so the rate of change of condition factor was constant in time. The intercept on the abscissa represents the net efficiency when there is no change in $q$, i.e. it is the efficiency of conversion during purely isometric growth. Linear regression of the data indicates the "isometric net efficiency", $E_i$, for these plaice to be 0·05, though the distribution of the points suggests that the true value might be slightly higher than this, between 0·06 and 0·12, i.e. conversion at between 6 and 12% efficiency resulted in the maintenance of $q$ at a constant value. The negative intercept on the ordinate represents a rate of loss of condition when $E$ is zero, that is, at the point at which maintenance is satisfied; this is approximately −2% per 10 days. Since the weight remains constant at this point, it is obvious that the length continues to increase. Levels of $E$ higher than the isometric net efficiency are correlated with increasing condition, up to a maximum in this set of data of 8·5% per 10 days, with $E \sim 0·2$.

Information of this kind is at present restricted to a small number of species, for which both length and weight data have been published;

apart from those already mentioned they include the whiting, *Merlangius merlangus* L., and haddock, *Melanogrammus aeglefinus* L., of Jones & Hislop (1971), and the small-mouth bass, *Micropterus dolomieu* (Williams, 1959). Few though these cases may be, they nevertheless indicate that a major part of the variance in experimentally determined net efficiencies is accounted for by changes in the condition factor; these changes may be regarded as indicative of the dynamic state of the reserves of materials rather than corresponding to true growth. Table I summarizes the isometric efficiencies estimated in each case.

### RELATIONSHIP BETWEEN RATE OF GAIN AND FEEDING RATE

In the last section, the nature of isometric weight gain was established. When the condition factor changes, the change in weight represents more than true growth. Reserve materials cannot be regarded as part of the feeding and metabolizing tissues of the body. The relative rate sof gain are presented here as a proportion of the mean of $(\bar{L}^3)$, where $(\bar{L}^3) = 0{\cdot}5 \{L_o^3 + L_t^3\}$ rather than $0{\cdot}5 (L_o + L_t)^3$.

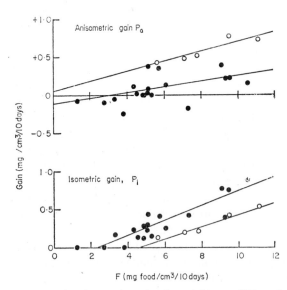

FIG. 3. Isometric and anisometric gains in weight are differently related to the feeding rate. When the initial condition factor $(q_o)$ is low, isometric gains are less important than anisometric; when the initial condition factor is high the converse is true. Data for maximum-fed plaice at Lympstone (Dawes, 1930, 1931). Solid circles, $q_o$ 10–11 mg/cm³; open circles, $q_o$ 7–8 mg/cm³.

The rate of total weight gain, $P$, is $(\Delta W/\Delta t)/(\overline{L^3})$. Isometric weight gain rates, $P_i$, are given by $q_o$ . $(\Delta(L^3)/\Delta t)/(\overline{L^3})$; and anisometric weight changes, $P_a$, by difference $P - P_i = P_a$. The feeding rate, $F$, is similarly given by $(\Delta I/\Delta t)/(L^3)$. These rates are all expressed in units of $mg/cm^3/time$. Figure 3 shows an analysis of the isometric and aniso-metric gain rates for Dawes' Lympstone plaice; both the 1929 and 1930 experiments, using maximum feeding rates, are included. The two groups of data shown represent growth periods, of up to 99 days, in which the initial condition factor was either 7–8 $mg/cm^3$ (open circles) or 10–11 $mg/cm^3$ (solid circles); other values are not shown, for the sake of clarity. It can be seen that the initial condition factor affected the conversion at any given feeding rate; those which started at 7–8 $mg/cm^3$ diverted more of the food to building up their reserves (thus increasing $q$) than those which started at 10–11 $mg/cm^3$. Conversely, the isometric gains were reduced by a low initial condition factor. The threshold for isometric gains was higher when the initial condition was 7–8 than when it was 10–11 $mg/cm^3$. Although not shown here, plaice with $q_o$ in excess of 12 $mg/cm^3$ actually gave negative values of $P_a$, that is, they lost condition. Similar results, though with slight differences in the threshold $F$'s, were obtained for the Cawsand, 1930, plaice.

Birkett's plaice, the haddock and whiting (Jones & Hislop, 1971) and the small-mouth bass (Williams, 1959) have yielded essentially similar results to those for the cod and Dawes' plaice. These few results, although they are not sufficient to draw general conclusions, nevertheless indicate that, even where only crude live weight or length gains have been recorded, there are qualitative distinctions between the utilization of absorbed materials for increasing the size of the body, on the one hand, and for increasing the weight of deposited materials on the other, which ought to be reflected in variations in chemical com-position; it is also clear that the relationship between these utilizations is extremely sensitive to the amount of materials already in deposit. There is as yet little information on changes in chemical composition induced by diet, or by feeding levels. The most important of such evi-dence relating to fish is Gerking's experiment with bluegill sunfish, *Lepomis macrochirus* (Gerking, 1955). Gerking fed his fish at various rates and compared the composition, after 30 days, in respect of total and protein nitrogen, and lipids, with the total intake of these materials (as contained in *Tenebrio molitor* larvae). Analysis of his data shows that the *Lepomis* accumulated almost 95% of the lipids they were supplied at any feeding level, but that the efficiency of nitrogen retention increased from zero, at maintenance, to almost 30% at its maximum. Thus, the lipid content of the *Lepomis* increased, but the protein-N content appeared to decrease; actually, the protein-N content of the lipid-free body increased slightly.

In young sole, Bromley (1971) showed that the nitrogen content per gram body weight increased as the condition factor increased, the relationship being as follows:

$$\text{mgN/g fresh weight} = a - \frac{b}{q}$$

where $a = 35\ \text{mgN/g}$ and $b = 84\ \text{mgN}$. An increase in $q$ from, say, 6 to 8 mg/cm$^3$, i.e. a 33% rise, was thus accompanied by an increase in nitrogen content of from 19 to 24·5 mgN/g, a 29% rise. Energy contents also showed parallel changes.

Blaxter (1967) showed that calves, feeding entirely on milk at different rates, retained energy as fats and proteins in different proportions; the threshold for fat retention was higher than that for protein retention, thus reflecting the situation for isometric and anisometric growth seen for plaice above. It is thus likely that the changing relationship between forms of weight gains in fish and intake rates is a reflection of the differing needs of the body for reserve materials. The dynamics of these reserve materials are in fact an important factor in growth/food relationships.

DISCUSSION

The apparently uncontrollable variations in efficiency of conversion which occur in most feeding experiments with fish have been interpreted in this paper as depending largely on changes in condition or in the storage of reserve materials. As might be expected, purely isometric growth is much the slower process, requiring less food, which is converted at a comparatively low "isometric" efficiency, than the corresponding rates during active fattening. It would obviously be advantageous, for productivity studies, to be able to express the relationship between food and growth by a series of "fixed points". It is probably just as true of juvenile fish, as of the mature ones on which the yield of exploited populations is based, that active feeding is seasonally distributed in nature, and that changes in the condition factor also occur seasonally. Thus, it would be reasonable to expect conversion efficiencies to be comparatively high in the active feeding periods, but for annual production to be achieved at a comparatively low efficiency because of the relative constancy of the mean condition factor. The part played by metabolism in determining efficiency has been deliberately left out of consideration here because there is little that can be said about this at present. It is likely that most fish in the free-living state are much more active than their captive counterparts; it can only be suggested, at present, that this would affect the storage of reserves more strongly than linear growth. But any factor which increased the metabolism would inevitably reduce the isometric efficiency, because of the greater demands on the food as a substrate for energy processes. Thus the isometric efficiency in the natural environment might be rather lower than the values quoted in Table I. For the plaice, for example, it

TABLE I

*Isometric net efficiencies of five species of fish*

| Species | Food | Approximate isometric net efficiency | Maximum net efficiency | Source |
|---|---|---|---|---|
| *Pleuronectes platessa* L. | *Mytilus* flesh | 0·06–0·12 | 0·2 | Dawes (1931) |
| *Gadus morhua* L. | *Gadus* flesh | 0·11 | 0·4 | Birkett (unpublished data) |
| *Melanogrammus aeglefinus* L. | Squid | 0·2 | 0·4 | Jones & Hislop (1971) |
| *Merlangius merlangus* L. | Squid | 0·2 | 0·4 | Jones & Hislop (1971) |
| *Micropterus dolomieu* | Live fish | 0·2 | 0·4 | Williams (1959) |

might be reasonable to use a figure approximately half of the value obtained from Dawes' data; this would give a food requirement of 15–20 g (as *Mytilus* flesh) for each 1 g of growth made isometrically during the year. During the active feeding season, however, since the intake is largely converted into stored materials, the efficiency would be higher and the food requirement per 1 g growth might reasonably be estimated as 3–5 g.

### SUMMARY

1. The efficiency of food conversion in fish, which is the ratio of total net gain: total food intake, can and does vary considerably.

2. Two ways of accounting for the variance, or of eliminating it, are discussed. The more important of these is that the variance can be explained as due to changes in condition factor and consequently to

the dynamics of stored materials within the body. These changes depend directly on the feeding rates.

3. That being so, isometric net efficiencies, at which the condition factor would be maintained without change, were calculated for several species. These values were 0·06 to 0·20 (6 to 20%) depending on the species, and the type of food.

4. Growth in length may require a different threshold feeding rate from growth in weight. The precise relationship between these threshold "maintenance requirements" depends primarily on the initial condition factor.

5. It is suggested that, in the natural environment, conversion efficiencies may well be high during the comparatively short periods of intensive feeding, when there is a rapid build-up of reserves; but that annual mean efficiencies will be low because the condition factor is independent of age.

## REFERENCES

Benedict, F. G. (1938). Vital energetics. *Publs Carnegie Instn* No. 503: 1–215.

Bertalanffy, L. von (1938). A quantitative theory of organic growth. (Inquiries on growth laws. II.) *Hum. Biol.* **10**: 181–213.

Bertalanffy, L. von (1964). Basic concepts in quantitative biology of metabolism. *Helgoländer wiss. Meeresunters.* **9**: 5–37.

Beverton, R. J. H. & Holt, S. J. (1957). On the dynamics of exploited fish populations. *Fishery Invest., Lond.* (2) **19**: 1–533.

Blaxter, K. L. (1967). *The energy metabolism of ruminants.* London: Hutchinson.

Brody, S. (1945). *Bioenergetics and growth.* New York: Reinhold.

Bromley, P. J. (1971). Relationships between the wet weight condition factor and nitrogen and energy content in the common sole (*Solea solea* L.). *J. Cons. perm. int. Explor. Mer* **34**. (in press).

Brown, M. E. (1946). The growth of brown trout (*Salmo trutta* Linn.). 1. Factors influencing the growth of trout fry. *J. exp. Biol.* **22**: 118–129.

Dawes, B. (1930). Growth and maintenance in the plaice (*Pleuronectes platessa* L.). Part I. *J. mar. biol. Ass. U.K.* (N.S.) **17**: 103–174.

Dawes, B. (1931). Growth and maintenance in the plaice (*P. platessa* L.). Part II. *J. mar. biol. Ass. U.K.* (N.S.) **17**: 877–947.

Elder, H. Y. (1962). Preliminary notes on the relationship between feeding and growth rate in the siluroid fish, *Bagrus docmac* (Forsk.). *Rep. E. Afr. Freshwat. Fish. Res. Org.* **1961**: 19–22.

Gerking, S. D. (1955). Influence of rate of feeding on body composition and protein metabolism of bluegill sunfish. *Physiol. Zool.* **28**: 267–282.

Graham, M. (1924). The annual cycle in the life of the mature cod in the North Sea. *Fishery Invest., Lond.* (2) **6**: 1–77.

Hickling, C. F. (1930). The natural history of the hake. Part III. Seasonal changes in the condition of the hake. *Fishery Invest., Lond.* (2) **12**: 1–78.

Johnson, L. (1966). Experimental determination of food consumption of pike, *Esox lucius*, for growth and maintenance. *J. Fish. Res. Bd Can.* **23**: 1495–1505.

Jones, R. & Hislop, J. R. G. (1971). Investigations into the growth of haddock, *Melanogrammus aeglefinus* L., and whiting, *Merlangius merlangus* L., in tanks. *J. Cons. perm. int. Explor. Mer* **34**. (in press).

Le Cren, E. D. (1951). The length–weight relationship and seasonal cycle in gonad weight and condition in the perch (*Perca fluviatilis*). *J. anim. Ecol.* **20**: 201–219.

Paloheimo, J. E. & Dickie, L. M. (1966). Food and growth of fishes. III. Relations among food, body size and growth efficiency. *J. Fish. Res. Bd Can.* **23**: 1209–1248.

Pentelow, F. T. K. (1939). The relation between growth and food consumption in the brown trout (*Salmo trutta*). *J. exp. Biol.* **16**: 446–473.

Putter, A. (1920). Studien über physiologische Ähnlichkeit. VI. Wachstums-ähnlichkeiten. *Pflügers Arch. ges. Physiol.* **180**: 298–340.

Rafail, S. Z. (1968). A statistical analysis of ration and growth relationship of plaice (*Pleuronectes platessa*). *J. Fish. Res. Bd Can.* **25**: 717–732.

Rafail, S. Z. (1969). Further analysis of ration and growth relationship of plaice (*Pleuronectes platessa*). *J. Fish. Res. Bd Can.* **26**: 3237–3241.

Williams, W. E. (1959). Food conversion and growth rates for large-mouth and small-mouth bass in laboratory aquaria. *Trans. Am. Fish. Soc.* **88**: 125–127.

Symp. zool. Soc. Lond. (1972) No. 29, 271–284.

# THE POSSIBLE CONTRIBUTIONS OF RADIOECOLOGY TO MARINE PRODUCTIVITY STUDIES

A. PRESTON, D. F. JEFFERIES and R. J. PENTREATH

*Fisheries Radiobiological Laboratory, Lowestoft, Suffolk, England*

SYNOPSIS

The scope of radioecology is outlined and some studies that are suitable for conduct in the labelled environments of radioactive waste disposal areas are discussed. In particular, the use of caesium-137 to trace the circulation of water in the north Irish Sea and to follow its distribution northwards and into the Atlantic over distances of several hundred miles is described. The use and limitations of radionuclides in delineating and quantifying trophic relationships are also mentioned and an attempt to use caesium-137 to derive estimates of food consumption for a young inshore plaice population is briefly described. Some problems of trace element cycling and the concept of a "biologically available" fraction in relation to trace elements in sea water are also presented.

## INTRODUCTION

Radioecology, sometimes called radiation ecology, is concerned with the behaviour of natural and artificial radionuclides in the natural environment—their transport and distribution and their interaction with the biota at the species, population and ecosystem levels—and with the effects of the accompanying radiation as one of many factors that may affect the structure of ecosystems. Studies therefore embrace not only the direct somatic and genetic effects of ionizing radiation, perhaps the most difficult studies to pursue under natural conditions and thus to date tackled principally at an experimental level, but also the environmental distribution of radionuclides and the mechanisms effecting these distributions.

These studies of the transport and distribution of artificial radionuclides may be considered in relation to deliberately planned tracer experiments or in relation to the extensive labelling of the natural environment brought about as a result of world-wide nuclear weapon testing and the controlled disposal of radioactive wastes. It is the latter aspect which will be discussed in this paper.

## MOVEMENT OF WATER

Some radionuclides when introduced to coastal waters act as effective labels of the water itself. Ideally, tritium in the form of tritiated water would provide the best label of all, but the concentrations generally available are too small, and the analytical effort involved proportionately too large, to indulge in the necessary large-scale sampling. However, increased rates of discharge of tritium which will occur in the future will make it possible to utilize it in studies of water circulation in the Irish Sea and several other smaller inshore environments near the more advanced nuclear power stations.

In the Irish Sea at the present time, caesium-137 released from the Windscale nuclear fuel reprocessing plant provides a good label for the water throughout the whole northern area, and offers an opportunity to observe the circulation of water labelled off the Cumberland coast (Preston, Jefferies & Mitchell, 1971). Samples for the inshore area, shown in Fig. 1, were collected at three-monthly intervals over a four-year period from a network of 25 stations covering an area of 1000 km². Sea water was sampled from surface, midwater and bottom in succession

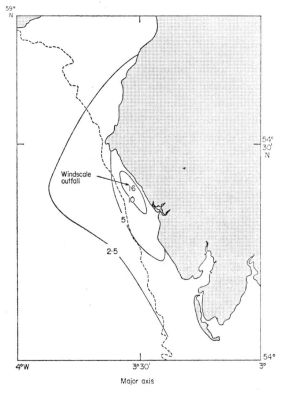

Fig. 1. Concentrations of caesium-137 in sea water off the Cumberland coast, 1963–1966 (pCi/litre) for a 1 curie/day discharge.

by pumping through a polyethylene hose. Equal volumes of membrane-filtered samples from each depth were bulked for analysis. The standing concentrations of caesium-137, based on the mean values for 15 cruises and corrected to unit daily discharge rates, are shown in Fig. 1. The inner contours are elliptical, their centres being displaced approximately 1·5 km in a southerly direction with the ratio of the major axis to the minor axis of approximately 4 : 1. This may be compared with a ratio of 5 : 1 which can be derived from the tidal stream data on the appropriate Admiralty chart. Further offshore the contours are displaced to the north, suggesting that the current system here may be different from that in the inshore area.

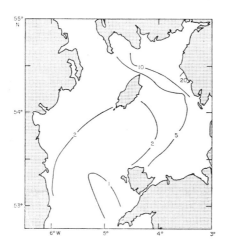

Fig. 2. Concentrations of caesium-137 in sea water of the north Irish Sea, September, 1968 ($p$Ci/litre).

The caesium-137 concentration contours over the whole sea area investigated during a research vessel cruise in 1968 (Fig. 2) show a pattern similar to that of the isohalines for the area (Bowden, 1955) and demonstrate the influence of incoming Atlantic water from the south on the circulation pattern of the north Irish Sea. The figure also demónstrates that caesium-137 is removed from the area by an outward flow through the east side of the North Channel, but that there is a fairly large eddy down the eastern Irish coast as far south as Wicklow, considerably further south than reported by Ramster & Hill (1969) from their studies with seabed drifters and current meters.

This distribution can be contrasted with that revealed by sampling carried out on a research vessel cruise in November/December 1969 following a period of strong westerly winds in early November, followed

L

by north-west to north winds later in the month. The normal pattern of concentration, achieved under the influence of Atlantic water entering from the south, had been displaced, suggesting a reversal of the normal water flow in the northern Irish Sea (Fig. 3). Salinity observations made

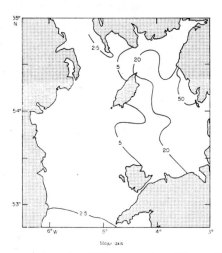

FIG. 3. Concentrations of caesium-137 in sea water of the north Irish Sea, December, 1969 (pCi/litre).

on this cruise, and on a cruise some two weeks earlier, confirmed this abnormal situation with water of high salinity across the North Channel and extending southwards to the west of the Isle of Man (Folkard, 1970).

This change, in the concentration contours, illustrates the extent to which abnormal wind conditions may be a contributory factor in influencing a largely confined water mass such as the Irish Sea, and which might be expected to have a short-term influence on biological productivity in the area (see Cushing, this Symposium, pp. 213–232).

Some data relating to the distribution of Irish Sea water as far north as the Minch and as far west in the Atlantic as longitude 7°W have been gleaned from more recent observations of surface water concentrations (Fig. 4); which show that Irish Sea water penetrates the Minch and may be traced over distances up to 400 km in a coastwise direction and out to 250 km north and west in the Atlantic.

SEDIMENT TRANSPORT

Other radionuclides discharged from Windscale, notably ruthenium-106 and zirconium-95/niobium-95, provide effective sediment

labels and it is possible to identify sediments, labelled in the Windscale
area, in river estuaries to the north and south up to 160 km away and

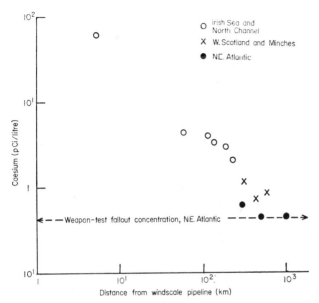

FIG. 4. The relationship between the concentrations of caesium-137 in sea water
and distance from the Windscale pipeline, 1968–1969.

to establish simple relationships between concentration and distance
from the discharge point (Jefferies, 1968, 1970). The recent advent of
high-resolution Ge(Li) gamma spectrometry techniques permits the
identification and measurement of isotopes of the same element with
distinct radioactive half-lives and thus, from relative concentrations at
varying distances, affords the possibility of deriving sediment transport
rates.

It may therefore become possible, with deployment of the requisite
effort, to examine much of the dynamics of water and sediment transport
in an area as large as the whole of the north Irish Sea. Indeed, provisional
estimates of the residence time of caesium in this area have already been
made, and suggest that water from the area of the Cumberland and
Lancashire coasts has a residence half-time of at least 12 months.

BIOLOGICAL RECONCENTRATION

Radionuclides are reconcentrated to varying degrees in biological
materials and use may be made of this in elucidating some of the

dynamics of mineral metabolism, particularly in relation to trace elements. The distribution of radionuclides through food chains may be used to delineate the trophic organization of complex ecosystems, and the quantitative developments of such data hold out the possibility of deriving estimates of feeding rates for some organisms under natural conditions. In aquatic environments the situation is complicated since both food and water may be significant contributory sources of radionuclides, and the contribution from water will be a significant one where the radionuclide exhibits only low concentration factors in food materials. For any given radionuclide the contribution to fish from water may also be more significant in the marine environment than in that of fresh water, due to the relative swallowing rates dictated by osmo-regulatory considerations.

### Estimates of food consumption

In principle, in a labelled environment the increment, over a given interval of time, of an organism's body burden for any suitable radionuclide may be used to derive estimates of food intake. It is necessary of course to establish a suitable model to describe the dynamics of radionuclide turnover, and to make due allowance for the relative contributions of food and water and the effects of growth and temperature. Intake of a radionuclide, neglecting radioactive decay, may be suitably described by the following simple equation:

$$I = \frac{KQ_t}{f(1 - e^{-Kt})} \tag{1}$$

where

$I$ = intake of radioactivity, units per organism per day;
$Q_t$ = body burden, in radioactivity units, after time $t$ days;
$K$ = excretion rate (day$^{-1}$) of $0.693/t_{\frac{1}{2}}$, $t_{\frac{1}{2}}$ being the biological half-time in days;
$f$ = fraction of the intake of radioactivity absorbed.

When the organism is in a steady state with its radioactivity intake

$$I = \frac{KQ_{ss}}{f} \tag{2}$$

where

$Q_{ss}$ = steady state body burden of radioactivity units.

The intake rate is dependent on both temperature and growth, and an increase in growth rate or temperature will accelerate the turnover of the radionuclide and thus shorten the biological half-life. Increase in body size associated with growth will, however, tend to lengthen the half-life, and will tend to outweigh the decrease in half-life caused by the associated increase in metabolic turnover.

Thus the pattern of concentration with time in an organism and its food and water supplies can be utilized to make estimates of food intake, provided that we know the contribution due to water, and this can be obtained experimentally by monitoring the organism in an aquarium containing the radionuclide of interest and feeding on inactive food; the temperature, body weight and growth dependence of this process may also be examined at the same time (Morgan, 1964; D. F. Jefferies, unpublished data). This has been done in the case of plaice in relation to temperature and body weight for the radionuclide caesium-134 (Morgan, 1964; Jefferies & Hewett, 1971), and recently field studies have been conducted at Windscale to examine the possibility of making estimates of the feeding rate of young plaice, utilizing caesium-137 as a label (Pentreath & Jefferies, 1971). A formula, derived from Equation 1, with due allowance for growth and temperature, can be used to make estimates of the amount of caesium-137 absorbed per day from both food and water:

$$I = \frac{(K_b + \lambda_g)Q_t}{f(1 - e^{-(K_b + \lambda_g)t})} \tag{3}$$

where

$\lambda_g$ = growth constant (day$^{-1}$), assuming exponential growth of the fish;

$K_b$ = excretion rate (day$^{-1}$), derived from experimental work in aquaria at very low growth rates (Jefferies & Hewett, 1971) and adjusted for body weight and water temperature;

$f = 1$.

The contribution from food has been obtained by subtracting from the measured flesh values a calculated water contribution, based on the observed sea water concentrations. However, it has not been possible to compute the fractions absorbed from various fractions of the diet, but assuming 100% assimilation of caesium (i.e. an $f$ value of 1) for any individual component of the diet, estimates can be made of the upper limit of consumption consistent with the calculated increment of caesium-137 body burden.

Utilizing the observed seawater caesium-137 values, and concentration factors of 4 and 14 for *Nephthys* and amphipods respectively, as measured in benthos samples, the derived values for caesium-137 intake from food are converted into weights of *Nephthys* or amphipods consumed per unit time. These values are given in Table I; the observed

TABLE I

*Daily food intake by I-group plaice in the north-east Irish Sea, 1969;*
*g/g fish per day*

| Month | Calculated assuming 100% assimilation of $^{137}Cs$ | | Observed weight of gut contents |
|---|---|---|---|
| | *Nephthys* | Amphipods | |
| May | 0·070 | 0·020 | 0·049 |
| June | 0·009 | 0·003 | 0·046 |
| July | 0·074 | 0·021 | 0·034 |
| August | 0·049 | 0·014 | 0·035 |
| September | 0·050 | 0·014 | 0·028 |
| October | 0·061 | 0·017 | 0·024 |

figures are of course averages, and represent mixed stomach contents. The calculated figures for *Nephthys* and amphipods may thus represent the possible range of values that might be encountered in individual fish existing solely on one component or the other.

Since there is evidence to suggest that the percentage assimilation of caesium-137 differs from one dietary component to another (Pentreath & Jefferies, 1971), the estimates given are probably too low, only slightly so for *Nephthys* but perhaps by as much as a factor of 4–5 for amphipods. It is not known to what extent the observed gut content figures, taken each month over a seven-day period, are in fact typical of that month. It has been assumed that the food in the stomach and intestine represents the intake for 24 h, though clearly this will be an underestimate since considerable digestion will have taken place. It is also evident from values of the dry weight to wet weight ratio of the gut contents that a large fraction is inedible silt, and thus intake on a conventional weight basis also suffers from considerable inaccuracies. It seems possible that food consumption during the growing season may be somewhere near 10% of body weight per day among the plaice population studied.

These estimates could clearly be improved by establishing the caesium assimilation factors for the various dietary components in aquarium experiments. There are suggestions that assimilation from the same dietary component varies with size of fish and possibly with feeding rate, and these variations might also need to be assessed. Further improvement in the accuracy of the estimates could be achieved by:

1. choosing an area sufficiently far from the Windscale outfall to smooth the month-to-month variations in radionuclide concentrations in sea water; with increasing caesium-137 concentrations in the Irish Sea this may already be possible in, for example, Red Wharf Bay;

2. refining estimates of the dependence of excretion rate on temperature and growth rate, which were allowed for in these recent studies by using data from experimental studies at very low growth rates; new values should be derived by experiments at higher growth rates or by actual field experiments in which fish are moved from the Windscale area to clean areas and their loss runs studied under near-normal growing conditions;

3. using a radionuclide where the increment from food is much larger than the increment from water; this may become possible in some nuclear power station environments in due course through the use of activation product radionuclides of high biological concentration factors, e.g. zinc and manganese.

### Trace element pathways to fish

Equation 2, the steady state equation, can be used to obtain estimates of the relative contributions of food and water to radionuclide intake by expressing both intake and steady state concentration in terms of sea water units, i.e. $Q_{ss}$ can be put in the form:

$$\frac{[\text{Concentration of radionuclide in fish}]}{[\text{Concentration of radionuclide in water}]} = \text{Concentration factor}$$

and

$$f[I] = K[C_{ss}] \qquad (4)$$

where

$[I]$ = input of radionuclides per g per day, in sea water units, to maintain $[C_{ss}]$;

$[C_{ss}]$ = steady state concentration of radionuclide per g in sea water units.

From Table II it can be seen that, assuming an $f$ value of 1, to maintain a concentration factor of $10^1$ with a biological half-time of $10^1$

days requires a daily input of 0·69 sea water units per g, whereas for a concentration factor of $10^4$ and an effective half-time of $10^1$ days, 690

TABLE II

*Input of radionuclides per g of fish per day* $[I]$, *in sea water units, to maintain* $[C_{ss}]$

| Biological half-time, days | $[C_{ss}]$ | | | |
|---|---|---|---|---|
| | $10^1$ | $10^2$ | $10^3$ | $10^4$ |
| $10^1$ | 0·69 | 6·9 | 69 | 690 |
| $10^2$ | 0·069 | 0·69 | 6·9 | 69 |
| $10^3$ | 0·0069 | 0·069 | 0·69 | 6·9 |

units are required. Reported values for the daily drinking rate of marine teleost fish approximate to 5% of body weight/day at 10°C (Smith, 1930; Evans, 1969) or 0·05 sea water units/g, and it has been demonstrated in the case of plaice that the daily intake of caesium from sea water is equivalent to 0·12 sea water units/g which includes a major fraction taken in across the gill surfaces (Jefferies & Hewett, 1971). Thus uptake from sea water is not a significant pathway in fish for a number of trace elements. Further reference to Table II suggests that the major radionuclide contribution can in fact only be provided from water when concentration factors are low ($10^1$) and/or biological half-times relatively large ($10^2$–$10^3$).

With food as a pathway, and assuming a concentration factor of $10^1$ in the food supply together with an $f$ value of 1, those fish which exhibit concentration factors and biological half-lives of the order of $10^1$ can meet their requirements with a food intake of 0·069 g per g of body weight (6·9%), a credible rate of food intake. Since, however, many essential metal metabolites exhibit concentration factors of $10^2$–$10^3$ in fish with biological half-lives between $10^1$ and $10^2$ (Table III), and assimilation factors are more likely to be in the range 0·1–0·3, organisms comprising the food supply will in turn therefore need to achieve concentration factors of at least the same order as the predator, and sometimes an order of magnitude greater. Indeed, evidence from most metal radionuclide studies does indicate a decrease in concentration factor with ascent of the trophic pyramid.

There must therefore be, at some basic level in the food chain, very rapid concentration from the water for most of those trace elements that appear at high concentrations at upper levels in the trophic pyramid. This process is probably too rapid to be a biological one, and

TABLE III

*The concentration factor $[C_{ss}]$, biological half-time $(t_{\frac{1}{2}}\,biol)$ of fish and fraction $(f)$ assimilated from the diet*

| Element | $[C_{ss}]$ | $t_{\frac{1}{2}}$ biol | $f$ |
|---|---|---|---|
| Cobalt | $10^2$ | $10^1$ | $3 \cdot 10^{-1}$ |
| Iron | $10^3$ | $10^2$ | $10^{-1}$ |
| Zinc | $10^3$ | $10^2$ | $10^{-1}$ |
| Manganese | $5 \cdot 10^2$ | $10^2$ | $10^{-1}$ |

is probably without physiological significance (Reichle, Dunaway & Nelson, 1970) at the level at which it occurs. Surface adsorption to a finely-divided matrix such as phytoplankton, or detrital material and sediment, is probably the underlying mechanism. Such radionuclide studies as have been conducted indeed show high concentrations in plankton (Rice & Willis, 1959; Chipman, Rice & Price, 1958) and on sediments (Preston & Jefferies, 1969) coupled with very fast rate functions, and trace element analysis of phytoplankton also indicates very high concentration factors for some trace elements (Bowen et al., 1971). The indiscriminate uptake by phytoplankton of elements such as cerium and zirconium, which are of no known biological significance but with marked affinity for surfaces, also suggests a straightforward surface adsorption phenomenon.

### Biological availability

The dynamics of trace element exchange in phytoplankton are of course themselves particularly attractive for the employment of radioactive tracer techniques, and yet much remains to be done here. A word of caution also needs to be sounded in relation to problems of biological availability, since evidence is accumulating from studies of fallout radionuclides in the Pacific (Robertson, Forster, Rieck & Langford, 1968), and from the behaviour of radionuclides in waste disposal areas (Preston & Dutton, 1968; Preston 1970), that there are very marked differences in the behaviour of artificial radionuclides and their stable analogues—which are due to differences in chemical and/or physical form between the material introduced and that naturally present in the sea water reservoir. Such differences may well be accentuated in aquarium-type studies and great care is needed in extrapolating results to natural conditions.

These differences of behaviour noted in the field, many of which refer to metals such as manganese, iron, cobalt and zinc which are regarded as essential metabolites, have drawn attention to the fact that sea water contains two or more separate compartments of differing "biological availability". From recent work (M. Bernhard, various Progress Reports and unpublished data) it seems virtually certain for example that only a small fraction of the zinc in sea water, 10% or so, is ionic, and that a large proportion of the remainder is complexed in some way, with a further small fraction in the particulate form. Anodic stripping voltammetry, the technique used in determining the ionic zinc fraction, has also been successfully employed to demonstrate that when zinc-65 in the form of chloride is added to sea water it remains for more than 100 days entirely in the ionic phase (Macchi, 1965; Barić & Branica, 1967). Experiments with phytoplankton show that specific activity of zinc-65 in the organisms after periods of uptake is different from the overall specific activity of the medium (Bernhard & Zattera, 1969). This suggests that only certain physico-chemical states are easily available to the organism and, since the rate of uptake of the zinc-65 is fast compared with that of the stable zinc, it is also possible to infer that the ionic phase was the one most available.

Perhaps future investigations should be directed to those physico-chemical states of trace metals that offer the greatest likelihood of surface adsorption; their employment in radiotracer experiments and their tentative identification in the environment might thus offer further data to explain some of the kinetics of trace element exchange at basal levels in the trophic pyramid. Certainly examination of the ratio of radionuclide: stable nuclide in sea water and in various lower trophic level components of the ecosystem is now becoming possible with the better techniques of trace element and radionuclide measurement available, which hold promise as a tool for investigating some of the mechanisms underlying the cycling of trace elements in the marine biosphere.

SUMMARY

The labelled environments of radioactive waste disposal areas offer unique opportunities to study the movement of water and sediments and the cycling of selected metals. Some aspects of mineral cycling in biological systems are particularly well suited to investigation by radiotracer techniques, and aspects of food consumption and utilization may also be illuminated by this approach. Greater appreciation of the potential of radioactively-labelled environments is required on the part of marine ecologists, and more awareness of the ecological problems on the part of the health physicist, before these opportunities can be realized.

## References

Barić, A. & Branica, M. (1967). Polarography of sea water. I. Ionic state of cadium and zinc in sea water. *J. polarogr. Soc.* **13**: 4–8.

Bernhard, M. & Zattera, A. (1969). A comparison between the uptake of radioactive and stable zinc by marine unicellular alga. In: *Symposium on Radioecology. Proc. 2nd Nat. Symp.*, Ann Arbor, Michigan, May 15–17 1967, 389–398, CONF 670503.

Bowden, K. F. (1955). Physical oceanography of the Irish Sea. *Fishery Invest., Lond.* (2), **18**, No. 8, 67 pp.

Bowen, V. T., Olsen, J. S., Osterberg, C. L. & Ravera, J. (1971). Ecological interactions of marine radioactivity. Section of *Radioactivity in the marine environment*. National Academy of Sciences—National Research Council, Washington D.C. 200–222.

Chipman, W. A., Rice, T. R. & Price, T. J. (1958). Uptake and accumulation of radioactive zinc by marine plankton, fish, and shellfish. *Fishery Bull. Fish Wildl. Serv. U.S.* **58**: 279–292.

Evans, D. H. (1969). Studies on the permeability to water of selected marine, freshwater and euryhaline teleosts. *J. exp. Biol.* **50**: 689–703.

Folkard, A. R. (1970). Hydrographic investigations in the English Channel and southern North Sea, January 1969, and Irish Sea, November–December 1969. *Annls biol., Copenh.* **26** (1969), 1970, p. 82.

Jefferies, D. F. (1968). Fission-product radionuclides in sediments from the North-East Irish Sea. *Helgoländer wiss. Meeresunters.* **17**: 280–290.

Jefferies, D. F. (1970). Exposure to radiation from gamma-emitting fission-product radionuclides in estuarine sediments from the north-east Irish Sea. In *Environmental surveillance in the vicinity of nuclear facilities. Proc. Health Physics Mid-Year Topical Symposium, Augusta, Georgia*, 1968: 205–216. (Reinig, W. C., ed.).

Jefferies, D. F. & Hewett, C. J. (1971). The accumulation and excretion of radioactive caesium by the plaice (*Pleuronectes platessa* L.) and the thornback ray (*Raia clavata* L.). *J. mar. biol. Ass. U.K.*, **51**: 411–422.

Macchi, G. (1965). The determination of ionic zinc in sea water by anodic stripping voltammetry using ordinary capillary electrodes. *J. electroanal. Chem.* **9**: 290–298.

Morgan, F. (1964). The uptake of radioactivity by fish and shellfish. I. 134-caesium by whole animals. *J. mar. biol. Ass. U.K.* **44**: 259–271.

Pentreath, R. J. & Jefferies, D. F. (1971). The uptake of radionuclides by I-group plaice (*Pleuronectes platessa* L.) off the Cumberland coast, Irish Sea. *J. mar. biol. Ass. U.K.*, **51**, 963–976.

Preston, A. (1970). Concentrations of iron-55 in commercial fish species from the North Atlantic. *Mar. Biol.* **6**: 345–349.

Preston, A. & Dutton, J. W. R. (1968). The application of neutron activation analysis to the study of trace elements in United Kingdom coastal waters. In *International symposium on the application of neutron activation analysis in oceanography*: 117–142. Inst. Roy. des Sci. Nat. de Belg., Brussels 1968.

Preston, A. & Jefferies, D. F. (1969). Aquatic aspects in chronic and acute contamination situations. In *Environmental contamination by radioactive materials*, IAEA/FAO/WHO, Vienna, 183–211.

Preston, A., Jefferies, D. F. & Mitchell, N. T. (1971). Experience gained from the controlled introduction of liquid radioactive waste to coastal waters. *Nuclear Techniques in Environmental Pollution*: 629–644. IAEA, Vienna.

Ramster, J. W. & Hill, H. W. (1969). Current system in the northern Irish Sea. *Nature, Lond.* **224**: 59–61.

Reichle, D. E., Dunaway, P. B. & Nelson, D. J. (1970). Turnover and concentration of radionuclides in food chains. *Nucl. Saf.* **11**: 43–55.

Rice, T. R. & Willis, V. M. (1959). Uptake, accumulation and loss of radioactive cerium-144 by marine planktonic algae. *Limnol. Oceanogr.* **4**: 277–290.

Robertson, D. E., Forster, W. O., Rieck, H. G. & Langford, J. C. (1968). A study of the trace element and radionuclide behaviour in a northwest Pacific Ocean ecosystem 350 miles off Newport, Oregon. *Pacific Northwest Laboratory Annual Report for 1967 to the USAEC Division of Biology and Medicine. Report BNWL-715*, **2**: *Physical Sciences, Pt 2, Radiological Sciences*, Oct. 1968 (BNWL-715: Part 2), 92–108. Battelle Memorial Institute, Richland.

Smith, H. W. (1930). The absorption and excretion of water and salts by marine teleosts. *Am. J. Physiol.* **93**: 480–505.

Symp. zool. Soc. Lond. (1972) No. 29. 285–296.

# THE POTENTIAL PRODUCTIVITY OF WATERS ON THE WEST COAST OF SCOTLAND

## R. I. CURRIE

*Dunstaffnage Marine Research Laboratory, Oban, Scotland*

SYNOPSIS

The coastal waters of the west of Scotland are discussed with particular reference to the large area of water partially enclosed within the fjord-like lochs.

The present fishing industry on the west coast derives its catches mainly from the area outside the lochs. Shellfish are currently leading in value of landings, closely followed by herring.

There seems little prospect of major improvements to these coastal fisheries and their future management must depend on exploiting them in a rational manner. The lochs, however, by virtue of their enclosed nature deserve consideration as areas of potential usefulness for aquaculture. Studies in progress towards this end are described and various possible approaches examined.

### COASTAL WATERS OF THE WEST COAST OF SCOTLAND

The continental shelf off the west coast of Scotland is about 100 miles (160 km) in width. Over the greater part of this shelf, depths lie between 100 and 200 m (Fig. 1) but a shallower sill area separates the west coast waters from those of the Irish Sea at a depth of some 50 m.

The land mass of the Hebrides is separated from the mainland by a channel exceeding 100 m in depth but it is bounded on the west side by an extensive area of shallower water, much of which is less than 50 m in depth.

The mainland coast of western Scotland, although only spanning about three and a half degrees of latitude is so deeply indented with fjord-like intrusions of the sea that the total length of coastline is well over 1000 miles (1600 km) between Cape Wrath in the north and the Mull of Galloway in the south. In addition there are numerous offshore islands spanning the length of the coast and likewise intersected to a varying degree.

These indentations in the coast, the sea lochs, bear a close similarity to the Norwegian fjords and one can identify a whole spectrum of types ranging from open embayments of the sea to arms of the sea, cut off from the main body of the ocean to a greater or lesser extent by shallow sills and/or constrictions at the mouth.

It appears, however, that over the whole length of the coast there is sufficient tidal rise and fall of the water to ensure an adequate flushing of the water inside these basins and in no instance at present do we know of any complete deoxygenation resulting from enclosure

(Craig, 1959), in the manner found on the southern part of the Norwegian coast where the tidal range is less pronounced (Strom, 1936).

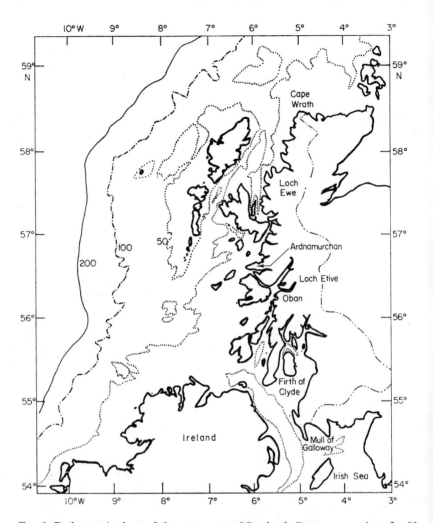

Fig. 1. Bathymetric chart of the west coast of Scotland. Contours are given for 50,
100 and 200 fathom depths. The approximate drainage area of the west coast is delimited
by the broken line (after Barnes & Goodley, 1958).

At the same time we must recognize that the bottom sediments of
these lochs, and particularly the deeper basins, have a high organic
matter content and that a comparatively delicate balance must exist
which maintains the present degree of oxygenation.

These lochs are also subjected to varying degrees of freshwater influence. This is evidently more pronounced on the more southerly part of the coast than in the north-west where the drainage area is more restricted so that the salinities in areas north of Ardnamurchan, the most westerly point of the mainland, are markedly higher than to the south of this point.

The main significance of this salinity reduction lies not so much in the overall reduction of salinity in the water column, but rather in the effect of the surface layer salinity reduction which leads to tremendous stability in the water column and a resulting resistance to vertical mixing.

A biproduct of this considerable freshwater input is the large amount of dissolved and particulate organic matter from terrestrial sources which is washed into the lochs and coastal waters and which may well make an important contribution to the organic system.

### THE WEST COAST FISHERIES

The annual Scottish Sea Fisheries Statistical Tables (HM Stationery Office) show the present status of west coast fish landings and their trend over the past decade (Figs 2 and 3).

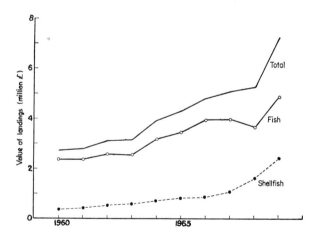

FIG. 2. Annual value of fish landings on the west coast of Scotland from British vessels in the years 1960 to 1969. The thin solid line is the total for pelagic and demersal fish combined. Data from Scottish Sea Fisheries Statistical Tables.

The recent increase in the value of shellfish landings is perhaps one of the most significant features, and in 1969 the shellfish taken in the west coast waters amounted to 42% of the total British shellfish catch. This appears to be related to a rapid growth in the landings of *Nephrops*

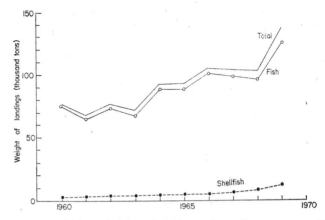

Fig. 3. Quantity of fish landed from British vessels on the west coast of Scotland in the years 1960 to 1969.

and scallops and the high market value of these products. Indeed the total value of shellfish landed in Scotland in 1969 exceeded the value of the entire British herring landings in that year. At the same time the landings of lobsters in Scotland although continuing to increase in value show a decline in quantity in recent years.

TABLE I

*Principal fish landings on the Scottish west coast, 1969 (from Scottish Sea Fisheries Statistical Tables, 1969, HMSO, 1970)*

|  | £ million |
|---|---|
| Shellfish | 2·36 |
| Herring | 2·30 |
| Haddock | 0·78 |
| Cod | 0·46 |
| Whiting | 0·43 |
| Hake | 0·24 |
| Skate | 0·12 |
| Plaice | 0·11 |

Of other fish in 1969, herring were of prime importance in west coast landings, followed by the demersal gadoids, haddock, cod and whiting, and then hake, skate and plaice (Table I).

The precise location of these catches is not available in the tabulated data but there is little doubt that the major part comes not from the sea lochs, but the adjacent coastal waters.

There is also a certain amount of fishing for salmon and sea trout in the west coast waters but data on the landings in different fishery board areas are confidential. The total value of salmonid landings in Scotland in 1969 was £2·35 million, but it is probable that only a small fraction of these came from the west coast, since the major salmon fisheries are on the east coast.

I do not intend making any appraisal of these statistics but merely quote them to illustrate the nature of the present fishing industry of this coast.

There is a further marine product of commercial importance on the west coast, the extraction of alginates from the large brown seaweeds *Ascophyllum nodosum* and *Laminaria hyperborea*. These occur in quantity in the west and north of Scotland and their commercial collection is organized by Alginate Industries Limited—mainly in the Outer and Inner Hebrides and the Orkney Islands. About 30 000 tons (wet weight) of Scottish weed is used annually; this is about 40% of the weed used by the firm, the remainder being imported mainly from Ireland. AIL has an annual turn-over of about £5 000 000 and exports about 70% of its production.

IMPROVEMENT OF PRODUCTIVITY

*Objectives*

There seems little prospect, at least in the immediate future, of making any significant change to the productivity of open sea waters and the conservation and rational exploitation of existing stocks of marine organisms still holds the best promise in these areas.

The west coast lochs, on the other hand, lend themselves, if not to physical enclosure, at least to a legal enclosure and they thus deserve consideration as an area in which techniques of marine cultivation might be employed to increase their production of useful organisms.

In the first instance, however, we must be clear about the objectives of introducing such an activity. The essential criterion spreads broadly across the field and viability must inevitably depend on an adequate return from the capital investment: it follows that those undertaking

M

the cultivation must be able to reap the benefits. Beyond this the objectives may be to maintain and supplement an existing industry, or to introduce a new local industry, or to develop a capital intensive exercise in food production. Furthermore, besides the objective of food production, the production of the basis for sport fisheries also has particular local relevance.

The objectives may thus differ considerably from area to area and on the west coast they may well be coloured by political factors such as the need to provide an industry supplementary to the other activities of a population dispersed over a wide area.

## Present status of cultivation

Commercial interest in marine cultivation in Scottish waters is in its infancy but nevertheless the important point is that in recent years it has become established, albeit on a small scale, and there is evidence of a growing interest.

The decline of the Scottish oyster fisheries in the last century led to studies of ways in which the young oyster might be helped over the stage of its life cycle to which the natural environment of these latitudes is hostile, one of the objectives of the Granton Marine Station opened in 1884. The first commercial oyster hatchery opened on the west coast in 1969 with the object both of producing spat for sale to other growers and also re-establishing some local oyster beds.

Mussels are not a significant item of the Scottish diet but profitable markets exist on the continent and in England. Pilot experiments in mussel culture, by suspended culture, have proved sufficiently encouraging to stimulate the beginnings of a small industry.

Rainbow trout are cultivated on a large scale in Denmark in fresh water. Better conversion rates appear to be obtainable in the sea and already Scottish waters have attracted capital investment for rainbow trout cultivation in the sea.

## Research in cultivation techniques

Various organizations are concerned in both the development of new techniques and in the application of techniques developed in other countries for cultivating marine organisms. The work of the White Fish Authority is probably of closest relevance to Scottish waters since much of it has been conducted on the west coast but at the same time it has not been orientated specifically at local problems, being a much more broadly-based study of fish cultivation. Probably their studies of marine fish rearing in sea enclosures come closest to the type of approach which might offer most promise on the west coast.

The choice of cultivation technique and of organism to be used not only depends on the objectives of the activity but also on the ability of nature to provide a suitable environment for it. There is, therefore, a need to understand the natural ecological cycle of these lochs, to identify what processes take place in them and the nature of the critical factors affecting the end result, so that one may see the way to profitable changes or evaluate the effect of cultivation undertaken on a trial and error basis.

The Department of Agriculture and Fisheries for Scotland has for some time conducted studies of an exposed loch system at Loch Ewe in Western Ross and to a lesser extent in a more sheltered loch, Loch Nevis. The Scottish Marine Biological Association is developing an extensive study of the more southerly Argyllshire lochs, and in particular Loch Etive.

Although the latter work in Loch Etive has only recently been started (Annual Report, SMBA, 1970), a number of significant questions have been posed by the observations to date.

Loch Etive is an extreme in the types of west coast lochs, displaying a considerable degree of enclosure and freshwater influence at the surface. The deeper basin of the loch ($\sim 140$ m) is typically marine, however, below the region of freshwater influence, and the hydrographic structure bears close similarity to that of a large estuary, and indeed resembles the Baltic Sea in some respects.

The input of dissolved and particulate organic matter from the land run-off is of such magnitude that it may well be a significant source in relation to the primary production *in situ*. There is evidence of a preponderance of omnivorous forms in the zooplankton and the rich detritus may well be the major energy input to the benthos. So far as the native fish population is concerned, it has become increasingly apparent that the loch is an important nursery area, while the adult fish population tends to be sparse. Comparisons with adjacent lochs and sea areas are being made to find out how far these features are common.

While it is hoped that these studies will elucidate the organic system characteristic of these lochs, there is a good prospect that they will tell us much about the marine organic cycle which is of much wider interest. A major difficulty in studying organic production in the open sea is that of identifying how much activity is brought about by *in situ* biological processes and how much change derives from movements of the water masses or organisms involved. It would seem that in a semi-enclosed loch system there is a much better chance of monitoring such changes and getting to grips quantitatively with the budget of events in the organic cycle.

FORESEEABLE DEVELOPMENTS

It seems probable that the criteria for cultivating the sea will differ markedly from those used in agriculture. In agriculture, only plants and herbivorous animals are cultivated. In the sea, the molluscs of commercial interest may be herbivorous, but apart from them we have to deal primarily with carnivorous animals. On land the removal of competitive crops and predatory animals is comparatively straightforward but in the sea these may have to be tolerated and this may dictate whether or not a particular mode of cultivation is possible. Even in restricted areas such as the west coast lochs it seems unlikely that direct fertilization will ever be a worthwhile proposition although it is the basis of most successful agriculture.

### Replenishment or supplementation of natural stocks

The organisms likely to offer the best prospect are those over which there is some limitation to dispersal. It is worth noting the very considerable success which has met the Japanese efforts to maintain their scallop fishery; the essence of this lies in annual stocking of beds which would otherwise be rapidly depleted by the intensity of fishing. The technical difficulties of spat collection, nurturing the spat and relaying on the beds have been overcome and there appears to be no real barrier to the success of similar techniques here. Similar achievements might eventually be possible with the lobster or perhaps *Nephrops*, but the necessary expertise is certainly not available at present.

### Low density "free range" cultivation

The essence of this approach lies in making better use of the natural environment either through fortification of some natural element of the fauna or through introduction of a new species. Depending on the capacity of the natural system, supplementary feeding may be required continually or at certain times of the year.

Physical enclosure of sea areas to retain the enriched stock is likely to require a prohibitive amount of capital investment except in a few instances and a more feasible approach might exist in controlling the behaviour pattern of the organisms involved, through suitable training. Carp responding to a bell at feeding time are but one illustration. In Japan a similar technique was used with rainbow trout in the Inland Sea but evidently met with unforeseen difficulties. The prospects in more enclosed waters seem sufficiently encouraging to warrant more detailed study of behaviour patterns and the influence of training on these in species of potential interest.

### High density cultivation

The suspended culture of mussels and oysters is well established in several countries. Suspension of these organisms in waters with rich natural feeding makes demands primarily on capital and labour. Provided sufficiently cheap means of support can be found there seems little barrier to the more extensive introduction of this technique in western Scotland. Difficulties have been experienced, however, with competitive settlement of ascidians in some areas and it is clear that the lochs are not uniformly good growing areas. Currently assessments are being made of the potential of different lochs.

Reference has already been made to the growing interest in marine cultivation of rainbow trout. Surprisingly, in Scotland freshwater cultivation is hindered by a lack of sufficiently constant and predictable water supplies and the sea consequently offers better prospects. Furthermore, it is claimed that better conversion rates can be achieved in sea water.

Other species worthy of consideration are salmon and sea trout and it may well be that certain white fish prove to have potential.

In this type of culture a greater capital input and labour requirement is needed and furthermore food must be supplied. Presently the latter is often supplied as trash fish and indeed in Denmark supports a subsidiary industry of fishing for this sole purpose. Thus association with fish processing plants or trash fish supplies can materially aid the development. At the same time the development of suitable dry foods would be an asset for enterprises not easily accessible to trash fish supplies.

Caution against over capitalization is emphasized by the simplicity of Japanese cultures of this nature and operating costs may well be reduced by the establishment of centralized marketing procedures, something along the lines of the Guernsey tomato industry.

Other questions which can only be answered by proper market analysis relate to how long or for how much of the life cycle of the particular fish it is profitable to keep it in cultivation.

The prospect of difficulty from disease must also be guarded against through further research and training.

### "Intensive" cultivation

I merely mention this here since it is but of fringe interest outside a few specialized localities, but when we consider the lengths to which the production of glasshouse crops have gone with carbon dioxide enrichment, artificial illumination, it does not seem ridiculous to consider similarly complex techniques for the growth of marine organisms.

The heated effluent water of power stations is already the subject of investigation in this respect and it may be in this context that the supplementation of light, inorganic nutrient control, etc. assume significance. The first quest would seem to be for the organisms which are of sufficient value to warrant the procedure.

The production of oyster spat is already established along these lines and there does not appear to be any invincible barrier to using a similar degree of sophistication with many other species.

### LEGAL ASPECTS

While one may contemplate hopefully the manipulation of nature, it is clear that little will be possible in the long run without attention to the legal aspects of the problem.

The present system of tenure of Scottish sea areas and of the sea floor does little to protect the sort of developments which have been discussed and indeed may serve as a considerable obstacle to their implementation.

Most of the sea lochs fall within the legislation of various salmon and freshwater fisheries acts and so far as the salmonid fisheries are concerned, within certain statutory limitations, are almost completely under the control of the fishery owner.

The sea floor, which is largely in the ownership of the Crown, may be leased for shellfish growing or to lay moorings for floating objects, but there appears to be little or no statutory protection for the individual undertaking the development.

Thus, while we as biologists may consider ways and means of making more use of the potential of these waters, we must look to our legal colleagues to ensure that the developments are both possible and worthwhile.

### POLLUTION

I have said sufficient about the potential of this valuable natural resource which we have in these semi-enclosed coastal waters. Its continued value, however, must depend on maintaining freedom from pollution. While this is a problem which has hardly arisen to date, we should remember that something like four and a half cubic kilometres of water pass daily up the west coast from the Irish Sea and Clyde estuary (Craig, 1959), and we must do all we can to avoid contamination of this source.

SUMMARY

The large area of sea water in the lochs of the west coast of Scotland is attractive from the point of view of cultivating marine organisms. The lochs lend themselves if not always to physical enclosure, at least to legal enclosure and there is consequently a good prospect that any investment in cultivation can directly benefit the investor.

The essential criterion of the viability of cultivation must be that the profits reaped are of sufficient magnitude to warrant the investment but in Scotland there is another factor of importance, namely that of maintaining a population dispersed over a wide area. Marine cultivation in this instance can be looked upon as a supplementary occupation.

Thus the objectives of endeavouring to introduce marine cultivation in this area can be to create an industry which barely exists at present, to sustain the existing industries, to provide an additional supply of food protein from marine sources and to provide the basis for sport fisheries with their lateral benefits to the community.

Currently, various techniques for cultivating marine organisms are being tried, and at the same time studies are being made of the natural ecological system in these lochs. It is important to establish what processes this system embraces and what determines its course so that one may identify the most promising means of altering or supplementing the natural system. This is a primary aim of the work of the new laboratory at Oban, but at the same time this work has still farther reaching implications, in that it presents an opportunity of examining the budget of the marine organic cycle in a manner not possible in the open sea.

It seems probable that even in such restricted areas of the sea as these west coast lochs, the most promising approach to cultivation will employ different criteria for improvement than in agriculture and parallel studies of the physiology and behaviour of potentially useful organisms are being undertaken, in conjunction with the field studies to identify possible approaches.

REFERENCES

Barnes, H. & Goodley, E. F. W. (1958). A note on rainfall in the west of Scotland. *Glasg. Nat.* **18:** 45–54.

Craig, R. E. (1959). Hydrography of Scottish coastal waters. *Mar. Res. Scot.* No. 2, 30 pp.

Scottish Marine Biological Association, Annual Report, 1969–70.
Scottish Sea Fisheries Statistical Tables, 1960–69. HM Stationery Office, Edinburgh.
Strom, K. M. (1936). Land-locked waters. Hydrography and bottom deposits in badly-ventilated Norwegian fjords with remarks upon sedimentation under anaerobic conditions. *Skr. norske Vidensk-Akad.* **1936**, No. 7, 85 pp.

Symp. zool. Soc. Lond. (1972) No. 29, 297–300.

# CHAIRMAN'S CONCLUDING REMARKS

## R. J. H. BEVERTON

*Natural Environment Research Council, London, England*

### SOME NON-BIOLOGICAL INTERESTS IN THE CONSERVATION AND PRODUCTIVITY OF THE COASTAL MARINE ENVIRONMENT

Dr. Cole, in his introduction, drew attention to the importance of coastal waters in the context of the conservation and productivity of the marine fauna, both inshore and in deeper water, and this significance has been illustrated by the contributions that have been presented. Several of these have been concerned with resources whose conservation has some immediate implications, perhaps because the information in that area tends to be most comprehensive, but comparable problems and mechanisms are being discerned throughout the field of marine productivity studies. The coastal and "shallow-water" environment is clearly of crucial importance to the well-being of many faunal resources, so it is appropriate to review briefly here the practical and scientific problems of coastal waters, other than biological, in order to indicate the breadth of other disciplines which also have interests relevant to the biologist.

It is convenient to start with a subject which appears to be remote from biological resources at the present time, the geology of the continental shelf. I expect you are all familiar with the dramatic story of the exploration of the North Sea leading to the discoveries of major gas fields in the south and recently of oil in the north. The pioneering work was done mainly by the universities in the 1950s, and these geophysical surveys established the presence in the southern North Sea of deep sedimentary basins having the characteristic structure of hydrocarbon reservoirs. It was that knowledge, coupled with the proof of gas in the adjacent Gröningen fields of north Holland and inference from extrapolation of the known land geology of the north-east of England and East Anglia, that led the oil companies to embark in the early sixties on the most intensive programme of detailed prospecting, comprising both seismic profiling and deep boring, that has yet been undertaken anywhere in the world. Something in the region of £200 million pounds has been spent by the companies in this search.

In 1966 the Institute of Geological Sciences itself began a systematic survey of the geological structure of the UK continental shelf. As well as its basic scientific interest, this programme has several practical objectives. One is to collate, by liaison with industry, all the available knowledge and thus obtain a strategic assessment of the hydrocarbon potential of the shelf which will assist both Government and industry in long-range planning. Another is to extend the primary geophysical reconnaissance to areas of the shelf outside those so far worked by the companies, where the geology is still largely unknown and in some cases, as in the Irish Sea, more complex than in the North Sea.

The IGS sea programme consists of these geophysical surveys linked with a shallow-boring network designed to establish the more detailed composition of the first few hundred feet of the shelf down to the bedrock. These shallow bore-holes serve two purposes. One is to detect the possible occurrence, in the top zone, of mineral resources other than hydrocarbons. The other is to enhance the interpretation of the geophysical information strata, with direct evidence where the deep strata slope up to relatively near the top of the sea floor.

Research on the shelf is also being undertaken by universities in coordination with the investigations of the IGS. For example, the Department of Geodesy and Geophysics at Cambridge, in conjunction with the National Institute of Oceanography, has recently investigated the Rockall Bank area, and the next few years will probably see an extension of this work by NERC institutes and universities to the continental slope and margins where, with the rapid advances in drilling technology, commercial exploitation may soon become feasible if sufficiently promising resources are located.

The surface of the seabed itself presents a number of scientific and practical problems. The systematic bathymetric surveys carried out by the Hydrographic Department of the Ministry of Defence (Navy) reveal that banks of soft sediments on the seabed are continually shifting in response to the action of tides and residual currents. This movement is complex and does not appear to conform to any simple pattern. Superimposed on the relatively slow build-up and recession of the larger banks is the faster movement in some areas of sand waves which may be a number of metres high and only a few hundred in wave-length.

Man has recently added his contribution to the problem by greatly increasing the extraction of sand and gravel from not only the near-shore areas but further offshore also. We have an inadequate understanding of what influence this will have on seabed topography but it may be considerable. Biological problems may also be created where the extraction takes place in localities associated with important animal resources. The effect may not necessarily be adverse; but when it is remembered, for example, how precisely the North Sea herring congregate for spawning on the Sandettié and adjacent banks one can hardly view the situation with complacence. The Lowestoft Fisheries Laboratory, the Hydraulics Research Station (now under the Department of the Environment) and NERC are collaborating in an attack on this peculiarly intractable problem.

A better understanding of these dynamic processes of the seabed surface is obviously of great importance with the advent of deep-draught tankers and bulk carriers, and the need to site offshore drilling rigs and pipe-lines on a safe substrate. It was to strengthen this research that the Unit of Coastal Sedimentation, which works in close cooperation with the Hydrographic Department, was established at Taunton a year or so ago.

Navigational demands are putting a premium on predicting sea-level variation to a new order of precision in which second-order and non-linear effects cannot be neglected. We are familiar with the hazard of positive surges caused by a coincidence of high tide and storm pressure in confined sea areas. The inverse of the positive surge is the so-called negative surge, that is, an extreme of low sea-level, and with large ships of perhaps 70 ft draught clearing the tops of offshore banks by only a few feet the margin of error is disturbingly small.

These are problems to which scientists in several laboratories are turning their attention. Numerical models of the combined effect of tides and wind pressure in a water basin of given shape and size can now simulate with considerable accuracy the main features of the outstanding storm surges of recent years, such as that which caused the disastrous flooding along the east coast in 1953. They have indicated the strategic locations in the North Sea where a few large moored buoys equipped with precision recording instruments could provide continuous observations which would enable the mathematical treatment to be further refined and, it is hoped, lead to better predictive methods. The development of buoy technology is now being taken up jointly by several European countries, including the UK.

The dynamics of the seabed surface cannot be understood without knowledge of the currents and tidal streams, and this brings me to the general question of water movements. Again, British coastal waters present a complex picture, with strong oceanic influence in the west and south-west on which are super-imposed local circulations in more confined areas. These differences of scale in space are associated with corresponding differences in time. For example, there are signs that the events of the 1920s in the English Channel (illuminated by the work of the Marine Biological Association), when the Plymouth herring disappeared and was replaced by pilchard, are beginning to be reversed.

We are probably seeing here the consequences of very long periodicity in the basic climatic regime, which will affect other regions than the English Channel. Such changes in the marine environment have obvious implications to coastal fisheries. They also demonstrate the importance of having adequate "baseline" information on such natural changes, both physical and biological, if we are to detect the real long-term effects of pollution. This is what is implied in the currently fashionable term "environmental monitoring", which at least has the merit of reminding us that unless our research is so organized that it is able to throw light on what is really happening in the environment much of its point will be lost.

I turn finally to the problems arising on the coasts themselves. Some of the research I have already mentioned is of immediate relevance here, notably that on storm and tidal surges as it relates to coastal and estuarine protection. The problem, at least as far as the east coast of England is concerned, is aggravated by the fact that the land itself is slowly sinking, at a rate of about one foot in a hundred years. This may not seem much, but it doubles the frequency probability of a major flood. The assessment of flood risk has therefore to be continually revised, and it was evidence of this kind for the Thames at London, provided by the NERC Institute of Coastal Oceanography and Tides, that contributed to the decision to construct a Thames barrage.

But the problems are not confined to protection against natural forces. One way of conserving water resources is to create large artificial impoundments by constructing barrages across the mouths of estuaries, and we have listened with great interest to the evaluation of the biological implications of analogous projects planned for in the Netherlands (Zijlstra, this volume, pp. 233–258). If that were done on a really large scale the effect of cutting off a substantial flow of freshwater on the dynamics of coastal seas could not be neglected. We have a fair idea of the circulatory patterns of the North Sea but I doubt whether it is sufficient to predict with any reliability what would happen in such circumstances, still less what the biological consequences would be.

In this brief review I have been able to touch only on some of what seem to me to be the main ways in which marine science is contributing to a better understanding of our coastal marine environment and its resources. I have not dealt, for example, with the special problems of estuaries, of the role of muds and sediments in relation to pollution, or the effect of sand and gravel extraction on the coastline itself. But I hope I have been able to convey something of the breadth of scientific disciplines which need to be brought to bear if science is to provide the answers to the practical problems of the future in our coastal waters.

# AUTHOR INDEX

*Numbers in italics refer to pages in the References at the end of each article.*

## A

Abram, F. S. H., 95, 96, *113*
Ahlgren, I., 46, *66*
Adams, J. A., 187, *198*
Alabaster, J. S., 89, 91, 92, 94, 95, 96, *113*
Allan, I. R. H., 89, 94, *113*
Allen, K. R., 77, 80, *85*, 120, 122, *131*
Andersen, J. K., 124, *131*
Anderson, G. C., 26, *40*
Anderson, R. R., 6, *16*
Andrew, T., 53, 57, 58, 62, *66*, *67*
Anon, 13, *16*, 254, *256*
Anraku, M., 187, *198*
Ascione, R., 5, 7, *17*
Atkinson-Willes, G. L., 145, *152*

## B

Baas Becking, L. G. M., 12, *17*
Backiel, T., 116, 127, *131*
Ball, I. R., 92, 93, *113*
Barić, A., 282, *283*
Barnes, H., 286, *295*
Baylor, E. R., 187, *198*
Beklemishev, C. W., 197, *198*
Benedict, F. G., 260, *268*
Bennet, A., *152*
Bennett, H. D., 7, *17*
Berner, A., 193, *198*
Bernhard, M., 282, *283*
Bertalanffy, L., von, 259, *268*
Beverton, R. J. H., 119, 130, *131*, 162, 169, *183*, 213, *230*, 254, *256*, 259, 262, *268*
Birge, E. A., 48, *66*
Bischoff, A. I., 146, *153*
Blaxter, K. L., 260, 266, *268*
Blok, E., 151, *152*
Blum, J. L., 11, *17*
Blumer, M., 194, *198*
Doddeko, R., 235, *256*

Boerema, L. K., 228, *232*
Böhnecke, G., 251, 252, 253, *256*
Bormann, F. H., 136, *152*, *153*
Bowden, K. F., 273, *283*
Bowen, V. T., 281, *283*
Bowers, A. B., 254, *256*
Boyd, H., 145, *152*
Branica, M., 282, *283*
Britton, R. H., 70, 75, 82, *85*
Brock, T. D., 4, 5, 7, 8, 13, 14, 15, 16, *17*
Brody, S., 260, *268*
Bromley, P. J., 266, *268*
Brook, A. J., 148, *152*
Brooks, E. R., 193, 195, 196, *200*
Brown, M. E., 260, 261, 263, *268*
Brown, V. M., 90, 91, 95, 96, 97, 99, *113*, *114*
Bückmann, A., 228, *230*, 235, 236, 237, 243, 244, 245, 249, 253, 254, *256*
Burns, C. W., 61, *66*
Butcher, R. W., 10, *17*
Butler, E. I., 188, 190, 191, 193, 194, 195, 196, *198*
Bye, J. A. T., 48, *66*
Bye, V., 149, *152*

## C

Carey, F. G., 190, *201*
Carroz, J. E., 173, *183*
Carter, G., 37, *39*
Castenholz, R. W., 4, 5, 6, 10, *17*, *18*
Chapman, D. W., 120, *131*
Chipman, W. A., 281, *283*
Christie, A. E., 14, *17*
Clarendon Press, 88, *113*
Clark, J., 255, *256*
Clayden, A. D., 170, *183*
Coche, A. G., 124, *131*
Colebrook, J. M., 203, 209, *212*
Collins, V. G., 62, *66*

Conover, R. J., 188, 190, 192, 193, 194, 198
Conover, S. A. M., 192, *199*
Cooke, G. W., 31, *39*
Cooley, H. L., 4, *18*
Cooley, P., 49, 50, *66*, *67*
Cooper, E. L., 124, *131*
Cooper, L. H. N., 186, *200*
Corkett, C. J., 193, *199*
Corner, E. D. S., 186, 188, 189, 190, 191, 192, 193, 194, 195, 196, *198*, *199*
Cowey, C. B., 186, 189, 190, 191, 192, 193, 194, 195, *199*
Craig, R. E., 286, 295, *295*
Cremer, G. A., 58, 62, *66*
Curl, H., Jnr., 186, *199*
Cushing, D. H., 162, *183*, 186, 197, *199*, 213, 216, 217, 218, 219, 223, 229, *230*, *231*

D

Dalton, R. A., 90, *113*
Das, N., 252, *257*
Davies, A. G., 189, *199*
Dawes, B., 260, 262, 263, 264, 267, *268*
Denko, E. I., 6, *17*
Department of Scientific and Industrial Research, 37, *39*
Dickie, L. M., 259, 261, *269*
Dickman, M., 14, *17*
Dickson, R., 215, 223, *231*
Dietrich, G., 220, 221, *231*
Dilz, K., 147, *154*
Doemel, W. N., 5, 15, *17*
Doudoroff, P., 89, *113*
Downing, K. M., 92, *113*
Dragesund, O., 218, *231*
Duffey, E., 138, *152*
Dunaway, P. B., 281, *284*
Duncan, A., 53, 57, 58, 62, *66*, *67*
Dutton, J. W. R., 281, *283*

E

Eaton, J. S., 136, *152*
Edwards, R. W., 46, *66*, 96, 97, *114*
Efford, I. A., 136, *152*
Egglishaw, H. J., 122, *131*
Eisma, D., 240, *256*
Elder, H. Y., 260, *268*
Ellis, E. A., 150, *152*

Ellis, M. B., *152*
Evans, D. H., 280, *283*

F

Fahay, M. P., 255, *256*
Feldman, N. L., 6, *18*
Feth, J. H., 25, *40*
Fiala, K., 145, *152*
Fish, G. R., 148, *153*
Fisher, D. W., 136, *153*
Fjerdingstad, E., 9, *17*
Foerster, R. E., 116, 124, 127, *133*
Fogg, G. E., 7, *17*
Folkard, A. R., 221, 222, 223, 226, *231*, 274, *283*
Ford, M. E., Jr., 50, *66*
Forster, W. O., 281, *284*
Fresco, J. R., 5, 7, *17*
Frost, W. E., 124, 127, 128, *132*
Fulton, J. D., 186, 197, *201*

G

Gambell, A. W., 136, *153*
Ganf, G. G., 55, *66*
Garrod, D. J., 176, 179, *183*, 215, *231*
Geen, G. H., 189, *200*
Gerking, S. D., 124, *131*, 265, *268*
Gessner, F., 240, *256*
Gibbs, M., 12, *17*
Glover, R. S., 203, *212*
Goedecke, E., 237, *257*
Goodley, E. F. W., 286, *295*
Graham, M., 262, *268*
Grygierek, E., 126, *133*
Gulland, J. A., 128, *131*, 169, 173, *183*
Gusev, M. V., 12, *17*

H

Hall, J. D., 123, *131*
Haq, S. M., 186, 188, 193, *200*
Harding, D., 221, *231*
Hardy, A. C., 203, *212*
Hargrave, B. T., 189, *200*
Harris, E., 192, *200*
Harris, J. G. K., 229, *231*
Harris, S. L., 49, 50, *66*, *67*
Harvey, H. W., 186, *200*
Hasler, A. D., 124, *132*
Hatch, R. W., 124, *131*
Haystead, A., 12, *18*

Hem, J. D., 7, 9, *19*
Hepher, B., 126, 127, *132*
Herbert, D. W. M., 89, 90, 91, 94, *113*, *114*
Hewett, C. J., 277, 280, *283*
Hickling, C. F., 126, 129, *132*, 262, *268*
Hidu, H., 124, *131*
Higley, D. L., 124, *132*
Hill, H. W., 273, *284*
Hislop, J. R. G., 264, 265, 267, *269*
Hoather, R. C., 36, *40*
Holden, A. V., 148, *152*, *153*
Holt, S. J., 119, 130, *131*, 169, *183*, 254, 256, 259, 262, *268*
Horsted, Sv. A., 176, *183*
Horton, P. A., 122, *132*
Hrbacek, J., 62, *66*
Hunt, E. G., 146, *153*
Hunt, R. L., 122, *132*
Hynes, H. B. N., 145, *153*

I

ICES, 164, 169, 176, 179, *183*, 252, *257*
ICNAF, 164, *183*
Illinois State Water Survey, 36, *40*
Irwin, W. H., 50, *66*, *67*
Ivlev, V. S., 116, *132*

J

Jefferies, D. F., 272, 275, 277, 278, 280, 281, *283*, *284*
Jennings, J. N., *153*
Jerlov, N., 224, 225, *231*
Jermy, A. C., *153*
Johannes, R. E., 190, *201*
Johansen, A. C., 235, 237, *257*
Johnson, L., 260, *268*
Johnson, M. G., 14, *17*
Johnson, N. G., 25, *40*
Johnson, N. W., 136, *153*
Johnson, W. E., 124, *132*
Johnston, R., 239, *257*
Jones, P. G. W., 239, *257*
Jones, R., 264, 265, 267, *269*
Jordon, D. H. M., 90, 91, 95, *113*, *114*
Joseph, J., 222, *231*
Joseph, J. M., 8, *17*

K

Kendall, A. W., Jr. 255, *256*

Kennedy, O. D., 186, 197, *201*
Keulgen, G. H., 48, *66*
Kibby, H. V., 58, *66*
Kipling, C., 124, 127, 128, *132*
Klein, L., 145, *153*
Knaggs, F. W., 151, *154*
Koberg, G. E., 50, *66*
Kolenbrander, G. J., 147, 148, *153*, *154*
Korringa, P., 194, *200*, 237, *257*
Kowalczewski, A., 70, 73, 75, 83, *85*
Krogius, P. V., 130, *132*
Krokhin, E. M., 130, *132*
Kühl, H., 239, *257*
Kullberg, R. G., 13, 14, *17*
Květ, J., 145, *152*

L

Lack, T. J., 70, 72, 73, 75, 83, *85*
Lackey, J. B., 8, *17*
Laevastu, T., 223, *231*
Laing, H. E., 12, *18*
Lambert, J. M., 149, *153*
Landsberg, H. E., 10, *18*
Langford, J. C., 281, *284*
Laurie, A. H., 50, *66*
Lebour, M. V., 186, *200*
Le Brasseur, R. T., 186, 197, *201*
Le Cren, E. D., 79, *85*, 116, 120, 121, 122, 123, 124, 125, 126, 127, 129, *131*, *132*, 255, *257*, 263, *269*
Lee, A. J., 213, 221, 222, 223, 226, *230*, *231*
Libosvarsky, J., 122, *132*
Likens, G. E., 136, *153*
Linford, E., 192, *200*
Lippman, H., 10, *18*
Lloyd, R., 90, 91, *114*
Ludwig, H. F., 13, *18*
Luknitskaya, A. F., 6, *18*
Lumb, F. E., 223, 224, *231*
Lund, J. W. G., 43, 45, 57, *67*, 146, *153*
Luther, H., 137, *153*
Lyutova, M. I., 6, *18*

M

McAllister, C. D., 187, 188, *200*
Macchi, G., 282, *283*
McDonald, I., 70, 75, *85*
Macek, K. J., 130, *132*
Mackay, I., 79, *85*

Mackenthun, K. M., 4, *18*
Makarova, N. P., 187, *201*
Mann, H., 239, *257*
Mann, K. H., 69, 70, 75, 79, 80, 81, *85*, 116, 122, 123, 125, *133*
Margalef, R., 13, *18*
Marine Biological Association, 189, *200*
Marshall, S. M., 187, 188, 189, 190, 191, 193, 194, 195, 196, 197, *198*, *199*, *200*
Martin, J. H., 186, *200*
Mathews, C. P., 70, 75, 79, 80, *85*, 123, *133*
Matthews, G. V. T., 145, *152*
Menshutkin, V. V., 130, *132*
Merkens, J. C., 92, *113*
Meyer-Waarden, P. F., 235, 250, *257*
Michalski, M. F. P., 14, *17*
Ministry of Technology, 90, 92, 93, 95, 99, 106, 107, *114*
Minshall, N., 25, *40*
Mitchell, N. T., 272, *284*
Mitrovic, V. V., 96, *113*
Moore, N. W., 151, *154*
Morgan, F., 277, *283*
Morgan, N. C., 136, 146, 148, 149, 150, *153*
Mortimer, C. H., 44, 46, *67*
Mullin, M. M., 186, 187, 188, 192, 193, 194, 195, 196, *198*, *200*
Munk, W. H., 60, *67*
Murphy, G. I., 56, 64, *67*
Murray, H., 5, 16, *19*

**N**

Nakken, O., 218, *231*
Negus, C. L., 77, 78, *85*
Neil, J. H., 25, *40*
Nelson, D. J., 281, *284*
Newell, B. S., 192, *199*
Newman, J. F., 151, *154*
Nicholls, A. G., 190, *200*
Nichols, M. S., 25, *40*
Nilsson, N. A., 126, *133*
Nizovtsev, G. P., 218, *231*
Novotna-Dvorakova, M., 62, *66*

**O**

Olney, P. S., 137, *153*
Olsen, J. S., 281, *283*
Olsen, S., 148, 149, 150, *153*

Omori, M., 187, *198*
Organization for Economic Cooperation and Development, 161, *184*
Orr, A. P., 187, 190, 193, 197, *200*
Osterberg, C. L., 281, *283*
Ottestad, P., 214, *231*
Owen, G. E., 25, *40*
Owens, M., 25, 26, *40*

**P**

Paffen, Kh., 10, *18*
Paffenhöfer, G-A., 187, 193, *200*, *201*
Pallis, M., *154*
Paloheimo, J. E., 259, 261, *269*
Parrish, B. B., 128, *133*
Parsons, T. R., 186, 197, *201*
Patrick, R., 6, 10, 15, *18*
Pearcy, W. G., 190, *201*
Pearson, E. A., 13, *18*
Pearson, H. W., 12, *18*
Peary, J., 4, 5, 6, *18*
Pentelow, F. T. K., 88, *114*, 260, *269*
Pentreath, R. J., 277, 278, *283*
Petipa, T. S., 187, 188, 189, 192, 194, 195, 196, *201*
Pierce, R. S., 136, *153*
Ponomarenko, V. P., 179, *184*
Postma, H., 239, 240, *257*
Postuma, K. H., 235, 252, *257*
Preston, A., 272, 281, *283*, *284*
Price, T. J., 281, *283*
Putter, A., 259, *269*

**R**

Rafail, S. Z., 261, *269*
Ramster, J. W., 273, *284*
Rauera, J., 281, *283*
Reichle, D. E., 281, *284*
Rice, T. R., 281, *283*, *284*
Ricker, W. E., 80, *85*, 115, 116, 119, 124, 127, *133*, 213, *231*
Ridley, J. E. A., 45, 50, *67*
Rieck, H. G., 281, *284*
Rigler, F. H., 61, *66*, 194, *199*
Riley, G. A., 60, *67*, 186, *201*
Robeck, G. G., 50, *66*, *67*
Robertson, D. E., 281, *284*
Robinson, E. L., 50, *67*
Robinson, G. A., 203, *212*
Rolley, H. L. J., 46, *66*

Rommets, J. W., 240, *257*
Roskam, R. Th., 237, *257*
Russell, F. S., 186, *200*
Ržoska, J., 137, *153*

S

Sachs, J., 6, *18*
Sawyer, C. N., 25, *40*
Schmidt, W., 48, *67*
Schroeder, H., 9, *18*
Schumacher, G. J., *19*
Scottish Marine Biological Association
   291, *296*
Scottish Sea Fisheries Statistical Tables
   287, 288, *296*
Seabloom, R. W., 26, *40*
Seber, G. A. F., 79, *85*
Shaw, D., 91, *113*
Shelbourne, J. E., 228, *231*
Shurben, D. G., 91, *113*
Shurben, D. S., 90, *114*
Simpson, A. C., 220, 221, *232*, 251, 252,
   *257*
Sládečkova, A., 6, *18*
Small, L. F., 190, *201*
Smed, J., 237, *257*
Smidt, E. L. B., 236, 240, 241, 244, 245,
   249, *257*
Smith, H. W., 280, *284*
Smith, W. G., 255, *256*
Sorokin, J. J., 62, *67*
Southgate, B. A., 89, *114*
Southward, A. J., 193, *199*
Southward, E. C., 193, *199*
Southwick, W., 5, 7, *17*
Sparrow, B. W. P., 189, *199*
Stann, E. J., 13, *18*
Stark, G. T. C., 96, *113*
Steel, J. A., 50, 52, 53, 57, *67*
Steele, J. H., 187, *198*, 225, *232*
Steeman, Neilsen, E., 9, *18*
Stewart, L., 143, *154*
Stewart, W. D. P., 12, *18*
Stockner, J. G., 5, 14, 16, *18*
Storrs, P. N., 13, *18*
Stratton, F. E., 37, *40*
Strickland, J. D. H., 187, *201*, 223, *232*
Strom, K. M., 7, *18*, 286, *296*
Struik, Ir. A., van der, 151, *154*
Sukopp, H., 144, 145, *154*

Sutcliffe, W. H., Jr., 187, *198*
Sverdrup, H. U., 56, *67*
Sylvester, R. O., 26, *40*
Symons, J. M., 50, *66*, *67*

T

Talbot, J. W., 221, *231*
Talling, J. F., 53, 55, *67*
Tåning, A. V., 235, 236, 237, 243, 254,
   *257*, *258*
Task Group Report, 25, *40*
Teal, J. M., 190, *201*
Thomas, D. W., 194, *198*
Tiews, K., 235, 250, *257*
Tijssen, S. B., 239, *258*
Tiller, B. A., 90, 95, *113*
Tomczack, G., 237, *257*
Tomlinson, T. E., 36, *40*
Trembley, F. J., 6, *18*
Troll, C., 10, *18*
Tümpling, W., von, 14, *18*

V

Van Denburgh, A. S., 25, *40*
Van Dorn, W. G., 48, *67*
Vandyke, Jennifer M., 90, *114*
Veen, J. F. de, 228, *232*
Vollenweider, R. A., 37, *40*, 52, *67*, 145,
   *154*
Vučetić, T., 186, 197, *199*

W

Walsh, R., 13, *18*
Walter, E., 126, *133*
Waring, G. A., 7, 9, *19*
Way, J. M., 151, *154*
Webb, K. L., 190, *201*
Webster, D. A., 124, *131*
Weimann, R., 10, *18*
Weiss, F. E., 5, 16, *19*
White, C. M., 49, *67*
White, D. E., 7, 9, *19*
Whitford, L. A., 7, *19*
Whittaker, R. H., 13, *19*
Whitton, B. A., 9, 10, 13, *19*
Wilber, C. G., 4, *19*
Wilhm, J. L., 14, *19*
Williams, P. M., 7, *19*
Williams, R. J. B., 31, *39*

Williams, W. E., 264, 265, 267, *269*
Williams, W. P., 79, *85*
Willis, V. M., 281, *284*
Wilson, D. F., 193, *201*
Wimpenny, R. S., 218, *232*
Windle, Taylor, E., 43, 62, *67*
Witzel, S. A., 25, *40*
Wium-Anderson, S., 9, *18*
Woldendorp, J. W., 147, *154*
Wolny, P., 126, *133*
Wood, E. J. F., 12, *17*

Woodhead, P. M. J., 237, *258*

Y

Young, L., 194, *199*

Z

Zattera, A., 282, *283*
Zavadskaya, I. G., 6, *18*
Ziegelmeier, E., 240, *258*
Zijlstra, J. J., 252, *257*
Zillioux, E. J., 193, *201*

# SYSTEMATIC INDEX

## A

*Abramis*, 62, 92
*Acartia*, 188, 189, 192, 195, 196, 207, 208, 209
*Acerina*, 94
*Achnanthes*, 10
*Acorus*, 70, 75, 78
*Acrocephalus*, 150
*Alburnus*, 79, 123
Amphibia, 138
*Anabaena*, 12
*Anguilla*, 92
*Anodonta*, 78
*Anser*, 145
*Aphanizomenon*, 43, 62
*Apium*, 142
*Artemia*, 187
*Ascophyllum*, 289
*Asterionella*, 58

## B

Bacillariophyta, 8, 60
*Bagrus*, 260
*Biddulphia*, 197
Bivalvia, 77
*Brenta*, 145
Bryozoa, 77

## C

*Calanus*, 186, 187, 188, 189, 190, 191, 192, 193, 195, 196, 197, 208, 210
*Calliphora*, 83
*Ceratophyllum*, 6, 149, 150
*Chara*, 5, 151
Chironomidae, 77, 78, 83
Chironominae, 78
*Chlorococcum*, 10
Chlorophyceae, 72
Chlorophyta, 8, 10, 60
Chrysophyta, 7, 8,
Chydoridae, 78
*Chydorus*, 79
Cladocera, 78, 84, 210
Cladophora, 10, 151

Cladophoraceae, 6
*Clupea*, 235
*Cocconeis*, 10
*Compsopogon*, 5, 6
Copepoda, 79
*Coregonus*, 138
*Cottus*, 122, 125
*Crangon*, 235
*Cricotopus*, 78
Cryptophyta, 8
*Cyanidium*, 5, 7, 15
Cyanophyceae, 10
Cyanophyta, 8, 60
*Cygnus*, 145
*Cyprinus*, 92

## D

*Daphnia*, 57, 58, 62
*Desmidium*, 8
Diamesinae, 78
*Ditylum*, 186
*Drepanocladus*, 9

## E

*Einfeldia*, 78
*Eleocharis*, 142
*Elminius*, 193
*Elodea*, 150, 151
*Equisetum*, 8
*Esox*, 124, 260
*Eucyclops*, 79
*Euglena*, 8, 9
Euglenophyta, 8
*Eunotia*, 9
*Evadne*, 210

## G

*Gadus*, 235, 261, 267
*Gasterosteus*, 109, 122
Gastropoda, 77
*Glyceria*, 142
*Glyptotendipes*, 78
*Gobio*, 02, 123

## H

*Hippuris*, 142
Hirudinea, 77
Hydrachnellidae, 79
*Hydrocharis*, 150
*Hydrurus*, 7

## I

*Icthyomyzon*, 123
*Isoetes*, 8

## L

*Laminaria*, 289
*Lemna*, 150
*Lepomis*, 124, 265–266
*Leuciscus*, 79, 123
*Littorella*, 142
*Lycaena*, 138
*Lyngbya*, 10

## M

*Melanogrammus*, 264, 267
*Melosira*, 57
*Mentha*, 142
*Merlangius*, 264, 267
*Metridia*, 188, 193
*Micropterus*, 124, 264, 267
*Microspora*, 10
Microsporales, 8
Mollusca, 83
*Mougeotia*, 5, 8, 10
*Myocaster*, 150
*Myosotis*, 142
*Myriophyllum*, 150
*Mytilus*, 267

## N

*Naias*, 5
*Nephrops*, 159, 288, 292
*Nephthys*, 277, 278
*Nitzschia*, 9, 10
*Nuphar*, 12, 70, 75, 78, 79, 83, 84, 149
*Nymphaea*, 149

## O

*Odontogadus*, 235
*Oedogonium*, 10
*Oikopleura*, 218
*Oncorhynchus*, 124

Orthocladiinae, 78
Oscillatoriaceae, 6

## P

*Perca*, 62, 79, 92, 123, 124
*Phaeothamnion*, 8
*Phoxinus*, 122
*Phragmites*, 144, 145, 150
*Pleuronectes*, 235, 260, 261, 267
*Plumatella*, 77, 83
*Podon*, 210
*Polygonum*, 142, 149
Porifera, 77
*Porphyridium*, 12
*Potamogeton*, 6, 150, 151
*Prasiola*, 7
*Prodiamesa*, 78
*Protococci*, 10
*Pseudocalanus*, 204, 205, 206, 207

## R

*Rasbora*, 96
*Rheotanytarsus*, 78
*Rhincalanus*, 195, 196
*Rhizoclonium*, 74
Rhodophyta, 6
Rotifera, 79
*Ruppia*, 6
*Rutilus*, 62, 79, 92, 123

## J

*Salix*, 70, 76
*Salmo*, 90, 122, 124, 260
*Salvelinus*, 122, 124
*Scardinius*, 92
*Scenedesmus*, 60
*Sida*, 79, 83
Sididae, 78
*Solea*, 235
*Spiratella*, 207, 208
*Squalius*, 94
*Stephanodiscus*, 55, 58, 60, 72
*Stichococcus*, 9
*Stigeoclonium*, 10
*Stratiotes*, 149, 150
*Synechococcus*, 4, 5, 6, 11

## T

*Temora*, 193, 206, 207
*Tenebrio*, 265

Tetrasporales, 10
*Tilapia*, 261, 262
*Tinca*, 92
Tubificidae, 77
*Typha*, 8, 150

**U**

*Ulothrix*, 8, 10, 11, 15
Ulotrichales, 6, 8
*Unio*, 78

**V**

*Vallisneria*, 6
*Vaucheria*, 12
Volvocales, 8

**X**

Xanthophyta, 60

# SUBJECT INDEX

## A

Abstraction, 42, 43, 51, 138–143, 144
Abundance, 12, 119, 125, 158, 159, 160, 176, 203–212, 236, 243, 245
Acid mine drainage, 8, 13, 14
Acidic environments, 7–9, 15
Acidic springs, 12
Activated sludge, 37, 99
Adsorption, 281, 282
Algicides, 62
Alginates, 289
Allen curve, 80, 81, 119–121
Ammonia, 37, 39, 89, 90, 91, 92, 94, 95, 97, 99, 103, 104, 105, 106, 108, 112, 192
Ammonium nitrate, 147
Amphipods, 277, 288
Anaerobiosis, 12
Anaerobism, 44, 149, 151
Anchovies, 219, 235
Angiosperms, 4, 5, 6, 8, 11, 12
Appendicularians, 228
Aquatic plants, 6, 37, 39, 75, 141, 151
Aquatic vegetation, 148–150
Ascidians, 293
Assimilation, 118, 193, 194, 197, 278, 279
Atlantic, 273, 274

## B

Bacteria,
flexibacteria, 11
purple sulphur, 4
Barrages, 135, 140, 300
Bass, small-mouth, 264, 265
Bicarbonate, 22
Biomass, 14, 37, 44, 55, 57, 58, 59, 61, 72, 75, 77, 80, 118, 119, 120, 128, 179, 218, 240
Birds, 138, 140, 143, 144, 151, 235
Bivalves, 218
Bleak, 79, 80, 81, 84, 125, 265
Bluegill sunfish, 265

Blue-green algae, 4, 5, 6, 11, 12, 14, 60, 61
BOD, 106, 107
Boron, 22
Bream, 62, 92, 93
Breckland Meres, 142–143
Brill, 158
Bryophytes, 7
Bullhead, 125
Buoys, 299

## C

Cadmium, 89, 90, 93, 94, 95, 98, 99, 105, 106, 107, 108, 110, 112
Caesium, 280
Caesium-134, 277
Caesium-137, 272, 273, 274, 275, 277, 278, 279
Calcium, 22, 123, 125
Calcium carbonate, 110
Canada geese, 145
Carbon, 15, 60, 63, 64, 65, 193, 196, 240
Carbon dioxide, 5, 92, 94, 116, 294
Carp, 92, 93, 94, 151, 292
Catch, 164, 168, 171, 172, 173, 176, 177, 214, 228, 236, 243, 244, 245, 246, 247, 248
Catchment, 22, 23, 24, 25, 26, 27, 28, 29, 30, 31, 35, 38, 39, 69, 88, 97–108, 136, 140, 146, 152
Centrarchids, 124
Cerium, 281
Chloride, 22, 23–29, 282
Chlorination, 44
Chlorine, 96
Chlorophyll, 14, 43, 53, 54, 55, 59, 72, 73, 191
Chromium, 89, 94, 98, 105, 106, 107, 110
Chub, 94
Circulation, 50, 59, 272, 300
Coalfish, 181
Cobalt, 282
Cockles, 240

Cod, 162–183, 213, 214, 215, 216, 218, 230, 235, 261, 262, 265, 288, 289
Coefficient,
  eddy diffusivity, 45
  extinction, 64, 65, 224, 225
  transmission, 225, 226
  turbulent transport, 45
Column compensation, 56
Column respiration, 53, 56
Competition, 64, 125, 126, 129, 213, 214, 218, 219, 227, 230
Concentration factor, 279, 280, 281
Condition factor, 262, 263, 264, 265, 266, 267, 268
Conservation, 115, 128–130, 135–152, 157, 159, 161–183, 203, 210, 233-256, 260, 289, 297–300
Continental shelf, 285, 297–298
Continuous plankton recorder, 203
Conversion efficiency, 57, 260, 263, 266, 267, 268
Cooling towers, 6
Copepods, 185–201, 217, 218, 228
Copper, 4, 9, 10, 62, 89, 90, 91, 93, 94, 97, 99, 105, 106, 107, 108, 110, 112
  nitrate, 237
  sulphate, 4, 62
Coypu, 150
Crowding, 254
Crustaceans, 159, 240
Cultivation, 159, 289, 290, 291, 292-294, 295
Culture, 126, 235, 293
Cultus Lake, 116, 124, 127
Currents, 299
Cyanide, 89, 90, 91, 93, 94, 95, 97, 99, 105
Cyprinids, 129

D

Dabs, 218
Dace, 79, 80, 94
Daily rations, 194–197, 198
Daphnids, 58, 61, 62
DDT, 95, 194
Denitrification, 37, 38, 39
Deoxygenation, 44, 45, 129, 130, 151, 285

Depth, 44, 46, 50, 56, 57, 59, 61, 64, 65, 69, 70, 73, 74, 84, 141, 149, 222, 239, 244, 246, 285
  compensation, 216, 223, 224, 225, 226, 229, 230
  critical, 216, 223, 224, 225, 226, 229, 230
  of mixing, 216, 219–220, 223, 229
Destratification, 48, 50, 51, 69
Detergents, 9, 96, 97, 129, 145
Detritus, 57, 63, 78, 82, 83, 116, 187, 188, 239, 281, 291
Diatoms, 4, 5, 6, 11, 12, 13, 16, 52, 55, 56, 57, 58, 60, 72, 82, 83, 151, 188, 193, 197
Diffusedair, 50
Dilution, 35, 36, 88, 96, 97, 111, 143
Distribution, 49, 56, 61, 73, 97, 102, 203–212, 221, 227, 236, 242, 243, 245, 248, 271
Diversity,
  floristic, 9
  habitat, 137
  indices, 13, 14
  species, 4, 11, 13, 14, 15, 151
Drainage, 5, 7, 22, 24, 25, 26, 27, 28, 29, 30, 31, 34, 35, 36, 38, 39
Ducks, 144

E

Ecosystems, 4, 14, 15, 70, 87, 115, 116, 128, 130, 135–152, 162, 203, 227, 271, 276, 282
Eels, 92, 123
Effluents, 12, 22, 25, 31, 35, 36, 96, 97, 100, 106
  discharge, 30, 35, 146
  flow of, 31, 32, 34, 35
  heated, 6, 103, 294
  sewage, 22, 23, 24, 25, 28, 29, 30, 31, 34, 35, 36, 37, 41, 83, 89, 91, 99, 100, 106, 112, 130, 136, 144
  thermal, 7, 15, 16
  warm water, 69
Elasmobranchs, 165
Energy, 64, 76, 116, 118, 121, 223, 224, 225, 227, 260, 261, 266, 267
  flow, 14, 52, 55
  relationships, 55
  requirements, 44–51, 81–82

Entrainment, 50
Escallops, 159
Esthwaite water, 46
Eutrophication, 129, 145, 203, 211

F

Fecundity, 79–80, 84, 88, 214, 216, 217
Feeding, 61, 84, 126, 127, 185, 186, 187,
    188, 197, 237, 246, 259–268, 276,
    277, 279, 292, 293
Fens, 150
Fertilization, 126, 129, 292
Fertilizer, 25, 26, 28, 38, 47, 146, 148
Fish, 4, 62, 69, 70, 76, 79–82, 83, 84,
    87–112, 115–131, 140, 141, 151,
    157, 158, 159, 160, 162, 164, 170,
    173, 178, 181, 182, 187, 213–230,
    235, 237, 240, 241, 243, 244, 247,
    248, 249, 250, 252, 253, 254, 259-
    268, 276, 277, 278, 279, 280, 281,
    287, 288, 291
  kills, 89, 51
  ladder, 140
Fisher Bank, 228
Fishery,
  freshwater, 22, 87–112, 127, 128, 129
    136, 139
  marine, 157, 158, 161–183, 203, 211,
    233–256, 287–289, 290, 294, 300
  regulation, 162, 181
Fishing amount, 162, 169, 173, 178,
    181, 182
  capacity, 161, 170, 174, 176, 178
  effort, 165, 166, 168, 169, 170, 171,
    172, 173, 174, 177, 178, 180, 181,
    182, 183
  electric, 122
  freshwater, 22, 87, 112, 127, 128, 129,
    136, 139
  marine, 161, 163, 164, 165, 168, 169,
    170, 171, 172, 173, 174, 176, 178,
    179, 180, 181, 182, 183, 243, 244,
    249, 250, 254, 292
Flagellates, 5, 151
Flamborough Head, 228, 252
Flow,
  chloride, 22, 33–34
  effluent, 31, 32, 34, 35
  energy, 14, 52, 55
  metals, 106–108

Flow, contd.
  nitrogen, 22, 33–34, 35, 36, 106, 107
  reservoir, 48, 53, 55·
  residual, 29, 31, 251, 252, 253
  return, 26
  river, 4, 23, 24, 26, 28, 30, 31, 32, 34,
    36, 43, 69, 72, 108, 139, 141, 143
  sea, 274
Fluctuations, 72, 94–96, 97, 108, 111,
    211
  annual, 204, 206, 207, 209, 211
  geographical, 205
  monthly, 208
  seasonal, 205
Food level, 190, 228, 261
Formaldehyde, 96
Fowlea Brook, 101

G

Gadoids, 289
Generation time, 78, 169
Geology, 297–298
German Bight, 215, 221, 228, 240, 241,
    243, 248
Germanium dioxide, 14
Grafham Water, 23, 139
Grayling, 100
Grazing, 26, 53, 57, 58, 59, 60–61, 62,
    64, 84, 186, 187, 188
Green algae, 4, 5, 6, 11, 12
Greylag geese, 145
Growth, 5, 6, 7, 9, 10, 11, 12, 14, 22, 37,
    53, 55, 57, 58, 60, 72, 77, 79, 80,
    84, 88, 109, 111, 118, 119, 120,
    123, 124, 125, 126, 127, 128, 148,
    158, 163, 169, 170, 171, 187,
    193–194, 195, 196, 216, 217, 218,
    227, 235, 237, 241, 252, 254,
    259–268, 276, 277, 279, 294
Gudgeon, 80, 92, 93

H

Haddock, 173, 177, 264, 265, 288, 289
Hake, 288, 289
Hall Beck, 123
Hard water, 90, 93, 97, 110
Hardness, 10, 92
Harlequin fish, 96, 97
Heavy metals, 9, 10, 15, 85, 105, 106,
    192

Herbicides, 95, 136, 146, 150, 151
Herring, 158, 159, 165, 173, 213, 217,
    218, 219, 230, 235, 236, 252, 253,
    255, 288, 289, 298, 299
Hook of Holland, 221
Hydrocarbons, 297, 298
  chlorinated, 97, 130
  polycyclic, 194
Hydrogen cyanide, 94, 104, 112
Hydrogen sulphide, 12, 43, 59
Hypolimnion, 44

I
ICNAF, 157, 163, 173
Industrial discharge, 34, 100
  waste, 22, 89, 91, 112
Insect, 138
Insecticides, 146
Instrumentation, 160
Invertebrates, 75, 76, 77–79, 84, 118,
    126, 138, 151, 182
Irish Sea, 272, 273, 274, 275, 279, 285,
    294
Iron, 282
Irrigation, 22, 26, 37, 136, 142

J
Jets, 49, 50, 51, 56, 61, 63

K
Kattegat, 241
Kola meridian, 215

L
Lake District, 123, 137
Lake Narrviken, 46
Land use, 25, 26, 28, 38, 39
Landings, 287–289
Larval drift, 214, 216, 217, 218, 219–
    221, 222, 226, 227, 229, 230
LC50, 90, 93, 94, 95, 96, 97, 99, 100,
    101, 103, 105, 108, 110, 111, 112
Lead, 10, 108
Life cycle, 158, 218, 219, 227
Light, 10–11, 52, 60, 64, 73, 74, 144,
    149, 294
Lipids, 265, 266
Liverworts, 8
Loads,
  grazing, 57, 58
  pollutants, 22, 24, 25, 26, 28, 36, 38,
    106

Lobsters, 288, 292
Loch Etive, 291
Loch Leven, 136, 146–147, 149, 150

M
Magnesium, 22
Maintenance requirement, 260, 268
Mallard, 145
Management, 3, 39, 84, 128–130, 135,
    136, 137, 159, 161, 162, 168–170,
    173–178, 182
Manganese, 279, 282
Margalef index, 13, 14
Marion Lake, 136
Mass, 22, 24, 25, 29, 30, 31, 32, 33, 34,
    35, 36, 37, 106–108
Maturity, 79, 163, 180, 216
Mercury, 194
Mesh aperture, 76, 79
  size, 173, 174, 244
Metabolic rate, 188–192
Metabolism, 118, 130, 185, 189, 190,
    193, 194, 196, 267, 276
Migration, 118, 128, 237, 245, 247, 248,
    252
  feeding, 237, 246
  spawning, 252
Mill Loch, 138
Minerals, 22
Mixing, 46–61, 74, 287
Molluscs, 159, 240, 241, 292
Morecambe Bay, 140
Mortality, 79, 118, 119, 120, 121, 123,
    127, 128, 151, 169, 170, 171, 174,
    176, 179, 187, 214, 217, 218, 227,
    248, 250, 259
Mosses, 5, 8, 9, 15
Mussel, 83, 235, 240, 248, 290, 293
Mute swans, 145

N
Nature Conservancy, 136, 138, 140, 143
NEAFC, 157, 163, 173
Nickel, 89, 90, 94, 98, 99, 105, 106,
    107, 108, 110, 112
Nitrate, 12, 16, 28, 36, 37, 72, 146, 147,
    148, 149, 239, 241
Nitrite, 239
Nitrogen, 22, 23–39, 76, 77, 146, 147–
    148, 193, 194, 196, 197, 239, 265,
    266

Nitrogen, *contd.*
  ammoniacal, 37, 38, 45, 107
  excretion, 189, 190, 191, 192
  fixation, 12
  inorganic, 22, 23, 24, 25–28, 31–38,
    106, 107
  organic, 190
  'sink', 38, 39
Norfolk Banks, 228
Norfolk Broads, 140, 145, 148, 149, 150
North Atlantic, 162–183, 213, 215
North Sea, 203–212, 213, 217, 218, 219–
    229, 230, 233–256, 297, 298, 299,
    300
North Wales, 10
Nursery, 214, 217, 218, 221, 228, 229,
    230, 233–256, 259, 291
Nutrients, 5, 12, 22, 24, 39, 41, 60, 116,
    139, 146–148, 149, 239, 240, 241,
    255, 294

O

Otoliths, 244
Oxygen, 56
  absorption, 45
  consumption, 6, 7, 45, 46, 81, 189,
    192
  curve, 14
  demand, 45
  demand of mud, 44, 45, 46
  demanding wastes, 21, 22
  dissolved, 11–12, 15, 37, 43, 44–46,
    51, 65, 72, 88, 89, 92, 94, 97,
    99, 102–103, 104, 105, 112
  production, 46, 73
  saturation, 51, 83
  tension, 44
  transport, 45
Oxygenation, 51, 286
Overfishing, 178–180
Oyster, 235, 290, 293, 294

P

Perch, 62, 79, 92, 93, 94
Pesticides, 89, 91, 95, 136
pH, 4, 7, 8, 9, 12, 15, 37–38, 92, 99
Phenols, 88, 90, 91, 92–93, 94, 95, 97,
    99, 104, 105, 108, 112, 194
Phosphate, 16, 72, 146, 148, 149, 239,
    241

Phosphorus, 22, 193, 194, 196, 197,
    218, 219, 239
  excretion, 189, 190, 191
Photosynthesis, 5, 11, 14, 52, 57, 83,
    116, 216, 225
Phytol, 194
Phytoplankton, 14, 42, 43, 44, 51–57,
    58–60, 61, 62, 63, 64, 65, 71, 72–
    74, 75, 83, 129, 146, 149, 151,
    186, 187, 188, 194, 197, 208, 281,
    282
Pike, 92, 124, 127, 128, 129, 140, 151
Pilchards, 218, 219, 230, 299
Plaice, 158, 159, 213, 218, 219–229,
    230, 235, 236, 240, 243, 244, 245,
    246, 247, 248, 249, 250, 251, 252,
    253, 254, 255, 261, 262, 263, 264,
    265, 267, 277, 278, 280, 288, 289
Pollutants, 3, 9, 13, 21, 22, 88, 91, 103,
    185, 193
  maximum permissible levels, 87
Pollution, 4, 11, 13, 87–112, 118, 130,
    144, 145–146, 150, 182, 190, 198,
    203, 211, 237, 255, 294–295
  domestic, 136, 145
  effects of, 4, 15, 16, 91, 157, 158, 160,
    211, 300
  industrial, 9, 10, 136, 145
  mine, 8
  organic, 6, 12
  studies, 14, 212
  thermal, 5, 6, 7, 15, 16
Population, 14, 21, 29, 30, 55, 56, 57,
    58, 59, 60, 62, 81, 83, 88, 94, 109,
    112, 118, 123, 124, 125, 127, 128,
    129, 130, 138, 150, 188, 189, 192,
    194, 197, 218, 219, 227, 228, 229,
    259, 271
  abnormal, 110
  density, 22, 24, 25, 29, 38, 39, 77, 79,
    84, 109, 124, 125, 126, 127
  dynamics, 115, 116, 119, 128, 130,
    225
  estimates, 122, 215
  mechanisms, 162, 163
  number, 116, 117, 118, 119, 121, 128
  parameters, 80, 81, 128
  size, 14, 172, 217, 244
  structure, 111, 123
  studies, 111

Potable supply, 22, 41
Potassium, 26
Potassium, chloride, 26
Power stations, 69, 103, 294
   nuclear, 272, 279
Predation, 61, 62, 118, 158, 159, 162
Predators, 259, 280, 292
Pressure, 190
Pristane, 194
Production, 44, 57, 61, 64, 65, 83, 225,
   226
   annual, 75
   cycle, 213–230
   egg, 194
   fish, 76, 80–81, 115–131, 177, 217,
   219
   food, 290
   gross, 52, 56
   net, 56, 57
   phytoplankton, 51–57
   primary, 13, 14, 73–74, 75, 85, 116,
   121, 126, 222–227, 240, 291
   secondary, 116, 121, 187, 188, 189,
   228
   zooplankton, 185, 192, 197, 198
Productivity, 42, 43, 148, 158, 181, 274,
   297–300
   primary, 15
   secondary, 84, 193
Protein-N, 265–266
Pteridophytes, 8
Pulmonate, 84

## Q

$Q_{10}$ value, 7

## R

Radiation, 10, 11, 48, 49, 65, 213, 216,
   223, 271
Radioactive decay, 276
   tracers, 281, 282
   wastes, 271, 282
Radioecology, 271–283
Radionuclides, 271, 274, 275, 276, 277,
   279, 280, 281, 282
Recruitment, 118, 128, 129, 158, 171,
   174, 176, 177, 178, 179, 180, 182,
   183, 213, 214, 215, 216, 217, 218,
   219, 226, 227–229, 230, 236, 237,
   250, 254, 259

Reddish Canal, 5, 16
Redfish, 167, 177
Reed warbler, 150
Reservoir, 22, 23, 41, 42, 43, 44–65,
   135, 138–142, 149, 281, 297
Resources, 128, 157, 160, 161–183, 203,
   233–256, 300
Respiration, 11, 14, 53, 55, 56, 65, 73,
   74, 188, 190, 192, 196, 216, 225
River
   Appletreeworth, 122
   Bere, 122, 124
   Black Brows, 122, 123
   Blackwater, 36
   Cam, 96–97, 110, 112
   Chelmer, 36
   Churnet, 10, 100
   Colne, 94
   Dee, 140, 141
   Delaware, 6
   Devil's, 122
   Docken's, 122, 124
   Dove, 100
   Great Ouse, 22, 23–25, 31, 33, 34, 35,
   36, 37, 38, 39
   Green, 6
   Hall, 122
   Horokiwi, 116, 122, 123
   Kennet, 69, 71, 73, 77, 82–83
   Kingswell, 122
   Lambourn, 142
   Lawrence, 122
   Lee, 37
   Loucka, 122
   Manistee, 123
   Nene, 108
   Nether Hearth, 122
   Patuxent, 6
   Sangamon, 36
   Shelligan, 122
   Soar, 100
   Stour, 28, 36
   Sydling, 142
   Tame, 100, 102, 103, 104, 106, 107
   Tarrant, 122, 124
   Tees, 12
   Thames, 37, 53, 58, 59, 64, 69–84,
   123, 125, 126, 221, 300
   Trent, 22, 23–25, 33, 34, 35, 37, 38,
   39, 88, 96, 97–112

River, *contd.*
    Tummel–Garry, 140
    Walla, 122
    Wear, 6, 11
    Wylye, 142
Roach, 62, 79, 80, 81, 82, 84, 92, 93, 94, 109
Romney Marshes, 150
R.S.P.B., 143
Rudd, 92, 93, 94, 95
Ruffe, 94
Run-off, 14, 22, 25, 26, 27, 28, 31, 32, 36, 39, 107
Ruthenium, 106, 274

S

Saithe, 158
Salinity, 92, 215, 220, 221, 230, 237, 239, 254, 274, 287
Salmon, 118, 129, 140,173,289,293,294
    sockeye, 116, 127
Salmonids, 122, 123, 124, 125, 130, 255, 289
Sampling, 14, 73, 97, 108, 112, 212, 236, 241, 244, 248, 249, 255
Sandeels, 218
Sand filtration, 42, 63, 65
Sardines, 219
Scallops, 288, 292
Schliensee, 46
Seaweeds, 289
Sedimentation, 53, 55, 57, 59
Settlement, 42
Shellfish, 157, 159, 160, 287, 288, 294
Shrimps, 235, 244, 248, 250, 251
Silica, 44, 55, 58, 72
Silver hake, 167
Size, 14, 109, 119, 277, 279
Skate, 288, 289
Soakage, 37
Sodium, 22
Softwater, 90, 97, 123, 124
Sole, 158, 159, 235, 236, 237, 243, 244, 245, 246, 247, 248, 249, 250, 251, 252, 253, 254, 255, 266
Southern Bight, 213, 220, 221, 222, 223, 224, 227, 228, 229, 230
Spawning, 80, 120, 121, 129, 179, 180, 216, 217, 226, 227–229, 235, 252, 299

Spawning *contd.*
    grounds, 214, 217, 220, 221, 227, 228, 229, 230, 251, 252, 253, 255
Species composition, 76, 125, 126
Sponge, 83
Squid, 267
Standing crop, 14, 53, 57, 60, 240, 241
Stickleback, 3-spined, 109
Stratification, 44, 45, 48, 49
    thermal, 45, 48, 49, 69, 209
Sturgeon, 120
Sulphate, 12, 22
Survival, 94, 95, 96, 111, 125, 127, 129, 130, 158, 159, 215, 241, 259
Suspended material, 239, 240, 255
    matter, 71, 72, 78, 83, 97
    particles, 11, 41, 42
    silt, 52, 63
    solids, 97, 99, 106, 107
Synergism, 89

T

Teleost, 280
Temperature, 4–7, 10, 14, 15, 37, 38, 46, 55, 56, 58, 65, 71, 72, 78, 82, 92, 93, 98, 102, 103, 112, 126, 127, 158, 190, 192, 193, 196, 215, 239, 261, 276, 277, 279
    critical, 6
    gradient, 13, 14
    lethal, 6, 7, 237
    optima, 5, 16
    range, 11
    tolerance, 5, 6, 7
Tench, 92
Texel, 220, 221, 222, 228
Thermal discharge, 6
    limits, 4
    springs, 5, 6, 7, 9, 10, 13, 14
    tolerance, 163
Thermocline, 41, 209
Toxicity, 9, 89–110, 111, 112, 189
    direct, 87, 88–89, 96
    measurements, 96–97
    median, 100, 102, 105
    predicted, 97–102
    selective, 14
    short-term, 91, 112
    of substances, 9–10, 13, 16, 89, 99, 192, 211

Toxicity, *contd.*
  tests, 13, 106, 111
  total, 99, 103, 105, 106, 110
Trawl, beam, 244, 249, 250, 255
Tritium, 271, 272
Trout, 92, 93, 94, 95, 96, 97, 100, 108,
    110, 111, 112, 116, 123, 124, 127,
    129, 140
  brown, 123
  rainbow, 90, 91, 92, 93, 99, 112, 290,
    292, 293
  sea, 140, 289, 293
Turbidity, 64, 69, 84, 220, 221, 222,
    223, 226, 230, 240
Turbot, 158
Turbulence, 37, 48, 52, 56, 60, 61

**V**

Van Dorn relationship, 48
Variations,
  annual, 72, 205, 206, 208, 209, 210,
    212
  geographical, 204, 205, 212
  seasonal, 31, 35, 190, 192, 204, 205,
    206, 208, 210, 211, 212
Vendace, 138
Vertical migration, 187, 192, 196, 198

**W**

Waddensea, 221, 223–256
Wash, 140
Waste discharge, 21
  disposal, 63, 282
Water alkalinity, 99
  column, 83, 287
  demand, 21
  landscapes, 143
  meadows, 143

Water alkalinity, *contd.*
  quality, 13, 21, 22, 23, 42, 89, 91, 92,
    106, 108, 111, 112
  shed, 152
  supply, 23, 42, 84, 136, 139, 277
  treatment, 41, 42, 65
  turbulence, 37
White Fish Authority, 290
Whiting, 158, 218, 235, 264, 265, 288,
    289
Wildfowl, 40, 136, 145
Willow Brook, 88, 108–110, 111, 112
Wind, 48, 49, 50, 51, 58, 61, 213, 215,
    216, 220, 223, 226, 228, 229, 230,
    273, 274, 299
Windermere, 124, 127, 128, 129
Windscale, 272, 274, 275, 277, 279
Woodwalton Fen Nature Reserve, 138
Worms, 218, 240
Wyland Lake, 124

**Y**

Year classes, 119, 127, 178, 180, 213,
    214, 217, 226, 227, 229, 230, 245,
    248, 251

**Z**

Zeeland, 234, 241, 245, 246, 247, 252
Zinc, 10, 89, 90, 91, 93, 94, 95, 96, 97,
    99, 105, 106, 107, 108, 112, 279,
    281, 282
Zinc-65, 282
Zirconium, 281
Zirconium-95/niobium-95, 274
Zooplankton, 57, 60, 61, 62, 63, 64, 78–
    79, 151, 185–198, 203–212, 291
Zuidersea, 234, 235, 254